# Praise for
## *Real Time Marketing for Business Growth*

"A wealth of approaches, methodologies, concepts and applications an effective marketing program in today's confusing and often confli Monique Reece has organized her wealth of marketing knowledge ence into a quick-reading but comprehensive approach to developin gram for almost any organization. Filled with not just 'how-tos' but 'whys' and 'so whats.' *Real Time Marketing for Business Growth* leads you through the 21st century marketing jungle in a proven and sound way. Learn how marketing can and should be done in today's global, interconnected yet very local marketplace."

**Don Schultz**
**Professor of Integrated Communication, Northwestern University, named One of the Most Influential People in Sales and Marketing**

"At Zappos.com, our #1 priority is our company culture. Monique explains how culture can drive profitability, and how your internal branding can drive your external branding. Monique shares ways to strengthen and deepen the linkages with your employees, customers, and other stakeholders to create a culture that drives sustainable, profitable growth."

**Tony Hsieh**
**CEO, Zappos.com**

"Read the text, do the exercises, and get ready to kick butt. Your competition will never know what hit them unless they read this book too."

**Guy Kawasaki**
**Cofounder, Alltop.com and author of The Art of the Start**

"An excellent extrapolation of the Kaplan/Norton strategy management framework. Linking strategy to execution through plans and measures is the secret sauce."

**David Norton**
**Professor, Harvard Business School, coauthor of The Balanced Scorecard and Strategy Maps**

"In *Real-Time Marketing for Business Growth*, Monique Reece gives business leaders state-of-the-moment marketing insights, presented engagingly, clearly and cogently. Anyone who takes marketing seriously will devour this book, discovering business enlightenment and reading enjoyment on every page."

**Jay Conrad Levinson**
**Author, Guerilla Marketing series**

"The title of this book might be a mouthful, but there's certainly lots to chew on for any CMO and staff. In today's hyper-sensitive, viral and virtual markets, annual planning is a pointless exercise. Take Monique's advice, embrace a marketing on-demand model that enables rapid response to ever-changing customer, competitor and business conditions."

**Donovan Neale-May**
**Executive Director of the Chief Marketing Officer (CMO) Council**

"There is a rule in football that says, 'Never, ever out kick your coverage.' If you do, your team could find themselves at a competitive disadvantage. The same holds true for marketing and sales. Marketing can easily out kick the sales coverage. In *Real-Time Marketing for Business Growth*, find out how to maximize that thin line between the two and stay ahead of the competition forever."

**Jack Stack**
**President and CEO, Springfield Re-manufacturing, author,**
**Great Game of Business**

# Real-Time Marketing for Business Growth

# *Real-Time Marketing for Business Growth*

## How to Use Social Media, Measure Marketing, and Create a Culture of Execution

Monique Reece

Vice President, Publisher: Tim Moore
Associate Publisher and Director of Marketing: Amy Neidlinger
Acquisitions Editor: Jennifer Simon
Editorial Assistant: Myesha Graham
Development Editor: Russ Hall
Operation Manager: Gina Kanouse
Senior Marketing Manager: Julie Phifer
Publicity Manager: Laura Czaja
Assistant Marketing Manager: Megan Colvin
Cover Designer: Chuti Prasertsith
Managing Editor: Kristy Hart
Project Editor: Jovana San Nicolas-Shirley
Copy Editor: Julie Anderson
Proofreader: Water Crest Publishing, Inc.
Senior Indexer: Cheryl Lenser
Senior Compositor: Gloria Schurick
Manufacturing Buyer: Dan Uhrig

© 2010 by Pearson Education, Inc.

Publishing as FT Press

Upper Saddle River, New Jersey 07458

FT Press offers excellent discounts on this book when ordered in quantity for bulk purchases or special sales. For more information, please contact U.S. Corporate and Government Sales, 1-800-382-3419, corpsales@pearsontechgroup.com. For sales outside the U.S., please contact International Sales at international@pearson.com.

Company and product names mentioned herein are the trademarks or registered trademarks of their respective owners.

Printed in the United States of America

First Printing March 2010

ISBN-10: 0-13-701010-9
ISBN-13: 978-0-13-701010-3

Pearson Education LTD.
Pearson Education Australia PTY, Limited.
Pearson Education Singapore, Pte. Ltd.
Pearson Education North Asia, Ltd.
Pearson Education Canada, Ltd.
Pearson Educatión de Mexico, S.A. de C.V.
Pearson Education—Japan
Pearson Education Malaysia, Pte. Ltd.

Library of Congress Cataloging-in-Publication Data

Reece, Monique.
  Real-time marketing for business growth : how to use social media, measure marketing, and create a culture of execution / Monique Reece. — 1st ed.
     p. cm.
  ISBN 978-0-13-701010-3 (pbk. : alk. paper)
  1. Marketing—Management. 2. Telemarketing. 3. Strategic planning. I. Title.
  HF5415.13.R367 2010
  658.8—dc22
                          2010001944

*To Isabella and Morgan, my two Angels,*
*for showing me what is really important in life.*
*I love you with all my heart.*

# Contents

Foreword . . . . . . . . . . . . . . . . . . . . . . . . . . . . . . . . . . . . . . . . . . . . . . . . xxi

Introduction . . . . . . . . . . . . . . . . . . . . . . . . . . . . . . . . . . . . . . . . . . . xxvii

**Section I**    **Purpose: Define Your Purpose** . . . . . . . . . . . . . . . . . . . . . . . . .1

**Chapter 1**    **What Is Purpose and Why Is It Important?** . . . . . . . . . . . . . . .2

Purpose-Driven Companies Make Higher Profits . . . . . . . . . . . . . . . .2

Create Raving Fans . . . . . . . . . . . . . . . . . . . . . . . . . . . . . . . . . . . . . . . .3

When Employees Leave at Night, So Does Your Business . . . . . . . . . . . . . . .4

Company Purpose: Intentional or Dysfunctional? . . . . . . . . . . . . . . . . .5

**Chapter 2**    **A Mission Statement Answers "Why Do We Exist?"** . . . . . . . . . . . . .6

Does Your Mission Statement Inspire? . . . . . . . . . . . . . . . . . . . . . . . . .7

**Chapter 3**    **Create a Compelling Vision** . . . . . . . . . . . . . . . . . . . . . . . . . . .8

Tell a Story . . . . . . . . . . . . . . . . . . . . . . . . . . . . . . . . . . . . . . . . . . . . . .10

**Chapter 4**    **Core Values Drive Behavior** . . . . . . . . . . . . . . . . . . . . . . . . .11

Make It Personal . . . . . . . . . . . . . . . . . . . . . . . . . . . . . . . . . . . . . . . . .11

**Chapter 5**    **The "C" Word** . . . . . . . . . . . . . . . . . . . . . . . . . . . . . . . . . . . .12

What Do Pizza and Shoes Have in Common? . . . . . . . . . . . . . . . . . . .13

Committable Core Values . . . . . . . . . . . . . . . . . . . . . . . . . . . . . . . . . .14

Zappos Core Values . . . . . . . . . . . . . . . . . . . . . . . . . . . . . . . . . . . . . . .15

**Chapter 6**    **How The Ritz-Carlton Creates and Sustains a**
**High-Performance Culture** . . . . . . . . . . . . . . . . . . . . . . . . . . . . . .17

How The Ritz-Carlton Mystique Works . . . . . . . . . . . . . . . . . . . . . . . .18

What Can 15 Minutes a Day Do for Your Company? . . . . . . . . . . . . . .19

The Transformation to Passionate Advocacy . . . . . . . . . . . . . . . . . . . .20

**Chapter 7**    **Defining Core Values** . . . . . . . . . . . . . . . . . . . . . . . . . . . . . .21

Defining Corporate Values . . . . . . . . . . . . . . . . . . . . . . . . . . . . . . . . .22

*PART 1: SELECT AND DEFINE* . . . . . . . . . . . . . . . . . . . . . . . . . . . .22

*PART 2: PRIORITIZE* . . . . . . . . . . . . . . . . . . . . . . . . . . . . . . . . . . . .22

*PART 3: TEST* . . . . . . . . . . . . . . . . . . . . . . . . . . . . . . . . . . . . . . . . . . .22

*PART 4: COMMUNICATE, EXECUTE, MEASURE* . . . . . . . . . . . . . . .23

**Chapter 8**  **Game Changers** . . . . . . . . . . . . . . . **24**

Purpose-Driven Companies Are More Profitable . . . . . . . . . . . . . . . . . . . . . .24

New Belgium Brewing: Passionate About Purpose, People, Sustainabilty, and of Course, Beer . . . . . . . . . . . . . . . . . . . . . . . . . . . . . . . . . . . . . . . . . .25

A Strong Internal Brand Equals a Powerful External Brand . . . . . . . . . . . . .27

**Chapter 9**  **Do What You Love and the Money Will Follow** . . . . . . . . . . . **30**

A New Wave of Entrepreneurship . . . . . . . . . . . . . . . . . . . . . . . . . . . . . . . .31

**Chapter 10**  **Measurable Goals Drive Success** . . . . . . . . . . . . . . . . . . . . . . .**32**

The Balanced Scorecard Goal Framework . . . . . . . . . . . . . . . . . . . . . . . . .33

Goal Categories . . . . . . . . . . . . . . . . . . . . . . . . . . . . . . . . . . . . . . . . . . . . .33

**Chapter 11**  **Situation Analysis and SWOT Analysis** . . . . . . . . . . . . . . . . . .**35**

Situation Analysis . . . . . . . . . . . . . . . . . . . . . . . . . . . . . . . . . . . . . . . . . . . .35

SWOT Analysis . . . . . . . . . . . . . . . . . . . . . . . . . . . . . . . . . . . . . . . . . . . . .35

Summary . . . . . . . . . . . . . . . . . . . . . . . . . . . . . . . . . . . . . . . . . . . . . . . . . .37

P • R • A • I • S • E™ Marketing Process . . . . . . . . . . . . . . . . . . . . . . . . . .37

*Purpose* . . . . . . . . . . . . . . . . . . . . . . . . . . . . . . . . . . . . . . . . . . . . . . . .37

Summary: Section I . . . . . . . . . . . . . . . . . . . . . . . . . . . . . . . . . . . . . . . . . .37

**Section II**  **Research: Market Opportunity** . . . . . . . . . . . . . . . . . . . . . . .**39**

**Chapter 12**  **The Biggest Mistake Entrepreneurs Make** . . . . . . . . . . . . . . . .**40**

Know What You Don't Know . . . . . . . . . . . . . . . . . . . . . . . . . . . . . . . . . . .40

**Chapter 13**  **A Micro to Macro Process** . . . . . . . . . . . . . . . . . . . . . . . . . . . .**42**

Goals of a Research Plan . . . . . . . . . . . . . . . . . . . . . . . . . . . . . . . . . . . . . .42

**Chapter 14**  **Micro Perspective: Focus on High-Value Customers** . . . . . . . . . .**44**

The Most Powerful (and Easiest) Way to Improve Profitability . . . . . . . . . . .44

Existing Customer Analysis and Segmentation . . . . . . . . . . . . . . . . . . . . . .46

*Step #1: Categorize Existing Customers by Revenue and Profit* . . . . . . . .46

*Step #2: Add Other Segmentation Characteristics* . . . . . . . . . . . . . . . . . .46

*Step #3: Define Service by Customer Segment* . . . . . . . . . . . . . . . . . . . .47

*Step #4: Customize Marketing Programs* . . . . . . . . . . . . . . . . . . . . . . . .47

**Chapter 15**  **Love Your Loyal Customers** . . . . . . . . . . . . . . . . . . . . . . . . . . . . . . . .**50**

How Do You Measure Loyalty? . . . . . . . . . . . . . . . . . . . . . . . . . . . . . . .50

Measure Customer Profitability and CLV . . . . . . . . . . . . . . . . . . . . .51

Building Customer Loyalty . . . . . . . . . . . . . . . . . . . . . . . . . . . . . . . .52

Measure Customer Delight, Not Satisfaction . . . . . . . . . . . . . . . . . .52

Net Promoter Score . . . . . . . . . . . . . . . . . . . . . . . . . . . . . . . . . . . . .53

Intuit: How the Best Get Better . . . . . . . . . . . . . . . . . . . . . . . . . . . . .53

**Chapter 16**  **1:1 Marketing: Treat Different Customers Differently** . . . . . . . . . . .**55**

Make Customers the Center of Your Universe . . . . . . . . . . . . . . . . . . .55

**Chapter 17**  **Marketing's Secret Weapon** . . . . . . . . . . . . . . . . . . . . . . . . . . . . . . .**57**

Tips to Create a Customer-Centric Culture . . . . . . . . . . . . . . . . . . . .59

**Chapter 18**  **Create Unique Customer Experiences** . . . . . . . . . . . . . . . . . . . . . .**61**

Customers for Life . . . . . . . . . . . . . . . . . . . . . . . . . . . . . . . . . . . . . .62

**Chapter 19**  **Customer Experience: The Dark Side** . . . . . . . . . . . . . . . . . . . . . . .**63**

Customer Experience: The Dark Side . . . . . . . . . . . . . . . . . . . . . . . .63

Why Consumers Are Skeptical . . . . . . . . . . . . . . . . . . . . . . . . . . . . .63

Live By the Golden Rule . . . . . . . . . . . . . . . . . . . . . . . . . . . . . . . . . .64

Customer Service Gone Bad . . . . . . . . . . . . . . . . . . . . . . . . . . . . . . .65

**Chapter 20**  **Why Do Customers Buy?** . . . . . . . . . . . . . . . . . . . . . . . . . . . . . . . .**66**

Why People Buy . . . . . . . . . . . . . . . . . . . . . . . . . . . . . . . . . . . . . . .67

Action . . . . . . . . . . . . . . . . . . . . . . . . . . . . . . . . . . . . . . . . . . . . . . .68

**Chapter 21**  **Real-Time Customer Research** . . . . . . . . . . . . . . . . . . . . . . . . . . . .**69**

**Chapter 22**  **Macro Perspective: Get the Big Picture** . . . . . . . . . . . . . . . . . . . . .**71**

Market Segmentation and Target Marketing . . . . . . . . . . . . . . . . . . .71

Identifying Target Market Segments . . . . . . . . . . . . . . . . . . . . . . . . .73

Business-to-Business (B2B) Target Markets . . . . . . . . . . . . . . . . . . .74

**Chapter 23**  **Market Segmentation for the Twenty-First Century** . . . . . . . . . . .**75**

Why Is Your Product or Service Hired? . . . . . . . . . . . . . . . . . . . . . . .77

**Chapter 24**  **Zeroing in on Consumer Target Markets** . . . . . . . . . . . . . . . . . . .**79**

**Chapter 25**  **Forecasting Demand** . . . . . . . . . . . . . . . . . . . . . . . . . . . . . . . . . . .**83**

Forecasting Believable and Realistic Demand (Not What You Think a
VC Wants to See) . . . . . . . . . . . . . . . . . . . . . . . . . . . . . . . . . . . . . . .84

**Chapter 26**   **Competition: Keep Your Friends Close and Your Enemies Closer** . . . . . . . . . . . . . . . . . . . . . . . . . . . . . . . . . . . . . . . . **86**

Observe and Learn . . . . . . . . . . . . . . . . . . . . . . . . . . . . . . . . . . . . . 87

Competitive Information Sources . . . . . . . . . . . . . . . . . . . . . . . . 89

**Chapter 27**   **Anticipate the Unexpected: Research Macro-Environmental Factors** . . . . . . . . . . . . . . . . . . . . . . . . . . . . . . . . . . . . . . . . . . . . **90**

Macro-Environmental Factors . . . . . . . . . . . . . . . . . . . . . . . . . . 90

*Political/Legal* . . . . . . . . . . . . . . . . . . . . . . . . . . . . . . . . . . . . *90*

*Demographic* . . . . . . . . . . . . . . . . . . . . . . . . . . . . . . . . . . . . *91*

*Economic* . . . . . . . . . . . . . . . . . . . . . . . . . . . . . . . . . . . . . . . *91*

*Ecological/Professional* . . . . . . . . . . . . . . . . . . . . . . . . . . . *91*

*Technological* . . . . . . . . . . . . . . . . . . . . . . . . . . . . . . . . . . . *92*

*Cultural and Social* . . . . . . . . . . . . . . . . . . . . . . . . . . . . . . *92*

Seize Advantage in a Downturn . . . . . . . . . . . . . . . . . . . . . . . . 93

Summarize the Secondary Research Plan . . . . . . . . . . . . . . . . 93

**Chapter 28**   **Get Smart: Talk to Your Customers** . . . . . . . . . . . . . . . . **94**

Developing Your Primary Research Plan . . . . . . . . . . . . . . . . . 96

Tips for Creating a Customer Survey . . . . . . . . . . . . . . . . . . . . 96

Online Survey Tools . . . . . . . . . . . . . . . . . . . . . . . . . . . . . . . . . 97

**Chapter 29**   **Social Media and Online Tools Enable Real-Time Research** . . . . . **99**

News Aggregators . . . . . . . . . . . . . . . . . . . . . . . . . . . . . . . . . . . 99

Using Social Media for Real-Time Research . . . . . . . . . . . . . . 100

Social Networking and Bookmarking . . . . . . . . . . . . . . . . . . . 100

Tools and Gadgets . . . . . . . . . . . . . . . . . . . . . . . . . . . . . . . . . . 101

Blogs . . . . . . . . . . . . . . . . . . . . . . . . . . . . . . . . . . . . . . . . . . . . . 102

Analysts Track Trends and Make Sense of Them . . . . . . . . . . 102

P • R • A • I • S • E™ Marketing Process . . . . . . . . . . . . . . . . . . . 104

*Research* . . . . . . . . . . . . . . . . . . . . . . . . . . . . . . . . . . . . . . . *104*

Summary: Section II . . . . . . . . . . . . . . . . . . . . . . . . . . . . . . . . . 104

**Section III**   **Analyze: Growth and Profit Potential** . . . . . . . . . . . . . . **105**

**Chapter 30**   **Business Expansion: Vulnerable or Poised for Growth?** . . . . . . . . **106**

Complementary Products and Services . . . . . . . . . . . . . . . . . . 107

**Chapter 31**   **Substitute Products and Services** . . . . . . . . . . . . . . . . . . **108**

**Chapter 32**   **Disrupt and Innovate** . . . . . . . . . . . . . . . . . . . . . . . . . . . . . . .**110**

    Finding New Value . . . . . . . . . . . . . . . . . . . . . . . . . . . . . . . . . .112

    Finding New Value: Part I . . . . . . . . . . . . . . . . . . . . . . . . . . . . .112

**Chapter 33**   **Finding New Value: Part Deux** . . . . . . . . . . . . . . . . . . .**114**

    Broaden the Buyers . . . . . . . . . . . . . . . . . . . . . . . . . . . . . . . . . .114

    Create Customer Experiences . . . . . . . . . . . . . . . . . . . . . . . . .115

    Tap into Trends . . . . . . . . . . . . . . . . . . . . . . . . . . . . . . . . . . . . .116

    Distinctive Delivery . . . . . . . . . . . . . . . . . . . . . . . . . . . . . . . . .117

    Imagine and Innovate . . . . . . . . . . . . . . . . . . . . . . . . . . . . . . .119

    Finding New Value: Part II . . . . . . . . . . . . . . . . . . . . . . . . . . .120

        *Buyers* . . . . . . . . . . . . . . . . . . . . . . . . . . . . . . . . . . . . . . . . . .*120*

        *Experience* . . . . . . . . . . . . . . . . . . . . . . . . . . . . . . . . . . . . . .*120*

        *Trends* . . . . . . . . . . . . . . . . . . . . . . . . . . . . . . . . . . . . . . . . . .*120*

        *Distinction* . . . . . . . . . . . . . . . . . . . . . . . . . . . . . . . . . . . . . .*120*

    Summary: . . . . . . . . . . . . . . . . . . . . . . . . . . . . . . . . . . . . . . . . .120

**Chapter 34**   **Pricing Strategy and Objectives** . . . . . . . . . . . . . . . . . .**121**

    Mapping Customer Value to Pricing Strategy . . . . . . . . . . . .122

        *Pricing Map Directions* . . . . . . . . . . . . . . . . . . . . . . . . . . . .*123*

    Training Industry Example . . . . . . . . . . . . . . . . . . . . . . . . . . .124

**Chapter 35**   **Analyze Price and Profitability by Product and Service** . . . . . . . . .**126**

    Revenue/Cost Analysis . . . . . . . . . . . . . . . . . . . . . . . . . . . . . .127

    Worksheet . . . . . . . . . . . . . . . . . . . . . . . . . . . . . . . . . . . . . . . .128

**Chapter 36**   **Distribution and Channel Sales Strategy** . . . . . . . . . . .**129**

    Choose the Right Channels . . . . . . . . . . . . . . . . . . . . . . . . . . .129

    Channel Considerations . . . . . . . . . . . . . . . . . . . . . . . . . . . . .130

        *Tiered Distribution* . . . . . . . . . . . . . . . . . . . . . . . . . . . . . . .*131*

        *Integrating Bricks and Clicks* . . . . . . . . . . . . . . . . . . . . . . .*131*

        *Internet Pure Play* . . . . . . . . . . . . . . . . . . . . . . . . . . . . . . . .*132*

**Chapter 37**   **Formula for Success: Real-Time Channel Development** . . . .**133**

    Real-Time Channel Development . . . . . . . . . . . . . . . . . . . . . .134

**Chapter 38**   **Analyzing and Selecting Channels** . . . . . . . . . . . . . . . . .**136**

    Avoid Channel Conflict . . . . . . . . . . . . . . . . . . . . . . . . . . . . . .137

    Channel Checklist: Devil's in the Details . . . . . . . . . . . . . . . .137

**Chapter 39**   **Strategic Alliances and Partnerships** . . . . . . . . . . . . . . . . . . . . . . . . . .**139**

Strategic Alliance and Partnership Success Factors . . . . . . . . . . . . . . . . . . . .139

Channel Mapping . . . . . . . . . . . . . . . . . . . . . . . . . . . . . . . . . . . . . . . . . . . . . . .140

P • R • A • I • S • E™ Marketing Process . . . . . . . . . . . . . . . . . . . . . . . . . . . . .141

   *Analyze* . . . . . . . . . . . . . . . . . . . . . . . . . . . . . . . . . . . . . . . . . . . . . . . . . . .*141*

Summary: Section III . . . . . . . . . . . . . . . . . . . . . . . . . . . . . . . . . . . . . . . . . . . .141

**Section IV**   **Strategize: Growth Opportunities** . . . . . . . . . . . . . . . . . . . . . . . .**143**

**Chapter 40**   **What Is Strategy?** . . . . . . . . . . . . . . . . . . . . . . . . . . . . . . . . . . . . . . . .**145**

Strategy Process . . . . . . . . . . . . . . . . . . . . . . . . . . . . . . . . . . . . . . . . . . . . . . . .146

**Chapter 41**   **A Framework and Process for Strategy Development** . . . . . . . . . . .**147**

**Chapter 42**   **Target Market Strategies** . . . . . . . . . . . . . . . . . . . . . . . . . . . . . . . . . .**149**

Rich, Niche Markets . . . . . . . . . . . . . . . . . . . . . . . . . . . . . . . . . . . . . . . . . . . . .149

Mass Market Penetration . . . . . . . . . . . . . . . . . . . . . . . . . . . . . . . . . . . . . . . . .150

Attract Early Adopters, Maximize Profits . . . . . . . . . . . . . . . . . . . . . . . . . . . .151

Market Penetration Strategy Requires Innovation . . . . . . . . . . . . . . . . . . . . . .152

**Chapter 43**   **Positioning Strategy** . . . . . . . . . . . . . . . . . . . . . . . . . . . . . . . . . . . . . .**154**

Types of Positioning . . . . . . . . . . . . . . . . . . . . . . . . . . . . . . . . . . . . . . . . . . . . .154

Create a Positioning Statement . . . . . . . . . . . . . . . . . . . . . . . . . . . . . . . . . . . . .156

   *Example Positioning Statements:* . . . . . . . . . . . . . . . . . . . . . . . . . . . . . . . .*157*

**Chapter 44**   **What Is Your Brand Worth?** . . . . . . . . . . . . . . . . . . . . . . . . . . . . . . . .**159**

Personify Your Brand . . . . . . . . . . . . . . . . . . . . . . . . . . . . . . . . . . . . . . . . . . . .159

**Chapter 45**   **Design Your Brand Personality and Essence** . . . . . . . . . . . . . . . . . . .**162**

**Chapter 46**   **Customer Strategies** . . . . . . . . . . . . . . . . . . . . . . . . . . . . . . . . . . . . . .**166**

Customer Loyalty Objectives and Strategies . . . . . . . . . . . . . . . . . . . . . . . . . .166

**Chapter 47**   **Listen and Respond** . . . . . . . . . . . . . . . . . . . . . . . . . . . . . . . . . . . . . . .**169**

Emotion Is Viral . . . . . . . . . . . . . . . . . . . . . . . . . . . . . . . . . . . . . . . . . . . . . . . .170

**Chapter 48**   **Customers Are Your Best Advisors** . . . . . . . . . . . . . . . . . . . . . . . . . .**172**

**Chapter 49**   **Customers Are Cocreaters** . . . . . . . . . . . . . . . . . . . . . . . . . . . . . . . . .**174**

The $1 Million Prize . . . . . . . . . . . . . . . . . . . . . . . . . . . . . . . . . . . . . . . . . . . . .174

Customer Engagement: A New Business Model . . . . . . . . . . . . . . . . . . . . . . .175

**Chapter 50   Product and Service Strategy** . . . . . . . . . . . . . . . . . . . . . . . . . . . . . . . . . **177**

Product Life Cycle Stages . . . . . . . . . . . . . . . . . . . . . . . . . . . . . . . . . . . . .177

*Introduction* . . . . . . . . . . . . . . . . . . . . . . . . . . . . . . . . . . . . . . . . . . .*177*

*Growth* . . . . . . . . . . . . . . . . . . . . . . . . . . . . . . . . . . . . . . . . . . . . . . . . .*178*

*Maturity* . . . . . . . . . . . . . . . . . . . . . . . . . . . . . . . . . . . . . . . . . . . . . . .*178*

*Decline* . . . . . . . . . . . . . . . . . . . . . . . . . . . . . . . . . . . . . . . . . . . . . . . .*179*

Are You a Pioneer or a Follower? . . . . . . . . . . . . . . . . . . . . . . . . . . . . . .180

**Chapter 51   Product Differentiation** . . . . . . . . . . . . . . . . . . . . . . . . . . . . . . . . . . . . **181**

Design with a Purpose . . . . . . . . . . . . . . . . . . . . . . . . . . . . . . . . . . . . . . .182

**Chapter 52   Competitive Strategies** . . . . . . . . . . . . . . . . . . . . . . . . . . . . . . . . . . . . **185**

Pick Your Battle Position . . . . . . . . . . . . . . . . . . . . . . . . . . . . . . . . . . . . .185

*Attack* . . . . . . . . . . . . . . . . . . . . . . . . . . . . . . . . . . . . . . . . . . . . . . . . . .*185*

*Flank* . . . . . . . . . . . . . . . . . . . . . . . . . . . . . . . . . . . . . . . . . . . . . . . . . .*186*

*Defend* . . . . . . . . . . . . . . . . . . . . . . . . . . . . . . . . . . . . . . . . . . . . . . . . .*186*

*Preemptive* . . . . . . . . . . . . . . . . . . . . . . . . . . . . . . . . . . . . . . . . . . . . .*187*

*Substitute Product* . . . . . . . . . . . . . . . . . . . . . . . . . . . . . . . . . . . . . . .*187*

*Retreat* . . . . . . . . . . . . . . . . . . . . . . . . . . . . . . . . . . . . . . . . . . . . . . . .*187*

The Downside of Winning . . . . . . . . . . . . . . . . . . . . . . . . . . . . . . . . . . . .188

**Chapter 53   Growth Strategies** . . . . . . . . . . . . . . . . . . . . . . . . . . . . . . . . . . . . . . . . **189**

Acquisition . . . . . . . . . . . . . . . . . . . . . . . . . . . . . . . . . . . . . . . . . . . . . . . .189

Strategic Alliances and Partnerships . . . . . . . . . . . . . . . . . . . . . . . . . . . .190

New Distribution Channels . . . . . . . . . . . . . . . . . . . . . . . . . . . . . . . . . . . .190

New Markets . . . . . . . . . . . . . . . . . . . . . . . . . . . . . . . . . . . . . . . . . . . . . . .190

New Customers . . . . . . . . . . . . . . . . . . . . . . . . . . . . . . . . . . . . . . . . . . . . .192

New Products . . . . . . . . . . . . . . . . . . . . . . . . . . . . . . . . . . . . . . . . . . . . . .192

**Chapter 54   Innovation Strategies** . . . . . . . . . . . . . . . . . . . . . . . . . . . . . . . . . . . . . **194**

Innovation Models . . . . . . . . . . . . . . . . . . . . . . . . . . . . . . . . . . . . . . . . . .194

**Chapter 55   The Long Tail** . . . . . . . . . . . . . . . . . . . . . . . . . . . . . . . . . . . . . . . . . . . . **197**

New Revenue Streams and Business Models . . . . . . . . . . . . . . . . . . . . . . .198

**Chapter 56   Nurture a Culture of Innovation** . . . . . . . . . . . . . . . . . . . . . . . . . . . . . **199**

Three Versus Drive Innovation and Growth . . . . . . . . . . . . . . . . . . . . . . .200

**Chapter 57   Sales Strategy and Plan** . . . . . . . . . . . . . . . . . . . . . . . . . . . . . . . . . . . **203**

Sales Strategy and Plan . . . . . . . . . . . . . . . . . . . . . . . . . . . . . . . . . . . . . .204

**Chapter 58**   **Marketing Objectives Drive Strategy** . . . . . . . . . . . . . . . . . . . . . . . . . . . . .206

**Chapter 59**   **The Art and Science of Developing Strategy** . . . . . . . . . . . . . . . . . . .208

Strategy Integration . . . . . . . . . . . . . . . . . . . . . . . . . . . . . . . . . . . . . . . . . .209

A Final Word . . . . . . . . . . . . . . . . . . . . . . . . . . . . . . . . . . . . . . . . . . . . . . .209

P • R • A • I • S • E™ Marketing Process . . . . . . . . . . . . . . . . . . . . . . . . . . .210

*Strategize* . . . . . . . . . . . . . . . . . . . . . . . . . . . . . . . . . . . . . . . . . . . . . .*210*

Summary: Section IV . . . . . . . . . . . . . . . . . . . . . . . . . . . . . . . . . . . . . . . . .210

**Section V**   **Implement: Traditional and New Media** . . . . . . . . . . . . . . . . . . . . .**211**

**Chapter 60**   **The State of Marketing Today** . . . . . . . . . . . . . . . . . . . . . . . . . . . . . . .213

Changes in Latitudes, Changes in Attitudes . . . . . . . . . . . . . . . . . . . . . . . . .213

Facts, Stats, and Key Trends . . . . . . . . . . . . . . . . . . . . . . . . . . . . . . . . . . . . .214

Key Trends Driving Marketing . . . . . . . . . . . . . . . . . . . . . . . . . . . . . . . . . . .215

**Part I**   **Social Media, Digital Media, and Personal Communication Tactics** . . . . . . . . . . . . . . . . . . . . . . . . . . . . . . . . . . . . **219**

**Chapter 61**   **Digital Base Camp: Create a Great Web Site** . . . . . . . . . . . . . . .**220**

Design for User Experience . . . . . . . . . . . . . . . . . . . . . . . . . . . . . . . . . . . . .221

Make Your Web Site Interactive and Targeted . . . . . . . . . . . . . . . . . . . . . . . .222

Integrated Technologies Deliver Better Customer Service . . . . . . . . . . . . . .223

Provide Value For Free . . . . . . . . . . . . . . . . . . . . . . . . . . . . . . . . . . . . . . . . .224

**Chapter 62**   **Search Engine Marketing (SEM) and Optimization** . . . . . . . . . . .**225**

Optimize Your Web Site . . . . . . . . . . . . . . . . . . . . . . . . . . . . . . . . . . . . . . . .226

**Chapter 63**   **Online Advertising** . . . . . . . . . . . . . . . . . . . . . . . . . . . . . . . . . . . . . . .**227**

Display Advertising . . . . . . . . . . . . . . . . . . . . . . . . . . . . . . . . . . . . . . . . . . .227

Sponsorships and Affiliate Advertising . . . . . . . . . . . . . . . . . . . . . . . . . . . . .228

Ad Exchanges . . . . . . . . . . . . . . . . . . . . . . . . . . . . . . . . . . . . . . . . . . . . . . .229

**Chapter 64**   **Email Marketing** . . . . . . . . . . . . . . . . . . . . . . . . . . . . . . . . . . . . . . . . .**230**

**Chapter 65**   **Mobility Marketing** . . . . . . . . . . . . . . . . . . . . . . . . . . . . . . . . . . . . . . .**232**

Widgets, Gadgets, and Mobile Applications . . . . . . . . . . . . . . . . . . . . . . . . .232

A Growing Tidal Wave of Opportunity . . . . . . . . . . . . . . . . . . . . . . . . . . . . .233

How Companies Use Mobile Phones to Drive Business . . . . . . . . . . . . . . . .234

**Chapter 66**  **Social Media: Build Your Brand and Connect with Customers** . . .**235**

A Shift of Power . . . . . . . . . . . . . . . . . . . . . . . . . . . . . . . . . . . . .235

The Real Value of Social Media . . . . . . . . . . . . . . . . . . . . . . . . . .237

Social Media Principles . . . . . . . . . . . . . . . . . . . . . . . . . . . . . . . .238

**Chapter 67**  **What We Know So Far: Surprising Statistics** . . . . . . . . . . . . . . . . . .**239**

Business Results from Social Media . . . . . . . . . . . . . . . . . . . . . . . . . . .240

**Chapter 68**  **Measuring the Effectiveness of Social Media** . . . . . . . . . . . . . . . . . .**241**

Operationalize Social Media . . . . . . . . . . . . . . . . . . . . . . . . . . . . .242

**Chapter 69**  **Social Media Networks** . . . . . . . . . . . . . . . . . . . . . . . . . . . . . . . . .**245**

LinkedIn . . . . . . . . . . . . . . . . . . . . . . . . . . . . . . . . . . . . . . . . . .245

Facebook . . . . . . . . . . . . . . . . . . . . . . . . . . . . . . . . . . . . . . . . . .246

Twitter . . . . . . . . . . . . . . . . . . . . . . . . . . . . . . . . . . . . . . . . . . .247

Social Bookmarking Sites . . . . . . . . . . . . . . . . . . . . . . . . . . . . . . .250

**Chapter 70**  **The Blogosphere** . . . . . . . . . . . . . . . . . . . . . . . . . . . . . . . . . . . . . .**251**

Getting Started . . . . . . . . . . . . . . . . . . . . . . . . . . . . . . . . . . . . . .253

**Chapter 71**  **Social Media Strategy and Planning Guide** . . . . . . . . . . . . . . . . . . . .**254**

Social Media Strategy . . . . . . . . . . . . . . . . . . . . . . . . . . . . . . . . . .254

*Purpose* . . . . . . . . . . . . . . . . . . . . . . . . . . . . . . . . . . . . . . . .255

*Purpose: What Do You Want to Accomplish?* . . . . . . . . . . . . . . . . . .255

*Research* . . . . . . . . . . . . . . . . . . . . . . . . . . . . . . . . . . . . . . . .256

*Research: Who Is Your Target Audience and Where Will You Find Them?* . . . . . . . . . . . . . . . . . . . . . . . . . . . . . . . . . . . . . .256

*Research to Listen, Understand, and Respond Effectively* . . . . . . . . . . . .256

*ANALYZE* . . . . . . . . . . . . . . . . . . . . . . . . . . . . . . . . . . . . . . .256

*Analyze: Statistics, Media Tools, Metrics, and Trends* . . . . . . . . . . . . . .256

*STRATEGIZE* . . . . . . . . . . . . . . . . . . . . . . . . . . . . . . . . . . . . .257

*Strategize: Create Your Game Plan* . . . . . . . . . . . . . . . . . . . . . . . .257

*Positioning: Articulate Your Brand Promise* . . . . . . . . . . . . . . . . . . .257

*Presence: Select the Types of Social Media to Use* . . . . . . . . . . . . . . .257

*Implement* . . . . . . . . . . . . . . . . . . . . . . . . . . . . . . . . . . . . . . .258

*Implement: Develop a Tactical Plan* . . . . . . . . . . . . . . . . . . . . . . . .258

*EXECUTE AND EVALUATE* . . . . . . . . . . . . . . . . . . . . . . . . . . . .259

                             *Execute: Link Strategy and Execution* .......................... .259

                             *Company Culture: Social Media Roles and Policy* ............... .259

                             *Evaluate: Metrics* ........................................ .259

                             *Reporting and Adjustments: Experimentation Criteria* ............. .260

**Chapter 72**    **Word of Mouth: Viral Marketing and Buzz** ..................... **261**

                  Stunts and Pranksters ........................................ .261

                  Historical Milestone ......................................... .262

**Chapter 73**    **Public Relations** ......................................... **265**

                  What's New, Who Cares? ..................................... .265

                             *Search* ................................................. .266

                             *Reach* ................................................. .266

                             *Frequency* .............................................. .267

                             *Pitching Your Story* ...................................... .267

                  The Mechanics ............................................. .268

                             *Search Criteria* ......................................... .268

                             *Links* .................................................. .268

                             *News Release* ........................................... .268

                             *News Advisory* .......................................... .269

                             *Media Kit/Media Room* ................................... .269

                             *You Got the Story...Now What?* ............................. .270

**Part II**        **Create a Tactical Plan with Execution Built-In** .................. **271**

                  Marketing and Sales Program ROI Analysis ...................... .272

**Chapter 74**    **Make Marketing Measurable** ............................... **273**

                  Individual Tactics Description ................................. .273

**Chapter 75**    **Implementation Calendar and Budget** ....................... **275**

                  Implement ................................................. .277

                             *P • R • A • I • S • E™ Marketing Process* ...................... .277

                  Summary: Section V ......................................... .277

**Section VI**   **Execute and Evaluate: Create a Culture of Execution** ...... **279**

**Chapter 76**    **The Problem with Marketing** ............................... **281**

                  How to Fix the Biggest Problems in Sales and Marketing .............. .282

                             *Break Down Sales and Marketing Silos* ....................... .283

                             *Change the Sales Pitch, Win New Business* ...................... .284

| | | |
|---|---|---|
| | *Organize Around Customers, Not Products* | .285 |
| | *Collaborate, Automate, and Get Smart* | .286 |
| | *Marketing Is Not a Department* | .288 |
| | *Measure Marketing, Continuously Improve* | .289 |
| **Chapter 77** | **Asset-Based Marketing Measurement** | **.291** |
| | Holistic Marketing Measurement | .292 |
| | Key Performance Measures | .293 |
| **Chapter 78** | **Evaluate: What Is Measured Improves** | **.295** |
| | Purpose | .295 |
| | Research | .296 |
| | Analyze | .297 |
| | Implement | .297 |
| | Strategize | .298 |
| | Evaluate and Execute | .298 |
| **Chapter 79** | **ROI Optimizer™: Increase the Effectiveness of How Marketing Is Measured** | **.299** |
| | ROI Optimizer™ Process | .300 |
| | *Step 1: Set Your Goals* | .301 |
| | *Step 2: Products and Services* | .302 |
| | *Step 3: Define Sales Channels* | .303 |
| | *Step 4: Define Target Customer Segments* | .303 |
| | *Step 5: Define Marketing and Sales Programs* | .304 |
| | *Definitions* | .305 |
| | Top-Down and Bottom-Up Analysis | .305 |
| | Demand Chain Optimization | .307 |
| **Chapter 80** | **The Balanced Scorecard** | **.308** |
| | What Is Measured Improves | .311 |
| **Chapter 81** | **The Art and Science of Execution** | **.313** |
| **Chapter 82** | **Real-Time Marketing Planning** | **.317** |
| **Chapter 83** | **Create a Culture of Execution** | **.319** |
| | Culture Rules! 10 Principles to Drive Business Success…and Have More Fun | .319 |
| | 1. It's the Economics, Stupid. | .319 |

2. Walk the Talk . . . . . . . . . . . . . . . . . . . . . . . . . . . . . . . . . . . . .321

3. Integrity, Accountability, and Trust . . . . . . . . . . . . . . . . . . . . .321

4. Create a Compelling Vision . . . . . . . . . . . . . . . . . . . . . . . . . . .322

5. Product Myopia Is the Death Spiral . . . . . . . . . . . . . . . . . . . . .323

6. Love Is the Killer App . . . . . . . . . . . . . . . . . . . . . . . . . . . . . . .324

7. Feedback Is the Breakfast of Champions . . . . . . . . . . . . . . . . .325

8. Relentless Communication . . . . . . . . . . . . . . . . . . . . . . . . . . . .325

9. Link Planning to Operations . . . . . . . . . . . . . . . . . . . . . . . . . .326

10. Marketing Is Not a Department: It's a State of Mind . . . . . . . .327

Evaluate and Execute . . . . . . . . . . . . . . . . . . . . . . . . . . . . . . . . . .328

*P • R • A • I • S • E™ Marketing Process* . . . . . . . . . . . . . . . . . .328

Summary: Section VI . . . . . . . . . . . . . . . . . . . . . . . . . . . . . . . . . .328

**Chapter 84   Now It's Up to You** . . . . . . . . . . . . . . . . . . . . . . . . . . . . . .**329**

**Endnotes** . . . . . . . . . . . . . . . . . . . . . . . . . . . . . . . . . . . . . .**331**

**Workshops and Training Programs** . . . . . . . . . . . . . . . . . . . . . .**337**

***Real-Time Marketing for Business Growth* Free Resources and Tools** . . . . . . . . . . . . . . . . . . . . . . . . . . . . . . . . . . . . . . . .**339**

**Appendix** . . . . . . . . . . . . . . . . . . . . . . . . . . . . . . . . . . . . . . .**341**

**Index** . . . . . . . . . . . . . . . . . . . . . . . . . . . . . . . . . . . . . . . . . .**347**

The following are available online at www.MarketSmarter.com:

• Research Resource Guide
• Competitive Research Guide
• Social Media Strategy and Planning Guide
• Marketing Plan Template
• Worksheets and Examples from each section
• Marketing Implementation Calendar
• Tactical Plan Template
• Traditional Media content
• …and other worksheets, tools and templates

# Foreword

*Real-Time Marketing for Business Growth* is an important book. Those of us who have been in business for a while know that business growth is rarely the result of one miraculous strategy or tactic. It's a series of small things that guide a business in upward growth. That's what I like about this book. It teaches people how to combine time-tested business concepts with new marketing tools and strategies. The result is an efficient and effective process to develop a plan—a roadmap for growth and success for your business.

This book presents marketing in an entirely new light. It highlights some of the problems in sales and marketing that have persisted for decades—and how to fix them. It shows companies how to organize around customers instead of products, and the need for companies to break down the silos between marketing, sales, customer service, and other teams to more effectively fulfill customer needs. It shows companies how to create a thriving culture that respects customers and employees—both of which are stakeholders.

This book was written for people like me—and most of you, I imagine—who are looking for something new in marketing. New and experienced entrepreneurs, marketers, and CEOs will find this book full of fresh new insights, including how to measure marketing and how to use social media to build customer relationships. Most importantly, it provides a process for writing a marketing plan—and smart business leaders know that the key to successful business growth is business planning. Monique teaches you a real-time planning process that keeps pace with change. It's a flexible, collaborative, and measurable process so your plan is a living, breathing operational document to help the entire business execute strategy and continuously improve.

*Real-Time Marketing for Business Growth* explains marketing in simple terms that can be understood by any business owner. This is not to say that this book oversimplifies. In fact, I have never seen a more comprehensive explanation of marketing. Many books deal with marketing as a tactic. This book presents marketing holistically through the P•R•A•I•S•E Marketing Process, which is a new paradigm that takes a fresh look at marketing planning. The plan it produces can make a company "'market smart" and improve profitability. How could it do anything else? To me, the most important concept I've ever taught is about praising—catching people doing something right. So I certainly would love a P•R•A•I•S•E Marketing Process.

There are four aspects of this book which I feel are unique in the field of marketing. First of all, *Real-Time Marketing for Business Growth* integrates culture throughout the marketing process. It starts with defining your company purpose, and I have always believed that a compelling vision and strong core values are the basic foundation of any business.

I know from experience that a healthy, thriving culture is woven into the fabric of every successful business. Companies that foster a thriving culture create a strong *internal* brand and that is the secret to creating a powerful *external* brand. This book will show you how to create happy, engaged employees—who in turn create delighted, engaged customers who become "raving fans."

Second, I like the fact that *Real-Time Marketing for Business Growth* simplifies and clarifies what can be a complex subject. The *One Minute Manager* series of books is focused and simple—and I have received considerable feedback that this is a powerful way to teach. Since I have made it my life's work to take the "BS" out of the behavioral sciences, I can relate to the power of simplicity when you want the learner to get full value from a book. Monique Reece has taken the "BS" out of the marketing planning process. Thankfully, this book avoids technical terms when possible and explains them when necessary.

Third, this approach focuses on customer experience and how to build customer loyalty. This is accomplished through ongoing real-time feedback from customers. I've often said that "feedback is the breakfast of champions." You'll get fresh ideas on how to attract new customers, retain them, and grow your relationships with them. This transforms customers into evangelists for your business—which of course increases profitability for your business.

Serendipity is the fourth fresh quality of *Real-Time Marketing for Business Growth.* Akin to luck, serendipity lets us know that there's a force greater than ourselves. Serendipity within the research step, for example, can reveal insights that dramatically influence the way a company chooses to market itself. And in a world that changes constantly, businesses must always adapt and change. I believe, as Monique does, that you should put your antennae up. If you are looking for something to happen, you'll get it.

Anyone wanting to increase profitability and reach a wider audience should venture through the P•R•A•I•S•E Marketing Process. It's a journey that can lead you to your greatest achievements. Thanks, Monique. All aboard!

**—Ken Blanchard**
Coauthor of *The One Minute Manager* and *Leading at a Higher Level*

# Acknowledgments

It started with one idea: to help CEOs, marketers, and entrepreneurs learn a better process for creating sustainable business growth. This book was written during one of the most difficult economic times in history, which sparked a question that I just couldn't let go of: If 87 percent of the businesses in the U.S. failed in the best of times, how would businesses succeed during one of the worst economic downturns?

It seemed like the right time to write a book that will teach people how to market smarter. Business leaders are more open and responsive to changing old, outdated methods of marketing that no longer work. We can change the business failure rate by helping businesses implement a proven process to plan, execute, and grow. As this recession gives birth to a new wave of entrepreneurship around the world, it is my dream to help businesses succeed.

This book is dedicated to the clients and alumni of the MarketSmarter Growth Plan Workshop who have learned and applied this process. As you have road-tested various iterations, your experiences have provided me with great deal of insight and invaluable feedback to continuously improve the process. I am so blessed to work with such amazing people—I really do love all of you!

It has been deeply rewarding to work with students in the Executive MBA program at the University of Denver. You're a smart and tough group of experienced corporate executives and entrepreneurs who have inspired me as you implemented so many of the ideas in this book with great success. We share a mutual passion for learning and you have taught me as much as I have offered to you. I also wish to thank Barbara Kreisman, Kerry Plemmons, Scott McLagan, and Kelsey Johnson at the University of Denver for giving me the opportunity to partner with such an outstanding university. Your leadership and entrepreneurial thinking is a breath of fresh air.

My deepest appreciation to Timothy Moore at FT Press and my brilliant editor, Jennifer Simon. This book is a reality because of your vision. I appreciate all the people at Pearson Education who have helped guide and shape this book. Russ Hall guided development, Jovana San Nicolas-Shirley was an absolute machine overseeing the entire production process, as was Kristy Hart, Managing Editor, and Julie Anderson provided meticulous copy editing. I would also like to thank Amy Neidlinger and Megan Colvin for their marketing expertise, as well as Amanda Moran, and Myesha Graham.

I have had the pleasure of working with Sharon Brandt and Steve Snyder over the course of nearly ten years. Not only are you the most talented people I have ever hired, I am also grateful for your friendship. Sharon, I appreciate your early feedback on the manuscript and continued support throughout the process. You write marketing plans better and faster than anyone I know! Steve, your brilliant insight on the ROI Optimizer has helped make a long standing goal a reality.

I would like to extend a heartfelt thank you to everyone who has contributed examples, case studies, and stories to bring this book to life including Denzil Samuels, Will Wade, Scott Nisbet, Andrew Graham, Michael Kuehn,Thomas Dahl, Luke Wyckoff, Tyler McCarty, Josh Fuller, Rob Silk, Sarah Mead, and Jessica McLean, my executive assistant who tracked down so many details for this project. A special thanks to Ryan Hunter, Lisa Johannes and Renee Armijo who provided early feedback on the manuscript and contributed great case studies.

If it hadn't been for a serendipitous meeting with Joel Appel and Frank Kvietok, this book would have never happened. Thank you for your inspiration and encouragement—and of course the excellent case studies and examples of kick butt product marketing.

A special thank you to Pamela Stambaugh, my coauthor of *Market Smarter Not Harder*, for collaborating with me on the first version of the PRAISE Marketing Process and encouraging me to do more with this fabulous model.

I am deeply appreciative of the "masters" who have shared their enduring wisdom and thought leadership: Clayton Christensen, David Norton, Robert Kaplan, Philip Kotler, Guy Kawasaki, Scott Bedbury, Kim Chan, Renee Mauborgne, Don Schulz, and so many others. I am especially grateful to Tony Hsieh for having the courage and vision to bring the topic of culture out of the closet and into the mainstream. Now about that topic of happiness….

A heartfelt thank you to Ken Blanchard for your wonderful support. Your insight and wisdom continue to inspire me.

My family has always been my biggest source of strength. Lynne, Mark, Michelle, and Colleen, my fun and amazing sisters and brother—and best friends. Mom and Dad, your love for us, and each other, has taught us all the power of unconditional love and the gift of family. Your encouragement has always pushed me to overcome any obstacle. Renee, Gina, and Jake—thank you for your patience and love throughout this process.

A huge hug and heartfelt thank you to my children, Isabella and Morgan. You have been so patient, understanding, and loving while I worked nights, weekends, and holidays on this project. And to Walter, you fill me up. You have given me so much support. Thank you for your amazing love…and for giving me the magic of Santa Fe.

And finally, I must say that this book was made possible through many long runs on the country roads of Santa Fe where I had many good conversations with God. I asked only for energy and wisdom so that I could put the tools and resources for business success into your hands. Now that you're holding it, *go do something with it!*

# About the Author

**Monique Reece** is the founder and CEO of MarketSmarter, a marketing consulting and training firm that helps companies improve strategy and implement real-time business planning processes to develop a culture of execution. MarketSmarter helps businesses create dynamic cultures that inspire innovation, employee commitment and customer loyalty. Monique has more than 20 years of marketing and executive management experience working with both Fortune 500 companies and fast-growing entrepreneurial businesses. She formerly served as Executive Vice President at Jones Knowledge and as Director of Global Market Development and Corporate Planning at Avaya. She has created business strategy, marketing plans, and training programs for several of the world's leading brands.

Monique is an Executive Education faculty member at the Daniels College of Business, University of Denver. She is also an Adjunct Professor at the Institute for Leadership and Organizational Performance at the University of Denver where she teaches marketing and customer experience in the Executive MBA program.

Monique is the creator of the MarketSmarter Growth Plan Workshop, a program that teaches CEOs, marketers, and sales professionals, and entrepreneurs how to develop growth strategies and marketing plans. She developed the MarketSmarter ROI Optimizer, a tool that helps businesses predict, measure, and continuously improve the results of sales, marketing and service programs.

As a columnist and writer, she has published hundreds of articles and is coauthor of *Market Smarter Not Harder*. She is also a frequent speaker for industry conferences such as the American Marketing Association and *Inc. Magazine*. She currently serves on the Chief Marketing Officer Council (CMO) Academic Liaison Board, the board of directors for The International Entrepreneurs (TiE Rockies), and several private companies.

Helping businesses learn and grow is Monique's biggest passion. She lives in Denver, Colorado and Santa Fe, New Mexico.

# Introduction

Predictable, profitable business growth is not as hard as you might think. Business growth is rarely the result of one miraculous strategy or tactic. It's the culmination of several small things that guide a business in upward growth. Sustainable business growth is also the result of business planning. Even though this fact is substantiated by countless studies and respected business leaders, most businesses don't have an *operational* marketing plan that is used daily to guide decision making, interactions with customers, and processes for people to collaboratively execute.

This book will show you the most effective way to create continuous, profitable growth. It combines timeless marketing concepts with many new marketing tools and strategies to provide you with the most efficient way I know to create a market plan—a roadmap for growth and success for your business.

You will learn a proven process that entrepreneurs and business professionals have been using for well over a decade to create significant success in their businesses. As an entrepreneur, marketing executive, and professor, I have helped business leaders launch and grow their companies for over 20 years, and I understand the challenge of finding time for business planning. That is why I made it a mission to develop the most efficient and effective method of planning that I possibly could.

Business owners are overwhelmed with information and the need to adapt to a constantly changing global market place—these factors highlight the need for business planning more than ever. How do we quickly assimilate and adjust strategies to respond? The answer is to apply *a new way of planning that is in real-time and has execution built into the process*. Planning and execution must be tightly integrated to occur not as an event or annual process, but part of day-to-day operations.

It's also time to fix the problems in sales and marketing that have persisted for decades, such as how to make marketing more measurable, organizing the company around customers instead of products, and breaking down the silos between marketing and sales teams to sell more effectively to customers. Marketing must also be flexible to integrate the latest marketing tools, social media, and online marketing strategies.

This book is written for CEOs, entrepreneurs, marketers, and sales professionals who are looking for a new, yet proven method to create business growth. This process and framework have been used to develop hundreds of marketing plans for companies in consumer, business, non-profit, retail, and manufacturing industries. Companies of all sizes and stages of maturity have used this process to increase revenue, profitability, and discover new business opportunities. Start-ups have used the planning framework as a feasibility study to test a new business idea or launch a new company. Fast-growing businesses use the process to grow at triple-digit rates. Even companies that have been in business for several decades have reaped tremendous value by developing a plan that keeps pace with customer needs in an ever-changing business climate.

In short, the process is flexible and proven to be successful. If you're tired of the same old marketing and business strategies and ready for growth, read on.

## Imagine

## A New Way of Marketing......

### ...in Real-Time

Eliminate the sacred and inefficient annual planning process and replace it with real-time planning that keeps pace with change. Use a process and tools that are flexible, collaborative, and measurable so the plan is a living, breathing operational document shared across the organization to help the entire business execute strategy and continuously improve.

### ...Improves Execution

Research proves that 90 percent of a company's strategy is not executed. Business planning cannot be disaggregated from execution; businesses need a planning process *with execution built in*. Learn how to create a culture of execution that is accountable and measurable.

### ...Makes Marketing Measurable, Predictable, and Successful

Introducing the ROI Optimizer, an industry-changing process that links and optimizes the entire demand chain so marketing and sales programs achieve increased levels of measurability and success. You will learn how to accurately predict the return on investment of sales and marketing programs by linking them to revenue goals, product and service forecasts, sales channels, and target market segments.

### ...Integrates Proven Concepts and Best Practices with New Tools

Even best practices need updating to reflect today's market realities.

Integrate best in class business tools like the Balanced Scorecard and strategy fundamentals from leading business experts into your plan. Combine proven marketing strategies with innovative new tools and techniques to target elusive buyers.

### ...Improves Customer Experience and Lifetime Value

Learn the easiest, most consistent way to create profitable business growth. Get fresh insight on how to attract new customers, retain them, and grow customer lifetime value. Learn how to create customers who are evangelists for your business and create increased levels of customer loyalty and profitability for your business.

### ...Develops Company Culture into Marketing's Secret Weapon

As former IBM CEO Lou Gerstner said, "Culture isn't part of the game. It IS the game." A thriving culture is woven into the fabric of successful businesses. Throughout this marketing process, you will learn how to create happy, engaged employees—who in turn create delighted, engaged customers. Businesses that foster a thriving culture create not only a powerful brand, they are *proven* to have substantially higher profits—up to 50 percent more—than businesses that don't.

### ...Innovates Using Social Media and New Media Marketing

New media tactics are rapidly beginning to overshadow, and in some cases replace, more traditional media channels. Build an integrated marketing plan that uses new media like search engine marketing, email marketing, viral marketing, social networking, and blogging. Learn how these tools will help you generate new leads as well as improve customer relationships and your company brand.

### ...Inspires by Producing Fast Results

Entrepreneurs and marketing and sales professionals aren't looking for "fill in the blank" exercises to help them run their business. Nor do they want to wade through long theoretical explanations of strategy. They need to know *how* to execute real-time marketing into a business plan that gets results. Learn a six-step process that provides your business with the fastest and most efficient method to create a plan for business growth...and lifelong skills that can be used to continuously improve your business.

*"A fool with a plan can outsmart a genius with no plan."*
*T. Boone Pickens*

## Decision-Making Framework

This book is organized in sections according to each step in the P •R•A•I•S•E™ Marketing Process (Purpose, Research, Analyze, Implement, Strategize, and Execute and Evaluate). Each step provides a decision-making framework that guides you to summarize your actions and decisions (see Figure I.1). Here's a quick summary of what we will cover in each section:

**Purpose:** Your company mission, vision, and values will define the direction for your business. You will define specific goals in several strategic areas and your marketing plan will be written to achieve these goals. You'll also create a situation analysis and SWOT analysis.

**Research:** The work you do in this section will lay the foundation for the rest of your plan. This part of the process may take you the longest, *but it is the most important so don't skip it!* The results are an understanding of customer wants and needs, customer segmentation, a definition of your target market, and a competitive analysis. You will also gain a deep understanding of the market forces impacting your industry. All of this information will be used to develop your strategies later in the process.

**Analyze:** In this section you will analyze research findings, distribution channels, and pricing to discover new product and service growth opportunities. You will also analyze competitors, market trends, and customer insight to identify new areas for business growth and improve customer experience.

**Strategize:** You will apply everything you have learned to develop a sales plan, marketing objectives, and marketing strategies. You will develop a positioning statement that differentiates your business and develop customer, target market, competitive, product, price, promotion, distribution, growth, and innovation strategies for your business.

**Implement:** You will learn how social media and other types of digital media can help you create brand awareness, drive leads, and engage customers. You will learn how to develop a tactical plan that defines the sales and marketing programs, timeline, budget, and resource needs. Apply these processes and methodology to improve execution, ROI, and sales for your business.

**Execute and Evaluate:** The "E" in P•R•A•I•S•E stands for Execute and Evaluate. You will identify critical metrics to track and evaluate strategies, and learn how to use the ROI Optimizer to measure and improve the results of marketing and sales programs across your entire demand chain. You will learn how to integrate marketing with operations and learn 10 principles that will improve your company's culture and ability to execute.

---

### Real-Time Marketing

Creating a marketing plan takes more time to develop the first time, but once it's written, it is much easier to update in real-time and keep it fresh. A good analogy is having a goal of getting fit. If you are out of shape, the first few weeks are tough. You can't delegate "getting in shape" to someone else; you have to do the push-ups yourself. But it becomes easier over time, and once you're in shape, it is much easier to stay that way. The same is true with your plan. Once it is developed, it is much easier to keep it current— and your business is in good shape to respond to changing market conditions.

---

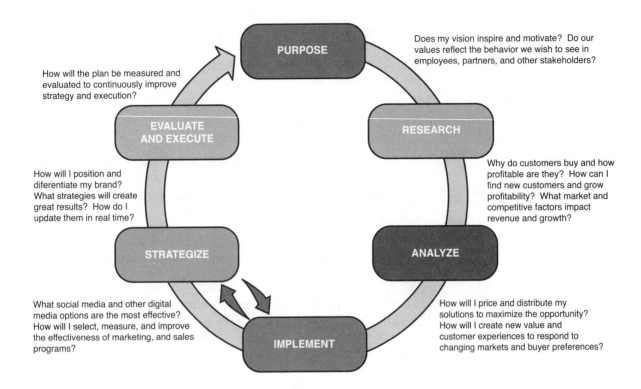

**Figure I.1** *Decision-making framework*

# Section I

# Purpose: Define Your Purpose

*"People want to be a part of something larger than themselves.
They want to be part of something they're really proud of,
that they'll fight for, sacrifice for, that they trust."*
—Howard Schultz, CEO, Starbucks

Defining your purpose is a critical first step in the process of any marketing plan because it describes why you are in business, where the business is headed, and how people will work together. Purpose characterizes the heart and soul of your business.

In this section of the marketing plan, you will define the following:

- Your *company vision,* which describes what your company will evolve to become in the future
- Your company *mission,* which summarizes what you sell, to whom, and how you deliver on this promise
- *Values* that people in the company must believe in and live by which is evidenced by their behavior
- Specific company *goals* that will be achieved during the defined planning time period
- A Situation Analysis to describe your company's current state
- A SWOT (Strengths, Weaknesses, Opportunities, and Threats) Analysis to define your company strengths and weaknesses relative to external opportunities and threats

# 1

# What Is Purpose and Why Is It Important?

If people understand where the company is headed (vision), what the company stands for (mission), how they will work together to get there (values), and what must be accomplished (goals), then the strategy to get there can be understood and executed.

These four elements will ultimately define your company culture, the kind of people you hire, suppliers you work with, how you treat your customers, and even the quality of the customers you attract. Ultimately, it is the best way you can create a solid foundation for your business that will set the compass in the direction you intend.

If you are an entrepreneur, your purpose is further refined by the reason you started your business. It's the passion, vision, and opportunity that inspired you to start the company. Company purpose is unique to every entrepreneur, just as personality is unique to every person. The goal in defining your purpose is to get clarity about what business you are in, how it is unique from others in the market, and the value you provide to all your stakeholders. A business does not exist solely to make money (although that is a nice goal). A business exists to provide value to customers who buy its products and services. If you focus on providing extraordinary value to customers, this alone can drive success.

Just to be clear, this section of your marketing plan is not about "fluff." Most of us have been in strategic planning sessions (or have worked at companies) in which considerable time was spent drafting mission statements only to wonder about the significance of what was really accomplished. And surely as a consumer, you have had an experience where you observed a mission statement displayed prominently on the wall of a business only to discover the words in the statement were anything but *your* experience with the company.

## Purpose-Driven Companies Make Higher Profits

If you want higher profits, have a purpose. Writing this section of your plan will increase profits while also creating a business that is more fun and meaningful for you, your employees, and your customers. *Companies that clearly define their mission, vision, and guiding principles, and communicate this consistently across the organization, have significantly higher profit per employee than companies who perform poorly in this area.*[1] Success Profiles, a performance management company, studied 600 businesses and found that the average profit per employee in the survey increased from $7,802 per employee to $27,401 in companies that make this a best practice in their organization.

If you think things like mission, vision, values, goals, culture, and company purpose are merely "soft," nice-to-have attributes for a business, this fact alone should change your mind.

As the leader driving the development of this important effort, you have the opportunity to create the experience people have with your company. If you are the company founder, you will develop the mission, vision, values, and goals to inspire your employees. If you are a marketing or strategic planning executive, you will have the opportunity to drive this process and communicate the messages in unique and creative ways so they are understood and integrated into the company culture. You will facilitate this important assignment and communicate the messages in your internal company brand campaign. As you will learn in the chapters that follow, an internal brand campaign is as important as your external campaigns because it inspires the actions and behaviors that ultimately become part of your brand.

We will explore several examples of companies that have done an exceptional job of defining their purpose. We will also look at a few special companies that have taken the road less traveled to create a company where company purpose is THE distinct competitive advantage for their company. Author Jim Collins defines the characteristics of companies like this in his book *Good to Great*. CEOs like Tony Hsieh of Zappos and Kimberly Jordon of New Belgium Brewery run companies powered by purpose.

## Create Raving Fans

While hundreds of companies are beginning to embrace the concept of a purpose-driven organization, these companies tend to be the exception, rather than the rule. I find this surprising given the fact that not only are these companies adored by their employees and customers, but they also *deliver consistent profitability and return to their shareholders.* Perhaps I am oversimplifying this concept, but when you have a choice to run a great company versus a mediocre company, *why not* create a great company? Not only will you have more fun; but you will create loyal employees and customers who are "Raving Fans."[2]

*Raving Fans*, the title of a book coauthored by Ken Blanchard, describes customers who believe so much in a company's people and products that they actually become a part of the sales force. The way to create customers who are raving fans is to first treat your employees with great care and respect. If you do this, they in turn will care for customers. The result of creating raving fan customers, being the employer of choice, and the investment of choice is a "triple bottom line." As Blanchard is famous for saying, "Profit is the applause you get for taking care of your customers and creating a motivating environment for your people."[3]

Blanchard not only writes about companies with extraordinary purpose, he runs a company that lives by these principles every day. As Chief Spiritual Officer of The Ken Blanchard Companies, Ken Blanchard's role is to lead others at a higher level. He not only does this in his organization, but he also teaches other companies to embrace this concept. If you don't think this concept is important, especially in tough economic times, read on to see how Blanchard handled a difficult choice in our last recession during the period of time immediately following the 9/11 tragedy.

## When Employees Leave at Night, So Does Your Business

In the first thirty days following 9/11, the Blanchard Company lost $1.5 million. During the economic downturn that affected most companies at this time, Blanchard was losing between $350,000 and $400,000 a month. He did not lay off people or shutter the business (as many other businesses did) because he said it would be the wrong thing to do. Instead he said, "Here's the deal. This is what we've got to do. Let's break into task forces and look for ways to cut costs and increase sales. Let's see how we can all pull together."[4] Employees responded by agreeing to cut their salaries and stop paying into the 401k. If people quit, it was agreed that they would not be replaced.

As Blanchard observed the sacrifice his employees made, he declared that when they pulled out of the slump, he would take everyone to Hawaii. In February of 2005, he followed through on his promise and took 350 people to Hawaii for a celebration.

When Blanchard discussed his decision to handle a crisis in this manner, he said, "You know, without your people, you are nothing. That is the biggest leadership mistake most people make. They think people and results are an either/or proposition rather than a both/and proposition. At the end of the day, when everybody heads home, your business just left. So leadership is about your people. If you turn around and nobody is following you, you are probably not leading."[5]

The result of a purpose-driven, triple-bottom-line company is a concept Blanchard calls the "Fortunate 500." What I love about this concept is that the meaning of business success is redefined. Companies in the future will be successful not by their size, but by the quality of service offered to customers and the quality of life experienced by employees.

## Company Purpose: Intentional or Dysfunctional?

This is what makes a purpose-driven company so unique: *The words in mission and value statements are supported by actions that drive behavior.* Company culture is ultimately (and simply) defined as "the way things are done around here." As actions and behaviors define the culture of a company, it would be wise to do this in a purposeful way. Companies that don't pay attention to culture or view it as unimportant will by default create an atmosphere that could be described as "dysfunctional."

If you have a company that has been in business for several years, it will be helpful to reflect on what your purpose is today and what you intended it to be when you started it. An important part of the marketing planning process is reflecting on past results and taking a series of small incremental steps to improve based on the new knowledge acquired throughout the process.

If you have already defined a vision, a mission, and values for your company, ask yourself if they are still relevant or if they need to change. Ideally, a company's mission and value statements stand the test of time; however, if you feel the statements do not accurately reflect where you are going today, now is the time to change them. The first few years of an entrepreneur's business tend to evolve opportunistically; therefore, it's extremely valuable to step back and evaluate whether your businesses is heading in the intended direction. Ask: "Have I communicated my company purpose so everyone understands where we are headed and why?" If not, this is your opportunity to create a solid foundation for the business. The future success and growth of your business depends on its purpose, so take time to complete this important first step in the planning process. As your marketing plan develops, you will see that purpose drives your marketing and business strategies.

# 2

# A Mission Statement Answers "Why Do We Exist?"

What is a mission statement? *A good mission statement is a concise statement that summarizes what you offer, to whom, and how.* I will provide you with a few examples of good mission statements, and then we will discuss vision and value statements and how they all come together to define your company purpose. I suggest that you read this entire chapter so you can see how all the elements work together, and then craft your own mission, vision, and values statements.

There is not a specific formula for writing a mission statement, but there are a few guidelines. First, make it brief. If you can't summarize your company mission in one or two sentences, it's not clear what you sell to anyone. Second, it ideally summarizes what you sell, to whom, and how. The best way to know if your statement is clear is to test it with customers, employees, and strangers. If they have a puzzled look on their face after hearing or reading it, try again. Good mission statements are clear and concise.

The following statement is an example of a good mission statement. Ron Phelps, Owner of RedShift Framing, says he regularly gets comments from customers about their mission statement. Customers say it's a perfect reflection of their experience with RedShift.

---

### RedShift Framing Mission Statement

Our mission is to produce a perfect package for art that exceeds industry standards using innovation, creativity, and environmentally sound products at a fair profit to fulfill our customers' expectation of value, aesthetics, quality, and conservation.

Source: Red Shift Framing

---

Clinic Service Corporation is a medical billing company that provides services to over 900 physicians. Medical billing is far from "sexy," but as you can see by the mission statement, they deliver more than just billing statements.

> ## *Clinic Service Corporation Mission Statement*
>
> Clinic Service maximizes the profitability of medical providers. We serve as the trusted business advisor, consistently producing and communicating relevant, high-quality business results for our clients. The Clinic Service team applies an untouchable ease of doing business grounded in integrity, discipline, and seasoned professionalism. We care and lead the market because of it.
>
> Source: Clinic Service Corporation

What I love about both of the statements is how they each demonstrate market differentiation in competitive markets. RedShift Framing is clearly not your average framing store, and Clinic Service Corporation delivers far more than just medical billing.

## Does Your Mission Statement Inspire?

*A mission statement is often expressed externally to customers. It can also be internally focused to provide employees with clarity and guiding principles.*

Great mission statements are inspiring. They create a sense of pride and ownership with employees and customers alike. Mission statements that are flat and lifeless have no purpose, and in fact can be de-motivating to employees if there is no substance to back them up. Keep in mind that if your employees do not feel happy, respected, and engaged, it is extremely difficult to create happy, engaged customers.

Companies that are both employee and customer focused often create an "employee pledge" in addition to a mission statement. Sometimes the statement is directed to customers and employees, and other times statements include suppliers, partners, investors, and the communities in which the company operates.

In an extremely tumultuous industry filled with bankruptcy proceedings, Southwest Airlines is one of the few consistently profitable airlines that has also maintained a thriving culture. The company puts its mission, vision, and values first because they realize their company purpose and culture drives shareholder value and satisfaction. This is a company that has always realized that customer satisfaction is the result of employee satisfaction, and their eyes have not wavered from that target.

If you are writing a mission statement for the first time, look for inspiration from companies that you admire. Also consider learning from best practice companies in completely different industries. For example, if you want your business to be known for its great customer service, you can use Nordstrom or The Ritz-Carlton Hotel Company as examples, regardless of the industry you are in.

# 3

# Create a Compelling Vision

An essential part of defining your purpose is creating a vision statement. A vision statement is a vivid statement or story that describes what the company will be like in the future. The future is defined as a point in time, perhaps twenty or more years from now. If this timeframe is too hard to grasp, think about ten years from now. *The purpose of a vision statement is to inspire and inform people about where the company is headed in the future.*

I do not endorse a specific process for writing a vision statement because I believe it should be an individual creative exercise. For some people, a clear concise statement works best. For others, vivid descriptions, pictures, or even stories are the most effective ways to communicate a vision. Several years ago I worked with Denzil Samuels, who at the time was General Manager for the Managed Services Organization at Lucent Technologies. Although Lucent had a broad overarching statement of purpose, Denzil wanted to create a vision for the new division he was leading that would communicate and align people toward the vision he had for the organization. As he was a new leader in the company, he also needed to convey his leadership style and beliefs so that people would understand what was expected of them.

I was consulting to Lucent at the time and asked Denzil to create his vision so that it could be shared in one of his first all-employee meetings about strategic direction. While I expected a paragraph or statement, what he created was something much better. He wrote a story that illustrated what the division would look and feel like to a new employee in ten years. The story was written several years ago, so the technology has changed; however, the impact of his story has not. The following is what he wrote.

> *Our latest recruit, Lee Wong, entered the beautiful marbled three-story atrium of our new Management Services delivery headquarters. As he walked past the rich, cherry wood reception area, he overheard receptionists speaking in French, Spanish, Italian, Russian, and English. Gazing at the magnificent artwork hanging on the wall, Lee couldn't help but notice the customer commendation letters that hung below both the Baldridge and ISO certificates.*
>
> *"Welcome to Management Services," a voice called out to him. "Thank you for joining us. You will be one of eight people joining our team today. Over the next two days, our orientation program should take you through everything you need to know about our successful business enterprise.*

*Lee gasped as he suddenly caught a glimpse of Bill Gates leaving a conference room with one of the management services associates. "Is that Bill Gates?" asked Lee. "No, that's Leonard Chavez with someone from Microsoft," remarked the receptionist.*

*The group walked further and was stunned when they reached the Operations Center. In front of them, covering one of the large walls within the center was an enormous electronic map of the world with a multitude of flashing lights, representing cities around the world. "Each light represents a city where we have our customers and our people," exclaimed the guide.*

*"In Management Services, we pride ourselves on three key elements. The first is* Superior Customer Service, *so it helps to be where our customers are.* Innovation *is finding creative ways to solve their communication challenges, and the third is* Leadership, *whether it's state-of-the-art technology, globalization, market leadership, or playing a key role in our communities. We want our customers to think of us as leaders. Of course we can't do any of this if we are not profitable."*

*Everyone smiled.*

*They were led to another room that was referred to as the "pride of the techies."*

*"Our technicians have built their own lab environment to help us understand and use new technology as it's released and the potential impact on our customers. It helps us understand the complex environments our customers have and how we can ensure new technology can be easily integrated into their environment. Actually what I often hear them say is that it's just fun to play with the new stuff."*

*As the group moved further into the Management Services center, they couldn't help but notice the impressive electronic notice board filled with information. The board was utilizing state-of-the-art technology and had information presented in a variety of colors, text, and graphics, which represented information about the business.*

*"This is like our own internal CNN," exclaimed the tour guide. "We get accurate information in a timely way to our people so that they can make the decisions that impact our business."*

*Lee couldn't help but notice that everyone they had passed, observed, or talked to seemed very upbeat, cheerful, and positive. In addition, he noticed the diversity of the organization, the mix of ages, cultures, and gender was both refreshing and encouraging.*

*It was now lunchtime and as they made their way to the dining hall, they passed a conference room filled with associates. "What's going on in there?" asked Lee.*

*"Oh, we have guest speakers from outside companies who come in to give free lunch-time seminars. Today's seminar is how to invest in stocks and shares. It helps our people stay in touch with important information outside the workplace as well as ensuring we keep in touch with key companies and people in the Denver area."*

*Over lunch, the team was greeted by one of the Management Services leadership team. "Welcome to our team," remarked Kathy. "The mere fact you are here today is a great tribute to your ability." We started with over 300 applicants for these 8 positions." The team gasped. "We pride ourselves on picking the best so that we can deliver excellence to our customers. But just because you are here doesn't mean you have arrived...it means your journey has just started. We demand that you give us better than your best. We expect you to grow and develop your skills and knowledge, while focusing on the core values of the team. You would do yourselves a disservice if you expected any less of yourselves. Thank you."*

*As Kathy sat down, Lee smiled to himself and thought, "I may just be starting on this journey but I can't help feeling I've arrived!"*

## Tell a Story

Denzil's story paints a vivid picture of what a customer or employee would see, feel, and experience when they entered the Lucent building. The basic message is that the company would be a global market leader, the employees are diverse and multilingual, and the company takes pride in offering the best technology to service customers. The story also describes a company culture that is professional, fun, and caring.

What if Denzil had written a statement such as: "Our vision is to be a diverse, innovative, global market leader that provides superior service and technology solutions to customers worldwide."

This would have been a perfectly acceptable and safe approach, but does it really mean anything? Which statement is more meaningful to you? I think most of us would appreciate the story more because it paints a vivid picture that is unique and inspiring. When you engage people at an emotional level, it will motivate employees who must execute activities every day to help you realize the vision. In fact, in just two years, the new division grew to become a $75 million (profitable) division of Lucent Technologies. It is a several hundred million dollar division today. When Denzil left the company a few years later, the employees printed the vision statement on a large canvas, signed and framed it, and gave it to him as a parting gift.

As you create a vision statement, or review an existing vision statement that is already drafted, answer the following questions:

- Is the vision clear?
- Is it future-based yet realistic enough to achieve?
- Is it inspiring to those who work here?
- If so, are there ways to make it even more compelling?
- If not, how does it need to change to be motivating for all stakeholders?
- Are all stakeholders aware of the vision? How is it currently communicated so there is a shared understanding of it? What can be done to bring it into focus and inspire everyone in the company?

### Marketing Tip

If you are a marketing executive facilitating this process, I recommend that you give your CEO the purpose of the assignment, and perhaps some examples. Then let him or her be creative. This is the one exercise in the entire process that the business leader must own. Your job is to bring it to life through the marketing plan and communication in your internal branding campaigns. In doing so, it will create ownership with other people in the company who contribute to the vision as the company grows and changes.

# 4

# Core Values Drive Behavior

The next step is to define values that reflect company beliefs. Core values ultimately drive behavior, so when values are clear and defined, it conveys what is expected of employees and it helps them make decisions. Speed of decision making results in an increased ability to execute because time is not wasted figuring out what is important or a priority. Values also drive what kind of people you hire, suppliers you work with, and even the type of customers with whom you do business. Core values are a fundamentally important driver of business success with many benefits.

## Make It Personal

Defining qualities like values requires that you dig deep to understand what drives you and what matters most, regardless of the job you have or company you create. If you reflect on a time you have ever compromised your values, you have likely paid a high personal price and perhaps regretted an action or decision. Values conflicts are often at the root of organizational performance (just look at the news headlines) as well as the cause of relationship conflicts.

Luke Wyckoff, President of Wyckoff Consulting, founded his company by following his gut and uncompromising core values. When he worked for a large national recruiting firm, he experienced a series of events that were red flags to his personal sense of integrity. Continuously frustrated, he thought about the kind of executive recruiting firm that he would like to start: a firm focused on integrity, trust, and honesty.

One day, as he drove to a client meeting to make a pitch to the board of directors, he had a crazy idea. When he was greeted in the lobby by the executive who was recommending his services, he was asked, "Where are your presentation materials?" Luke said," They're in the car. If you trust me, just go with it." Luke walked into the board meeting and spontaneously presented his own company, making a very passionate speech about the principles and values of his firm. The board liked what his company stood for, and he walked out with an immediate assignment and a $20,000 retainer. This gave him the seed money and the courage to leave a company that had different values from his own to start his own firm. Lesson learned: Follow your gut and don't compromise your values.

# 5

# The "C" Word

Up to this point, I have made a few references to the "C" word, Culture, but I have not yet explained why it's so important. During the more than 20 years that I have developed marketing and business strategies, I've noticed something quite interesting: A company could develop the best kick-butt strategy to win in the market—and still fail to realize the potential of what was possible. What kept a company from achieving what it was clearly capable of? Some people might say "execution," but if you dig deeper, you have to ask, "What keeps a business from executing?"

The answer is culture. A company that has no soul, no sense of purpose, no passion for serving customers, and no desire to foster happiness and trust among employees can't possibly win in the market. A company without culture will never achieve greatness or even a fraction of what it could achieve with a healthy, vibrant culture.

So what is a healthy, vibrant culture? I could tell you, but I think it's better to show you. As I mentioned in the Introduction, culture is a theme woven throughout this process. You will learn from examples throughout the book and you will also have the opportunity to develop your own culture plan in the last chapter of the book. But for now, learn from a few of the masters. The examples in the rest of this section will show you how to create a truly amazing culture: a company where it's not only more fun to work, but more profitable and satisfying to all stakeholders as well. Let's start with a company that has recently become the poster child for culture and values-based leadership.

Las Vegas-based Zappos is anything but a typical online shoe retailer. Company culture and values do not simply differentiate the business, but seem to fuel the very idea of why the company exists. Founder and CEO Tony Hsieh attributes Zappos's overwhelming success (and over $1 billion in sales) to a culture that thrives on unique values and delivers exceptional levels of personalized customer service. In less than ten years, Zappos has created a customer base that exceeds 10 million, and an impressive 75 percent of customers return to buy an average of 2.5 times a year.

Truly exceptional customer service is the norm at Zappos. They have a 24/7 service, a 365-day return policy, an 800 number on every web page, free shipping, and free return shipping. When was the last time you placed an order through a customer service agent and finished the call actually feeling better than you did before you made the call? That's the goal at Zappos. Your experience with a customer service agent is anything but typical. In fact, the friendly, caring agents have been known for cheering up a customer who is having an exceptionally bad day by sending flowers, a note, or spending extra time trying to make a customer's day a little happier.

## What Do Pizza and Shoes Have in Common?

When Hsieh spoke at a recent conference, he shared a story that described just how service oriented his employees are. He was in Santa Monica with a group of people including a vendor from Sketchers who was hungry and craving a pizza at 3:00 a.m. When she became frustrated after making call after call to find a pizza place that would deliver at 3:00 a.m. with no success, Hsieh suggested that she call Zappos to see if the customer service agent who answered the phone could help. "You must be kidding," she said. Hsieh gave her the number and when the agent answered the phone, she gave him her request (remember she is in Santa Monica looking for a pepperoni pizza delivery at 3:00 a.m. and the agent works for a shoe company in Las Vegas). After a brief hold, the agent comes back on the line and gives her five phone numbers for pizza places that were still delivering. Now that's service. Great service is the core purpose at Zappos. The company is a service company that just happens to sell shoes and other items.

Since Zappos is "Powered by Customer Service," one of the biggest challenges is finding people who love working with other people to deliver "Wow!" customer service.

New candidates are screened in two interviews. One interview is focused on skills and the other on core values and cultural fit. Questions like, "On a scale of one to ten, how weird are you?" help sort out the cultural fit.

Once hired, every employee goes through five weeks of training in culture and core values as well as customer service and warehouse training. Zappos wants people who are there for the culture, not for the paycheck. In fact, they are so adamant about this that they offer new hires $2,000 to quit after their initial five weeks of training. If you stop to think about this for a moment, you realize just how unusual Zappos is. Two-thousand dollars is a really good incentive for call center employees looking for a nice bonus to go find another job, but surprisingly few actually take them up on it. In 2007, three percent took the payout to leave, and in 2008, only one percent took the offer.

## Committable Core Values

Hsieh says the secret sauce to a great culture is having "Committable Core Values." This means that whatever a company's core values are, people must commit to them, evangelize them, and be willing to hire and fire based on the core values. Hsieh says he wasn't always enlightened about the importance of culture to business success. He learned this the hard way that most entrepreneurs do: through personal experience, trial and error, and mistakes. Although Hsieh's first company, LinkExchange, was very successful (he sold it to Microsoft for $265 million when he was only 24 years old), he said he didn't know any better to pay attention to company culture. By the time the company grew to 100 employees, he no longer wanted to work in the company because it had become too impersonal.

Hsieh has clearly put his "lessons learned" to work at Zappos where culture and core values are talked about every day, just as revenue and market share are talked about in most companies. Culture is so important that they have developed a more than 350 page manifesto called "Zappos Culture" that is updated yearly (it was more than 470 pages in 2008). The highly transparent company extends the same courtesy to suppliers, vendors, and customers by offering several views into the company:

- An extranet gives vendors access to the same database as Zappos employees. Hsieh says, "This means we have 1,500 vendors helping us co-manage the business."
- An "Ask Anything" newsletter.
- Tours for customers, reporters, or anyone that just wants to visit their company headquarters and warehouse. Just make a request at tours@zappos.com. During a visit, you can walk around and talk to anyone you want. Zappos will even pick you up at the airport!
- Communicate with Hsieh or other Zappos employees through Twitter (twitter.com/zappos) or through one of several blogs (blogs.zappos.com).

So what's next for a company that has set a new benchmark for employee engagement and customer service? Hsieh says he wants the company to be known for "Three C's," which are clothing, customer service, and culture—three attributes that align with the customer value chain. Customers come to the company for the clothing (awareness); customer service helps retain them and bring them back; and culture is the platform that makes it all possible.

The July 2009 merger of Zappos and Amazon could be a match made in heaven. The merger combines two strong visionary leaders, a customer-driven online experience, and technology directed toward a 1:1 learning relationship with customers. If Hsieh can infuse the union with his personalized approach to customer experience, we may see a new business model—a perfect combination of technology and caring, personalized service.

"It's all about delivering happiness," says Hsieh.

## Zappos Core Values

The Zappos core values are expressed next. The explanation of each value is actually in the words of an employee, Donavon Roberson, from the Zappos Culture Book. The book is published by Zappos every year and is largely a compilation of what the culture means to each Zappos employee. It's really a brilliant idea to create a culture book that is written by employees. Although CEO Tony Hsieh developed the ten core values, it's the employees who own them, live them, and make them real.

Roberson's introduction to the ten values begins with "…I love what I do! I love this company! I love the culture, the people, the mission, and the passion to do whatever it takes to provide the greatest customer service possible. I was attracted to the culture and the fact that it is a living, breathing, active aspect of who we are. Many organizations that I have been involved with in the past have had mission and value statements, but they were simply put into publications and posted on walls. Many companies talk about culture, vision, or values but many times it ends there, a plaque on the wall. Not in the case with Zappos! Our culture is what sets us apart from would-be companies that try to mimic what we do here."[1]

## *Zappos Core Values*

### 1. Deliver WOW Through Service

Go the "extra mile" to make sure that the customer is completely taken care of.

### 2. Embrace and Drive Change

Realize that we are a growing company and that change is inevitable if we are going to stay relevant.

### 3. Create Fun and a Little Weirdness

To ensure that our customers catch our enthusiasm, we need to create an environment worth passing on…not to mention the importance of not taking ourselves too seriously.

### 4. Be Adventurous, Creative, and Open-Minded

In a setting that is going to change, an attitude of open-mindedness is key. Besides…who knows when the next big idea is going to hit; think "outside the box."

### 5. Pursue Growth and Learning

Pushing yourself to the next level benefits the individual and the company as a whole.

### 6. Build Open and Honest Relationships with Communication

It has been said, "Teamwork makes the dream work." Communication is the key to strong teams moving in the same direction for the common good of the company.

### 7. Build a Positive Team and Family Spirit

Since the majority of one's week is spent at work, it seems only fitting to create an atmosphere worth coming to.

### 8. Do More With Less

Money is not always the key to success. Sometimes solving the task at hand with limited resources brings about a greater sense of accomplishment and satisfaction for a "job well done."

### 9. Be Passionate and Determined

Go for your dreams and desires and don't let anyone or anything stop you from doing what you want to do within the company.

### 10. Be Humble

The truth is that it is not about me; keeping this in mind makes all of the other Core Values not only possible but attainable.

©2010 Zappos.com, Inc.

## rlton Creates and Sustains a
## erformance Culture

oncepts of mission, vision, and values by illustrating
haps the best example of how a company integrates
ir culture on a *daily* basis (if you know of others,
s I love hearing about creative, effective ideas on this
plished seamless processes and rituals into daily busi-
the flexibility of delivering exceptional levels of serv-

exceptional service to customers in a service busi-
siness because each customer interaction is unique.
of processes and rituals is too structured or rigid to
u will see that it actually provides a framework for
employees to add their own creativity to each service interaction, and this is what creates
the magic.

Ritz Carlton's unique approach earned the Malcolm Baldridge National Quality
Award twice, and they now teach other companies to use the same principles that have
helped them to become so successful. Recipients of the coveted Malcolm Baldridge
award are required to teach others the principles of their best practices so companies can
learn and apply these strategies to their own company.

Diana Oreck leads The Ritz-Carlton Leadership Center, a leadership training organization that provides a broad spectrum of classes for senior executives, managers, and
employees. The center is a resource for companies that would like to learn how The
Ritz-Carlton defined their principles and how the company integrates them into processes. What is so wonderful about the Leadership Center is that any business owner or senior executive can learn and experience The Ritz-Carlton "Mystique" first-hand (yes, they
actually share everything). You can then apply what you learned in a creative way that
makes sense for your company. I'm speaking from experience as I have used what I
learned at the Center to develop several organizational change programs.

The key to The Ritz-Carlton's success is employee commitment and engagement,
which is created by their foundational principles called The Ritz-Carlton Gold Standards.

The principles are comprised of elements the company uses to describe mission, vision, values, and service principles to create a culture of committed employees who in turn create engaged, loyal customers. The Ritz-Carlton Gold Standards include the following five components:

- **The Credo:** This is similar to a mission statement and conveys the essence of the brand: "The Ritz-Carlton experience enlivens the senses, instills well-being, and fulfills even the unexpressed wishes and needs of our guests."
- **The Motto:** The well-known statement, "We Are Ladies and Gentlemen Serving Ladies and Gentlemen," describes the spirit of Ritz-Carlton employees.
- **Three Steps of Service:** The three service steps describe how guests will be greeted, how their needs will be fulfilled, and a sincere farewell that will make guests long to return again.
- **Service Values: "I Am Proud to Be Ritz-Carlton."** This statement is the heart of the Gold Standards. Twelve simple but powerful statements define what is expected of everyone in the company. Employees are expected to know every word of every principle, but more importantly what each statement means. One of the twelve principles is discussed every day during the daily line up.
- **The Employee Promise:** This statement defines managements' commitment to employees.

## How The Ritz-Carlton Mystique Works

If you are thinking, "But any company can come up with great words," you should note that creating inspiring mission, vision, and values statements is only the first step. What makes the statements come to life is the rigorous processes put in place to support them. Every employee, without exception, must go through seven days of training before ever working in a Ritz-Carlton. Two full days of the orientation are indoctrination in The Ritz-Carlton values and philosophy. The goal is to create a significant emotional experience for new employees during their first few days. This happens the moment new employees arrive for training at 6:00 a.m. and see senior leaders lined up outside the doors of the hotel, clapping and cheering as they greet them. The message is clear: *You are important and we will treat you exactly as we want you to treat customers.*

The leadership team is involved in facilitating the program, sending a powerful message about the importance of consensual commitment. "For these next few days, we will orient you to who we are—our heart, our soul, our goals, our vision, our dreams—so you can join us, and not just work for us."[1] When management affirms what is expected of every employee, they also communicate what employees can expect of leaders.

Horst Schultz, former president and COO of The Ritz-Carlton, implemented the motto "We Are Ladies and Gentlemen Serving Ladies and Gentlemen" in the mid-1980s, and the motto is still at the heart of the company's values today. In an address to employees, Schultz said, "You are not servants. We are not servants. Our profession is service. We are Ladies and Gentlemen, just as the guests are, who we respect as Ladies and Gentlemen. We are Ladies and Gentlemen and should be respected as such."[2]

When new hires have worked a few weeks with a coach to learn the skills of their job and apply the Gold Standards to their daily work, they return for a third day of training on their 21st day of employment so they can talk about their experiences. In this session, the goal is to assess how well The Ritz-Carlton has lived up to the commitments that management made during initial training and orientation. Management pays close attention to the feedback from employees so training can be continuously improved. On an employee's 365th day of employment, he or she returns for a fourth day of training where he or she is psychologically "rehired" and reenergized with The Ritz-Carlton philosophy.

## What Can 15 Minutes a Day Do for Your Company?

In my opinion, the most powerful aspect of The Ritz-Carlton culture is the fact that every person in the company (management included) receives 15 minutes of training, *every single day.* This is accomplished through the "daily lineup" that serves as a mini-training session held at every Ritz-Carlton hotel across the world, as well as the corporate office. Employees and management gather to hear one of the featured "Service Values" read by an employee or manager. This is followed by an example of how an employee has exhibited the principle through specific action or behavior, or how it could be applied through various actions and behavior. This reinforces the company's philosophy and helps employees develop the skills and behavior necessary to deliver high levels of service. This practice also recognizes outstanding employees, thereby creating even greater motivation to excel.

Another example of employee recognition and positive behavior reinforcement occurs when a "Wow Story" is shared two days a week. This is a real story of how an employee created a great experience for a customer. The story is often read from customer comments but it can also be an experience that was observed by a manager or fellow employee. This simple yet powerful daily ritual is an opportunity to remind and teach employees about the values and beliefs of The Ritz-Carlton. Employees hear it, get an experience of it, and are motivated and encouraged to act in ways that will enhance the company culture and deliver exceptional customer experiences.

Contrast The Ritz-Carlton process with those in your company or with companies you have worked at in the past. Do employees even know what the company values are? How are they expressed so everyone has a common understanding of them? Are employees rewarded for exhibiting values? Are they reinforced daily so they always remain on an employee's mind? Are employee behaviors directly correlated to customer value and customer experience? Are employees recognized for their engagement with customers and contributions to the organization?

Most businesses will train new employees about values and beliefs during the first week of employment and perhaps only once or twice a year thereafter. As a result, employees can't even remember what the statements are, let alone tell you how they are woven into the fabric of the culture or used to drive individual behavior and customer experience.

## The Transformation to Passionate Advocacy

Cultural transformation is achieved as employees progress through their own personal experience with a company. A new employee might hear what your company values mean, but he will not believe, trust, or understand them until he sees real proof that there is substance behind the words. At this point, an employee begins to internalize what the company culture means to him and exhibits the values in his daily behavior. It takes considerable effort and commitment to build this level of trust in an employee, but the result is a culture that separates the mediocre from extraordinary. It's what makes companies (like Zappos, Southwest Airlines, and The Ritz-Carlton) that are competing in commodity markets excel over their competitors.

The financial results of a healthy culture are significant for any business. For The Ritz-Carlton, a one percent increase in customer satisfaction results in a 2.5 percent increase in revenue per available room. Employee turnover is only 23 percent in an industry where normal turnover is 100 percent. Stop and think about this for a moment. This is quite an achievement considering most employees are hourly workers. There are very few companies that can take a young man or woman out of some of the worst neighborhoods in the world and turn them into respectful leaders who are valued contributors to a company's success.

Most businesses can only dream of being this successful, yet many of the processes just described can be duplicated. Several industries, such as those in the call center market where turnover rates exceed 125 percent a year, can learn to apply the same principles to improve their businesses. Here is my challenge to you: Apply just one idea from The Ritz-Carlton. I *guarantee* it will improve your company culture, customer experience, and bottom line.

# 7

# Defining Core Values

As you converse, debate, and prioritize a list of values with your leadership team, you have an opportunity to build a solid foundation of shared values that are a collective expression of principles and beliefs. The following exercise will take you through a process to define, prioritize, and evaluate values for your organization. The result of your efforts will ultimately drive the behavior of everyone in your business, and it will become a business tool to drive decision making. During the process of evaluating the best values for your business, keep three primary measures in mind. Values must be 1) distinctive—unique to the company; 2) able to stand the test of time; and (3) drive decision making and behaviors.

On the following page is a list of values to give you some ideas to get started. Like a mission or a vision statement, there is no "right" way to define your values. You can choose a standard approach, or you may want to define principles, as Zappos did.

It's valuable to do this exercise with others in the company so there is a lot of stimulating discussion to select the values that most reflect your company purpose. Debate the choices people make and be highly selective. As a guideline, select three to five core values or define a small set of principles. You want to purposefully narrow and refine your choices. After selecting three to five core values, define them further in statements so there is absolute clarity about their meaning. Arbitrary statements such as, "We value quality, teamwork, and innovation" mean nothing without a definition of what each word means. When you do this exercise with a group of people, you will find that people define values in very different ways.

Another problem with an arbitrary statement like this is it contains three different values. You can't give a clear example of what the values statement means if you have more than one in a sentence. If you base performance evaluations on the way people behave and perform against the values, it's too murky. Are they being evaluated on quality, teamwork, or values? This exercise will force you to be selective and discriminating in your choices.

# Defining Corporate Values

## PART 1: SELECT AND DEFINE

Select three to five values from the following list or define your own.

- Quality
- Excellence
- Innovation
- Profitable
- Honesty
- Integrity
- Reliability
- Creativity
- Dependability
- Dedicated

- Competitive
- Entrepreneurial
- Highly Specialized
- Efficient/Effective
- Responsiveness
- Honesty
- Accountability
- Growth
- Authenticity
- Education

- Performance
- Knowledge
- Security
- Customer Focus
- Precision
- Affordability
- Value
- Competitive
- Other

## PART 2: PRIORITIZE

Now prioritize and define the three to five values (less is better) deemed by the entire team to be a truly authentic representation of your company values.

## PART 3: TEST

As you deliberate values, ask the following questions, which will help you prioritize those that are most important:

1. Which values are so much a part of your company that if they ceased to exist, your company would cease to exist as it is?
2. Are these the values you believe your company can remain committed to under pressure and obstacles?
3. When you look at each value, does the word passionate come to mind?
4. Ask why a value was selected. (Why did you select that specific value? Why is that important? And why is that important? Keep asking why until you are certain this value is the right one.)

Example: The value "quality" is debated against the value "innovation." Both values are important to leaders but innovation is selected on the basis that quality is always important, but it has become an expectation customers now have.

## PART 4: COMMUNICATE, EXECUTE, MEASURE

Similar to most projects, the hardest part of this exercise is not development, but execution. Now that you have put time and energy into developing values you are passionate about, you need to communicate them and build them into the daily operations of your business.

The only way to do this is through relentless communication and mechanisms that are built into the processes and the fabric of the company culture. Simple things such as a small desktop reference or framed description of the values, mission, and vision are good reminders to help guide people every day. An even better way is through rituals. As shown in Chapter 6, "How The Ritz-Carlton Creates and Sustains a High-Performance Culture," The Ritz-Carlton integrates daily rituals into their culture that provide daily training. Ken Blanchard leaves a daily voicemail for employees, reminding them of mission and purpose. Use your imagination to come up with creative internal campaigns that will serve not only to teach or remind, but inspire. Better yet, ask your employees how they would bring the company values to life for everyone in the company. You will probably get your best ideas this way.

Vision, values, and culture are driven top-down in a company, so the business leaders (the company owner, C-level executives, and business unit leaders) must walk the talk. Leaders in senior positions must model the behavior they wish to see in other people. If senior leaders do not emulate the values, you can never expect employees to do so.

Lastly, the best way to motivate employees to embrace company values on a daily basis is to measure and reward employees through their performance appraisals. On the performance appraisal, ask employees to describe and give examples of how values are exhibited in their everyday work. If performance measures and salary are tied to how well employees execute value-driven behavior, you will surely see results.

# 8

# Game Changers

Concepts such as corporate social responsibility, eco-tourism, environmentalism, and "green" products have become increasingly more important to both consumers and businesses in recent years. So has the growing concern over companies that exploit child labor, disrespect diversity, or ignore personal and environmental safety. Values are no longer a nice-to-have. They are growing in awareness and significance as a key business success factor—and becoming an expectation we have of the companies that we do business with.

While a select few companies would dare say values and core purpose drive business success, others are courageously beginning to use this as a means to differentiate their brand and their company. They have abandoned the old ways of doing business and have chosen a new business model that operates with integrity, values, purpose, passion—and yes, profitability.

## Purpose-Driven Companies Are More Profitable

A new kind of business referred to as Firm of Endearment (FoE) describes companies that embrace this operating philosophy. The book *Firms of Endearment* illustrates the fascinating connection between operating a purpose-driven company and financial outcomes. The authors researched companies people truly love and respect and compared traits each firm has with key stakeholders in five groups: employees, customers, suppliers, society, and shareholders. Similar to The Fortunate 500, in an FoE business model, no stakeholder comes first. FoE companies achieve their financial objectives through *endearing* themselves to *all* stakeholders by addressing their needs.

According to Firmsofendearment.com, "These companies pay their employees very well, provide great value to customers, and have thriving, profitable suppliers. They are also wonderful for investors, returning 1025 percent over the past ten years, compared to only 122 percent for the S&P 500 and 316 percent for the companies profiled in the bestselling book *Good to Great*—companies selected purely on the basis of their ability to deliver superior returns to investors."[1]

Who are these companies? Only 28 companies meet the criteria for being an FoE company. Amazon, eBay, and Google are just a few. Check out www.firmsofendearment. com to learn more.

FoE are known for challenging industry standards and beliefs, operating with great transparency, decentralizing decision making, and operating with the company's long-term interests in mind. Because these companies favor organic growth and don't believe in traditional tradeoffs (such as blending work and play), they attract loyal employees who are usually paid more than industry averages. Loyal employees attract more customers and increase customer loyalty, resulting in improved bottom-line measures of performance.

What can you learn from companies like this? It pays to be nice (and it's a lot more fun!)

## New Belgium Brewing: Passionate About Purpose, People, Sustainabilty, and of Course, Beer

New Belgium Brewing founders Kim Jordon and Jeff Lebesch met over a beer at a friend's house in 1990. A year later, they founded their own brewery, which has grown to become America's third-largest craft brewery and the eighth-largest overall with sales of $96 million in 2007 and projected to grow eight percent in 2008. As of August 2009, the brewery grew to 348 employees who are as passionate about the company's purpose as the founders.

Purpose is a powerful driving force at New Belgium. Even before the first beer was bottled and sold, Jordon and Lebesch decided to craft a vision and values that would make their new company a direct reflection of their personal core values. They hiked into the woods with a jug of beer, pen, and paper, to craft a vision for the company they wanted to create. This vision, "To operate a profitable brewery which makes our love and talent manifest," is still the driver of their success today.

Part of what their love and talent manifest is their strong belief in sustainability. As early adopters to the movement toward sustainability, employees voted to make New Belgium Brewing the first 100 percent wind-powered brewery in 1998, even if it meant forfeiting their yearly bonus. That first vote created the momentum for the significant progress the company has made, and continues to make, in their commitment to sustainability. A few of their goals are to reduce their carbon footprint by 25 percent, reduce water usage by 10 percent, offset eight million car miles in the next year by riding bikes (Team Wonderbike has over 10,000 member pledges), and many other projects you can review by visiting this section at www.newbelgium.com/sustainability. The company is also a member of 1% for the Planet, meaning through donations and fund-raisers, the company contributes one percent of their revenue to environmental non-profits.

The company founders and employee owners clearly put actions behind their words. A key business practice that drives the company culture of commitment and execution is a policy of open book management. New Belgium Brewing shares financials, business strategies, and branding plans, creating a culture of transparency that fosters trust and respect. CEO Jordon says, "We care deeply about one another, and we also care deeply about being very good at what we do."[2]

The result of New Belgium's passion and purpose tied to business practices is an amazing employee retention rate of 92 percent. On one-year anniversaries employees are rewarded with a bike (the one famous on the Fat Tire label) and stock ownership. Employees who have been with the company for five years are rewarded with a trip to Belgium.

---

### *New Belgium Brewing Purpose Statement*

To operate a profitable brewery which makes our love and talent manifest.

**Company Core Values and Beliefs:**

1. Remembering that we are incredibly lucky to create something fine that enhances people's lives while surpassing our consumers' expectations.
2. Promoting world-class beers.
3. Promoting beer culture and the responsible enjoyment of beer.
4. Kindling social, environmental, and cultural change as a business role model.
5. Environmental stewardship: Honoring nature at every turn of the business.
6. Cultivating potential through learning, high-involvement culture, and the pursuit of opportunities.
7. Balancing the myriad needs of the company, our coworkers, and their families.
8. Trusting each other and committing to authentic relationships and communications.
9. Continuous, innovative quality and efficiency improvements.
10. Having fun.

Source: New Belgium Brewing

---

Many companies develop exceptional statements reflective of their purpose, but fail to execute in a way that employees are inspired and motivated by them so that their behavior is a mirror reflection of the company's values. If your goal is to create a great company known for its values, culture, and unique customer experiences, you have to go far beyond just creating great vision and values statements. It's all about execution, and it's surprisingly harder to do than you think. It takes commitment, relentless focus, and dedication. In Section VI, "Execute and Evaluate," we will discuss specific actions you can take to create and build your own culture of excellence.

## A Strong Internal Brand Equals a Powerful External Brand

It makes complete sense that cultivating a thriving internal brand would be reflected in a stronger and more powerful brand externally. It not only serves to differentiate a business in a competitive market, it also drives down marketing and branding costs. A common benefit of companies with strong internal brands is that they spend considerably less than other companies on sales and marketing.

Scott Bedbury is one of the leading marketing and branding experts in the world. He built the Nike and Starbucks brand from their infancy to become among the world's leading brands. I had an opportunity to interview Bedbury and ask him how he did this. As you will see, it was not through cleaver marketing strategies and tactics. It was a relentless focus on the company's purpose.[3]

---

### *"Just Do It" Campaign Among Bedbury's Accomplishments*

Scott Bedbury, former senior vice president of marketing at Starbucks, was instrumental in creating the Starbuck brand. Prior to that, he was head of advertising for Nike, where he launched the "Just Do It" campaign. A resident of Seattle, he is CEO of Brand-stream, an independent brand consultancy.

**Reece:** How do you build a great brand?

**Bedbury:** With people that are passionate and care about the company and the brand. Every great brand starts with a passionate, visionary CEO, like Phillip Knight at Nike and Howard Schultz of Starbucks. They focused on creating a great product. But what increasingly separates product A from product B is how people feel about the brand and all the details that go around the experience—what happens after you buy and how you are treated during the purchase.

**Reece:** At Nike, you had a multi-million-dollar ad budget to help you build the brand, but at Starbucks you spent very little money on advertising. What did you focus on to build the Starbucks brand with a limited budget?

---

**Bedbury:** The "Just Do It" campaign was launched with $8 million, and when I left, we were spending $200 million on media worldwide. At Starbucks, Howard realized the single most important thing was the people, and what set Starbucks apart was the health benefits and stock ownership for people who work part time. It had never been done before, and it came with a cost.

The dollars to build the brand were put into operations to create an experience that would enable the brand to endure and be sold profitably for many years to come. It really came down to experiential marketing.

The stores were once four white walls. There was no comfortable furniture or fireplaces or music. So we set out to create an experience in the stores and a level of brand equity that most traditionally marketed brands couldn't touch. That meant constant creative development of products, and the look and feel in the stores. It wasn't cheap. The first year, we spent $100 million building out stores, which is a significant marketing budget for anyone.

**Reece:** Did you set out with the mission to define your brand by focusing on a stock option and employee benefit plan or did this happen by accident?

**Bedbury:** That was Howard's mission. When he took over the company, he was not a rich man and he didn't own a house or even a car. Howard grew up poor in Brooklyn and was influenced strongly by his dad, who never got health benefits from any of his employers. This fueled Howard's drive to create a company that put employees first.

He is passionate that when it comes to customers versus employees, employees will always come first. He knows if he does this, he has employees that value their job, and if they feel valued and respected, they will in turn take care of customers—and that formula has always worked.

**Reece:** It really has worked. Why don't more companies do this?

**Bedbury:** It takes a lot of courage. When Howard tried to raise $2.8 million to buy the company from the three founders, he made 220 presentations and he got shut down in all but 12 of them. He was seen as an idealist who was going to put an unnecessary burden on the bottom line by offering benefits to part-time employees who viewed this as a temporary job.

But Howard convinced them that turnover would drop, which it did. Store manager attrition was 15 percent, part-time hourly employees was 65 percent, compared to McDonalds and Taco Bell, which were about 200–300 percent a year. That's turning over your work force every four months, and when you do that, your service suffers and there are all kinds of problems. I don't know why more people don't do it. If you give up some equity to employees, they'll reward you for that.

**Reece:** When will people cease to pay $5 for a designer cup of coffee?

**Bedbury:** I don't think they ever will. I have a Starbucks close to my house in Seattle and I go there for the coffee and also for the peace of mind and to see friends. It's not just about the coffee; it's about the experience.

**Reece:** What are the most important things you learned from building two of the world's leading brands?

**Bedbury:** The No. 1 thing is everything matters and you should sweat the small stuff. I think Starbucks has the best restrooms in the world. We paid attention to that.

The other is never underestimate getting the brand positioning right inside your company first so everyone understands what the values are and what it means. It's not about reciting a mission statement, it's about understanding what is Nike and what's not Nike. You would hear that all the time in the halls of Nike. There was no mission statement. It all came down to what was honest and what was not honest. What was consistent and what was not consistent. It was highly judgmental, but everyone felt the scrutiny of their peers to honor the brand. So make sure everyone gets it and honors it. And the ones that don't, you get them the heck out of the company.

**Reece:** What is the most important element to focus on when building a brand?

**Bedbury:** Exceeding customer expectations. We are coming off three decades of businesses in every industry failing to meet customer expectations. The sad part is they have done that while communicating promises they are not keeping, or inconsistently meeting. People just want a product they can trust. Less than 10 percent of product claims are believed today.

**Reece:** How does a company understand its brand essence, what you call its DNA?

**Bedbury:** It starts with an audit. If you ask employees to use three adjectives to describe the brand today, good or bad, what would they say?

The second question in this two-question survey is, "If everyone in the company did their job at the highest level and pulled together, how would you want the brand to be described as in three years?" There is always a gap.

# 9

# Do What You Love and the Money Will Follow

If you own a small business, you don't have to look far to find examples of companies that are integrating passion and purpose in their businesses. At first glance, Cru Vin Dogs appears to be an odd mash-up of products: wine and dog portraits. But a closer look reveals a thriving business fueled by the interests and passion of three owners.

Cru Vin Dogs is a business operated by husband and wife team, Jay and Mary Snellgrove, and partner Bill Foss. Jay is a gifted artist who draws meticulous portraits of dogs. A small number of prints are signed, numbered, and made available for sale in the gallery and wine store. Portraits can also be commissioned by loving pet owners.

The three partners combine their passion and skills to create limited edition wines featuring portraits of a dog (created by Jay) and are marketed under the label Cru Vin Dogs. Several types of wines are made including Cabernet Sauvignon, Pinot Noir, Cabernet-Syrah, Cabernet Merlot, Chardonnay, Sauvignon Blanc, and, most recently, a Shiraz-Grenache-Mourvedre blend. The creative product portfolio is comprised of three major lines, as shown in Figure 9.1.

**Puppy Series**: 2008 Greyhound Sauvignon Blanc; 2008 "Blue Heeler" Shiraz-Grenache-Mourvedre.

**Portrait Series**: "Yogi" Cabernet/Shiraz (the name of their beloved golden retriever), 2005 "Yogi" Cabernet-Syrah in a collectable 1.5 liter bottle in cedar box, and "Lucky" Cabernet/Merlot.

**Best in Show**: 2007 Pinot Noir.

Image Source: Cru Vin Dogs Wine Group.

**Figure 9.1** *Cru Vin Dogs product portfolio*

In addition to selling wine and portraits of dogs, the gallery and wine store sells clothing with the company logo and dog portraits, note cards (with dog portraits of course), and various wine accessories. Central to Cru Vin Dogs's business philosophy is charitable giving to organizations and foundations that support dogs. Ten percent of all revenues are split between Canine Companions for Independence and the Morris Animal Foundation's Cure Canine Cancer Campaign. Specific releases of wines are given to organizations such as the Ali Foundation and other charities to help them with fundraising.

When I asked the business owners why they chose to create a business with such an unusual combination of products, they said they simply wanted to combine their passions to create a business they loved. Their background and experience was in the wine importing and wholesaling business, but they wanted more from life. They wanted to do what they love as well as give back to the organizations they passionately believe in. The strategy has worked for these entrepreneurs. Since the 2007 launch of the company, Cru Vin Dogs has donated over $100,000 to dog-related charities.

## A New Wave of Entrepreneurship

The intent of this story and the previous example of New Belgium Brewing (in Chapter 8, "Game Changers") is to illustrate how purpose can be the central business driver for a company's existence. As the economy rebounds, I predict there will be a new wave of entrepreneurial business that is bigger than anything we have seen in history. As many people make a conscious choice to leave corporate life and create a new business, many will pursue a business that is central to their values and passions. There has never been a better time to be an entrepreneur, and you really can "do good" and be financially successful. As the saying goes, "Do what you love and the money will follow."

But we're not going to leave it to chance. The next step is to define your goals, break them down into executable steps, and put a plan in place to execute them.

# 10

# Measurable Goals Drive Success

The goals in your marketing plan will describe very specific objectives you want to achieve as a result of implementing your marketing plan. The marketing plan goals should tie back to the overarching goals of the company to create alignment and momentum. Be as specific as possible when describing your goals so they are measurable. Follow a framework to create SMART goals, which are Specific and Measurable, Motivating, Achievable, Relevant, Trackable and Time-bound, as described below:

- **Specific and Measurable:** State your goals in a way they can be measured. Break big goals down into manageable chunks so you can define the steps to achieve big goals.

- **Motivating:** Describe goals that you want to achieve and can achieve. People excel when they do things they like. As goal achievement is delegated to employees in your company, the goal should also motivate them, so it's important that they understand their role in achieving the goal. Consider tying performance measures to the goal as incentive.

- **Achievable:** Describes goals that are realistic yet challenging to you and your team. Nothing is more de-motivating than having a goal that is completely unrealistic.

- **Relevant:** Define goals that drive short-term objectives like revenue as well as goals that are congruent with the long-term vision. Both short-term and long-term must be balanced.

- **Trackable and Time-bound:** Define the timeframe each goal must be completed, as well as how it will be tracked, measured, and reported. If possible, state who is responsible for the goal (this could be a person, department, division, or region). For large overarching goals, you may want to consider assigning an executive sponsor.

To achieve a short-term plan, it's important to state very specific goals and milestones. Consider how the 80/20 rule (Pareto principle) drives most businesses. If 80 percent of your revenue comes from 20 percent of your customers, then it's critical to focus goals on that 20 percent of your customer base.

To balance both long-term and short-term goals, you will define one-, two-, and three-year goals. Obviously there will be more detail developed for one-year goals, but your marketing plan should also include long-term growth strategies. Your strategy should have consistency while remaining fluid and responsive to changing market conditions.

# The Balanced Scorecard Goal Framework

The Balanced Scorecard is an effective framework for categorizing goals into financial, customer, process, and culture segments. Section VI, will explain how you can use the Balanced Scorecard (BSC) framework to align activities to achieve your goals. For now, I would like you to think about your goals in each of the four overarching goal categories used in the BSC:

- **Financial:** Think long-term *and* short-term. What are the revenue and profitability goals related to growth? What are the cost containment goals?
- **Customer:** What is the value provided to the target segments of customers?
- **Internal Processes:** What processes must be in place to deliver value to customers?
- **Learning and Growth:** What skills do people need to implement the processes? How will culture inspire employees to deliver extraordinary value to customers?

# Goal Categories

In addition to the BSC categories, additional categories are listed below for you to consider, such as business growth and specific marketing and sales categories. Please customize the goals to correspond to the needs of your business. Write your goals using the SMART framework described earlier. When you have finished, edit the list to select and prioritize those that will have the most impact on business success. Fewer goals result in more focus. Summarize the goals in the marketing plan template.

If you have a small company you can group all your goals together. If you work in a large company, you may wish to divide goals (and your plan) by divisions, product and service lines, or geographic regions.

**Financial**

- Revenue
- Profitability
- Gross margin
- Operating costs
- Other key financial performance metrics

**Customer**

- Value proposition goals
- Number of customers
- Number and revenue of customers by market segment
- Market share
- Customer retention
- Customer satisfaction (Net Promoter Score)
- Customer lifetime value

### Process and Innovation

- New processes to deliver greater customer value
- Process integration
- Number of new products
- New services
- Awards and patents
- Research and development
- Time to market
- Improve customer experience

### Growth

- Number of employees
- New customer segments
- New products and services
- New markets, geographic regions, stores, offices, and so on
- Acquisitions, alliances, new channels, and so on
- Revenue, market share, and so on

### Learning and Culture

- New positions and skills needed
- Performance measures
- Employee satisfaction
- Culture programs
- Employee retention
- Training and Development

### Marketing and Sales

- Lead generation
- Marketing program ROI
- Brand awareness
- Lead to proposal to close ratio
- Sales funnel effectiveness

As you develop your marketing plan, your goals will change and evolve because you will learn more about the market. This section will also be fluid as you develop your plan, so don't worry about writing "perfect" goals before moving on to the next section. In Section VI, you will review and evaluate the goals you are creating now to make sure they are still relevant based upon what you have learned during the course of writing the plan.

# 11

# Situation Analysis and SWOT Analysis

## Situation Analysis

A Situation Analysis is a brief overview of company's current situation. It's similar to a balance sheet as it provides a brief snapshot of the company's current situation. It provides enough of an overview that the reader will understand the company's products and services and the value its products and services provide to customers. The key issues, concerns, and business drivers are summarized to give the reader a good idea of the business environment. This section may also include *brief* information about competitors and past financial performance as well as a brief summary of the products and services in the marketing plan.

All of this information should total two or three pages. Detailed information about the market, competitors, and target market will be developed in the Market Opportunity Analysis in the next section.

## SWOT Analysis

A SWOT (Strengths, Weakness, Opportunities, and Threats) Analysis is an important outcome of the situational analysis. It is a simple and effective way to summarize your company's internal strengths and weaknesses, relative to its external opportunities and threats. The outcome of the SWOT matrix is that it helps company leaders develop contingency plans to overcome threats and understand the best opportunities to pursue where the company has a competitive advantage. But remember that competence alone does not constitute a competitive advantage. You must be able to perform and execute better than your competitors. The following summary outlines additional benefits and outcomes from doing the SWOT Analysis.

Use the chart in Table 11.1 to create your SWOT Analysis. Create bullet points in each category and then summarize actions in the marketing plan template to do the following:

1. Expand and leverage your strengths.
2. Understand your weaknesses and seek to overcome those that you can control.
3. Identify opportunities and create strategies to act on them.
4. Reduce threats where possible and create a defensive plan.

**Table 11.1**  SWOT Analysis

| Strengths | Weaknesses |
|---|---|
|  |  |
| Opportunities | Threats |
|  |  |

## Summary

Now you are ready to summarize the first section of your marketing plan. Using the following checklist to summarize this section in the marketing plan template in the Appendix.

## P • R • A • I • S • E™ Marketing Process

### Purpose

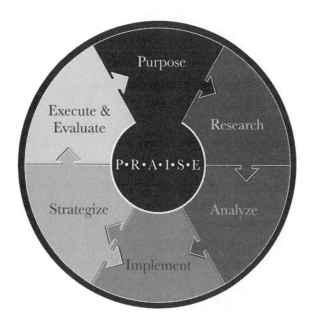

## Summary: Section I

✓ Create your company values with buy-in and commitment from senior leaders.
✓ Write a vision statement that summarizes the future direction of what the company will become in the future.
✓ Write a mission statement that incorporates the company values and vision.
✓ Create goals for the desired timeframe of the plan (usually three to five years).
✓ Summarize the Situation Analysis:
  • Key issues the plan will address and the business drivers
  • Brief product and services description
  • SWOT Analysis
✓ Review and finalize goals following completion of the marketing plan.

# Section II

# Research: Market Opportunity

*"We have for the first time an economy based on a key resource [information]
that is not only renewable, but self generating.
Running out of it is not a problem, but drowning in it is."*
—John Naisbitt

This step in the marketing planning process is considered by most business leaders to be the most important. Why? Business decisions are often made without having enough—or the right—information, to make an intelligent assessment regarding the future direction of their business. This part of the process is critically important to your overall plan as it will help you understand the market opportunity, revenue potential, your customer's wants and needs, and your competitive advantage. You will also learn new ways to use social media and other tools to seamlessly update your plan on an ongoing basis. After completing this section, I guarantee you will emerge with new knowledge and enlightenment about potential growth opportunities. With that bold statement, here is what we will cover in this section:

- How to drive more profitability and revenue from your customers
- The most effective way to define your ideal target market
- Why your customers buy from you
- How to develop your market and competitive intelligence
- Simple steps to build a customer relationship management program
- How to increase customer retention, customer loyalty, and customer lifetime value
- Successful tips to create a customer-focused culture
- Competitive differentiation
- New media and social networking tools to get research done fast and efficiently
- Define and scope your research plan for primary and secondary research

# 12

# The Biggest Mistake Entrepreneurs Make

Do *not* be tempted to skip the research phase of the marketing planning process! It does not matter if you are writing a plan (1) for a new business; (2) if you have been in business for awhile and you are writing your first plan; or (3) you are updating an existing marketing plan—*do all of the exercises*. I promise you will gain tremendous insight from doing them. Once you have written the plan at least once, then you can begin to update it using the real-time methods outlined throughout the book. Remember, writing a plan is always harder the first time, but once it is done, it becomes easier to keep it current.

The *biggest mistake* that entrepreneurs make, which causes most business to fail, or at least fail to grow, is that they don't integrate research into the planning process. Entrepreneurs love to jump right in to creating marketing strategy and tactics, which is a huge mistake. When a business takes the time to understand how their solution solves customers' problems, who is buying and why, then strategies and messages that are conveyed through marketing tactics are targeted and effective.

## Know What You Don't Know

Research has become considerably easier now that a myriad of Internet resources are available at your fingertips. The problem is not finding information because we are barraged with it. The problem is assimilating it and turning it into actionable knowledge to make decisions. Throughout this process, you will learn new tools and techniques to keep pace with information overload, as well as simple methods you can integrate into daily business processes so this information is organized and updated into your plan in real-time. Another technique you will learn is to use real-time research tools. We will explore how you can integrate social media, social networking, blogging, customer advisory boards, and other tools for getting actionable information in a fast and efficient way.

If you are creating your first marketing plan and have been in business for a couple of years, research will be valuable for several reasons. First, you can validate the assumptions you made when you first started your business. How has the current economic climate impacted sales and customer buying behavior? How has the economy changed the competitive environment? Is the market more price competitive or are there new opportunities in the current economy that you can take advantage of? How has your target market changed over time? Do customers value your products and services as they once did or have their wants and needs changed? All of these questions and more underlie the reason why research must become integrated into regular business practices.

Second, you will research and analyze new areas where you can grow your business based upon the successes you have had so far. It's valuable to learn from situations that did not turn out as expected. Was the end result due to improper assumptions based on not understanding the market or customer needs? Was it an issue with execution, or was it due to market or competitive factors you did not anticipate?

Third, a marketing plan is a valuable historical document that you can review to see what assumptions you made as you evaluate business results over time. One of the biggest mistakes entrepreneurs make is the false belief that they have a marketing plan because it exists "in their mind." This simply doesn't work. Marketing strategy and plans must be written to completely understand, communicate, and execute them.

As you embark on your research, you will discover many benefits from the experience. One of the biggest is: *You Will Know What You Don't Know.* My experience working with businesses is that they see this part of the marketing process as a journey of discovery. Entrepreneurs feel humbled from the experience, and greatly excited about the new growth opportunities they discover. They learn to be more prepared to respond to changing market conditions, and become more agile to capture new opportunities. Throughout the research phase of marketing planning, one of the biggest benefits you will receive from the process is serendipity, which is discovering pearls of wisdom and insight that you didn't know or were unaware of. This can take your business in an entirely new direction. It happens to everyone going through this process, so remain open to new ideas.

### Marketing Tip for Start-Ups

If you are creating a marketing plan for a *new* business, your research will be based on a set of assumptions about the market opportunity, and your objective will be to validate those assumptions. Even though you do not have historical data, do the exercises making a best guess and assumptions using best-case/worst-case scenarios. A valuable outcome of doing the exercises for start-ups is that you will understand what kind of information is important to track on an ongoing basis. The process of learning how to find and analyze the most relevant data and metrics will be applied continuously to adjust your strategies as your business grows. *This gives you a huge advantage over competitors who don't create a marketing plan during the critical start-up stage.*

# 13

# A Micro to Macro Process

An easy way to think about research is to break it down into two main chunks: micro and macro research. Micro research is internally focused, and it will help you understand who your customers are and why they buy from you. It involves analysis of your customer data and usually some primary research. Primary research is information you will need to gather on your own using tools like surveys and customer interviews. This research often consists of information gathered directly from customers, or potential customers, and will help you understand buyer needs and preferences.

Macro research is externally focused to help you understand the market, your industry, and the competitive landscape so that you can begin to anticipate market forces impacting your business. Most of your macro research is gathered from secondary research, which is information that has already been collected by someone else for a different purpose, but is useful to you. Examples include information found in research reports, industry periodicals, and articles.

## Goals of a Research Plan

There are several overarching objectives of research for a marketing plan. The primary goals are to:

- Gain a competitive advantage by knowing more about your competitors and market trends.
- Understand customer preferences.
- Validate the viability of new product and/or service opportunities for your customers.
- Identify additional target markets for existing products and services.
- Learn about new communication technologies that will help you create richer experiences with your customers.
- Anticipate changes in market conditions.
- Find answers to challenging issues affecting your business.

The end result of your research is to make well-informed decisions. William Pollard said: "Information is a source of learning. But unless it is organized, processed, and available to the right people in a format for decision making, it is a burden, not a benefit." The best way to organize and prioritize what is needed is to create a research plan. The research plan will define questions that need to be answered, researched, and then analyzed in order to make decisions and take well-calculated risks that lead you to business growth.

As you go through this section and complete the exercises, write down the issues and questions that arise. Most of the questions can be answered through secondary research; however, it's also advisable to engage your customers and/or potential customers using primary research. At the end of this section, you will find a process and explanation that will teach you how to create a primary research plan. For now you only need to be concerned with listing research questions as you go through this section.

It's important to define questions so that they can be clearly answered. Ambiguous questions produce ambiguous answers, so you don't want to ask an open-ended question that is hard to research or will not yield actionable information. An example of an ambiguous question for a financial service firm might be, "What are the trends in financial services?" A more specific question would be, "As divorce rates climb above 50 percent, what are the specific needs women have for financial planning services and investment advice if they have typically relied on their spouse for this? What do they *need* and who do they currently purchase the services from?" This type of question will help you drill into specifics that will help shape strategies.

Focus and prioritize the research plan on the topics you need to learn about in order to make decisions during the rest of the planning process. Research categories to consider are

- New target markets
- New potential products and new service offerings
- Buyer behavior and needs
- Market situation and key trends
- Market sizing by product or service
- Competitors
- Macro environmental factors
- Customer relationship management processes
- Distribution channels
- Other

---

**Marketing Tip**

Research is the most important part of the marketing planning process, and the results of your work in this area will create the primary drivers of your business growth and success. This step in the process is the most significant, and it may also be the most difficult; however, it will make the rest of your plan much easier to develop—and grounded in facts instead of assumptions!

*"In the long run, a short cut seldom is."*
—Malcolm Forbes

---

# 14

# Micro Perspective:
# Focus on High-Value Customers

The heart of micro research is analysis of your existing customer base. Learning more about your current customers is a critically important step in your growth plan. The outcome of the next exercise has eight benefits:

- Segment customers based upon revenue and profit.
- Segment customers by characteristics to improve target market criteria.
- Create a profile of your best customers to use this to target new customers.
- Create different levels of service for different customer segments.
- Align everyone, especially those in sales, marketing, and customer service, on the definition and criteria of different customer segments.
- Reduce customer defection.
- Create strategies to build customer loyalty with your best customers.
- Develop marketing programs for distinct customer segments.

## The Most Powerful (and Easiest) Way to Improve Profitability

This exercise is my favorite in the entire planning process because I have seen how this simple analysis adds significant value to every business that has used it. It helps focus companies on attracting higher value customers, it refines marketing strategies for customer segments, and it will help you find new customers who match your ideal target market profile. It is a very simple yet powerful segmentation process.

The first step is to segment your customers according to revenue and profitability in four quadrants: A, B, C, and D customers. Here is a definition for each category:

A Customers = High Profit, High Revenue

B Customers = High Profit, Low Revenue

C Customers = Low Profit, High Revenue

D Customers = Low Profit, Low Revenue (Therefore, the "D" stands for "Deadbeat.")

"A" customers are your most profitable and highest revenue-generating clients that you want to love individually and often. "B" customers represent an opportunity because business transactions with this customer segment are profitable, but these customers do not purchase very much from your business for some reason. Is it because they are giving part of their business to a competitor? Is it because they make only occasional purchases? Do they tend to buy only in small amounts or in one product category versus across your product or service lines? Are the customers in this segment aware of the full range of products and services your business has to offer? A thorough analysis of buying behavior and decisions will help you take the necessary action to help transform these customers into "A" customers.

"C" customers are those who may purchase a lot from your business and therefore generate a lot of revenue, but transactions are not profitable for some reason. Perhaps these customers are demanding price concessions and discounts. Maybe they only buy "loss leaders" and purchase more profitable items from someone else. Or perhaps your "C" customers require more service from employees? As you analyze this group of customers, the goal is to understand why business transactions with this customer segment are not more profitable and figure out what you can do to change this.

Often businesses will discover large revenue-generating customers are in this segment and these customers receive a substantial discount. If your goal is to increase brand awareness by securing a powerful customer, then this may be an acceptable strategy. If you have customers in this segment that receive large discounts and also bring in a substantial amount of top-line revenue, this *may* also be acceptable. The most important question to ask as you evaluate customers in this category is to ask, "By servicing customers in this segment, what am I giving up by continuing to put resources toward these customers instead of 'A' customers?"

The customers that are low revenue and causing a drain on your profits are your "D" customers, otherwise known as "Deadbeats." When companies look at the customers in this category, they almost always discover that these customers are very difficult to deal with. They may be unpleasant, demanding, or just rude. In other words, it's painful to do business with them and they cause a drain on resources, or worse, negatively affect employee morale.

You need to do one of two things with this group of customers. First, you should look for ways to develop them into "C" or "B" customers. Review the list of questions and issues listed in each category to see if they apply to this group of customers. Create a plan of action to see if you can increase the value of these customers and move them to a higher segment. If this doesn't work, you will need to make the tough decision to "fire" them—or you can refer them to a competitor.

# Existing Customer Analysis and Segmentation

## Step #1: Categorize Existing Customers by Revenue and Profit

Start with what you know. Separate your existing customers into one of the four categories defined by revenue and profitability according to the A, B, C, and D definitions.

## Step #2: Add Other Segmentation Characteristics

After you have segmented customers by revenue and profitability, the next step is to look at the customers in each of these categories to describe the characteristics that make each of these customer segments unique. What do you notice about "A" customers? Are there common demographic criteria that describe these customers such as size of company, geographic area, certain industries, amount of revenue, number of employees, primary decision-maker level, or other characteristics? Do these customers make referrals and tend to buy across multiple product and service areas of your business? Are "A" customers the most enjoyable and fun to work with?

When my company went through this process of segmenting customers several years ago, we discovered unusual criteria that we eventually made part of our target market criteria. This criteria was (1) they were in a specific profitability range; (2) they were smart, and we enjoyed learning and collaborating with these companies; and (3) they were fun to work with! As you can see, the definitions you ultimately assign to each customer group are both quantitative and qualitative. *The goal for this portion of the exercise is to think creatively and objectively to define the characteristics of your best customers—the criteria will be used to define your primary target market.*

Now evaluate your "B" customers; what do you notice? Do they only buy one or two products instead of several products and services from your company? Do they give you only a portion of their business while they give your competitors more? Are these customers from a particular industry or geographic area? How would you describe the target market criteria for these customers?

Now look at your "C" customers for common characteristics that could describe this group of customers. Why are these customers high revenue, but low in profitability? Do these decision makers consist of purchasing agents from large companies who purchase in volume at lower prices? Does only one department do business with you instead of the entire company? How is the decision maker different from customers in the other categories? What other characteristics would you use to describe customers in this segment?

As you ask similar questions for your "D" customers, you may notice that there is one particular aspect of this group of customers that is different from the others. Hint: It's usually tied to the "likability" factor. Is this group of customers difficult to work with? Do these customers require a lot more service or "whine" more than any other customers? Do your employees cringe when they hear a particular customer is on the phone? Look at the group of customers in the group you have identified as "D" customers and define as many common characteristics of this group as you can.

## Step #3: Define Service by Customer Segment

When you have finished the first two steps of this exercise, step three is to describe how you provide different levels of service to customers in each of the segments. Some companies may note that they don't treat customers in each of the segments differently. This is not smart. "A" customers should be loved individually and often and your "B" customers require different handling than your "C" customers. Each customer segment should be entitled to different levels of service.

For example, first-class and million-mile business members get higher levels of service compared to coach passengers who fly infrequently and are interested in a discount price. All customers get to the same destination safely and at the same time, but the customer experience is different.

If you discover that you do not provide differentiated levels of service in each of these segments, you have made an important discovery. When you develop customer service strategies later in book, you can create strategies for each of the customer segments.

## Step #4: Customize Marketing Programs

The final step in this exercise is to determine how you market to each customer group. Just as different service levels are needed, marketing programs for each customer segment should also be unique. As you consider your existing marketing strategy and communication programs, think about the types of special offers, rewards, and incentives you offer, as well as the frequency of your communication with segments of customers and/or individuals. Note how existing marketing programs vary (or not) for each of the four customer segments. Later in the planning process, you will put this idea to work to develop different marketing strategies and programs for customer segments.

I mentioned earlier that this one exercise has proved to be a goldmine for some businesses. Here's why: Once you know who your best customers are, and why, this information can be used to target new customers who meet the same criteria. You simply use the criteria that you defined for an "A" customer as your ideal target market profile. Your observations about the characteristics in this segment may also lead to additional targeting criteria. Also note that if you have not maximized the revenue and profit potential for "A" customers and there are still considerable products or services to sell to these customers, then this group of customers might actually be your "B" customers. In this case, you need to set the bar higher and define new target market characteristics for "A" customers. This exercise will also help you increase both revenues and profits with your existing customer base by evaluating how to migrate them up another level or two, transitioning "B" customers to become "A" customers, "C" customers to "B" customers, and so on.

Every company I have worked with has found this exercise to be extremely valuable because it shines a bright light on information they didn't know about customers. It also helps establish more effective marketing and sales strategies, as well as processes.

A healthcare company did this exercise and was shocked to learn that the 80/20 rule was actually reversed. Most of their customers were in the "D" category. By simply understanding this and defining what an "A" customer looked like, they were able to completely refocus the sales force on a new set of target prospects, resulting in a huge uplift in new sales. They also "fired" their "D" customers by politely referring them to a competitor, and this enabled them to focus their energy and build a new sales funnel of profitable customers very quickly.

Following completion of Figure 14.1, summarize your findings and decisions in the marketing plan template in the customer segment and target market sections. You will continue to refine this information as you complete additional exercises in this section.

**Marketing Tip**

If a marketing team is working on the plan, it is extremely valuable to do this exercise as a group. You may want to invite the sales team to participate in this exercise. It can be done individually first, then shared as a group to see if everyone has similar or different perspectives, and why.

# PRIORITIZE CUSTOMERS BY VALUE

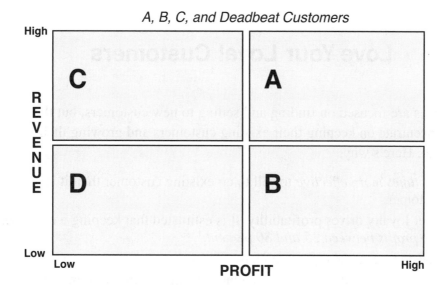

(1) Segment customers by revenue and profit.

(2) Define other characteristics that are similar in each segment.

(3) Define how customer service is different in each customer segment.

(4) Define how marketing programs are different in each segment.

I know this about my class **A** customers: _____

_____

I know this about my class **B** customers: _____

_____

I know this about my class **C** customers: _____

_____

I know this about my class **D** customers: _____

_____

**Figure 14.1**   *Prioritize customers by value*

# 15

# Love Your Loyal Customers

Many companies are focused on finding and selling to new customers, but the smartest companies concentrate on keeping their existing customers and growing their relationships with them. Here's why:

- It is *five times more effective* to sell to an existing customer than it is to find a new customer.
- Customer loyalty drives profitability. It is estimated that keeping a customer can *increase profits between 25 and 80 percent.*[1]
- Loyal customers make repeat purchases.
- Loyal customers tend to buy across your portfolio of products and services.
- Loyal customers give referrals.
- Loyal customers tell their friends and spread good will.
- Loyal customers are immune to the pull of competition.
- Loyal customers require less marketing.
- Loyal customers help you co-design new products and services.

Do you know what drives customer loyalty in your company? In addition to an analysis of your customer base, it is important to understand WHY customers choose to do business with your company. What drives them to do business with you instead of your competitors? What do your customers value the most? It's easy to form assumptions about why customers do business with your company instead of competitors, but the only real way to know is to *ask them*. Surveys, focus groups, and behavior research can help you understand what customers want and gauge how well your company actually meets their needs.

## How Do You Measure Loyalty?

You now know that great customer service and experience creates customer loyalty, which in turn creates more profitability, but how much profitability? Research shows that a *one percent increase in customer retention is equal to a five percent increase in business value*, which is significant. Research also has proven that companies with the highest level of customer loyalty *grew revenues at twice the rate of their competitors.*[2]

There are several metrics you can use to track customer loyalty. Two of the most effective are customer lifetime value (CLV) and customer delight using the Net Promoter Score (NPS). These concepts are explained below.

## Measure Customer Profitability and CLV

A basic measure of customer profitability is the revenue a customer generates over a period of time, minus the cost of attracting, selling, and servicing the customer. Activity-based cost is another way some businesses calculate customer profitability. This method is more complicated and involves subtracting all costs and resources to make and distribute the product or service, including all expenses to service the customer (travel, entertainment, phone calls, and so on). This is a much more granular method of estimating customer profitability, and if you don't have the luxury of time or an accounting department to crunch all these numbers for you, I suggest you stick with the simple calculation previously described. This basic measure will give you a good estimate of customer profitability and you can also use the same method to evaluate profitability of channels and market segments.

CLV is based on the concept that a customer profit rate increases the longer they do business with a company. Depending upon the industry, this number can be substantial. According to James Putten of American Express, a company's best customers outspend others by:[3]

- 16 to 1 in retailing
- 13 to 1 in restaurants
- 12 to 1 in the airline business
- 5 to 1 in lodging

CLV can be calculated in several ways. Many companies use the same calculations described above (annual customer revenue minus costs to arrive at profitability rate and the number of loyalty years) plus estimating the net present value. But again, if you have not estimated CLV before, I recommend a basic approach (customer revenue - costs = profitability × years) so you have a good estimate of present and future CLV and how loyalty transfers to profitability in your business.

## Building Customer Loyalty

It's a fact that loyal customers create sustained, profitable growth. You now know *why* you should focus on creating loyal customers and how to measure it, but *how* do you do it? Here are a few methods you can learn and apply to your business:

- Measure customer delight, not customer satisfaction.
- Measure customer loyalty using the Net Promoter Score.
- Create customer relationship management strategies for profitable customer segments.
- Build a customer and employee centric culture.
- Engage customers in unique customer experiences.
- Know why customers buy your products/services and why they choose to do business with your company.

## Measure Customer Delight, Not Satisfaction

Measuring customer satisfaction will not be an indicator of customer loyalty. Yes, you read that correctly. In fact, customers who are merely satisfied are at risk of defecting to a competitor. Why? Like a business attribute like "quality," customer satisfaction is becoming a given, a baseline assumption that customers expect. Consumer needs have become more fickle as products and services have evolved to become more sophisticated and a vast array of choices has been made available for consumers to choose from. This means businesses need to ask different questions to understand whether they are meeting customer needs.

Fredrick Reichheld, author of *The Ultimate Question* and *The Loyalty Effect*, has studied customer loyalty and how to measure it for more than a decade. He discovered there is really only one question that a business can ask its customers to know if they are loyal:

"How likely is it that you would recommend this company to a friend or colleague?"

## Net Promoter Score

Reichheld's question results in a metric called the Net Promoter Score (NPS). The NPS is derived from measuring customer satisfaction by the criteria in three groups:

- **Promoters** are loyal enthusiasts who continually buy from a business and encourage their friends and family to do business with the company.
- **Passives** are satisfied but unenthusiastic customers who would easily move to the competition.
- **Detractors** are unhappy customers who no longer wish to buy from a company.

Reichheld advises companies to measure customer loyalty by asking the "Ultimate Question" and using a ten-point scale. Promoters score a 9 or 10, Passives a 7 or 8, and Detractors score 6 or below. Therefore, the best way to gauge customer loyalty (profitable growth) is to subtract the number of detractors from the number of promoters to calculate the NPS  (P - D = NPS).

The best companies average an NPS between 50 and 82 percent. Sadly, the average U.S. company has an NPS of less than ten percent. Some firms even have a negative NPS. It's no wonder so many businesses fail. They don't know how to keep their existing customers; therefore, how could they ever be successful in growing their business with new customers? The NPS is a remarkably simple methodology to track customer loyalty and understand customers' constantly evolving wants and needs.

Both small and large companies are integrating the NPS score into their business processes and using it as a key metric. Take a look at how Intuit uses the NPS to measure and improve customer relationships and develop new products.

## Intuit: How the Best Get Better

Scott Cook, former CEO of Intuit, was passionate about creating customer loyalty. When Intuit adopted the NPS to measure customer loyalty, they implemented a two-question phone survey to determine how many promoters, passives, and detractors there were. They asked:

1. What is the likelihood that you would recommend TurboTax to a friend or colleague?
2. What is the most important reason for the score you gave?

The result of asking these two questions resulted in an NPS of 27 to 52 percent across Intuit's product lines.[4] While this is above the national average, Intuit's goal was to achieve a much higher ranking. Intuit launched a 6,000 member "Inner Circle" of customers to get ongoing feedback about how the company could improve. As customers joined the virtual community, they were asked to answer the "Ultimate Question" and make recommendations for improvements to TurboTax. They could also vote on the suggestions other people made. Intuit's software team then ranked and prioritized the suggestions so the most popular and valuable suggestions were implemented first.

But Intuit didn't stop there. They discovered that priorities were different across the Promoters, Passives, and Detractor segments. Curious, executives called customers to learn more. (Note: The task was not delegated to a research manager.) This resulted in several discoveries and subsequent improvements in the products. The final outcome was an increase in new user NPS from 48 to 58 percent, and scores for the desktop version of TurboTax jumped from 46 to 61 percent.

If your company has several metrics, you might find it refreshing—and immensely more valuable—to focus on one measurement. Cook said, "We have every customer metric under the sun and yet we couldn't make those numbers focus the organization on our core value of doing right by the customer. The more metrics you track, the less relevant each one becomes. Each manager will choose to focus on the number that makes his decision look good. The concept of one single metric has produced a huge benefit for us—customers, employees, and investors alike."[5]

Current CEO of Intuit Brad Smith has continued to foster Intuit's maniacal focus on understanding customer needs and using non-traditional market research to do so. Follow Me Home is an observational research project started several years ago. Intuit representatives go to a customer's home or office and observes them as they load the software and use it. Intuit knows they can only learn so much by talking with customers and asking questions. Often it's far more effective to watch what customers do when they use a product. This sheds light on how the product is used, the features customers use and appreciate the most, and those that are not used at all. Over time, this helps Intuit modify products to meet customer needs based upon what they value the most. It's so important that Intuit invests more than 10,000 hours a year with customers on this project alone.

# 16

# 1:1 Marketing: Treat Different Customers Differently

So far, you have learned how to segment customers and why customer loyalty is important to the profitability of an organization. The process of understanding how your company collects and analyses this information has probably shed light on how well this information is tracked and stored in a database. If you currently segment customers based upon their value to your business, great. You may use this information to provide different levels of service and marketing to different segments. If you do not currently track this information, or only track some of it in a sales database program, then now would be a good time to assess your current and future needs. Ongoing tracking and analysis of customer purchases and buying behavior is a critically important aspect of your marketing plan. This information will be used to develop your customer relationship management (CRM) strategies.

The basis of CRM is simple: Rather than trying to sell a product to as many customers as possible, focus on selling as many products or services to each customer over their lifetime. Rather than organizing the company around products, divisions, and sales channels, organize around the customer. Instead of trying to sell to as many new customers as possible, focus on getting, keeping, and growing customers. This is the basis for profit growth.

Most marketing and sales teams are using some type of CRM program to track customer information. For those that do this well, the core of a CRM program is a database that enables a learning relationship with customers. It tracks what customers buy, their preferences, and a company's profitability, activities, and communication with customers. By tracking information on an individual customer basis, anyone in the company can have the information they need to have the next conversation with a customer.

## Make Customers the Center of Your Universe

An effective first step of developing and implementing a CRM program is to focus on creating a CRM strategy for your most profitable customers. Don't extend it to other customer segments until after this first step is implemented and tested. When this process has become successful, you can choose another segment and roll out programs to the next customer group. This process of slow, incremental implementation has proven to be one of the most critical success factors for companies implementing new CRM programs.

A CRM strategy begins with defining the type of information that is important to know about customers, as well as how this information will be tracked and reported. For some businesses, it is useful to report this information weekly; for others, it is useful on a monthly or quarterly basis. If you don't have a person responsible for CRM programs, assign a customer relationship manager who is responsible for a certain set of customers. This person can come from sales, marketing, customer service, or another area of the company. On a monthly or quarterly basis, have the CRM managers organize and share what has been learned about customers.

Cross-functional team dialogue is often overlooked, but it is critically important. By distributing CRM responsibilities across several people and sharing customer feedback, it takes the burden off one or two people to be responsible for this information. It will also help the broader team become smarter about customers as people learn from each other. This type of process achieves the outcome of improved customer relationships and helps your business become a customer-focused learning organization. The product marketing teams will begin to design new products and services to more effectively meet the needs of customers. The marketing team will know how to craft new messaging that is more relevant to its most valuable customers. And it will help break down the barriers between sales and marketing teams by engaging in a dialogue about what customers want, and how to improve sales, marketing, and customer service.

Maintaining or growing customer relationships may require new customer service strategies directed toward major accounts or valuable market segments. Major account service may require a restructuring of the sales force to allow salespeople more time with customers. If a company differentiates itself from competitors based on knowledge and service, then training programs may need to be developed for several audiences who interface with customers, including salespeople, distributors, customer service agents, and operations teams.

If delivery, integration, or logistics is a priority for customers, business processes may need to be redesigned to fulfill customer requirements. A customer that demands reliability and responsiveness may require a 24/7 help line. Initiatives such as these improve customer service and differentiate a business as a result of being customer focused rather than product focused. When businesses allow customers to challenge them to improve service and experience, the company will be better as a result.

# 17

# Marketing's Secret Weapon

So far, we have discussed how to analyze and segment your existing customers and track customer information to develop effective CRM strategies. These are the basic mechanics for fostering customer loyalty and building a more profitable customer base. Customer experience and a customer-centric culture are the elements that add the magic.

A strong customer strategy requires a company culture that values customers and nurtures this philosophy among employees. It's easy for business leaders to talk about creating a customer-focused culture, but actually doing it is a completely different matter. Companies that are customer-centric do more than put programs in place. *They design a culture that values creating a rich customer experience, and strives to exceed customer satisfaction.* Employees in companies like this realize that customer satisfaction is important, but it's just the price of admission for competing in their industry. They know that *exceeding* satisfaction creates customer loyalty and a high-performance organization.

Many companies adopt a "customer is always first" mantra, but it's my experience that this is wrong—it's backwards. If you put employees first, they will always move mountains to take care of customers. It just doesn't work the other way around. If you have ever experienced an employee who is complaining about how the company treats them poorly while trying to service you, then you know what I mean. Customers will not feel valued unless employees feel valued, too. Companies that truly value and appreciate their customers create a culture that is respectful to both customers and employees. It's really quite simple. Employees want to please customers. The biggest reason they don't is because they don't feel valued or don't understand how; therefore, how could they provide great customer experiences? Employees need to know the rules of customer engagement and what their boundaries are so they feel empowered to do the right thing for customers. It's simply playing by the Golden Rule: "Do unto others as you would have them do unto you."

It may sound easy to build an employee- and customer-centric strategy, but don't be fooled. According to a survey of CRM users, 87 percent of those surveyed said the failure of their programs was largely due to the lack of adequate change management. Even though there was a desire to be customer focused, the culture did not support the strategy. If customer strategy is not crystal clear and integrated into company values, culture, and daily processes, even the best of intentions will be disappointing.

A company's ability to foster customer loyalty is closely linked to the company purpose and culture. When a company has a strong foundation of values and principles, and has processes in place to nurture them, executives and employees can naturally do the right things to stimulate customer loyalty. If you did a good job of defining your company purpose in Section I, "Purpose," you have taken a huge leap in the right direction.

## Customer-Focused Culture at OrangeGlo

One day I was visiting the office of OrangeGlo, a family-run business that was on a path to turn its small cleaning business into a multi-million dollar brand. (It was eventually sold to Church and Dwight, makers of Arm and Hammer products, for $325 million.) When I walked through the front door, it appeared that nearly every employee in the company was packed into the front office. Entrepreneur Joel Appel was sharing a story about how two of the drivers had just returned from a long trip delivering product across the country when they received a call from one of their best customers, Wal-Mart.

Wal-Mart was in process of opening one of their biggest stores in Texas and realized they were out of stock of OrangeGlo and OxiClean, two products that Wal-Mart customers expected to find in the store. They asked OrangeGlo if they could possibly arrange to have the products there the next day, which was not possible using typical transportation methods. So the two drivers offered to load up a truck and drive it day and night in order to please the company's most valuable customer.

Appel could have rewarded the two men with additional pay or a "thank you" and left it at that. Instead, he chose to recognize the two men for their dedication and commitment for doing something so important to both Wal-Mart and OrangeGlo. If you could have seen the smiling, beaming faces on the two men, and all the other employees who were smiling, clapping, and patting them on the back, you would realize there is nothing more important than rewarding employees for their actions. There could not have been a more powerful training moment than this to teach other employees the value of customer service.

Another great lesson about creating a customer-and employee-centric culture can be learned from The Ritz-Carlton. In Chapter 6, "How The Ritz-Carlon Creates and Sustains a High-Performance Culture," I described how all new employees at The Ritz-Carlton are required to attend training prior to ever setting foot on the job. There is strict adherence to this rule because the company realizes that they are in the business of creating unique customer experiences. In order to do this, employees must understand the company values, principles, and what it means to "anticipate and respond to a customer's unexpressed wishes." This is very hard to do in a service environment where every customer service moment is unique.

A company can only teach employees what their values mean, provide them with examples, and clearly state what their boundaries are to meet this goal. To this last point, The Ritz-Carlton's employees are allowed to spend up to $2,000 a day to make sure a customer is satisfied. Employees rarely tap into this fund because they know they have a high degree of flexibility and creativity to make customers happy—and happiness is not usually tied to money.

Company culture is the secret weapon of good marketing. A talented marketer can create brilliant marketing programs, but if the underlying culture can't support it, even the best programs will fall short.

The following is a list of a few rules of the road to keep in mind as you design a company culture linked to customer strategy.

## Tips to Create a Customer-Centric Culture

1. Company culture starts at the top. If the CEO or senior leadership team does not value culture, you have quite the battle in front of you. If you are a marketing executive in a company with a problematic culture, focus on the things you *can* do to help your company move toward building a customer-centric culture.

2. A powerful external brand begins with a strong internal brand:
   - Is there regular, ongoing communication across the organization so people understand the company strategy, goals, and how their daily work contributes to this?
   - Do people understand the company purpose, mission, vision, and values?
   - Are values defined and communicated often so people understand what types of behaviors are associated with the values?

3. Educate and train employees to do the following things:
   - Treat different customers differently. To do this, they will need to understand who your best customers are, as well as understand the criteria and rational for customer segmentation. Share the outcomes of the A, B, C, D exercise.
   - Handle difficult customer situations. If employees are trained and armed with ideas and examples about how to handle a variety of customer situations, they will be much more relaxed and feel more capable to respond.
   - Set broad boundaries. Give people the latitude to solve customer problems. If they understand what the boundaries are, you can leave it to them to be creative and do the right thing for customers.
4. Invest in training for new employees, especially in areas like company culture and values. This will set them up for long-term success.
5. Provide feedback mechanisms so that front-line employees can easily communicate customer needs to the rest of the organization. Feedback should not be limited to only the marketing and sales departments, but should be shared throughout the organization so everyone can learn, interact, and respond to customer feedback.
6. Reward employees who provide outstanding customer service. Not only will you retain your best employees, you will set an example for others in the company.

# 18

## Create Unique Customer Experiences

One of the most interesting and creative ways successful companies create competitive differentiation is by creating unique customer experiences. Peter Drucker said, "The aim of marketing is to make selling superfluous." In today's market, this could be updated to: "The aim of great customer experiences is to make marketing superfluous."

Perhaps the best expression of this is the growing trend of customers taking a more active role as co-producers in experiences. For example, Nike's web site allows customers to custom design their own athletic shoes based upon individual preferences. Oakley sunglass fans can design and order their own shades on the company Web site.

Converse has been selling shoes for decades. If you're a Gen-Xer, perhaps you wore a pair of the famous black and white tennis shoes. Was it ever a good shoe? I don't think so. In my humble opinion, it has absolutely no arch support or performance capabilities, but the brand has been revitalized and has made a comeback by designing shoes that appeal to a new generation. Visit www.converse.com and you'll experience a young, spunky, and user-friendly site. Browse their diverse array of clothing and shoes, including those by designer John Varvatos. The most engaging aspect of Converse.com is the excitement of concocting your own unique pair of designer shoes. Choose from twelve basic designs, a deluge of fabrics, threads, patterns, lace colors, and even the hue of your rubber insole. Converse.com elicits a delightful creativity that, for a decent price, can be yours with a simple click.

You don't have to have a consumer product or retail store to create a unique customer experience. Citizen's Bank in Boston installed a "Dog Spot" in the lobby of a bank to cater to dog lovers. A special area features water bowls, a doghouse, and dog biscuits so canine-loving customers could bring their best friend with them while they took care of banking needs. Suddenly a typically mundane activity like making a deposit became a warm and friendly experience.

Business-to-business markets can foster customer loyalty by hosting customer advisory boards or creating unique events that foster customer intimacy. The following stories illustrate a few examples.

## Customers for Life

When a new business division at Avaya was created to focus on Service Providers, I was brought in to lead global market development with our customers. It was a unique business model. We bundled Avaya's communication solutions with those of large service providers like Sprint, France Telecom, Telecom Italia, AT&T, British Telecom, and other tier-one service providers around the world. Our objective was to partner with these companies and build a new revenue stream for both Avaya and the service provider by selling solutions to the service provider's customers. Hosted, on-demand services required the implementation of a new business model (from hardware to hosted solutions), so it was critical to build relationships with executive decision makers.

As our team designed the launch of this new service, we knew that traditional marketing programs would be useless in reaching the CEO and other executives unless we implemented a compelling customer intimacy strategy. A key part of this strategy was sponsorship of The World Business Forum, a two-day conference for C-level executives to listen to the world's leading thought leaders such as Jack Welch, Richard Branson, Tom Peters, Jim Collins, and respected CEOs from the world's best companies.

Over the course of two days, we had the opportunity to spend quality one-on-one time with our customers and get to know them on a level that would have taken years of business meetings to develop. We hosted lunch and cocktail parties with the conference speakers so customers had the opportunity to talk with them about specific business challenges. In the evening, small dinners with customers were arranged so everyone could share perspectives about the topics that were presented that day and get to know each other on a personal level. Over the course of two solid days with customers, business issues were discussed, and much of the conversation was personal. As relationships developed, it opened the door to talk with customers about the advantages of implementing a new business model. It was a priceless experience with customers—who became friends for life. Had we taken a more traditional sales path, it would have taken many months to have quality conversations with these individuals.

# 19

# Customer Experience: The Dark Side

## Customer Experience: The Dark Side

In the new economy, there is little margin for error. Companies that do not pay enough attention to customer service are prey to agile competitors who see an easy opportunity to strike and take advantage of a vulnerable customer base. It's not just poor customer service that causes customer defection: The growing use of social media can quickly accelerate a company's demise.

Once upon a time (pre-Internet), customers who had a bad experience would tell nine or ten people about it. Now when a customer has a bad experience, they tell thousands—even tens of thousands of people about it around the globe.

People don't just tell others about their bad customer experience, they may post a video on YouTube or a blog that *shows* people just how badly they were treated. Ouch. And it won't be long before customers are streaming live audio and video of the mishap for the entire world to see. Marc Andreessen, founder of Netscape, the first Internet browser that was sold to AOL for $4.2 billion, is involved in a new company called Qik. This technology has the ability to turn every mobile device with a camera into a source of streaming video and audio. Just imagine the effect of this. Qik's technology could record a firestorm of customer service disasters.

## Why Consumers Are Skeptical

Clearly consumers are more skeptical today than they have ever been before. Who can blame them? Enron was essentially fictitious; executives at Tyco, Qwest, and a host of other firms lied and cheated all the way to the bank. Once solid financial firms crumbled like a house of cards. Even our former president, George W. Bush, lied about "weapons of mass destruction." And then there's Bernie Madoff, who has forever changed the look a consumer has in her eye when talking to her financial advisor. There's plenty of reason for even the most optimistic of folks to be skeptical.

But what has led to consumer skepticism is not caused so much by the big issues just mentioned. It's the small ways companies, even entire industries, take advantage of their customers. Airlines are probably the worst. You will never know what the best fare is when booking a flight. You could have easily paid hundreds of dollars more for your ticket than the guy sitting in the seat next to you. Making last-minute travel plans? Most companies would love to give you a discount for potentially unused inventory, but airlines find this a good excuse to charge you even more. If you are traveling last minute to attend a funeral, you may get a generous $100 off the price of the inflated ticket, but the customer service agent will press you to produce verification from a physician or funeral home that your loved one is indeed dead. Just what a grieving customer needs.

Most major airlines charge their customers $100–$150 to make a ticket change, and $50 to check a bag. As fuel costs soared, consumers were nickel and dimed for a cup of coffee or a soda on a flight they paid more for than they did a year ago. Airline execs blamed Wall Street traders for higher costs due to soaring fuel costs, but when the price of oil dropped to half of what it was, airlines continued to charge customers the same price for a ticket and charge for the basics such as having your luggage accompany you on a trip. In a recent Jay Leno monologue, Leno quipped that it won't be long before airlines start to charge consumers for basics, like arriving at their destination safely. Want a smooth landing? That will be another $50.00.

## Live By the Golden Rule

Southwest Airlines is one of the few airlines that remains profitable and has a stellar reputation for employee and customer satisfaction. They simply follow the Golden Rule: *Do unto others as you would have them do unto you*. Ask any Southwest Airline employee or executive, and they will tell you they practice the Golden Rule in everything they do. But there is no need to ask because you will *experience* it.

Other industries are also guilty of poor customer experience. Car rental companies charge consumers two or three times above normal gas rates if they bring back a car without a full tank of gas. Imagine a car rental firm that filled up the tank for you when you returned it, charging you the market rate? Wouldn't people flock to do business with the company? But it may not necessarily be for the great experience as much it would be for the thrill of just being treated fairly. This is one industry that has opportunity written all over it.

Another industry that comes to mind when thinking about customer service is the communications industry. Mobile phone carriers won't hesitate to send a customer a $1,000 phone bill because her teenage son downloaded ringtones and music from the

Internet without a data plan. But how would a teenager know the phone company charges ridiculous data transfer rates for a slow download of a song? If only mom had known she could have signed up for a $25 a month plan for unlimited Internet access and saved $975!

## Customer Service Gone Bad

Perhaps the darkest side of customer experience is the way in which some companies take advantage of their most loyal customers. If you are a loyal cable subscriber, you are probably paying more for your service than a new customer who just got a deal for switching carriers. If you are a magazine subscriber, you are probably being asked to renew your subscription at a much higher price than if you just let the subscription lapse and subscribed as a new customer. *Why are some companies penalizing their best customers?*

Do companies really think they are making more money with this bait and switch tactic? All the switching, paperwork, and hassle of dealing with companies like this is frustrating for customers, as well as for employees. Do companies think consumers are too stupid to notice? Or that employees don't know they are duping customers? If bad behavior like this is just company policy, why on earth would an employee ever trust the company they work for?

Treating people fairly is a pretty simple concept. So is the idea of giving good customer service. As we get back to basics in this new economy, maybe more companies on the dark side of customer service will see the light.

# 20

# Why Do Customers Buy?

The "A, B, C, and Deadbeat Customers" exercise in Chapter 14, "Micro Perspective: Focus on High-Value Customers," helped you segment and analyze your customer base. The next step is to analyze why your customers buy from you. Do you know what your customers value the most? What drives them to do business with you instead of your competitors? To answer these questions, you will create a "working hypothesis," or best guess, about why your customers choose to do business with you. This question can only be answered one way: You need to ask them. The outcomes from the "Why People Buy" exercise later in this chapter will become part of your primary research.

Entrepreneurs have a sense of what motivates customers to do business with them, but as I have worked with hundreds of entrepreneurs on this exercise, they usually discover that their initial assumptions are incorrect. This causes a whole chain of marketing mistakes: Sometimes brochures do not describe the actual benefits customers derive from a product, service, or company; or the company emphasizes low price when price is not even important to the customer buying decision. Factors like timeliness of delivery or what constitutes quality are very different between what the company assumes and what the customer really wants. The "Why People Buy" exercise will help you separate facts from assumptions. Like the "A, B, C, or Deadbeat" exercise, there are many benefits to this exercise including improved marketing strategies, focused messaging, and improvements in the results of marketing programs.

Mac McConnell, who owns Artful Frame Gallery in Fort Lauderdale, Florida, thought for a long time that his customers bought because of price. He advertised low prices and competitive research revealed he was indeed the cheapest in town. Frustrated with business profitability, he decided to ask each customer who came in the door over a six-week period to fill out a one-page questionnaire about his or her experience with Artful Frame and the reasons why he or she buys from him. Much to his surprise, McConnell discovered that his customers prized quality, creativity, and service. Price finished near last as a priority in his shoppers' minds.

As a result of this simple questionnaire, McConnell's entire strategy shifted from being the low-price provider to being a quality framing shop. His employees are trained to skip a conversation about price and engage the customer in a creative discussion. McConnell changed his inventory to emphasize high-end pieces. The average invoice rose from $67 to $167. Sales tripled to almost $600,000 and net profits increased 26 percent. Not only is McConnell happier because he is making more money, he and his staff are happier because they are doing more creative work for customers.

## Why People Buy

Create a working hypothesis, or best guess, of why people buy from you. Your goal will be to validate your working hypothesis in your primary research. This information will be used in several areas of the planning process including the development of several business strategies. It will also be used to create focused communication and messaging to increase the effectiveness of your sales and marketing programs.

A. **Select and Define Attributes:** Review the following list of attributes and select those that you believe are the primary reasons your customers buy from you. If these attributes don't fit for your business, write your own attributes in the blanks below. Select and define no more than five attributes.

| **Attribute** | **Definition** |
|---|---|
| Price | _____ |
| Quality | _____ |
| Customer Service | _____ |
| Reputation | _____ |
| Relationship | _____ |
| _____ | _____ |
| _____ | _____ |

B. **Prioritize and Rank Attributes:** Based on why you believe your customers choose to buy from you, rank the attributes in order of importance: 1 is the least important and 5 is the most important. Prioritize each attribute so you have a ranking of most important to least important. Prioritize and rank exactly the same number of attributes that you defined above.

**C. Translate Attributes to Benefits:** Write the prioritized ranking of attributes in the area below. Now translate each of the attributes into features and benefits customers receive from them. Describe the benefits from your customers' perspective.

| ATTRIBUTE | FEATURES | BENEFITS |
|-----------|----------|----------|
| 1. | | |
| 2. | | |
| 3. | | |
| 4. | | |
| 5. | | |

**Marketing Tip**

If you are taking a team-based approach to writing your company plan, have everyone in the group begin by brainstorming a list of possible attributes and vote on the top five. Then have everyone define and rank each attribute separately. When finished, go around the group and have each person describe how and why they answered as they did. You will be surprised how different the responses can be!

Decide as a group how you will choose to define and prioritize each attribute. If you are doing this exercise as part of a strategic planning session, this should be one of those "Ah Ha" moments as you realize how internally focused ideas and messaging can be. It should stimulate interesting discussion because people will have differing opinions. The secret to this exercise is to realize that *only your customers* can really define their buyer motivation.

## Action

After you have completed this exercise, the next step is to validate your assumptions with customers and dig deep to understand what motivates them to do business with you. This will be done using primary research such as a customer survey or customer interviews. This process will be explained later in this section. For now, summarize what you learned in the "Customer Behavior" section of the marketing plan template and write down questions you would like to have answered when you develop your primary research plan.

# 21

# Real-Time Customer Research

The concept of customer focus groups usually creates an image of a group of 10–12 people who meet anonymously behind a two-way mirror to discuss a company's products or services. While this primary research method can be an effective way to get customer feedback, I would like to share a very different approach for learning about customer preferences. This approach can be used for any size of company, but it is exceptionally valuable for companies that are in the early-stage launch of a product or service.

Launch Pad is a business that was founded by Joel Appel and Frank Kvietok. Both Joel and Frank have deep consumer products experience. Joel and his family founded OrangeGlo (specializing in cleaning products), which was sold in 2006 for $325 million. Frank was a "creative PhD" scientist with Procter and Gamble. The two young entrepreneurs founded Launch Pad with the intention of funding and rapidly launching innovative new consumer products.

How do they know if a product will be successful or not? Aside from experience and "gut feeling," they use consumer focus groups to test and validate their assumptions about the go-to-market strategy. But focus groups are not simply used as a research tool. It's actually part of the underlying fabric of their business operations. Here's how it works.

Every Wednesday, a group of people, mostly women who have been a part of this group for a long time, meet to give their opinions about various products. During the course of an hour, product managers from Launch Pad present concepts and ideas to the group who in turn give their opinions about the products and the way they are marketed. There are no two-way mirrors, no set agendas, and no formalities—just honest direct feedback.

The day before the meeting, the agenda is penciled out. Topics range from discussion about the likes and dislikes of a product, packaging design, messaging on a Web site, pricing, promotions, or advertising, to questions about who would buy the product and why, among other topics.

One of the most unique and valuable outcomes from the focus groups is the ongoing interactivity that potential customers have with the products. All of the products are in various stages of product launch and the group gives ongoing feedback throughout the launch process and product life cycle.

This group has the power to shape the strategic and tactical launch of the go-to-market strategy. The Launch Pad team actively listens to the comments and suggestions, makes adjustments, and the cycle repeats. Every week the goal is to get permission to move to the next level. As the product progresses through the launch process, it is progressively tested in target markets so the strategy can be refined. It's one of the most effective processes I have seen for launching new products. It enables a company to see if a product or product strategy will be successful—or not—before thousands of dollars are wasted.

While this process is ideal for a new product launch, you can modify it for testing products and services in new markets, evaluating new features, advertising campaigns, and other important marketing criteria.

Ongoing research to understand the ever-changing wants and needs of customers is an important part of every marketing plan. As you read through this section and go through this process, you will learn various techniques for integrating customer feedback into your everyday business activities.

---

### Marketing Tip for Large Companies

If your company or agency has done recent customer research to understand buyer behavior, review this information to see if you can use the findings in your marketing plan.

You may discover that the type of research your company conducts annually does not include the right type of information to update your plan, or enough specifics into what drives buyer behavior. If this is the case, make new recommendations about the type of research criteria that will be more useful in the future.

---

# 22

# Macro Perspective: Get the Big Picture

The first part of this section focused on the micro, or internal, aspects that drive your business. The research up to this point has been focused on your customers and has been gathered from company database records (or your best guess if you don't collect this information). Now we'll shift to an external perspective to seek information about market segments, competitors, and the market environment. The blending of information about both the internal and external environments will help identify opportunities for business growth. The combination of both the micro and macro research becomes the Market Opportunity Analysis (MOA) section of your plan.

A macro perspective is an understanding of the market and industry in which you compete, the potential market size for your solution (projections of the available market size, revenue, and market share), and your competitors. Macro research will include examining the issues and events outside of your control (such as the economy) that may impact your business. Companies that learn to anticipate market, industry, and competitor dynamics have a distinct competitive advantage. They discover opportunities and quickly respond to them because they have already thought through their next strategic move. Businesses that are not prepared for obstacles and uncertainties are often blindsided. These companies can get derailed for periods of time; or worse, they can fail due to unforeseen issues.

Your research in this section will include the following:

1. Sizing the market opportunity for your products and services.
2. Defining your target market.
3. Competitive research to determine your unique differentiation in the market.
4. Macro-environmental issues and trends to anticipate changes that are outside of your control but still impact your business.

## Market Segmentation and Target Marketing

Clearly and accurately defining your target market(s) is one of the most important, if not *the* most important, part of developing your marketing plan. If the target market description is not accurate or is too broad, the rest of your marketing plan will not be on point.

If your messaging and marketing strategies are directed to the wrong target market, how could they possibly be effective?

Identifying a target market starts with market segmentation. Market segmentation is the process of defining and selecting all the possible segments of customers who would be interested in buying your products. Begin by identifying the broad market segments that buy your products and services, then narrow this to the one or two markets that have the strongest need and ability to purchase your solutions. Factor in issues such as the ease of reaching and selling into the markets, competitor market share, and other factors.

If you sell many diverse products and services, or if you sell into many different industries or geographic locations, you may have several target market definitions. They may be defined by demographic and psychographic characteristics. Demographics are items like age, income, gender, occupation, and so on. Psychographics are lifestyle traits, such as hobbies, sports, and special interest groups. Market segments should be mutually exclusive with no overlaps.

### Marketing Tip

Review the definitions you developed for your "A" customers in the "A, B, C, or Deadbeat" exercise of Chapter 14, "Micro Perspective: Focus on High-Value Customers." If these characteristics represent the optimal buyer for your products and services, you should integrate these characteristics into your target market description.

Use the following criteria to define your target market. The first section, "Identifying Target Market Segments," summarizes common characteristics of primarily consumer buyers, although several factors can be used to target business buyers. The second section, "Business-to-Business (B2B) Target Markets," summarizes the attributes of buyers in a business market. Be as specific as possible to define an accurate description of your customers. The more you narrow and focus on precise characteristics of buyers, the more targeted your marketing becomes.

# Identifying Target Market Segments

1. **Demographics**

   *Consumer:* Criteria such as age, sex, income, occupation, education, household size, geography, home ownership, marital status.

   *Business-to-Business:* Criteria such as industry specialty groups, geography, level in organization (C-level), size of organization, number of employees, revenue, type of asset, buying cycle, seasonality.

2. **Psychographics**

   How do a prospects' lifestyles, interests, activities, and opinions affect their buying behavior?

3. **Need and Problem**

   What problem are you solving for the target customer? How much time or money will your solution save? How big is the problem for various target markets?

4. **Revenue Potential**

   How much revenue do you anticipate each segment will generate?

5. **Growth Potential**

   How much do you anticipate the target market will grow and change?

6. **Loyalty Potential**

   Does the target segment(s) tend to be loyal customers or do they buy based on price?

7. **Responsiveness**

   How fast is a prospect likely to respond to your products and services? What are the "no haggle" factors you should consider?

8. **Ability to Target**

   The ability to reach a customer through a targeted marketing program is an important consideration, and will impact marketing expenses and budgets.

9. **Lifetime Value**

   What is the estimated lifetime value for a specific market?

10. **Decision-Making Power**

    Who is the buyer versus the user? Who makes the actual purchase decision and who is involved in the decision-making process?

11. **Usage**

    Are users of your product or service high, medium, or low users?

# Business-to-Business (B2B) Target Markets

1. **Specific Industries**

   Include the SIC/NASICC number for each of the industries in your target market. Defining the specific codes will be valuable to you as you create marketing programs to reach these audiences.

2. **Specialty Groups**

   Groups may consist of trade or professional organizations, government sectors, exclusive clubs, special interest groups, and so on.

3. **Geographical Regions**

   Some businesses are exclusively local while others use technology to find a broader reach. Large companies typically have geographical regions defined using their own unique descriptions, such as North America, CALA (Caribbean, Latin America), EMEA (Europe, Middle East, and Africa), and APAC (Asia Pacific and China).

4. **Job Title and Responsibility**

   C-Level (CEO, CFO, CMO, COO), Senior Executives, Directors, Senior Managers, Managers, Procurement Officer, and so on followed by their area of concentration (human resources, marketing, sales, operations, and so on).

5. **Size of Organization**

   Target based on company size that may include total revenues and/or number of employees. Try to go beyond broad descriptions such as small, medium, and large. These descriptions vary widely by company. For example, the Small and Medium-Sized Business Market (SMB) could be defined as fewer than 500 employees in some companies, and another company might define small as less than 50 employees.

6. **Type of Asset**

   This is critical information for anyone targeting technology or manufacturing businesses. For example, if you sell a software product, you will need to understand what type of operating system the company currently uses and perhaps what enterprise applications are installed. If you are trying to sell a certain type of machine, you can target companies with an install base of certain equipment.

7. **Price Range of Buyers**

   How sensitive to price are the buyers of your product or service?

8. **Buying Cycle**

   Does your market buy products or services on a seasonal basis only at a certain time of the year?

# 23

# Market Segmentation for the Twenty-First Century

Marketers are challenged to keep pace with constantly changing consumer buying habits. Consumers are confronted with making choices from an enormous array of new products. The proliferation of new media and access to products and services through new channels has changed the way people buy. All these factors result in fragmentation of market segments and distribution channels and the need for new methods of market segmentation.

One approach that is highly effective is an extension of what marketers call observational research, but it adds a new spin that attaches consumer behavior with brand purpose. The result of successful branding and marketing is customer perception that a product or service has significant meaning in their life. This can only be achieved when marketers understand how a product is used and valued by customers. When you understand this, you can then define targeted segments and more effective marketing communication focused on those characteristics. Clayton Christensen, a Harvard professor and best-selling author, discovered a simple way to segment customers that companies are finding immensely valuable.

The premise is based on a statement made by revered Harvard professor Theodore Levitt back in the '60s. He told his students, "People don't want to buy a quarter-inch drill. They want a quarter-inch hole!" Despite the fact that marketers know this to be true, marketing is still focused on the features and functionality of the drill, not the hole. This causes misguided marketing messages and strategies and subsequently marketing is directed toward solving the wrong problem. The product is marketed in ways that is irrelevant to customers.

Christensen takes Levitt's premise "that people just want to get things done," and puts a new spin on it. He says, "When people find themselves needing to get a job done, they essentially hire products to do that job for them."[1] It's simple: If you understand the job that needs to get done, design the products and services to do that job, and market the product to reinforce how the product does the job, consumers will hire the product when they need to get the job done.

Sheraton Hotels is a good example of a company that offers an entire portfolio of products directed to various customer segments that are looking for different products and experiences to hire for a specific job. In this case, the job is to find a place to sleep in a hotel overnight that fits the customer's need for price and comfort. Low-budget travelers might choose to stay in the Four Points brand, and business travelers may choose a Westin or a Sheraton because they love the "Heavenly Bed" in their home-away-from-home. Discriminating travelers who appreciate luxury can choose from the St. Regis or The Luxury Collection hotel brands. Hip travelers may prefer the W Hotel, or the new modern Aloft hotel brand. Travelers who are looking for a completely different experience may choose to stay at an Element hotel. This new hotel brand focuses on the attributes of balance, health and fitness, green and sustainability, and modular design so travelers can design the room space as they wish to use it. All of these brands belong to Sheraton; however, each individual hotel is branded and targeted to a customer segment who wants to get a specific job done.

A few years ago, I had the opportunity to interview Clayton Christensen following the release of his successful book, *The Innovators Solution*. He shared an interesting story about the way a company applied this concept to get a much better understanding of the job consumers hired their product to do for them. Here is an excerpt from the interview.

---

### *Clayton Christensen on Market Segmentation*

**Christensen:** ...How do you know if customers will buy the product or not? The answer to that is you have to segment markets differently. Companies today segment markets by the attributes of products, or by the attributes of customers. But rather, you need to segment markets by the jobs customers are trying to get done for themselves when they buy a product.

**Reece:** Give me an example of this.

**Christensen:** A major fast food chain was trying to accelerate the sales of its milkshake, so they kept trying to improve the taste of the milkshake by making it tastier, creamier, and so on. They interviewed customers in the demographic segment that were more likely to buy the product and tried to understand what they wanted, but it didn't make any difference in sales. And finally, the market researcher from our organization just stood in the restaurant for 18 hours and watched people to observe what they were trying to do when they bought a milkshake. What were they trying to accomplish for themselves, or what job did they need to get done? It turned out the milkshakes were bought for a couple of different jobs. The main one was that people wanted something to keep them busy during a long, boring commute to work. That was the purpose for which they bought the product. And if you understand what these jobs are, then making a product that does the job well vastly increases the probability they will buy

---

the product. The reason most products fail is that companies segment their markets in ways that are irrelevant to the purposes for which customers buy the product.

**Reece:** How did this change the way the company marketed their product? Was it brand message? Because you could argue that a cup of hot coffee would keep them busy in their car for a long time too. Although coffee is usually purchased because it's caffeinated.

**Christensen:** That's right. Once you understand what the job is, it means the competition is not a Burger King milk shake; it's the other products they might hire to get the same job done. People are not hungry yet, but they will be by 10:00, so they need something that will sit in their stomach for a while. So they compete against coffee, donuts, bagels, bananas, and Snickers bars.

**Reece:** What did this company do to change their strategy?

**Christensen:** Once you know the job, you can figure out how competitors do that job well. Then you can ask, "How can I improve my product so it does the job perfectly, and what entails making it even more viscous?" Well, you can stir little chunks of fruit in it to make it even more viscous. Not because it makes it healthier (people aren't hiring the milkshake to become healthy), but because it just makes the commute more interesting. Now you bring the dispensing machine out in front of the counter and let people just swipe a card through so they can get it and go. It's all of those kinds of things that once you understand the job, you make it easier and simpler for them to do the whole job more effectively. Then you know the customer will value it and gain share against the real competition.

## Why Is Your Product or Service Hired?

In the "Why People Buy" exercise (in Chapter 20, "Why Do Customers Buy?"), you created a working hypothesis about why your customers buy from you, and converted the attributes into benefits. As you look at these benefits, how would they translate to the specific job your customer is trying to do? Be as precise as you can and answer the following questions:

- Do my solutions provide what the customer wants?
- Do my products and services add more than what the customer wants?

- Does it do the best job in the market considering what customers want?
- How does my marketing communicate the outcome customers are looking for?
- What other ways can the customer get the job done?
- Should changes be made to my product, service, or marketing communications?

Think broadly about this last question because you will use this information later in the chapter to define substitute solutions in the competitive analysis. In Table 23.1 summarize the benefits that your product or service delivers. Then, define what job you believe your customers are trying to get done. In the third column, define substitutes and observations.

**Table 23.1** Why Is Your Product or Service Hired? What Is the Job Customers Want to Get Done?

| Customer Benefits | What Job Does the Customer Want to Get Done | Substitute Alternatives/ Observations |
|---|---|---|
|  |  |  |
|  |  |  |
|  |  |  |
|  |  |  |
|  |  |  |
|  |  |  |

If this segmentation method stimulates questions (and it should!), you should add them to your primary research plan to increase your understanding of what customers want and what drives them to buy. Remember, your focused attention and efforts on this subject now will not only save you time later, but could potentially save you tens of thousands of marketing dollars that might be wasted communicating the wrong message.

# 24

# Zeroing in on Consumer Target Markets

If your market is consumers, consider using a segmentation tool like PRIZM (Potential Rating Index by Zip Codes), a clustering tool developed by Claritas Inc. Consumer groups are broken into 39 different sectors within five different categories, comprised of education and affluence, family life cycle, urbanization, race and ethnicity, and mobility. The sector clusters are names of fun and descriptive groups such as The Cosmopolitans, Blue Blood Estates, and Hometown Retired. Each of the clusters is segmented by zip code so you can easily target like-minded individuals.

As you become more experienced in understanding your target market segments, your goal should be to continuously refine how this is applied to target customer segments and marketing programs. A company that does this really well is Globus family of brands, an international travel organization that has been in business since 1928. In an initiative launched to improve their understanding of how and why diverse groups of customers purchased trip packages, Globus discovered very unique qualities and preferences among people who purchased travel packages.

Scott Nisbet, COO of Globus, was Executive Director of Customer Acquisition and Retention at the time the segmentation project was initiated. He said the ability to creatively and specifically define customer segments enabled them to create new customer segmentation strategies and customize messaging that was more precisely directed toward the needs of each group. For example, a traveler who craves adventure in exotic locations would never appreciate a well-organized trip around the UK and Scotland. Likewise, a traveler who appreciated the group interaction and an informative guide would be a fish out of water in the jungles of Ecuador. If a customer prefers guided travel, this group of customers fit into a segment they called "Hold My Hand."

On refining its understanding of customer psychographics and travel styles over several years, Globus developed new target market segmentation descriptions. The company now overlays three different databases, each with specific segmentation criteria. They use segmentation developed by a company called Cohort that is comprised of demographic and psychographic data. Through database analysis, Cohort identified cohesive segments of U.S. households. The households are grouped into 30 cohorts based on overall similarity across 7 demographic and 40 behavioral characteristics (see Burt and Marilyn and Alex and Judith in Figure 24.1, who are creatively named after typical names in the groups of survey participants). The groups included 13 married segments, 9 single female segments, and 8 single male segments. Cohorts were appended to the database to further analyze and segment customers so they could surmise if a person would be more interested in a trip to Egypt or Italy.

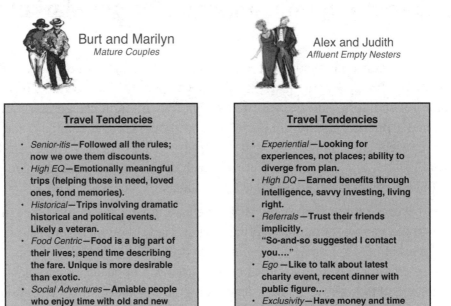

**Burt and Marilyn**
*Mature Couples*

**Travel Tendencies**

· *Senior-itis*—Followed all the rules; now we owe them discounts.
· *High EQ*—Emotionally meaningful trips (helping those in need, loved ones, fond memories).
· *Historical*—Trips involving dramatic historical and political events. Likely a veteran.
· *Food Centric*—Food is a big part of their lives; spend time describing the fare. Unique is more desirable than exotic.
· *Social Adventures*—Amiable people who enjoy time with old and new friends.

**Alex and Judith**
*Affluent Empty Nesters*

**Travel Tendencies**

· *Experiential*—Looking for experiences, not places; ability to diverge from plan.
· *High DQ*—Earned benefits through intelligence, savvy investing, living right.
· *Referrals*—Trust their friends implicitly. "So-and-so suggested I contact you...."
· *Ego*—Like to talk about latest charity event, recent dinner with public figure...
· *Exclusivity*—Have money and time for more exclusive trips.

**Figure 24.1** *Globus customer segmentation example*

This data was then overlaid with an Equifax database of demographic data and preferences. For example, if the Equifax database shows the traveler is a dog owner, this person is less likely to take a trip than a someone who does not own a dog. Several data points like this serve as indicators of who is more or less likely to travel.

The third database integrated into segmentation is the one million customers in the Globus customer database, which contains profiles of customer preferences gathered over many years. The information was collected through surveys after every customer trip. It defines how likely a customer is to travel again with Globus (see Figure 24.2), as well as when and where they want to go. Segments define the number of times a person has traveled with Globus and the likeliness of the customer wanting to travel with them again. Travelers in the Platinum segment have traveled with Globus four or more times and will likely travel with the company again. Gold travelers have traveled with Globus two or three times and are likely to travel with the company again. Shooting Stars are defined as travelers who have traveled with Globus only once but are very likely to travel with Globus again based on their positive first experience; therefore, this segment requires special nurturing to increase travel over time. The bottom tier is "Tin" because these people have traveled with Globus once but are not likely to again.

As you can see in Figure 24.2, the result of the company's ongoing segmentation efforts is a very specific and targeted list of customers to whom Globus can direct specific marketing campaigns. Each campaign describes exactly the kind of trip the customer would be interested in taking. Globus direct mail campaigns do not result in paltry industry averages of one to two percent return on investment—they average 14 percent.

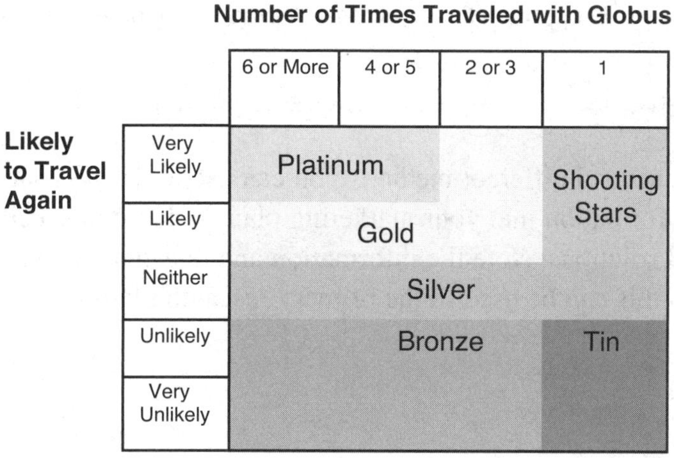

**Number of Times Traveled with Globus**

| Likely to Travel Again | | 6 or More | 4 or 5 | 2 or 3 | 1 |
|---|---|---|---|---|---|
| | Very Likely | Platinum | | | Shooting Stars |
| | Likely | Gold | | | |
| | Neither | Silver | | | |
| | Unlikely | Bronze | | | Tin |
| | Very Unlikely | | | | |

**Figure 24.2** *Globus family of brands loyalty tiers*

Businesses continue to find ways to segment their products to capture new, more precisely defined target markets that have more precisely defined needs. This is part of a growing trend of micro-niching that is enabled by the ability to capture information about customers using sophisticated software programs, bar codes, and RFID technology. By cross referencing where people shop, when people shop, what people buy, and how products are used, more information can be learned about customers, allowing you to hone marketing strategies and programs.

**Marketing Tip for Mid-size and Large Companies**

Take your existing target market profile and evaluate if your assumptions and descriptions are accurate. Pay close attention to how you can make them more specific or refine the description based upon the results of the "A, B, C, and Deadbeat Customer" exercise from Chapter 14, "Micro Perspective: Focus on High-Value Customers."

Also look across business units to see how markets are segmented and target markets are defined. If markets are defined as large, medium, and small businesses, is this too broad to effectively target market programs? Are target market segments organized around products instead of customers? If this is the case, your company is probably missing opportunities to expand the account. Another common occurrence of targeting based on products instead of customers is several salespeople from the same company may be calling on the same customer. Not good.

Look for new ways to fine tune target market profiles based on the information in this chapter, with an eye on opportunities to cross-sell products and services across the organization.

You now have several different methods you can use to define your target market. Summarize this information into your marketing plan so that it is specific for each of your products and solutions. Note the information and questions you need to ask customers directly so this can be used in the primary research plan.

# 25

# Forecasting Demand

A marketing plan must include a forecast of the market opportunity size, which is the estimated number of potential buyers of your products and services. From this, the addressable market size is estimated by analyzing who is available to purchase the product, has the means to do so, and has access to your products. This number will be a more conservative subset of the market size. From this, the company must decide what portion of the market it will penetrate. For example, if a new snack product will be launched by a company, it probably won't launch in all markets at once. The company would select a few test markets to roll out first. The target market number would be projected from the addressable market.

New markets are more difficult to size and forecast because so little information is available about the industry. Therefore, the best method to size an emerging market is usually primary research combined with available facts found through secondary research.

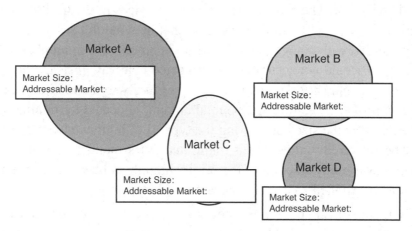

**Figure 25.1**  *Market forecast*

After you research the market opportunity size for your product or service, you will need to narrow the number to those qualified to purchase (interest, income, and access), then narrow that number to the target market (see Figure 25.2). Further refinement of buying criteria as described in the next section will help you arrive at a realistic target market size.

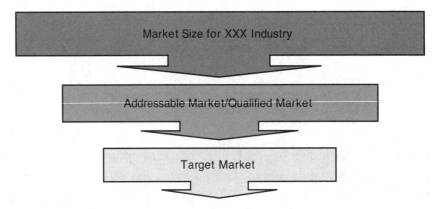

**Figure 25.2**  *Estimating market demand*

## Forecasting Believable and Realistic Demand (Not What You Think a VC Wants to See)

One mistake companies often make is overestimating market demand, or confusing the definition of market sizes. I remember being in a strategic planning meeting where a salesperson was making a case for how big the market was for a particular industry and why we should pursue it. The product was training services in the healthcare market, which he claimed to be a $70 billion market. So that he wouldn't shoot himself in the foot by being saddled with a huge quota based upon an unrealistic number, I explained that market demand could not accurately be projected that way. Instead, the company needed to look at the industry size, narrow the opportunity to the market we served (nurses), narrow further by estimating the total amount allocated to training in this segment, and then narrow the size considering the type of training we were delivering and how it would be delivered (online versus traditional assessments and instructor-led training). The market was a tiny fraction of the original numbers he claimed, but a realistic market size was determined so a sales forecast could be developed.

The example illustrated above was an everyday occurrence during the early 2000s. Many business plans were funded based on poor and unrealistic projections of market demand. Over-eager entrepreneurs mistakenly cited total market opportunity numbers (or the number of eyeballs they could drive to a website), and assigned an arbitrary percentage of market share to estimate demand. It's no wonder so many of these businesses are no longer around.

Let's look at another example. Let's say a company wants to introduce a Chardonnay wine. They would start by looking at the market size population where the product will be introduced, and then narrow to the average amount of discretionary income spent on food and beverage, the amount spent on beverages, the amount spent on alcoholic beverages, the amount spent on wine, then the amount spent on white wine. If the marketer thought she could pull from several categories of white wine drinkers (Chardonnay, Pinot Grigio, Chenin Blanc, Sauvignon Blanc, and so on), she would select this total market size. If she was looking for a conservative estimate, she may forecast demand solely on the population of Chardonnay drinkers in a market.

Forecasting demand is a science, but there is also some art involved. Additional considerations in the forecast include the amount of marketing budget allocated to drive demand, the number of salespeople who are able to sell into a market, and of course, what the company is able to produce. If you sell a technology product or manufacturing part, you will also need to account for the installed base. Competitor market share is also essential to take into consideration, especially if the competition has a very loyal customer base.

Another way to size the market is by the job that needs to get done. If you choose to segment and measure your market this way, you will likely find that the market size is bigger than you thought. By factoring in the complementary and substitute products that can get the job done, you will get a new perspective on market size.

Industry growth rates are yet another consideration that you may wish to factor into your equation. If the healthcare industry, for example, is growing at the rate of 20 percent annually, you can factor this into your estimates and compare your company growth rates to industry averages to see if you are growing at the same rate as other companies in your industry.

Your industry association(s), or associations of your target markets, will be an excellent resource to you as several industries track this type of information for members. For consumer markets, Nielsen Media Research monitors sales on a per-product basis to aid companies in market sizing on an industry level by competitor. Industry information can be found using the North American Industry Classification System (NAICS). Federal agencies classify businesses in order to collect, analyze, and publish statistics related to the U.S. business economy.

If you are launching a product in an entirely new market space, you may need to look at adjacent industries and also research reports compiled by futurist firms that specialize in estimating demand. As mentioned earlier, you can also use primary research to forecast demand.

# 26

# Competition: Keep Your Friends Close and Your Enemies Closer

Competitive research is an important part of your marketing plan. You need to understand the strategies of your most direct competitors, as well as those of your indirect competitors. As you develop this section of your marketing plan, you should become aware of three types of competitors:

1. **Direct competitors who sell the same products or services that you do**

2. **Indirect competitors**

   These are companies that do not compete head-to-head with your firm, but nonetheless compete against your business because they offer a similar product or service. For example, a mid-size consulting firm that provides a specialized type of consulting may compete with a large multinational firm that provides similar consulting, but derives a larger percentage of their business from global clients in conjunction with other consulting services they provide.

3. **Competitors who supply a substitute product or service**

   These are alternative choices a person considers as a way to meet their needs. The solution provides the customer with the same or similar result, but does so in a different way. If you want to watch a movie, you have many choices. You can record a movie and use TiVo to watch it at your convenience. Or you can order a movie from your cable or satellite system and watch it on demand as you like. Another choice is to go to the movie theater. All of these options are forms of substitute products. If the goal is "entertainment," then the list of substitute products grows to sporting events, theater, opera, and a myriad of other choices.

   A B2B example is using mediation services instead of an attorney for certain types of legal mitigation. A person may choose to use a financial advisory firm instead of a banking representative or an investment strategist for long-term retirement planning. Another example is the choice to work with a CPA on a tax return instead of using a software program, or just doing it with pen and paper.

4. **Competitors who compete for the same budget or wallet share**

   Who is competing for the same budget as you? You may not have thought about this kind of "competition" before, but it's important to consider. Companies have many projects under consideration at the same time and different departments compete for the same budget. So, your "competitor" may be another project within a company. If you have ever been blindsided by a lost sale just as you thought you were going to win a deal, you know how frustrating it can be. The only way to try to potentially alleviate this up front is by asking and drilling into buying criteria and conditions. A similar form of competition in this area is the decision for companies to make versus buy. Instead of outsourcing a capability, the company may decide to do it internally.

## Observe and Learn

Throughout the marketing planning cycle, it is valuable to track a few of the top competitors in your industry. There are many reasons for this. It will help you gain valuable insight about innovative strategies they are deploying across various aspects of their business such as new products and services, growth into new markets, or sales and marketing strategies. You will also learn about their customer base and potentially discover new opportunities to win market share.

Whatever size of business you have, and no matter how new or mature your market is, you will see value in tracking your competitive market. This will come from not only tracking direct competitors, but indirect competitors, companies that provide substitute solutions, and innovative new companies in your industry or adjacent industries. *Tracking different types of competitors will help you think more creatively and strategically about marketing and sales strategies and create innovative solutions to business problems.*

If you are one of the few people who say, "But I don't have any competition," think again. It's a global marketplace, and someone out there is making and selling something like yours, or at the very least a substitute like yours. During this step in the process, it's your job to find out who it is. Think broadly about who is fulfilling the customer need today, and how. Refer back to the "Why Is Your Product or Service Hired" exercise you did in Chapter 23, "Market Segmentation for the Twenty-First Century," which identified alternative ways for a customer to get a job done that is similar to your solutions. If you have the opposite problem and have dozens of competitors, your job is to select the top three or four companies to track during the planning process. If you try to track too many, it becomes a cumbersome process, and you'll get bogged down in this step.

Marquis Banking Partners had a difficult time finding a competitor who offered a similar full range of services to what they did. In this case, Marquis chose to track a national staffing firm, Bank Temps, which provides interim staffing for positions like tellers, even though Marquis focuses on C-level interim staffing for banks. One of Marquis' goals is to broaden the reach within their existing customer base, so tracking a firm like this would be advantageous to learn about strategies to target and sell interim staffing to bank directors and other decision makers within a bank.

In Table 26.1, "Competitive Tracking Information," select three competitors and write their names in the boxes labeled Competitor A, B, and C. The vertical axis lists several topics that you can research for each competitor. Every company is unique, so customize the topic areas most relevant for your business. For example, a small consulting company would not see much value from trying to ascertain market share, but this is a critical data point for large companies. You will use the same three competitors as a point of reference throughout the planning process, and the information you gather now will be particularly valuable as you develop marketing strategies and tactics.

**Table 26.1**   Competitive Tracking Information

|  | Your Company | Competitor A | Competitor B | Competitor C |
|---|---|---|---|---|
| Annual Sales Revenue | | | | |
| • This year | | | | |
| • Last year | | | | |
| Market Share Growth Rate | | | | |
| Number of Employees | | | | |
| Geographic Coverage | | | | |
| Target Market | | | | |
| • Primary | | | | |
| • Secondary | | | | |
| Clients | | | | |
| Products and Services | | | | |
| • Uniqueness | | | | |
| Distribution Channels | | | | |
| Major Suppliers | | | | |
| Pricing | | | | |
| Marketing Strategy | | | | |
| Sales Strategy | | | | |
| Other | | | | |
| Observations | | | | |

Summarize this information and your observations in the marketing plan template so you can use it when you develop strategies.

It's a good idea to transfer this table into a spreadsheet or other document that will help you track this information not just once, but on an ongoing basis. In the marketing plan template, there is a place to include the competitive chart as well as a summary of the key findings on each competitor (which I discuss later in this chapter). Another way to include competitive information in your plan is to write a narrative of the competitive environment. Choose whatever style is best for you, or use both methods for a snapshot view and a more thorough briefing.

**Real-Time Marketing Tip**

To accomplish two goals, (1) keeping competitive information updated on a regular and seamless basis, and (2) fostering a collaborative approach to marketing planning, consider using this process:

**Collection:** Create folders in a shared workspace so that when information such as articles, earnings release, and press releases are discovered, they can be stored in separate folders within the competitive folder. That way, all the competitive information is stored in one place.

**Collaboration:** This is one section of the marketing plan where it is easy to spread responsibilities across a team of people. Assign a competitor to different individuals on your planning team. Engage a cross-functional team of people from customer service, sales, operations, and marketing to collect and assimilate information for each competitor. Each person or team can also be responsible for communicating updates in monthly sales meetings and/or quarterly reviews.

By assigning competitors to different individuals, it spreads the workload, it educates more people about the competitive environment, and it is much easier to adjust strategies to respond to changing market conditions. This process also keeps the marketing plan updated in real-time.

## Competitive Information Sources

The Competitive Research Guide is a comprehensive list of resources that helps you discover where to look for certain types of competitive information. It can be found in the resources section of www.MarketSmarter.com.

# 27

# Anticipate the Unexpected:
# Research Macro-Environmental Factors

The macro environment is comprised of events that are outside your direct control that nonetheless can impact and influence your business success. The recent economic and political activities have presented us with lots of surprises. Some of these we can see coming and others are much harder to predict. The goal of the following exercise is to look ahead, notice trends, and create contingency plans to counter potential issues. This proactive work can also help you discover new growth opportunities before your competitors do.

## Macro-Environmental Factors

Review the following six macro-environmental categories and consider how these factors impact your business and industry. The categories are artificially distinguished from one another in the sense that it is not necessarily possible to differentiate political/legal issues from economic ones. To assist you in asking the right questions about your business, there are examples within each category.

### Political/Legal

Political and legal impacts on business include legislation, government intervention, changing government agency enforcement, and political activity.

Example question:

How will the proposed congressional bill affect the budgets available for my product in primary education? What program budgets have been increased and what is the timing for when the programs will be funded?

## Demographic

Basic demographic information defines key target market criteria for most companies.

Example question:

> The existing target market of donors/subscribers for our chamber orchestra is adults 50–70 years old. We need to foster a new market of followers in the Gen Y demographic who will become dedicated, loyal customers. What is their level of interest in this type of music? Where are the best places to reach them with advertising and marketing? How much does this segment donate to groups like ours?

## Economic

The economy affects businesses every day. Inflation swings, the stock market, business cycles, savings rates, and debt burdens all take their turn impacting business.

Example question:

> How will the changing bank lending practices affect my real estate business with corporate clients in the next six months? As interest rates increase, what percentage of new home buyers be able to secure a mortgage? What obstacles will they face?

## Ecological/Professional

The global climate and move toward green, environmentally safe products impact consumer and business buying decisions. The huge interest in this topic is rapidly changing the competitive landscape as new companies rush to take advantage of this growing trend.

Example question:

> If the lettuce crop freezes in California again, what alternative sourcing is available in Florida or Mexico? What price increase can we expect this year and should we absorb the costs or pass them along to consumers? What should our contingency plan be?

Example question:

> As banks are required to train employees in regulatory issues quarterly rather than yearly, how can I adjust my consulting services to capture this growing demand?

## Technological

Rapid technology changes influence all industries. How will advances in telecommunications, software, operating platforms, science, biomedical, and other industry-specific influences impact your business?

Example question:

The newest version of X software will be released in six months, affecting the functionality and reliability of our software, which integrates with this software. How will this affect our customers? How can we predict additional changes or protect our software so we are not affected by future surprises?

## Cultural and Social

People relate to each other in ways that can be categorized by lifestyle and preference descriptors. Behaviors are formed around these values and beliefs. Trends indicate changes in cultural and social values. For example, flexible work schedules, telecommuting, virtual corporations, environmental consciousness, and green manufacturing are all recent trends. The earlier you perceive a trend, the more opportunity you have to be the first to capitalize on related business opportunities. How will these trends and others impact your business?

Example question:

As the price of gasoline rises, are more companies beginning to offer virtual offices as a benefit to keep employees? How do companies manage their employees who work at home part time and what tools are needed so they can collaborate with others?

---

### Marketing Tip: Expect the Unexpected

In addition to creating contingency plans for potential negative influences, your research in macro-environmental factors will help you become more prepared to take advantage of opportunities when the moment arises so that you can seize the opportunity instead of your competitors. Unique situations that you cannot control, such as the economy and legal regulations, will always arise. While some businesses will only see the downside of these effects, you can look for the opportunity in every situation and use it as a catalyst for growth.

---

## Seize Advantage in a Downturn

Tyler McCarty's business, Wirth Business Credit, was focused on providing financial services such as leasing for companies buying capital equipment, like printing, machinery, or farm equipment. When the financial crisis resulted in tighter bank lending to businesses, McCarty realized his company was in a unique position to help several new types of businesses that could no longer depend on banks for financing.

Additionally, he saw the opportunity to be a resource to banks. The last thing a banker wants to tell his long-time customer is that he can't help him. McCarty became a valuable resource to banks by giving them an alternative solution for business lending. Bankers could refer customers to McCarty, which helped them preserve valuable customer relationships. It was a perfect win/win situation for everyone—bankers, customers, and McCarty.

## Summarize the Secondary Research Plan

At the beginning of this section, you began a list of the possible research topics to consider for your research plan. Now that have completed all the exercises, it's time to define your market research plan.

Review the list of topics at the beginning of this section, and the list of questions and issues you have made throughout your work in this section. Prioritize the research and review the Research Resources Guide to determine the best places to search for each topic. There are many excellent resources listed in this guide that will help you find information on many topics. One of the best is usually your industry association. Others include articles, subscription databases such as Lexus-Nexus or Dun and Bradstreet, government reports, and analyst reports. Remember that it is less expensive and usually faster to do secondary research than it is to do primary research so consult with this guide to discover new sources of information. It can be downloaded from the *Real-Time Marketing for Business Growth* book resource section at www.MarketSmarter.com.

It's easy to get lost in this part of the process if you have an extensive list of topics to research, so remember to focus on the topics that are most pertinent to your business goals. The objective during this phase of the process is to research the most important topics—the topics that will help you make decisions and develop strategies. Also keep in mind that business research is an ongoing process, so it won't start and end here.

# 28

# Get Smart: Talk to Your Customers

Research studies have proven that an organization can only learn about 30 percent of what customers need, want, and expect through normal business interaction. The other 70 percent must be revealed by targeted research, ongoing communication, and constructive feedback.

Primary research typically focuses on specific information you want to directly ask customers, or potential customers, in order to help you understand buyer needs and preferences. This information will be very valuable as you evaluate a business idea, new product, or service concept, channel buying preferences, assess media and marketing likes and dislikes, or come across other issues you will use to refine your strategies.

Primary research can also be used to refine messaging and communications and provide valuable insight about the ways a product can be positioned and sold. Several years ago, Arm and Hammer watched as baking soda lost market share as a prime ingredient in baking. They conducted research that analyzed their customers' tastes and lifestyle. They learned that women had less time and inclination to bake from scratch. Arm and Hammer repositioned baking soda as a cleanser and refrigerator deodorizer. A year later, 33 million refrigerators in the U.S. had baking soda in them.

Several methods are used to conduct primary research, including focus groups, interviews, surveys, and observational studies. If you have not done primary research before, you may want to use professional researchers who can help you design, administer, and compile results. If you wish to try it on your own, it's a process you can learn, and there are many technology solutions to streamline the process for you to do so.

If you want to use an online survey, it's best to stick to quantitative questions. Responses to open-ended questions are often brief and ambiguous, and answers can be misleading. Qualitative questions are excellent for interviews and focus groups because you can dig deeper into responses and increase your understanding of the issues. See Table 28.1 for more information about the use and application of qualitative and quantitative research methods.[1]

**Table 29.1** Primary Research Methods

| | Description | Typical Uses | Methods | Examples |
|---|---|---|---|---|
| Qualitative | Exploratory and open-ended<br><br>Subjective in nature<br><br>Not necessarily projectable<br><br>Effective early in project | When trying to answer:<br>Why?<br>Who?<br>What?<br>How?<br>Where?<br>When? | Focus groups<br>Interviews<br>Customer visits<br>Pilots | Identify gaps in current product features<br><br>Reasons for customer attrition<br><br>Learn how product is used |
| Quantitative | Uses structured questions where response options are predetermined<br><br>Respondents are representative of the target market<br><br>Results are projectable | When results need to be objective, quantitative, and statistically valid across the population<br><br>% population<br><br>Price points<br><br>Ranking<br><br>Rating | Surveys (phone, online, mail, in person)<br><br>Choice models | Interest level in new product idea<br><br>Buyer preferences<br><br>Pricing<br><br>Determine which market uses a product more, or how frequently |

Source: Sharon Brant

Ken Blanchard, well known co-author of the *One Minute Manager* series, is famous for saying, "Feedback is the Breakfast of Champions." This is the goal of primary research: To get feedback from the people who use your products and services and are therefore in the best position to tell you what they *really* think. Your job is to ask, listen, and respond to the feedback. Notice I didn't say "react." If a customer gives you some tough feedback, look at it as a gift. You may not agree with the comments, but it would be wise to step back and consider the comments and suggestions carefully in order to better understand the needs of your customers, and hopefully gain new insight about how you can improve what you offer to customers.

If primary research is new to you, the first few projects present you with a learning curve, but you will quickly learn that Blanchard's quote has a new, richer meaning to you. Feedback is indeed a gift, and I can guarantee that once you begin to implement your customer strategies, you will find that ongoing feedback becomes a healthy addiction. You will look for new and varied ways to learn more about your customers' preferences. As information is accumulated in your database and you can retrieve and study it, you will be able to better anticipate and respond to changes in purchase needs and behaviors.

## Developing Your Primary Research Plan

A research process is comprised of five major steps:

**Define the Problem and Objectives:** Focus on what you really need and want to know that will make a difference in your go-to-market strategy. Possible topics are new product/service offerings or enhancements, pricing, media preferences, purchase decision drivers, buying habits, and many other topics.

**Develop a Plan:** Define the research method to be used and the questions you want to ask. Choose the tool(s) you will use to implement the research (online survey, phone interviews, mall intercept interviews, focus groups, in-person interviews, and so on). Determine how much the research will cost.

**Execute:** Determine how long it will take and how much it would cost to administer and collect the data.

**Analyze Results:** Collect the data so it can be presented to decision makers who can act on the data. What did you learn? What recommendations will you make?

**Decide and Take Action:** Make decisions based on the research. What actions will you take based upon what you learned? Concisely summarize the information and enter the results and decisions into your marketing plan. Create a plan for integrating the results into your plan.

Using these five steps, create a primary research plan. Review the results of the exercises you have completed throughout this section. Your research may focus on new concept testing and market sizing, or you may choose to learn about customer needs and preferences using a voice of the customer (VOC) method. If you choose VOC research, consider measuring customer satisfaction (delight) of existing products and services, understanding customer needs, and why customers buy. The last two areas of research will tell you if customer needs are met or not and give you insight into what drives purchasing decisions, which can be used in messaging, positioning, and marketing programs.

## Tips for Creating a Customer Survey

1. Define the purpose of the primary research. What do you want to learn from it?
2. Who is your audience? Is it current customers and/or potential customers? Decision makers, influencers, and/or users?

3. Keep it short, simple and easy to interpret. A common mistake is unclear directions. If you ask a person to rank their preferences in terms of importance on a scale of one to five, make sure you tell them which is the most important: one or five. Another common mistake is asking a person to circle all potential attributes that are important to them rather asking them to RANK them. You need a ranking of prioritized items to draw good conclusions.

4. Keep the questionnaire to one or two pages, and 10–12 questions.

5. Make sure that you send the survey out to a large-enough sample size to be statistically valid based on the size of your target market.

6. Qualitative questions used in VOC research invites customers to elaborate on answers, and you will get a more precise understanding of customer needs. For surveys, quantitative data is best because qualitative questions may be harder to interpret.

7. Be sure to ask the "Ultimate Question:" "Based upon your experience with our company, would you recommend (your business name) to others?"

8. Set a short timeframe for customers to fill out the questionnaire and return it.

9. Consider offering an incentive for filling out the survey.

10. Share the results with your customers.

This last point is important. If your market is a group of influential C-Level executives, you may wish to summarize the anonymous responses to the survey and distribute them to participants. If people are taking time out of their busy schedule to share their perspective with you, it's important that they know it was worthwhile and valued. Send a note summarizing what you learned and the action you plan to take.

## Online Survey Tools

Internet-based survey tools have made it easy for anyone to design and launch their own questionnaire to customers and prospective customers. There are several reasons to consider using online tools versus more traditional survey instruments. Speed and lower cost are among the top two reasons people prefer to go online. Here are others:

- Surveys can be delivered in hours versus days, allowing you to respond much faster.
- Internet-based surveys generally cost 20 to 50 percent less than conventional surveys, especially if postage is involved.
- Online surveys can generate up to a 50 percent higher response rate.

- A broader audience can be reached on the Internet; however, not all target markets can be reached via the Internet.

- Interactive graphics can show products to customers, and audio can be incorporated into a survey.

- Many customers today prefer to respond online versus mailing in a survey or responding to a phone call.

- Several reports state that people tend to be more honest online than they would be otherwise.

One of the most important aspects of your research is asking the right questions. You can hire a marketing consultant who specializes in research to develop, administer, and analyze the research for you, or you can learn to do it yourself. Many books and articles have been written on the topic. If you study the basic research protocol guidelines, you can learn the process. Additional information and resources can be found on the MarketSmarter Web site.

Zoomerang was one of the first Internet survey tools, and you can test the service with a free 30-day trial. Zoomerang also maintains a panel of over 3 million consumers that can be used (for a fee) to field your survey if you don't have a customer base to select from. SurveyMonkey is another popular tool. It allows you to choose from several different types of service plans and select from several styles of questions, template designs, and reporting tools as well. Learning from your customers has never been easier—so no more excuses!

> ### Marketing Tip
> "Marketers need to get back to listening and engaging customers, everywhere, all the time. Marketing is a continuous process of organizational learning by continuously interacting with customers and the marketplace in order to learn, adapt, and respond creatively and competitively."
> —Regis McKenna

# 29

# Social Media and Online Tools Enable Real-Time Research

Every company wanting to keep pace with change faces the challenge of staying current with the massive amounts of data available. Several companies have emerged to answer the need for more information, and to filter that information so you can find just what you need when you need it. Search engines, research aggregators, Internet resources, and a vast number of innovative new media tools can help you research and find information so you're never behind the learning curve.

## News Aggregators

As the Internet continues to grow by millions of new users a year, and thousands of new Web sites are created each day, you probably have the same problem most people suffer from: information overload. Many new media services and tools have risen to the challenge to help with this problem. News aggregators will help you filter large amounts of web-based content by delivering information that is relevant and timely right to your desktop. Instead of remembering to constantly check Web sites, blogs, news wires, and podcasts, or subscribing to content that clutters your inbox, you can subscribe to content feeds and news aggregators that track and organize information for you.

More than 2,000 different news feed tools have been created that distribute content from a huge array of sources. Simply subscribe to the content you want from multiple Web sites and have it delivered to a central news aggregator to read when and where you want. This allows you to scan headlines in one place and directly access content that interests you with a single click.

RSS creates a win/win situation for both the consumer of information and the publisher. Publishers benefit from the ability to syndicate their content very quickly and send it to people who are truly interested in it. Readers benefit from subscribing to content that is delivered directly to them, and they can receive automatic updates from their favorite Web sites that can be read where and when they choose.

Unlike email subscriptions, it's easy to unsubscribe to feeds by simply removing the feed from the aggregator. Another important benefit is that users of news aggregators do not supply their email address, which mitigates any risk from viruses, spam, and phishing.

## Using Social Media for Real-Time Research

Many people think of social media as a form of implementation to create leads and build a brand. It does indeed do these things, and it's also a fabulous tool for conducting research—in real-time. Because you have gone through this section, you are now aware of several areas you would like to research on an ongoing basis that would be beneficial to your business. There are several social media, networking, and bookmarking sites that will speed this process for you. Here are just a few ways you can use social media to increase your marketing intelligence:

- Most sites have robust search capabilities (Twitter search, Facebook search, and so on). Add key words to track topics, such as the following:
  - Competitors
  - What is being said about your company and key executives
  - Trends in your industry
  - Products and services in your industry
  - Flag key conferences for information and presentations
  - Get feedback from people in your network
  - Exchange ideas with others in your network
  - Discover new resources

## Social Networking and Bookmarking

**Twitter** is a social networking site where you can send and receive information with people whom you choose to follow, or who follow you. Like social bookmarking sites, you can share information with business associates to stay up-to-date on the topics most relevant to you. It's also a valuable tool for research projects because you can tell people what you are working on and ask them to share ideas. If you follow people who share similar interests, you will begin to discover hundreds of resources with interesting and timely information you would not otherwise find. Several other tools are listed in the social media tools strategy and planning section in Section V, "Implement."

If you are just getting started on Twitter, I recommend checking out several resources that will help you navigate the "How Tos" such as the Twitter Guide Book on Mashable or the growing number of resources available on social media.

And of course, don't forget that **Google** has great search capabilities. Customize your own search terms with keywords, names, companies, and other topics. Google will send you email messages right to your inbox as often as you like.

**LinkedIn** is a fabulous social networking service for business professionals to connect and network with each other. Many people use the service for finding new jobs and careers, and others use it for research purposes when they want to hire someone with specific skills, locate someone in their network who works for a particular company, or connect with others who share similar interests. Sign up for membership in the thousands of professional and association groups that are in your industry, or with whom you are affiliated. It's a great way to communicate, share, and get ideas. Use LinkedIn Answers to pose a question to your connections and get feedback.

**Delicious** and **Stumble** are just two of the most popular social bookmarking sites to tag, manage, and consolidate Web sites and resources. Sites like this give you a heads up on what other people are interested in knowing because the most popular Web sites are sorted by topic.

## Tools and Gadgets

You can use social media sites for research and there are also several tools that can help you streamline the process of real-time customer feedback.

**WuFoo** is a service that will let you create any kind of survey or form and embed it on your Web site or blog. You can use an existing survey or create a new one with multiple choice questions, open-ended questions, and quick polls. The report feature will give you real-time results so you can modify the feedback form as needed.

**PollDaddy** has a polling feature similar to WuFoo, and a special function for Twitter polls. Simply create the question, log in to Twitter, and the question is automatically sent to all your followers.

**TwtPoll** is similar to PollDaddy and includes an option that allows the poll recipients to ReTweet your poll questions to their networks, giving your research a much wider audience.

## Blogs

If you like blogs, check out **Technorati,** the number-one blog index. Using either simple keyword and blog directory searches, or advanced tagged searches, you can easily access blogs about your company, industry, or any other subject of interest. Another useful Technorati tool is its "watchlist" option, where you can save your searches in RSS format and thus follow a particular blogger or story. If you have a company blog, you can tag it for certain searches, such as "Lifestyle," or "Business," to ensure higher hits. Fundamentally, Technorati allows you to read what "real" people are thinking about your company or industry, and what they're disseminating on the Web.[1]

**Alltop** is the online magazine rack of the Internet. The site is an eclectic collection of some of the most interesting stories, blogs, and Web sites you may never find on your own. Alltop's goal is to aggregate information from thousands of resources into individual Web pages, making searching a whole lot easier. As Alltop says, it's "aggregation without the aggravation." If you are researching market trends, this is an Internet resource you definitely want to visit. And don't forget to check out the Holy Kaw section.

**Mashable** is the largest blog focused on social media news and Web 2.0. It's one of the best resources for discovering what's new, which is incredibly valuable since there is something new every day. You can also read reviews on new Web services, Web sites, and blogs. Check out the "How To" section for useful social media resource guides.

## Analysts Track Trends and Make Sense of Them

During this research process, one of your goals should be to identify resources that can regularly keep you updated on the latest news and trends in your industry, what your competitors are doing, and the changing buying habits of buyers and decision makers. A few of my favorite sites are the analyst firms such as Forrester, Gartner, IDC, Data Monitor, Deliotte, and McKinsey who regularly publish in-depth reports on certain topics. The firms employ analysts who are experts on specific topics and several publish blogs and studies that will keep you informed of the latest changes in your industry. Subscribe to their newsletters and the information is automatically delivered to you.

Some research reports from these firms are expensive; however, if you should find just the right information you need, it is less expensive than hiring a consultant or making a bad decision based on wrong or incomplete information. Just remember a MasterCard analogy: The price of a research report: $2,500. The price of just the right research to launch your new business: Priceless.

All of these tools can be used for the purpose of research while also increasing the effectiveness of your marketing and communications strategies. Social media as a strategy and tactic will be covered extensively in Section V.

*The bottom line*: Use social media and online tools to aid your research. It's a smart way to save time, stay informed about topics that are important to you, stay connected with business associates, and expand your network. Add mobility tools, and you can mix, mash, browse, blog, text, and tweet your way to a real-time marketing plan.

---

**Marketing Tip**
**Stay Smart and Current: Simple Ways to Integrate Real-Time Research**

- Create folders (paper based and/or computer based) with the headings or research topic areas of your marketing plan. For example, competition, target markets, pricing, trends, new markets, CRM, strategy ideas, and so on.

- As you come across research information on Web sites, articles, and blogs, cut and paste the information, or make a copy of it, and put it into the relevant folder.

- Use news aggregators, social media search functions, and online Internet resource aggregators to find and deliver relevant information to you.

- Summarize the relevancy of an article in a "working draft copy" for the next release of your marketing plan.

- Post the marketing plan folder and the topic-specific folders on your Intranet or in shared folders on sites like LilyPad or Groupsites so key stakeholders can easily add information as they come across it.

- To add even more accountability and ownership to the plan, assign different topics to stakeholders and have them report on their findings once a quarter in strategy review meetings. This way, important information can be acted on immediately.

- Use these techniques to create a dynamic marketing process that fosters a team-based approach to marketing planning across the marketing and sales teams.

---

If you follow these suggestions, it will keep your planning information organized and updated, and also easily access and shared with other people to encourage continuous learning. When it's time to update sections of the plan, you will have a lot of the heavy lifting already done.

# P•R•A•I•S•E™ Marketing Process

## Research

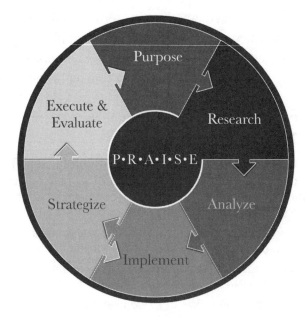

## Summary: Section II

✓ Summarize market segmentation and target markets in your marketing plan.

✓ Create an action plan for how you will drive more profitability and revenue. How can you transition "B" and "C" customers to become "A" customers?

✓ Summarize findings on customer retention, customer loyalty, and CLV.

✓ Create a working hypothesis for why your customers buy from you.

✓ Define and scope your secondary research plan.

✓ Create a primary research plan for information you need to get directly from customers to validate assumptions.

✓ Determine what competitors you will track through the planning process and complete the Competitive Tracking Form.

✓ Develop macro-environment questions that will be answered through research.

✓ Evaluate how social media tools will help you get research done more efficiently.

✓ Research is a process. Set up a system for collecting and organizing information.

✓ Summarize findings into Section II of the marketing plan template so you complete the Market, Company, Customer, and Competitive Analysis sections.

# Section III

# Analyze: Growth and Profit Potential

*"We are* drowning *in* information, *while starving for wisdom.
The world henceforth will be run by synthesizers, people able to put together
the right* information *at the right time, think critically about it, and make
important choices wisely."*
—Edward O. Wilson

The outcome of doing the research outlined in the last section, as well as the research you discover throughout this process, is a new perspective on your market opportunity. You should now understand your target market, factors that influence buyer behavior, and market drivers that impact your business.

With this knowledge, you will now analyze this information with several other subjects before you develop marketing strategies. You will analyze your pricing strategy relative to competitors and consumer buying criterion. An analysis of revenue and profitability by product and/or services will enable you to make better decisions based on the target profit levels you would like to achieve. You will also evaluate new distribution channels that give you access to your target market, as well as new buyers. Perhaps the most important part of this chapter is the new perspective and business growth you can achieve from disruptive innovation. The analysis phase of the process allows you to:

- Analyze your pricing strategy and find new opportunities for increased profitability.
- Identify complementary products to expand revenue and new market growth.
- Evaluate substitute products to determine how they may be a threat—or a new opportunity to capture new customers.
- Analyze the best distribution channels to reach your customers.
- Evaluate the profitability of your products and services.
- Develop new growth opportunities by creating greater differentiation and value for your solutions.

Each topic in this section builds upon the next so when you finish this section, you will have completed all the foundational work to create effective marketing strategies and tactics.

# 30

# Business Expansion:
# Vulnerable or Poised for Growth?

In your research, you may have discovered unmet service needs or discovered new product ideas. Now you will analyze your products, services, and target markets to find new ways to expand your business. You will also examine expansion risks.

Two basic issues must be considered when evaluating expansion of products or markets: costs and complexity. Let's look at three different scenarios. Many businesses start by selling one product to one market, and they ask, "Where do I go next?" Note that if this describes your situation, you are in a pretty vulnerable position should there be a major change in either area.

You can expand by adding more products. If you sell several products to one market, you may increase your costs in production but you save marketing costs by offering multiple solutions to a single market. Not only are you not as vulnerable as in the first scenario, you will see profitable growth from selling multiple products and services to your existing customers.

Another option is to expand by selling your product or service into new markets. In this scenario of selling one product into three markets, you may triple your marketing costs while realizing some cost efficiencies in production.

To further extend this example, assuming you have three products and three markets, you potentially multiply your costs to both areas. Marketing costs such as product development, packaging, distribution, advertising, and promotion will increase. As you add additional products, it potentially impacts not only production costs, but the number of people you employ and perhaps the size of your facility. The point of analyzing marketing and production together is to understand growth opportunities on both sides of the equation and to make mindful decisions about expansion.

## Complementary Products and Services

Growth opportunities come from selling new products to your existing markets and identifying new underserved markets where you can sell your products and services. I'm sure your research revealed several new ideas in these areas. Now you need to analyze the potential for each new solution. If you have not already researched the market size and opportunity, you will need to do so. Evaluate the target market, the benefits potential buyers would receive, the price, possible distribution channels, and marketing strategies. Your analysis should include how many current customers may potentially buy the solution and the number of competitors who sell competing solutions.

Large companies typically run their new ideas through a product development process consisting of a number of phases and gates. I have seen this process take so long (even in companies that profess to be industry-leading innovators) that by the time the product is ready to ship, it's no longer viable. Either the laborious process causes early evangelists to lose interest and the project is forgotten, or nibble companies hungry for growth come from behind to capture the market.

### Marketing Tip: Real-Time Product Development

A better way to test a new idea is to use the real-time research process that was outlined in Section II, "Research." Assemble a group of customers or prospects in your target market and test various concepts with them. If you keep them involved throughout the development cycle you receive valuable feedback on topics ranging from features and functionality to product design and marketing.

Markets are changing too fast to get bogged down in old product development and product management processes. Guy Kawasaki once said, "If the software industry were honest, they would admit the algorithm is ship, then test." He offers two tips on product development:

1. **Don't Worry, Be Crappy.** Ship before you believe the product is perfect.
2. **Churn Baby Churn.** Build in a process to revise your product after it has shipped. Ship the product quickly, get feedback, modify the product, send it back to the consumer, and keep making improvements.

# 31

# Substitute Products and Services

The explosion of new products and services during the last decade has created entirely new industries, as well as huge demand for products that didn't even exist a year ago. Industry lines are blurred. Is a mobile phone in the telecom, mobility, or application industry? The answer is "yes." And as new platforms and applications enable new capabilities, the mobile phone will touch dozens of industries including education (to deliver training and education on-demand), banking (swipe your phone to pay for coffee), and many other industries.

The future of new companies, even those like Digg and Facebook that are immediately successful by creating millions of users and vast business wealth, have yet to be defined. Is Digg a search engine, publisher, social networking platform, syndicator, software application, or…? We'll see. The great news for growth-hungry companies is that new markets expand the number of buyers.

A consistent theme throughout this book is reinventing old marketing processes to adapt to a constantly changing global marketplace. In the next several exercises, you are going to test your thinking about the market size and buyers for your solutions. In some cases, this will reveal that you have more "competition" than you thought you did. On the other hand, you may discover new buyers and new markets for your solutions that you never even considered.

Let's begin with a quick recap of what you learned in Chapter 23, "Market Segmentation for the Twenty-First Century," in Section II. When customers have a need or a specific job to do, they hire a product to do it for them. Your task was to consider all the possible alternatives a customer would consider when making that buying decision. These alternatives are called substitute products and services.

For example, if the job is to acquire specific legal services, you can choose to hire a lawyer or mediator. If the job is entertainment, there are lots of ways to do it. Going to the theater, ballet, cinema, restaurant, or video store are just some of the ways a customer could hire a product to do the job for them. Customers going from point A to point B have lots of choices. They can drive, fly, take a train, a bus, or even a boat to commute to work. Your job is to figure out the reasons why people make various choices when they need to get a job done.

Your earlier work in Chapter 20, "Why Do Customers Buy?" will help you with the next exercise. You identified why people buy, the benefits they value, and hopefully validated your assumptions by asking customers when you implemented your primary research. In Chapter 26, "Competition: Keep Your Friends Close and Your Enemies Closer," you were asked to identify substitutes for your solutions. We'll now use that information to analyze potential growth opportunities.

In the Table 31.1, summarize the products and services that can be substituted for your solutions, because they produce approximately the same benefit or outcome.

**Table 31.1** Substitute Products and Services

|  | Product or Service A | Product or Service B | Product or Service C | Product or Service D |
|---|---|---|---|---|
| Job It Accomplishes |  |  |  |  |
| Who Buys It |  |  |  |  |
| How Else Can the Buyer Do the Job? |  |  |  |  |
| Price Range |  |  |  |  |
| Observations |  |  |  |  |

This exercise should expand the boundary lines for how you currently think about your competitive market space. When companies break out of what they perceive as industry constraints, they no longer compete against other like-minded businesses. They gain new insight and perspective, which can present new opportunities and buyers.

# 32

# Disrupt and Innovate

Now you will shift your thinking completely outside the box to consider ways you can become a market leader. The exercise in the previous chapter, "Substitute Products and Services," got you thinking about natural extensions in your current market. The next exercise will ask you to change the way you think about your business so that you can create new value for your customers. This is done through radical rethinking outside of typical industry solutions and competitive offerings to consider what customers really want.

Philip Kotler says marketing is about knowing "where your customer is going and [being] one step ahead to offer it to them." Seth Godin, author of several marketing books including *The Purple Cow* and *Permission Marketing*, refers to the process of creating something remarkable as the creation of a "Purple Cow." Renee Monbourge and Kim Chan, authors of *Blue Ocean Strategy*, call it finding your Blue Ocean. In my workshops, I call it "Finding New Business Value." Whatever you want to call it, it's the process of creating increased **customer value** and **business value** by offering a solution to customers that results in market differentiation. The result is different from current industry standards, competitor's standards, and perhaps typical business models. It may also be different because it offers customers a unique *experience*.

At the heart of the value creation process is a focus on what the customer wants. Disruptive innovation rarely comes from looking at how to take costs out of the organization. Remember what Peter Drucker said: "The most important aspects of business are marketing and innovation." If marketing is about fulfilling customer needs and innovation is the application of new ideas, then you must start with what the customer wants and innovate from this point.

Let's look at a few examples of companies that have created new business value in their industries. NetFlix is an example of a company that changed the way people rent movies. If people don't want the hassle of driving to a neighborhood video store, movies can be rented by ordering them online. The industry game changer is the Netflix expansive distribution system that allows customers to receive the movie, usually the next day after ordering it. Also, Netflix is easy to get: A new customer simply fills out a profile of their movie preferences and selects a monthly subscription plan that fits their frequency and price preferences. And like Amazon, the system learns more about users' preferences every time they shop and makes movie recommendations based upon previous customer selections. Add to this the ease of shopping online, free shipping, no hassle returns and delivery, no late fees, and the ability to cancel a subscription at any time, and Netflix was able to create new business value in an industry in which "copycat" companies compete for the same customer base with basically the same products and services. Now that Netflix has added new services like movies on demand, this service will create even more disruption in the cable and television industry.

When companies break out of what they perceive as industry constraints, they no longer compete against other businesses. They enter into new uncontested market space where they no longer compete on the basis of price. What is surprising is the simplicity in which they do it. The result is greater business focus, more customer value, and often the ability to offer lower prices. To learn more about this concept, I highly recommend reading *Blue Ocean Strategy*, by Renee Monbourge and Kim Chan, who have studied this concept extensively.[1]

Whether you are starting a company in a new industry or if you are already in a mature, established industry, it is valuable to look for new models and concepts used in completely different industries that can be applied to your business. Southwest Airlines discovered their competitive advantage by going outside their industry to study airline efficiency and find ways to speed up ground turnaround time. They studied Indy 500 pit crews and were able to use these benchmarks to improve their on-ground turnaround time and set a new industry standard. Competitive advantage comes from being the first to do something old in a new way.

Many airlines have attempted to copy the 15-minute turnaround time established by Southwest, yet Southwest Airlines remains the industry leader because they deploy other strategies that are much harder to copy. No other airline has created the same warm and friendly environment that Southwest has been able to establish with their customers. United tried to compete by starting TED, a low-cost subsidiary that aimed to compete with Southwest, but failed to achieve this goal. Why? One of the big reasons is that the culture never changed. The same surly stewardesses that served on United Airline flights also worked for TED. From the customers' perspective, there isn't a noticeable difference between a TED flight and a United flight. But there *is* a difference when comparing a TED flight to a Southwest Airlines flight. Southwest fares are always low, and they continue to let you make flight changes and check your baggage for no additional fee. They even give you snacks for free. Good luck even finding so much as a bag of peanuts on a TED flight.

## Finding New Value

In the next two exercises, you will be examining your business model to gain a new perspective. In the first exercise, you will evaluate common characteristics in the industry in which you compete and look for ways to eliminate the things customers really don't care about. Then, in Chapter 33, "Finding New Value: Part Deux," you will look closely at the benefits customers want and need when they hire a product to get a specific job done. How can you respond to offer a solution completely focused on these benefits? Is there a way to deliver a solution with greater service but at a lower cost because the solution has been simplified? What ways can you create value that no one in your industry has thought of yet? The outcome of this should help you simplify your business model, and bring greater customer focus to your solutions.

## Finding New Value: Part I

Discovering new value in your business requires questioning assumptions about common industry practices (see Figure 32.1).

## Finding New Value

Discovering new value in your business requires questioning assumptions about common industry practices.

### De-Emphasize
What elements of your industry *add minimal value* to your customer?

**Destroy**

What elements *should be destroyed* that your industry has taken for granted?

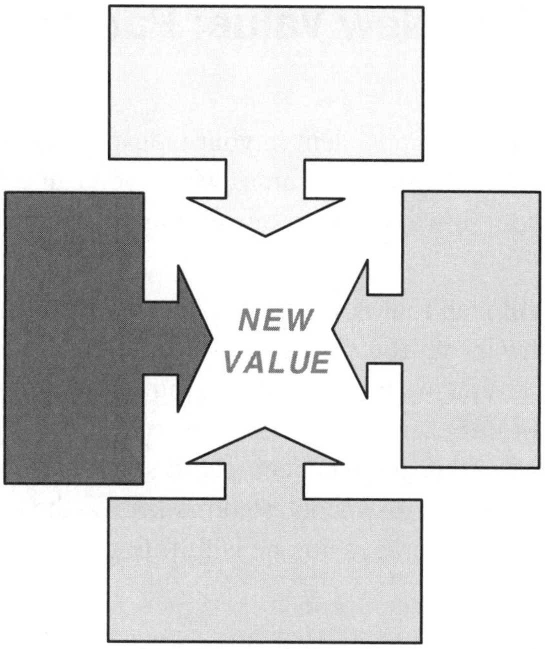

NEW VALUE

**Create**

What qualities *should be developed* that your industry has yet to offer?

### Promote
What qualities *add the most value* for the customer?

Summarize Opportunities and Actions: _____
_____
_____
_____
_____
_____

**Figure 32.1**   *Finding new value*

# 33

# Finding New Value: Part Deux

You now have an idea of the areas prevalent in your industry that are irrelevant or add minimal value. You have also identified the areas where you can create and promote value to customers, and do it in ways that no one else in your industry has yet discovered.

In this chapter, you will map four new areas against the job customers hire your product or service to do for them. You will explore broadening your audience of buyers, adding new experiences, leveraging trends, and looking for new ways to deliver the solution to buyers. The goal of this exercise is to find new ways to study what customers want. The difference between this and what competitors provide is the opportunity to provide new value and compete in an uncontested market. Or the opportunity may have nothing to do with competitors: Perhaps no one is fulfilling an unmet customer need.

## Broaden the Buyers

Expand and redefine how you think about the buyers for your product or service. Begin by thinking about current buyers, and then consider all the people who influence the buying decision. In business markets, what people (roles) in what departments influence buying decisions? How much interaction does your company have with these influencers? Do industry experts and gurus influence buying decisions? Do trade and industry associations influence buyers? What about distribution channels?

In consumer markets, women influence 85 percent of all buying decisions. But what other family members contribute to purchasing decisions? What factor do children play in influencing purchases simply by accompanying mom or dad when they make a purchase? Is there an experience you can add so children actually remind their parents to do a rather mundane task like grocery shopping, banking, or shopping at *your* store just because they like to go there? Some businesses create an area to keep kids busy while parents shop, but could you go beyond this concept to create an *experience* for dad and son to have fun and bond? Also consider the role the community plays in influencing events and consumer behavior.

As you think about what your solution has to offer, who is buying it, and who influences purchasing decisions, are there buyers you have not yet considered? Do sales and marketing programs consider all buyers and influencers?

This concept can also be applied to a different product development approach. How will different buyers respond if you make it easy for them to understand how your solution applies to a variety of jobs? Arm and Hammer made it easy for consumers to think about using the product as a carpet deodorizer (Arm and Hammer Vacuum Free carpet deodorizer); a kitty litter deodorizer (Arm and Hammer Super Scoop); a detergent to clean and freshen clothes (Arm and Hammer laundry detergent); and a toothpaste to make mouths feel clean (Arm and Hammer Complete Care toothpaste).[1] Arm and Hammer didn't burden customers with thinking about how to use the product in different ways. *They made it easy by creating new products targeted to different uses, and attracted new buyers.*

## Create Customer Experiences

Logic can sway some purchases, but emotions are the real driver of buyer behavior. When you think about the job that buyers hire your product or service to do, what experiences can add value and excitement? A better customer experience can result in new ways to differentiate your business and attract new buyers. They can also lead to increased revenue and profits because buyers will pay for an experience that provides them with more value.

What is interesting, however, is that often when a business decides to get rid of the things customers really don't value, it simplifies its offering and the price of their product or service actually becomes lower. When businesses can offer customers a better experience at the same or lower cost than competitive choices, they find new value in an uncontested market place. This is how disruptive innovations are created.

Landmark Theaters has changed the experience of going to a movie theater. Moviegoers can order tickets online and reserve a first-class seat. This lets the buyer walk right into the theater (no waiting in line or risk of driving to a sold-out show), and sit in a large, luxurious leather recliner to watch the movie. And forget paying a ridiculous sum of money for a bucket of popcorn (it's free at Landmark) or the basic high-calorie candy and soda. Choose from a whole menu of good foods like quiche, a chicken baguette sandwich, and delicious desserts. Order a glass of wine, a beer, a cappuccino, or an exotic tea. And it doesn't stop there. You can enjoy the food from the café and wine bar in the lobby, or you can have your own personal waiter bring it to your seat. Now you can enjoy a dinner and movie date—in one single experience.

Many predicted that cinemas would be in trouble due to substitute offerings like video stores, Netflix, pay-per-view, and on-demand movies. If you're like me, you have to look at the simplicity of what Landmark has done and ask: *"Why did it take so long for someone to think of this?"*

Retailers like REI added experience to several of their flagship stores years ago. In addition to shopping, consumers can rock climb on the indoor wall or try out a kayak in the small river outside the store. Why don't other retailers do things like this...or something more?

When I was in Paris with my daughter recently, I thought she would enjoy visiting the Louis Vuitton store in the eighth arrondissement. The breathtaking storefront features a huge Louis Vuitton bag that can be seen for blocks away. It's an attraction for first-time shoppers, but I wonder how many repeat visitors they have? Once inside, the experience is anticlimactic. It's just a regular store with Louis Vuitton bags. I observed the number of people filing in and out of the store as the clerks and security guards passively stood buy with an air of indifference. There was nothing inviting about the store except the rather unusual architectural building. Shoppers must think, "Okay. Been there, done that." But what if the shopper had a real experience while shopping?

Perhaps a small section of the store could be devoted to the history of Louis Vuitton. Louis Vuitton aficionados might be thrilled to walk through displays featuring vintage bags and interesting facts about how he influenced fashion. Assuming the shoppers are high-end (bags are $200–$6,000—so it's a safe assumption), why not pamper them in special ways? The store could feature a wine bar, which is a natural in Paris (not to mention one might cast away all doubt about spending $2,000 on a bag after a glass of wine) or create other ways to pamper discriminating shoppers. And I'm sure businesses in the area could offer dozens of ideas for complementary products or services. Paris is my favorite city in the world because I love the people, the style, the food and wine, the architecture, and the history. In this example, how can a fabulous Parisian lifestyle be integrated into the store environment to enhance the brand and customer experience?

## Tap into Trends

Instead of adapting to trends, create and influence them. In the previous chapter, "Disrupt and Innovate," you researched macro-environmental issues that were shaping your industry. How can you take these trends and use them to your advantage? How can you tap into trends like the abundance of information, the ease of communication through social networks, the ability to reach an expansive number of people globally, use tools like blogs and social networks, support the Green movement, alleviate growing consumer skepticism, or enable individual preference through mass customization? All of these trends can be leveraged to create new business success.

The iPhone changed consumer experiences and expectations of mobile devices. The creation of the iPhone set off a huge wave of entrepreneurs rushing to create mobile applications resulting in dozens of I-can't-live-without-it tools. More than 100,000 people visited the iTunes Application store in its first weekend alone. Linux created a similar stir with open source computing. New technologies give birth to all kinds of new businesses that in turn inspire other new markets and businesses.

When Ted Turner created a new way of delivering television, he launched an entirely new industry. The industry responded by creating new types of programming we have now come to expect, like HBO. The outcome of HBO series like *The Sopranos* and *Sex in the City* influenced television, entertainment, and fashion industries.

Today's equivalent to Ted Turner might be Kevin Rose, founder of Digg, the new Internet company that has created 30 million raving fans since its launch in late 2004. Company valuation is estimated between $60 million and $300 million. The power of this company and Internet tool is unknown because it's so new, but like Google and the iPhone, with this much interest and a huge user base, the future will be written by customers. And this in turn will give birth to a new wave of businesses and trends.

Work with your team to create a list of trends. What trends are influencing your customers? How have they impacted what customers want or expect? What trends are changing the way your business, or others like it in your industry, are doing business? Objectively look at the gap between these two areas and identify opportunities for change, growth, or expansion.

## Distinctive Delivery

The Internet has created disintermediation between businesses, channels, and consumers. As customer needs and preferences change, they also look for new channels to access and buy products. For example, if the job a customer wants to get done is learning new knowledge, he can access education and training in several ways including books, CDs, seminars, university courses, online resources and articles, consultants, and third-party providers. Depending upon the level of value and price, people buy from these sources for lots of different reasons.

Several years ago, if a business person wanted luxury air transportation, the only way she could get this was to reserve a first-class or business-class seat. The only other option appeared to be buying a corporate jet, but this option is cost prohibitive for most businesses. NetJets examined this market need and how they could deliver a similar outcome to customers who wanted premium air travel service. NetJets invented fractional jet ownership, which allows business executives to use a private jet for a certain number of hours a month. The company offers a simple, affordable solution to business travelers who desire fast, personalized, no-hassle transportation at a reasonable price.

Netflix did the same thing in the entertainment business, disintermediating video stores to sell direct to consumers. The result is entertainment delivered to your doorstep or personal computer. Amazon took a similar approach by selling books, music, and more directly to consumers, and forever changed the way consumers buy books and now many other items. Online retail marketplaces like Amazon Marketplace and eBay allow small businesses access to millions of consumers.

As you examine the job that your customers want done, and the methods of access to get it done, think about whether you deliver it in the best possible way. In what ways can you provide ease of access, or perhaps greater access to your solutions? Examine your current channels and consider other ways you can get your product in the hands of buyers using new distribution channels. Sometimes this is a change in delivery methods or channels, but it can also mean a change to your products and services. Look at the benefits your customers want and figure out different ways to give it to them. Do you need to simplify your solution or add more benefits? Maybe you need to add complementary products that will give you access to new distribution channels, and therefore, new buyers.

Match what customers want to the way they buy and access it. Do buyers want the solution to be:

- Fast or slow
- Basic or robust
- Serious or fun
- Independent or collaborative
- Available everywhere or a selective few

- Practical or luxurious
- Low price or high
- Available instantly online or through brick and mortar
- One-stop shopping or a highly specialized business

These are just a few attributes to consider as you look for new ways to create value. As you have progressed through this marketing process, you should now understand what your customers want. Ask yourself, "How is my solution different from what competitors provide?" Is there a gap of unmet customer needs? Or perhaps you are thinking, "It has nothing to do with competitors." Maybe no one is fulfilling the need—and therein lies the opportunity.

## Imagine and Innovate

Let's look at an example of how these four concepts could be applied to a rather ordinary transportation service: Trains. What if the rail transportation in the U.S. could be completely reinvented? If the goal is to get people from point A to point B in a reasonable time, like Europe and Asia do with high-speed trains, there is a vast array of creative ways in which to do this. A company (it probably won't be the railroads) could deliver a unique experience by adding capabilities and attributes like wireless and conferencing capabilities, meeting rooms, or a theater. This would allow business travelers to enjoy affordable luxury to work and be productive between cities. Imagine the joy of a commuter who travels weekly between L.A. and San Francisco when she discovers that she has other choices!

Just think of the endless possibilities in consumer trains that carry families from one place to the next. Why not have cars with movie theaters, or other forms of entertainment? A family could actually spend time together without the hassle of stuffing everyone into a car, spending an exorbitant amount of money on plane tickets, or tolerating the hassle and impersonal experience of air travel. What are the possibilities of a "green service?" Imagine a mode of transportation that doesn't burn gas or coal, doesn't pollute the environment—maybe it even gives energy back to the environment somehow. Some smart entrepreneur will figure it out.

The next exercise is designed to build upon what you have learned so far during this process. It is designed to help you discover and summarize how you will differentiate your business by creating better customer experiences resulting in deeper relationships with them. This is what will add value to your business. It isn't about building a better product. Marketing is about delightfully satisfying the wants and needs of your customers, and if you can figure out innovative new ways to do this, you will be far ahead of most companies that still operate with a product mentality.

In the last exercise, "Finding New Value: Part I," you analyzed how you can eliminate the things most competitors in your industry offer that your customers just don't value. This may simplify your offerings and make your business more efficient. Now you will expand on the concepts you applied in the "Promote" and "Create" categories.

# Finding New Value: Part II

Creatively explore and analyze new approaches to reach a broader market of buyers, create unique customer experiences, leverage growing trends, and find new methods of delivering your solutions.

## Buyers

How you can broaden the buyers you sell to, or gain a better understanding of others who influence the buying decision? If you made a change to customer experience or delivery, would this change the number of people you could sell your solutions to?

## Experience

What experiences can you add to create new value for your customers? What experiences would people value enough to pay more for? How can these experiences create market differentiation so you no longer compete on price, or you attract new customers?

## Trends

What trends are evolving that you can leverage in new and valuable ways to improve customer value and access to more buyers and influencers? What trends impact buyers, customer experience, and delivery?

## Distinction

What new channels and attributes can you add to reach new buyers in new markets? How can improvements in efficiency, quality, timing, availability, and other factors improve customer access and preference for your solutions?

## Summary:

Brainstorm each of these areas with your team to create a list of ideas in each category that are unique and create differentiation. Summarize the recommendations and next steps, then experiment and test the ideas with your customers.

# 34

# Pricing Strategy and Objectives

The way in which a company positions and prices its products and services may be the most visible evidence of how a company values its brand. A company that seeks product or service leadership is less concerned with pricing than it is with innovation.

A company's pricing strategy is an important and complicated decision. To make matters worse, there are dozens of different pricing methods companies use. I want to simplify the process as much as possible and present you with a process that will be used to help you develop a pricing strategy aligned with your business strategy. The first goal is to understand your objectives. There are four main pricing objectives that work for most businesses:

- **Profit Maximization:** Companies that successfully differentiate their brand from others in their category can maximize prices to what the market will bear. The target market may be smaller than if you were pursuing a different objective, but higher profits will provide your company with more strategic options. The cosmetics industry provides several examples of profit maximization. The cost to produce some cosmetics is minimal, and even after adding the cost of expensive packaging and marketing, the profit is substantial.

- **Market Leadership:** Companies perceived to have the highest level of product or service quality, service excellence, and/or luxury create a very loyal base of customers. Unique brand positioning and effective marketing strategies reinforce their leadership position. Brands such as SubZero and Viking continue to grow and avoid the competitive pricing wars prevalent with other competitors in the appliance market.

- **Market Share Penetration:** If you are introducing a new product and your goal is to get the product into as many users' hands as possible, your objective should be to price your product as low as possible to gain new customers and win market share, or to steal market share from existing competitors. This strategy is effective if the market is price sensitive to products in your category, or if there are many substitute products available.

- **Survival Pricing:** Products or services are priced at or below cost to get rid of excess inventory or respond to competitive pressure. Companies may need to adopt this strategy to avoid losing customers or going out of business. This is a short-term strategy that should only be applied in extreme cases. The business must learn how to add value and differentiate from the competition, and to up-sell customers to more profitable products and services.

You will notice that "low price leader" is not on the list. I don't believe this is a good strategy for any business except big companies like Wal-Mart that can actually deliver on the promise. Besides, who wants to operate a business based on having the lowest price? Where's the fun in that strategy? First, it's a difficult claim to make and you'll always be looking over your shoulder to substantiate the claim. Second, there are so many alternatives to differentiate and add value to your solutions, resulting in profitable growth for your business.

Companies approach pricing strategy in various ways. One approach that works for many businesses is market-based pricing using target margin as the pricing floor. This will allow everyone (executives, finance, marketing) to sleep at night without worrying about damage to the bottom line or to brand equity. It will also provide more discipline for the sales force. If prices fluctuate, it may encourage bad behavior from sales people who offer customers a low price just to close a deal. It can also train customers to expect and demand price concessions.

Keep in mind that once the general price is set, consideration must be given to modifying the base cost to geographical regions, sales channels, and the different types of customers who purchase (large volume purchasers versus occasional buyers). Contract terms, guarantees, and other factors also weigh in to pricing decisions.

The relationship between price and quality isn't as predictable as it once was. Consumers favor low prices on commodity goods and in situations where it is difficult to ascertain the value for paying a slightly higher price. At the same time, consumers value quality, convenience and service on some items and they don't mind paying a premium when they perceive equitable value in return. These are just a few of the things that will impact price. Others are product awareness, marketing effectiveness, product positioning, and brand.

## Mapping Customer Value to Pricing Strategy

To help you create your pricing strategy, or evaluate if your current strategies are aligned with your objectives, you will create a Pricing Map for your business. The steps are outlined below and this is followed by an example of a completed Pricing Map for the training industry. The goal of this exercise is to evaluate your products and services against competitors and substitutes, as well as to the perceived value and budget of your customers.

## Pricing Map Directions

The pricing map illustrates the relationship between commodity and specialty products on the vertical axis, relative to price on the horizontal axis. In some B2B examples, the description of the vertical axis can change to decision maker target markets and the horizontal axis represents the budget ranges, or price. Select the best criteria for the vertical and horizontal axis that is most relevant to your business.

A diagonal line runs through several semicircles. The diagonal line assumes a direct relationship between perceived value and price. Each of the semicircles represents similar competitive products corresponding to a price point. The semicircle also represents substitute products of similar products in a budget/price range that provide the same perceived benefits. Substitute products and services are generally at the lower level along the price axis as they tend to be less expensive (for example, renting a movie versus going to the theater).

Some companies sell products or services at all price points up and down the line, maximizing their growth across products and markets. Other companies only sell products or services to one market. As you analyze the data from the research you collected on market opportunity and buyer needs within various target markets, you can evaluate market expansion opportunities.

What differentiates companies who sell at the high end of the pricing map versus those who sell at the lower end? They have created a perception of value by adding unique services, personalized service, higher quality, faster turnaround, or some other special aspect that elevates their brand above competitors. Market leaders can command a higher price because they have proven a direct relationship between quality and price.

When you have completed the pricing model, evaluate your current pricing structure relative to the entire choices available to your target market. The highest-priced product in the market sets the price ceiling and your break-even point sets the floor. ("Break-even" is the point where total revenues equal total costs.) Demand is what consumers are able and willing to buy at a certain price. Most businesses will set prices somewhere in the middle of the two spectrums. A low price may be charged for a specific item or service at break-even if the goal is to get new customers in the door that have the potential to buy additional items or services.

If your goal is to be the lowest priced in the market, I would urge you to rethink your strategy. As discussed earlier, unless you are Wal-Mart, offering the lowest prices is not a sustainable strategy in the long run. It is, however, clearly acceptable to give discounts for large volume purchases, early payment discounts, or other price incentives to purchase. But discounts should be the exception, not the rule. A justifiable discount should reward the customer for having saved you time or costs, so you both win. In short, there is a reason for the discount; it is not arbitrary.

Consider this: Have you ever lowered your price for a customer because you perceived it was necessary to win a sale? If you provided the same value and benefits when you charged the same customer more for the next sale, you may have ended up losing the customer. The price difference only served to confuse the customer, resulting in a short-term gain and a long-term loss.

Some businesses believe that an economic downturn is justification for lowering prices. I strongly caution you to think about the consequences of doing this. Research from past recessions confirms that it takes six years for businesses to return to normal pricing after making price cuts. Ouch. A recession is bad enough without prolonging the pain even further.

## Training Industry Example

Figure 34.1 illustrates a Pricing Map example for the training industry. It demonstrates the Pricing Map concept so you can apply similar thinking to competitive and substitute products or services in your industry.

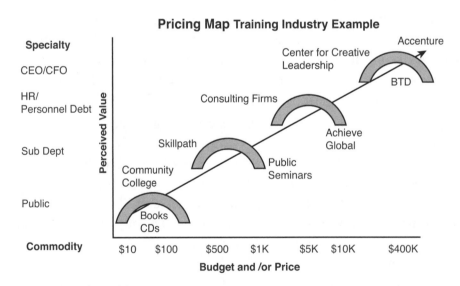

**Figure 34.1** *Pricing model for the training industry*

The training industry provides a good B2B example of buyer groups that make purchase decisions based upon value and budget. Beginning at the top of the vertical line and moving down to the left corner, you can see that the CEO/CFO would consider purchasing a highly customized training program that typically has a high price tag, while a human resources department typically has a budget for purchasing training services or products for the organization. Specific departments and/or business units have discretionary dollars to purchase skill-specific training through public seminars, custom training, or products like audio, video, and online training solutions. Large companies may also develop their own internal training using the expertise of its staff.

The lower end of the diagram represents substitute products like books, CDs, and community college courses. All of these sources provide training at the commodity price level which is a substitute for higher-priced training options. In each instance, the price range changed *and* the target market may have changed based upon what the buyer perceived as the best value for his or her budget.

Some companies sell training products at several price points, to several different buyers, meaning they have expanded their product line and their markets. In other situations, a company may sell only specialty products or services to one market. An analysis of the entire market offerings will highlight potential areas where you can expand your business, or it may shed light on competitive alternatives you have not yet considered. Keep in mind that the customer is looking for a solution to get a job done, and will base buying decisions on price, value, brand, and other considerations.

If your goal is to maximize profits, what price point best supports that goal? If you wish to compete at the top end of the scale, what attributes create differentiation? Relationship building activities add value, but they can also add costs. However, customers will pay a higher price for a product or service that is differentiated and provides value.

Develop your own pricing map using the blank pricing map worksheet in the *Real-Time Marketing* book resources section at www.MarketSmarter.com.

# 35

# Analyze Price and Profitability by Product and Service

Working with companies both large and small over the years, I have noticed that a lot of time and attention is invested in developing marketing strategies without fully understanding the internal costs and profitability of the products or services being sold. It's surprising—shocking, actually—that so few business professionals understand their costs and margins. In Section VI, "Execute and Evaluate," we will explore new, more efficient methods of budgeting and forecasting that are cross functional across operations, finance, marketing, and sales. For now, let's make sure we have at least the basics in place.

The purpose of the exercise is to help you understand how you can increase profitability across your product and service lines. This evaluation must be done before you develop your pricing strategy. If you are a marketer who breaks out in hives at the very word of "finance" or "budget," don't worry. The process you are about to learn is made just for you. It's simple and easy to understand. Please note that the next form and several others are available for you to use in the *Real-Time Marketing for Business Growth* book resources section at www.MarketSmarter.com. The exercises and forms are designed to work together to allow you to "plug and play" different variables to analyze price and profit points.

> ### Marketing Tip for Large Company
> If you are a marketing professional in a large company, your finance team should be able to provide you with the information you need to understand the cost, revenue, and margin on a per-product and service basis. If not, now is a good time to work with others in your company to fully understand this information.

# Revenue/Cost Analysis

The revenue/cost analysis worksheet summarizes recent sales history and variables impacting sales. Two simple examples are provided to help you understand a product business (Tony's Surf Shop) and a service business (Larry the Lawyer). The goal of the sales budget is to calculate revenue, profit, and contribution to revenue on a per-product and service basis.

The worksheet will ask for fixed costs and variable costs. Fixed costs are costs that continue regardless of the volume of sales. Rent, salaries, insurance, interest charges, and property taxes are examples of fixed costs. Variable costs are costs that fluctuate based on production and sales volume. In retail business, they may include freight, commissions, shipping, and handling. In manufacturing, the variable costs might include molds, assembly, cleanup, set up, and freight. In service businesses, commissions, consulting, or contractor fees used in providing a service are examples of variable expenses. Some service companies allocate costs as a percentage of the service's revenue contribution to overall revenue. Others choose to allocate costs based on time spent on projects. Work with your accountant or finance team to make a list of the fixed and variable cost items so there is agreement about what costs go where. Explain your objectives to the finance team so they can understand your goal is to make marketing decisions on a per-product and service basis.

If you have a new company that does not yet have a sales history, the budget will be based on projections. Consider using industry standards from your industry association or from Risk Management Association's (RMA) Annual Statement Studies.[1]

The following worksheet summarizes the income and costs for both the product and the service businesses. The examples reflect two small businesses and are intentionally simple to explain the concept. The same methodology can be applied to any size of business. If you are a marketer in a large company, your finance team can hopefully provide you with the information you need.

The worksheet provide examples for three products or services. It can be easily modified to suit the needs of your business. You will note that there are letters next to each line item. The letters match those in another worksheet titled Target Profit Analysis. Simply plug the numbers from the line items in the Revenue/Cost Analysis worksheet into the line items with the corresponding letters in the "Target Profit Analysis" worksheet. This will give you an easy way to experiment with changing different variables to see how you can achieve a higher profit. Blank worksheets and examples are in the *Real-Time Marketing for Business Growth* book resource section at www.MarketSmarter.com.

# Worksheet

**Revenue/Cost Analysis**

Date:

*$$$ Dollars*

|  | | Tony's Surf Shop | | Larry Lawyer | |
|---|---|---|---|---|---|
|  | | Actual Last Yr | Budgeted Current Yr | Actual Last Yr | Budgeted Current Yr |
| A. | Number of Employees (Full-time equivalents) | 1 | | 7 | |
| B. | Quantity Sold | 1) 240 Surfboards<br>2) 268 Wetsuits<br>3) 402 Body boards | | 1) $ 3,380 Hrs<br>2) $ 3,900 Hrs<br>3) $ 2,080 Hrs | 1) Document Preparation<br>2) Legal Research<br>3) Counseling and Litigation |
| C. | Retail Price per Product/Service (Amount retail purchaser pays) | 1) $ 500<br>2) $ 150<br>3) $ 55 | | 1) $ 50/Hr<br>2) $ 75/Hr<br>3) $ 175/Hr | |
| D. | Revenues per Product/Service (Amount you receive B x C) | 1) $ 120,000<br>2) $ 40,200<br>3) $ 22,110 | | 1) $ 169,000<br>2) $ 292,500<br>3) $ 364,000 | |
| E. | Overall Gross Revenues | $ 182,310 | | $ 825,500 | |
| F. | Allocated Overhead per Product (Fixed Cost) | 1) $ 37,079<br>2) $ 12,360<br>3) $ 6,742 | | 1) $ 63,360<br>2) $ 95,040<br>3) $ 158,400 | |
| G. | Variable Cost per Unit | 1) $ 250<br>2) $ 90<br>3) $ 35 | | 1) $ 18<br>2) $ 42<br>3) $ 85 | |
| H. | Total Cost of Product/Service | 1) $ 97,079<br>2) $ 36,480<br>3) $ 20,812 | | 1) $ 124,200<br>2) $ 258,840<br>3) $ 335,200 | |
| I. | Pre-Tax Profit per Product/Service (Revenue per product less allocated overhead and direct costs per product [D-H]) | 1) $ 22,921<br>2) $ 3,720<br>3) $ 1,298 | | 1) $ 44,800<br>2) $ 33,660<br>3) $ 28,800 | |
| J. | Percent Contribution to Revenues per Product/Service [D / E] | 1) 66%<br>2) 22%<br>3) 12% | | 1) 20.5%<br>2) 35.4%<br>3) 44.1% | |

*Assumptions:*

*example*

# 36

# Distribution and Channel Sales Strategy

Distribution is the process of getting a product or service to the buyer or end user through a channel. Selecting the right sales channels is one of the most important strategies you will execute because channels give you access to buyers. Channels in consumer, B2B, and manufacturing businesses each have unique distribution characteristics. This chapter will examine the primary issues and considerations of different types of channels and hopefully spark new ideas for channels you have not yet considered.

## Choose the Right Channels

Examples of distribution channels include direct sales, agents, brokers, dealers, value added resellers, licensing, franchising, wholesalers, retailers, distributors, catalog/direct mail, telemarketing firms, inside sales (outbound and inbound), and the Internet. A company may use several types of distribution channels to reach buyers in different market segments and geographies.

To choose the right channels for your business, define your objectives and analyze the benefits to be gained through each channel opportunity. The primary considerations include selling costs, revenue generation, geographic needs, expertise and reach of channel partners, and branding. A cost and benefit analysis should be done to evaluate how much it will cost to sell and service the channel, and the benefits and estimated return expected by using each of the channels.

For example, if you sell a software product, you have several channel options, each with its own benefits. You could sell or OEM to a hardware company that sells the product with a hardware component like a computer. You could integrate or bundle the software with other complementary software products. It could be sold through computer specialty stores or to mass market retailers. Another choice is to sell through a catalog retailer that sells products to a particular target market, or you may choose to sell software online directly to consumers.

Evaluation of channel options also includes decisions about who you want to sell and represent your solutions, which affects your brand. You can sell directly to customers using a dedicated sales force, or sell through a value added reseller (VAR), independent software vendors (ISV), or specialized channels. These are just some of the options for a software product. Each has its unique advantages and disadvantages that should be weighed carefully.

A factor that influences channel strategy is the decision to use a push or a pull strategy, or both. A push strategy is enticing distributors to carry and sell your products to the consumer. In this case, a company may rely heavily on its own sales force and trade promotions (channel incentive) to create demand. Campbell's Soup is an example of a well-known commodity product that is pushed through several channels.

A pull strategy is common among well-known brands, like the iPod. Large amounts of advertising and promotion are invested to create a strong, visible brand to pull the consumer to purchase it. Many companies use a combination of both push and pull strategy to maximize sales. Pharmaceutical companies that market directly to consumers are a good example. Many use broad-reaching television campaigns urging patients to ask their physician for a certain drug and pharmaceutical sales reps market directly to physicians.

## Channel Considerations

To determine the best distribution strategies for your products and services, you should analyze the advantages and disadvantages of each channel. The following issues are the prime points of consideration:

**Cost:** It generally costs less to employ a sales agency or middleman to sell your products than it does to pay salary and commission to your own sales force, or to open a new sales office. However, commissions paid through sales representatives are usually higher.

**Revenue:** How many sales reps does the channel have? If you have 10 sales reps working for you, this dedicated sales team may be more knowledgeable of your company's offerings, but they don't have the scale of an intermediary with 100 sales reps. You will need to estimate the additional revenue that can be generated through external sales teams.

**Geographic Territories:** You will likely need different types of distribution for different geographical regions. In small rural locations, it may be more cost effective or even necessary, to employ a firm that covers a rural territory. If you are expanding into foreign markets, it would be wise to distribute through a company that has already established markets and customers in those regions and knows the unique characteristics of each country.

**Expertise and Reach:** Intermediaries have expertise, specialization, scale, and contacts into well-defined markets. All of these factors enable a company to reach new customers it otherwise could not reach on its own or it would take considerable time and expense to build.

**Brand and Position:** Brands that have been sold exclusively by a company and choose to expand by selling their products or services through distributors will need to be careful to protect their brand. Brands like David Yurman and Armani sell products through retailers who match their brand image. Companies like Bobby Brown cosmetics use an **exclusive** distribution strategy, such as selling through Neiman Marcus and Nordstrom versus many department stores, which gives them greater control. This not only adds to the prestige of the brand, the distributor will benefit by offering an exclusive product or service, have specialized knowledge of the product, and also enjoy the revenue from being an exclusive sales channel. Companies that seek mass distribution will implement an **intensive** distribution strategy to sell products or services through as many places as possible. A **selective** distribution strategy is used by companies that want to sell between these two extremes.

## Tiered Distribution

Companies that sell direct to end users or consumers use a direct sales approach. Examples include the Internet, telemarketing, infomercials, and mail order. Companies that sell through one or more channels have a tiered distribution strategy. For example, a company selling to a retailer that sells to a consumer has a one-tier distribution strategy. If the company sells through a wholesaler or VAR that sells to a retailer that then sells to the end user, it has a two-tier distribution strategy. If the company sells through a distributor that sells to a sales agency that sells to the retailer that in turn sells to the end user, it uses a three-tier distribution strategy. Simply stated, each tier between a company and the customer equals a distribution channel.

The same tiered distribution scenario is applied to B2B and industrial industries, but the types of distribution channels change to manufacturers, manufacturing reps, brokers, industrial distributors, and others.

## Integrating Bricks and Clicks

Customers are increasingly looking for integrated solutions to purchase products. They may want to do their shopping online but have the flexibility to return the merchandise at a store, or to have an item that was purchased online serviced at a location convenient to where they live or work. If your goal is to offer your customers an integrated channel experience, your strategy and processes must be clearly defined and tightly integrated to create consistency in both environments.

Some of the basics of a successfully integrated channel are consistent return policies, discounts, promotional prices, inventory of advertised items, and product availability. There are many real-time inventory needs and complexities that must be considered as channels are integrated. One of the most important must be consistency of brand image and customer service. A call center representing a company must have the same level of care and service that a consumer would expect to find when shopping in a store.

## Internet Pure Play

In contrast to the integrated channel strategy described previously, many companies use the Internet exclusively as a channel for selling products and services. Examples of this business model include Amazon, Expedia, and Lending Tree. Clearly the advantage of a pure ecommerce business is the expansive reach to potential customers worldwide, and the cost savings from not having to maintain a brick and mortar presence.

Even traditional brick and mortar businesses are moving to the Internet to take advantage of cost savings. The banking industry is going through significant changes and is offering more choices for consumers who prefer doing online transactions versus the hassle of visiting a location. The average transaction at a full service bank is $4.07 compared to a phone transaction costing 54 cents, an ATM transaction costing 27 cents, and an online transaction costing just 1 cent. This stark reality has created Internet-only banks that are very price competitive. Cost savings in one area can be passed along to consumers in the form of higher interest rates on savings accounts and investment plans. This creates more stress on traditional banks that cannot compete at the same level and gives Internet-only banks a distinct competitive advantage.

# 37

# Formula for Success: Real-Time Channel Development

Selecting distribution channels is a combination of art and science. Mass distribution may sound like a desirable strategy, but timing is critical if this is your goal. One mistake that businesses make is choosing this strategy too early in the product life cycle. If your product does not have brand awareness, selling through mass retailers and distributors could prove to be fatal to your business or product line. You need to create market demand for your products first, or you risk low sales and being abandoned by the channels you worked so hard to establish.

Unless you can make a significant investment in marketing and advertising, your strategy should be to build brand awareness through channels that can help you establish your brand. Launch Pad, the innovative company described in Section II, has implemented a distribution strategy and process that has been highly effective for launching products. As you recall, Launch Pad launches unique new consumer products using a process of real-time research gathered in focus groups and testing with potential customers. The process gives them the ability to test product concepts, packaging ideas, messaging, advertising, and so on as they move through the product development and commercialization stages.

As the products transition from development to launch, the company continues to test and carefully measure response as it is sold through progressively larger channels. The objective is to test response to consumer demand in low-cost environments. Products go through a "Pyramid Principle" that moves products up the distribution chain through increasingly larger channels. Figure 37.1 shows how it works.

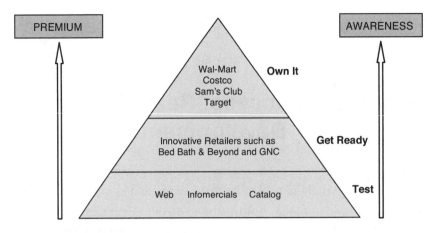

© Launch Pad. Reprinted with permission.

**Figure 37.1**    *Launch Pad's Pyramid Principle*

## Real-Time Channel Development

Products are launched at the bottom tier of the pyramid, primarily direct to consumers, so that the product can be refined as consumer feedback and demand are analyzed. Selling through low-cost channels like the Internet, infomercials, and specialty catalogs is low risk and more flexible than other channels. If the product isn't successful, it is either killed (it's okay to fail fast) or changes are made to one or more of the marketing mix elements (product, price, promotion, and place). Refinements and testing continue until everyone feels it's right to move up the pyramid to the next level of distribution.

In the middle tier of the pyramid, Launch Pad enjoys working with what they call innovative distribution channels like Bed Bath & Beyond. Retailers like this are open and flexible to testing and understand the value of partners working together to make a product successful for both companies. For example, Bed Bed & Beyond will merchandise products using floor space and displays to promote the products, giving Launch Pad feedback as the product is tested through various merchandising displays, price points, and geographical locations.

Building great supplier and customer relationships is one of Launch Pad's critical success factors. Their goal is to make the product successful for their channel partners, so they are responsive to their needs and requests. Launch Pad makes it extremely easy for distributors to do business with them. For example, if the product doesn't sell as well as expected, they give the retailer funds to mark down the product and get rid of the inventory. This alleviates risk for the channel and builds confidence in the ongoing relationship they have with Launch Pad. It's a win-win partnership for both companies.

Launch Pad has a similar relationship with Wal-Mart. As products are tested in various Wal-Mart locations, they give Launch Pad ongoing feedback on customer response and demand generation. Founder Joel Appel says, "Wal-Mart is such a great company to work with. It's a myth that they are difficult to do business with. They make the right decisions for their company and their customers, and the feedback we get back, good or bad, allows us to make adjustments so the product is ultimately successful for both of us. They drive innovation and solid performance from their suppliers and help us make better products."

The preceding example illustrates a retail channel strategy, but conceptually it can be applied to other types of businesses. Incremental phased distribution can help any business increase its chances of success.

Several other lessons can be learned from this example:

**Build Strong Relationships:** Treat your channel partners with the same respect you give to customers and employees.

**Ongoing Testing:** Never assume you have the optimal scenario figured out. Create a healthy aptitude for ongoing learning and continuous improvement.

**Remain Flexible:** Flexibility requires that you solicit ongoing feedback about what's working and what needs to change. Build flexible terms into your agreements.

# 38

# Analyzing and Selecting Channels

In this chapter, you will map the current and potential channels that can be used to reach your ultimate end user customer. Consider who buys your solutions, as well as the ultimate end user of the solution. How many new channels can you identify?

Every company has unique needs and challenges with respect to selecting the best channels. Channel decisions can be complex, and developing the best strategy to access new markets and buyers is one of the most important marketing decisions you will make. In Table 38.1, consider your buyers and end users. Define the current channels where you sell your solutions; then indicate other possible channels to reach your target segments and target customer. Evaluate the costs and benefits of using different channels to extend your reach to end users.

**Table 38.1**   Channel Analysis

**Product or Service:** _____

|  | Channel #1 | Channel #2 | Channel #3 | Channel #4 |
|---|---|---|---|---|
| Reach | | | | |
| Projected Revenue | | | | |
| Projected Costs | | | | |
| Geography | | | | |
| Expertise/Brand or Company Strength | | | | |
| Other Observations | | | | |

# Avoid Channel Conflict

Channel conflict is common if there are not clear agreements about mutual objectives and selling terms. The most common sources of channel conflict involve issues related to geographical boundaries, customers, industries served, and pricing. Give considerable thought to the channel issues in advance to alleviate the chance there will be channel conflict down the road. The channel checklist below will guide your decision making in several critical areas.

Dilution and cannibalization are concerns as companies expand. No one knows this better than Starbucks. In July 2008, Starbucks announced that after several years of rapid expansion both domestically and internationally, they would close 600 stores. In January 2009, Starbucks announced it would close another 300 stores. Although a slow economy is certainly to blame, the aggressive growth plan was also a factor. As the number of Starbucks stores swelled with locations in grocery stores, shopping malls, airports, retail stores, and locations within a block or two from an existing Starbucks, the market became oversaturated. Stores begin to suffer from cannibalization and brand dilution. You know you have a problem when jokes start to surface: *Did you hear about the Starbucks opening inside the Starbucks?*

# Channel Checklist: Devil's in the Details

Distribution strategy and channel selection is a critical component of your marketing strategy. The next step is making sure you have covered all the details to effectively execute the strategy. There are many issues that must be considered in advance of formalizing and implementing a strategy, and the following checklist will assist you in finalizing the details:

- ✓ **Pricing and Discounts:** Consider how prices and discounts will be given to certain distributors who purchase large quantities, pay in advance, or guarantee selling a specific amount of goods or services. Distributors will want to ensure there is price parity or consistency of discounts and allowances. Some brands set the same price across all channels and rely upon the brand awareness and value added services of the channel to differentiate the product or service.

- ✓ **Geographical rights:** Distributors may want geographic exclusivity or credit for sales based on geographic borders.

- ✓ **Terms and Conditions:** What guarantees will be made on prices or products? What terms will be established for payment, delivery, returns, pricing, and servicing?

✓ **Training:** What training and support will the different types of channels need to be effective? What tools will be provided to them? What is the frequency of the training?

✓ **Support:** If you have a licensing or franchise channel strategy, you will need to define the company support that will be provided. This might include administrative, advertising, technology, marketing, training, promotion, supplies and equipment, and process and procedures support.

✓ **Reporting:** How will you track and measure the effectiveness of each channel? How will you measure the success of a channel relationship? What is the frequency and means by which you will measure performance? How will this information be integrated and communicated with channel partners to increase effectiveness of execution?

✓ **Contract Length:** Carefully consider the terms and conditions of your distribution agreements, and conduct periodic reviews to make sure the relationship is a win-win for both the company and the distributor. If a distributor does not live up to commitments that were made at the beginning of the contract term, you should have the mechanisms in place to make changes.

✓ **Incentives:** If your plan includes sales promotions to channels, include incentives and commissions in your budget. Keep in mind that your incentives budget may need to grow as the product matures.

✓ **Relationship:** Channel relationships need to be nurtured. Your strategy should include a plan for ongoing communication and joint planning, as well as ways you and your team can develop and grow the relationship.

# 39

# Strategic Alliances and Partnerships

Strategic alliances or strategic partnerships should be approached with the same rigor as a channel relationship in order for the partnership to be mutually successful in the long run. Companies that take a passive role with their alliances, such as putting the partner logo on their web site and creating loose agreements to promote each other's products, do not enjoy nearly the same level of success as businesses that put structure, commitment, and energy toward making the partnership successful.

For example, a company once said they had a "great" strategic alliance with another company because it gave them access to over 1,200 worldwide locations. Further examination revealed there was only a master services contract in place, but nothing else. Did they just expect the service to sell itself and create a new revenue stream? My advice to this company outlined a process and approach that you can use to make your strategic alliances and partnerships more successful. Use the eight steps below as a guideline to develop your plan.

## Strategic Alliance and Partnership Success Factors

The following process will help you structure new alliance partnerships, as well as keep the relationships with your existing partners on solid footing. These success factors do more than build good partnerships; they will build revenue streams that will grow steadily over time:

1. When establishing a partnership, hold a strategic planning meeting between the key stakeholders of both firms. This needs to include a cross-functional team of people from product management, marketing, sales, finance, and the executive sponsors.
2. Agree on the joint revenue and benefits each party will receive. Both parties need to have some "skin in the game."
3. Determine the marketing support that the sales teams will need to be successful. If joint marketing is needed, create a partner marketing plan that outlines all the programs, costs, roles, and responsibilities. The marketing staff from each company can develop the plan and meet as necessary to refine it.

4. Determine the training that is needed for various functional teams, paying special attention to training for the sales force. The sales team usually needs ongoing training, not just a one-time training event.

5. Agree on how each company will support the sales teams in sales calls. If your product or service is technically complex, a joint sales team with a sales and technical expert should meet with customers. This is the best way for each company to learn from each other and it will also create momentum and accountability.

6. Find a "sales evangelist" who is having early success selling the product or service and making significant commissions. Find out what he or she is doing and promote this to the larger sales teams so they can learn how to be more successful and make money from the strategic alliance.

7. Agree on the measures of success up front. Meet as a team at least quarterly to review results and adjust the game plan.

8. Create quick wins. Don't take on too much too fast; otherwise, the alliance will just be viewed as another "program of the month" that didn't work. Start small and build momentum and success stories. Both teams should agree on what the early wins will be so there is focused energy toward realizing the goals.

## Channel Mapping

The process of visually linking product and service goals to channels and target market segments will help you estimate revenue generation through each of the channels and sales groups for each of your products and services. In Section VI, you will add marketing programs to estimate the number of leads and projected revenue created from channel marketing programs. You will learn a process for defining top-down and bottom-up metrics to measure the effectiveness of not just your channels, but your entire demand chain using a tool called the ROI Optimizer.

# P•R•A•I•S•E™ Marketing Process

## Analyze

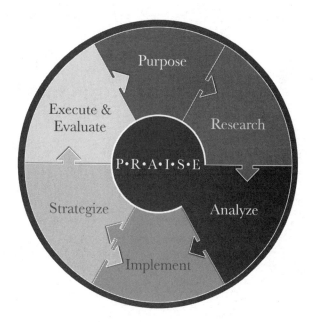

# Summary: Section III

- ✓ Analyze new complementary products/services to sell to existing customers.
- ✓ Analyze substitute products and the value customers receive from them. Are they potential threats, or can you change your solutions to more effectively compete?
- ✓ Complete the two "Finding New Value" exercises and summarize the outcomes.
- ✓ Create a Pricing Map to analyze competitive and substitute products. This process may also reveal new opportunities to sell additional solutions or target new buyers.
- ✓ Analyze the revenue, costs, and profit associated with each product and service.
- ✓ Evaluate and select distribution channels using the channel strategy tools.
- ✓ Project revenue through distribution channels to each market segment.
- ✓ Create an initial draft of channel and pricing strategies. Finalize this in the next section when other strategies are defined.
- ✓ Summarize findings and actions in Section III in the marketing plan template.

# Section IV

# Strategize:
# Growth Opportunities

*"The essence of strategy is in the activities—choosing to perform activities differently or to perform different activities than rivals. Otherwise, a strategy is nothing more than a marketing slogan."*
—Michael Porter

The two arrows in the P•R•A•I•S•E Marketing Process between Implement and Strategize imply a reciprocal relationship between the two elements. They are intended to convey the *continuous process* of strategy development and implementation, measuring results, and developing new strategies based on the outcomes and what you learned.

Strategy *always* comes before implementation. But stop for a moment and think about how businesses typically approach marketing. The goal is often to start producing leads and finding new customers. If a business owner is starting a new business, he or she can't wait to create a logo, brochure, direct mail piece, web site, and so on. What happens is programs are implemented before strategy or a marketing plan is created, and they are often based on a best guess of who will buy the products and services and why they buy. Marketing messages convey the benefits the marketer or business owner believes are important, not necessarily what drives the customer to buy. Often the results fall short in generating leads, sales, or the targeted return on investment.

I imagine that nearly everyone reading this book can relate to this scenario. Consider the reciprocal relationship between "Strategize" and "Implement" as you read this chapter. You will reflect on the past marketing strategies and tactics you have implemented and how to make them more effective and measurable in the future. Most important, you will apply what you have learned from the research and analysis you have completed up to this point in the process to develop new strategies to grow your business and market share.

Renowned management expert Peter Drucker said the best learning in life comes from a very simple process. When you begin something new, write down what you believe will happen. Then write down what really happened. Is there a substantial difference between what your expectations were and what actually happened? If so, what did you learn from the experience?

A similar process will be applied to strategy development. As strategies are executed, you will evaluate the cause and effect of the results. Was your strategy on target? If results are less than expected, was this due to the strategy, strategy execution, unexpected changes in market conditions, or something else? If you have followed this process so far, your strategies will yield much better results than you have experienced in the past. In this section, you will learn how to:

- Create effective positioning and value propositions.
- Understand what makes an effective brand.
- Develop a sales forecast and a sales plan.
- Evaluate competitor strategies to determine your competitive advantage.
- Define specific marketing objectives.
- Analyze several types of marketing strategies to determine the optimal strategic direction for your business.
- Evaluate strategic opportunities based on the competitive landscape.
- Create effective strategies to achieve your business and marketing objectives.

# 40

# What Is Strategy?

I find it interesting that there are so many different methods and theories about strategy, yet few describe a process for *how* to create them. Michael Porter defines strategies as fitting into three generic categories: (1) cost leadership (competing on the basis of low production and distribution costs), (2) differentiation (superior products or service), and (3) focus (on only a few product or market segments).[1] He says the evidence of strategy in a company is when it "performs different activities from rivals or performs similar activities in different ways." Michael Treacy and Fred Wiersema, authors of *The Discipline of Market Leaders*, write that companies should focus strategy on one of three value disciplines: Operational Excellence, Product Leadership, or Customer Intimacy.

What all marketers seem to agree on is how to evaluate *what makes a good strategy.* I believe Phillip Kotler summarized it best when he said, "Companies will have a unique strategy when (1) they have defined a clear target market and need, (2) developed a distinctive and winning value proposition for that market, and (3) arranged a distinctive supply network to deliver the value proposition to the target market."[2] Nirmalya Kumar has a similar strategic method that he calls the "Three Vs," which are value target, value proposition, and value network. His concept is explained in an article interview in Chapter 56, "Nurture a Culture of Innovation."

All of these "strategies to create strategies" are valuable and yet there are other factors that must be considered. It's easy to get lost in the complexity of strategy, so my goal is to take the "BS" out of strategy development and provide you with a process and the most essential information you need to know to develop successful strategies. Strategy will always be an art, but it you apply science and process it will be far less risky. The information in this section builds on everything you have already learned throughout this book, so the new information is concise, but meaty.

Selecting the right strategies to implement for your business depends on many factors, including product life cycle, market size, number and strength of competitors, and customer characteristics and buying behavior. You will also consider other factors such as: Is the market growing or mature? Is your company a market leader or one of many competitors vying for customer mind share? What resources do we have available for growth? Do our people have the skills needed to execute the strategic plan? All of these factors will influence the strategic direction and pace of growth. Competitive intensity is another factor. If the market is growing, it is much easier to win market share and market share gains are worth considerably more in a growth cycle than they are in a mature market.

## Strategy Process

As you progress through this section, you will note the following:

- Target Market, Competition, and Customer strategies have been discussed in previous chapters; therefore, the new information is provided to help you consider additional factors and refine your strategies in these areas.
- Pricing and Distribution strategies that you drafted in Section III, "Analyze: Growth and Profit Potential," can now be finalized and integrated with the other strategies you are about to develop.
- Growth and Innovation chapters will give you ideas to help you develop long-term strategies with an eye on differentiation, innovation, and business growth.
- Promotion strategies will be developed after you complete Section V, "Implement."
- And finally, please note that Chapter 43, "Positioning Strategy," is the most lengthy in this section as this topic has not been discussed yet; it is a catalyst for strategy development in other areas.

While individual strategy topics are discussed throughout this section, you will notice that many of the strategies you create are not discrete, but integrated. After you have learned about different types of strategies, you will define your sales goals and learn to write marketing objectives that are clear, concise, and measureable. The final step is developing your own strategies to achieve these objectives.

Keep in mind that strategy requires you to make tradeoffs. As you review concepts and examples for different types of strategies throughout this section, you will need to make choices and purposefully limit the size and complexity of your go-to-market strategy. It's just as important to figure out what to *stop* doing as it is to focus on what needs to be done. Prioritize strategies and tactics to achieve the most important goals, both short- and long-term, so that you can realize your long-term objectives.

---

### Marketing Tip

Jim Collins wrote a fabulous article on this topic several years ago called "The Power of Catalytic Mechanisms," which can be found on his website at www.jimcollins.com. I recommend reading this article at some point during this marketing process, as it will present you with a simple yet innovative decision-making process to evaluate activities against the strategies and goals you wish to achieve.

---

# 41

# A Framework and Process for Strategy Development

I have observed that marketers are often frustrated or perplexed by the lack of a process that describes how to develop strategy. On the following pages, you will learn a process that is both streamlined and explained with examples and case studies. Every business is unique, and therefore, many different variables must be considered when developing your own strategies—but the process will work for most businesses. A few adjustments will need to be made depending upon whether you are developing strategies for an existing business, or launching a new business. Here are a few guidelines:

**New Businesses:**

Begin by developing target market and positioning strategies that will drive all other strategies. A market plan is created to influence the buying behavior of a target audience, so if this strategy is not clear and focused, the rest of your marketing plan will be off target. Positioning is also an important strategic driver because it will determine how your brand is unique.

**Existing Businesses:**

Begin by creating strategies in the three areas of customers, target markets, and positioning. We have discussed the importance of customer loyalty and its direct correlation to profitability. If you focus on maximizing the value delivered to customers, this will increase retention, loyalty, referrals, profitability, and other positive outcomes.

As you read this section, keep an open mind to strategically explore ideas you may not have considered in the past. Market growth comes from offering increasing levels of differentiation and value to current customers, as well as expanding into new markets. Figure 41.1 illustrates the strategies we will cover in this section.

**Figure 41.1**  *Marketing strategies*

# 42

# Target Market Strategies

In Section II, "Research," you defined your primary and secondary target markets and learned why focusing on a specific target market is one of the most important strategies for your business. The information in this chapter will help you refine strategies to reach your target audience.

## Rich, Niche Markets

Although mass marketers benefit from higher sales volume than niche marketers, there are many reasons to choose a strategy focused on penetrating niche markets. A company that delivers products or services to a niche market understands the needs of its customers in ways that a mass marketer can never achieve. A deeper understanding of customer needs enables a company to provide better products and services, and add additional value to fulfill these needs. Companies focused on mass markets also find it more difficult to create customer intimacy than niche players. As you learned in earlier chapters, building deeper customer relationships has many advantages, the biggest of which are customer retention, customer loyalty, and referrals. Marketing resources allocated to becoming a bigger player in a small market will also increase brand awareness.

Niches can be defined in several ways. It may be a specific type of customer defined by demographics, psychographics, geography, or industry. It can also represent a channel or a specific type of consumer. Or niche players can target an ideal customer such as a large retailer, government entity, or a manufacturer that will buy large volumes of a specific product. Another way to focus on a niche market is to produce or sell only one product. An example is a company that makes only one part but sells it to multiple car companies, or a specialty store that sells only one type of product, such as high-quality pens.

Niche marketers usually respond more quickly to trends and macro-environmental issues impacting their industry. The pet food industry reached $17 billion in U.S. sales in 2008 with 60 percent coming from dog food. Until very recently, the majority of dog owners purchased "mass market" dog food for their pets. Brands like Purina, Pedigree, and Iams were market leaders. Small, niche players such as Innova, Wellness, and Prairie entered the market appealing to pet owners' need for organic or grain-free dog food options for their pets. While these niche players were only a small part of the pet food market, they quickly gained market attention and market share after the pet food recall of 2007. Natural pet food sales topped $1 billion that year and revenues are expected to more than double by 2012 to $2.5 billion.

When a company can deliver better products and superior service to a niche market than its competitors, it can usually charge higher prices, therefore realizing higher margins. The only real downside to a niche penetration strategy is the risk of other competitors entering the market, or potentially saturating the market. If you choose to pursue a niche strategy, your plan should identify and prioritize several target markets so you have a contingency plan in place to grow into other niche markets. When a particular niche strategy succeeds in one market, the same strategy can be applied to new niche markets you want to pursue over time. This continuous strategy of penetrating new markets is highly successful for companies.

## Mass Market Penetration

The objective of a mass market penetration strategy is to create high-volume sales, capture market share, and build a large customer base. Can anyone remember what life was like without Post-its, the magical cubes of paper that can stick to almost anything without damaging its surface? The invention by 3M, rumored to be a mistake, is now seen on every employee's desk, from entrepreneurs to CEOs of Fortune 500 companies. The product line has been expanded to include note pages as well as easel paper that can be stuck on conference room walls. This is truly one product that has mass market appeal.

To capture market share, the mass marketer will need to spend heavily in advertising and promotion, as well as invest in manufacturing to ramp production and inventory. Marketing, advertising, and sales programs should focus on capturing as many new customers as possible within a short period of time. Free trials, discounts, and other sales promotions will increase adoption quickly, resulting in a strong customer base and increased market share.

Penetrating the mass market requires significant investments to allocate internal resources across several departments to serve customers, as well as build multiple distribution channels. The good news is that as volume increases, production costs will be reduced.

A solid baseline of market share and customers may either deter other competitors from entering the market, or it may (and most likely) attract competitors who want a piece of a desirable, growing market. New product pioneers would be wise to have patent protection to bolster competitive entry barriers. But even this doesn't deter some companies from trying. Crocs shoes took the market by storm, but several copycat manufacturers have tried to steal a piece of the lucrative "ugly shoe" market. Crocs, Inc. is now defending their position with 11 patent infringement suits.[1]

Mass market strategies are not only for large companies—they are also often used by small companies that market products which appeal to a large customer base. Just think of the products that are marketed through infomercials, and you will recall many small companies that market to the masses. While businesses that deploy a mass market strategy do not usually focus on creating customer intimacy, there should be customer relationships management programs to build customer loyalty, stimulate re-orders, cross sell products, and help prevent defection when competitors do enter the market. When this happens, be prepared to extend product offerings through line extensions as quickly as possible in order to retain customers, or modify the product for new markets.

## Attract Early Adopters, Maximize Profits

Many businesses initiate a skimming strategy when launching new products. This is technically a pricing strategy, although it is also a target market strategy when directed toward a specific buyer profile. If your business incurred significant expenses in research and development, production, and commercialization, a skimming strategy may be part of your plan to recover some of these initial costs. The idea is to enter a target market with an initial high product price, and get out early as competition enters the market. You can then choose to enter a new market with the same product, introduce a "new and improved" product to the existing market, or exit completely if the market no longer looks attractive. If you have little or no patent protection, other competitors may have greater resources for quickly capturing market share.

If you choose to adopt this strategy, focus on attracting early adopters within target segments to penetrate the market more quickly. The sales force should focus on selling into the largest segments first. A skimming strategy does not typically involve sale promotions as the goal is to achieve sales at high margins; but limited-time free trials can encourage early adoption, and trials can convert to sales quickly. If selling through distributors, consider offering volume discounts to those willing to buy large volumes of product. Skimming can be an effective strategy in segmenting the market. A firm can divide the market into a number of segments and reduce the price at different stages in each, thus acquiring maximum profit from each segment.

A company adopting this strategy should define a transition or exit strategy in advance, and build this into the marketing plan. This will protect margins and eliminate a potentially difficult (and emotional) decision among product managers and other stake-holders. Perhaps most important, you will be prepared to execute the next set of strategies in your marketing plan.

## Market Penetration Strategy Requires Innovation

A market penetration strategy stimulates a target market to increase the rate at which they use a product. This strategy is highly effective for products in a mature or growing life cycle phase. This shows customers new ways to use a product, encouraging them to either use a product more often or to buy it in larger quantities.

Educating customers about new ways to use products will drive increased usage. A few well-known examples with which you are probably familiar include the Fruit Growers Association, which stimulated sales of fruit with the "five times a day cam-paign." Kodak increased sales by showing customers how any event is worth capturing in pictures. Kraft cheese is promoted as a snack, a topping, an ingredient in a recipe, or a dessert. Campbell's soup was repackaged and marketed to show customers how soup can be a great snack in the late afternoon when energy is low and one's thoughts drift to the nearest vending machine for relief. Campbell's also promotes soup as a key ingredient in recipes for main-dish casseroles.

Premium products that were once purchased for special occasions can be marketed as an everyday indulgence. Godiva Chocolatier introduced specialty coffee to turn the everyday ritual of drinking coffee into a rich, indulgent experience. Four of the seven coffee varieties are infused with the rich indulgent flavors of Godiva truffles. Companies with products such as lingerie, beer, or specialty soaps and lotions often market their products as a special or luxury product for everyday use. If you want more examples of how companies stimulate the purchase of their products or extend the life of a product in a mature market, look no further than the aisles of your local grocery store. Consumer product companies will show you how it's done—again and again.

Similar concepts can be applied to B2B markets. In B2B or industrial markets, vol-ume purchase discounts will stimulate demand. This is done by bundling items, offering a "two for one" discount, and giving incentives to stimulate sales and move more prod-ucts. Increased advertising and sales promotions can increase sales by offering discounts or incentives to stimulate purchases.

New target customers also increase product usage. Tums targets not only people with upset stomachs, but it also touts the additional benefits of being a calcium substitute for women who use the product. A Sprint family plan extends the benefits of individual mobile phone use to the entire family. Johnson's baby oil, a product once reserved for babies, is now a perfect choice for anyone wanting softer, smoother skin.

Ingredient branding is another way to leverage and extend brand equity. Ingredient branding is leveraging the brand cachet in one product to develop a new product that has more value as a result of the ingredient brand. This can create new markets, channels, and products. Examples of ingredient brands include Intel, Gore-tex, and Nutrasweet.

In Chapter 43, "Positioning Strategy," you will learn how to effectively communicate and position the value of your solutions to affect the behavior of the specific target market(s) you have selected.

# 43

# Positioning Strategy

The value proposition, positioning statement, and brand identity are three elements at the heart of your marketing plan. Everything you have learned about brand differentiation must now be expressed creatively in your marketing communication programs through these three elements. As Lynn Upshaw, author of *Building Brand Identity*, states so eloquently, positioning sets the direction for all further marketing activity:

> *"A brand's positioning is the compass of its identity, pointing it toward the place where it can leverage the most power in the category in which it competes, and establish the most powerful leverage within the lives of its potential users. How a brand is recognized in the marketplace is based largely on its personality, but what it means in someone's life is derived from its positioning."*

**Positioning** is a term used to describe how customers perceive a product when considering all the competitive alternatives to choose from in a product category. It is the distinct position of your products and services in the mind of your prospective customers. It is not a tag line or a slogan, but a carefully crafted statement that defines the key benefit you would like targeted customers to think of given all the other choices available in the market. The most critical element of a positioning statement is differentiation. A brand cannot be created unless it is differentiated in the market.

In a moment, you will learn how to write a positioning statement that will focus and articulate the unique benefits and differentiation of your solution to targeted customers. This statement will be used in every aspect of your marketing, including collateral, advertising, and promotion—essentially every message and channel in which you communicate.

## Types of Positioning

First, let's look at different ways you can position your solution. There are six primary positioning methods that describe the most common types of positioning strategy for a product or service:

- **Positioning by attribute,** which the automobile industry clearly demonstrates. BMW stresses handling and engineering efficiency; Volvo emphasizes safety and durability; Volkswagon emphasizes practicality.

- **Positioning by price or quality,** which is how consumers distinguish between a low-price leader like Wal-Mart and a high-end retailer like Neiman Marcus.

- **Positioning with respect to use or application,** such as Johnson & Johnson did with baby shampoo. They repositioned the product for people who wash their hair frequently and wanted a mild shampoo, increasing market share from 3 percent to 14 percent.

- **Positioning by the product user** to deliver a target message, such as "Choosy Mothers Choose Jif."

- **Positioning with respect to a competitor,** as Avis famously did with the "We're #2 So We Try Harder" campaign.

- **Positioning by problem,** which is targeting a product or service as a solution to solve a specific problem. An example is Federal Express: "When it absolutely, positively has to be there overnight."

As you begin the process of developing your positioning statement, answer the following questions (see Figure 43.1):

- How are your products and services positioned now? Examine your current marketing materials and advertising messages.

- How do you want your target customers to think about and position your products and services in the future?

- What actions must you take to get from your current position to what you envision for your brand?

- How is this position different or better than your competitors?

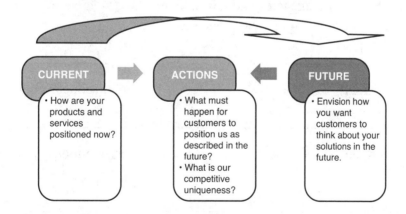

**Figure 43.1** *Positioning your brand*

Positioning statements are comprised of five elements: **target market, product/service identification, frame of reference, point of difference or uniqueness,** and **justification** for the uniqueness. Except for two, most of the elements are obvious. A product's frame of reference refers to the options your target market has available to them to fulfill a specific need. While it is important to narrow focus on a specific target market, it is usually (but not always) best to expand the frame of reference because you want to include possible substitutes. For example, if the product was an iPod, the frame of reference may be "portable music devices."

Differentiation is the attribute that sets your product apart from all others. It refers to the one specific benefit (two at the most) that you want people to associate with your solution. It's tempting to say, "Yes, but my product does X, Y, and Z"—but if you try to communicate more than one or two benefits, it will only confuse a prospective customer and the product will be dropped completely out of mind. Differentiation is the key to positioning and branding.

The last element in the positioning statement is justification, and this is the evidence or facts that back up the promised results. This needs to be a fact, not wishful thinking or an opinion. It is a fact that gives the buyer justification for why your solution is better.

## Create a Positioning Statement

Now write a positioning statement for your solution. If possible, do this with your marketing team to brainstorm all the possible options to arrive at the best possible outcome. The draft wording of your positioning statement may seem a bit contrived, but remember it *is not intended to be used literally in a tag line or messaging*. It is meant to be used internally (and shared with agencies and consultants who develop marketing materials) to guide and focus your messaging and strategies.

To_____         _____
        (Target Market)                                    (Product/Service)

is the _____ that _____
             (Frame of Reference)                        (Differentiation/Key Benefit)

because

_____
                      (Justification)

## Example Positioning Statements:

### Federal Express:

*To deadline-oriented business people, Federal Express is the overnight package delivery service that is the most reliable because of its sophisticated package tracking system.*

### Clinic Service Corporation:

*To physician's office administrators who manage an office with 4–8 physicians, Clinic Service Corporation is the medical billing company that provides intimate, personalized customer care for every client while delivering industry leading ROI and profitability to physicians because we collect 99.7 percent of total billed revenue.*

Positioning is a key component of brand equity. Strong positioning infers differentiation which leads to the ability to command a higher price. Higher prices should translate to higher profits, which is the reward for differentiating your product from competitors.

The outcome of a positioning statement is a **value proposition** that is a simple and concise statement of the benefits for your targeted customer. For example:

- Volvo: The safe, durable car for your family.
- Geiko: The money you could be saving.
- DiGiorno: It's not delivery. It's DiGiorno.
- Southwest Airlines: The no-frills, low-cost, fun airline.

Several factors ultimately influence a brand image. Companies like Ben and Jerry's, The Body Shop, Starbucks, and Apple have very strong brands that are linked to social responsibility and innovation. What makes the brands unique and memorable is consistency of messaging across integrated marketing programs.

Another factor is *uniqueness* of position in the marketplace. For example, Starbucks CEO Howard Schultz believes the quality of the company's work force is their "only sustainable competitive advantage." Starbucks' relentless focus on employees is visible in the ground-breaking health insurance plan for part-time employees and in the way employees are trained. Even though the company has grown from a small coffee shop in Seattle to one of the world's most recognizable brands, the company has maintained a culture that is hard for even mom and pop coffee shops to imitate.

## *Characteristics of Successful Positioning*

The message is clearly **targeted** toward the audience you are trying to reach:

- "Gillette, the best a man can get"
- "Choosy Moms Choose Jif"

The brand promises **relevant** benefits connected to the customer's life:

- Staples: "Easy Button"
- Clairol Hair Color: "You're worth it"

Supporting **facts** back up the stated benefit:

- "Trident is recommended by four out of five dentists for patients who chew gum."
- "Children's Tylenol. The first choice of pediatricians."

The positioning and brand personality communicate a **congruent** message:

- Wheaties: "The Breakfast of Champions"
- IBM: "Think"

# 44

# What Is Your Brand Worth?

The term "branding" was first associated with ranchers burning a mark on a steer so that one rancher could identify his steer from another. The idea of branding a product or service is really the same; you are burning your brand image in the minds of consumers. Building a strong brand image and personality demands that you understand the essence of your product or service and succinctly convey it to your target customer. Creating and communicating your company's brand identity is critically important in a competitive and volatile marketplace.

The evidence of a strong brand is its **Brand Equity**. It is the total accumulated value or worth of a brand, which consists of the tangible and intangible assets that the brand contributes to the company, both financially and in terms of selling leverage. Brand equity, while hard to measure, is worth a considerable amount on a company's P&L statement. Coca Cola's brand equity is estimated to be worth $67 million, and even relatively new companies like eBay and Google have earned considerable brand equity in a short period of time.

## Personify Your Brand

The position of a product is strengthened when it is personified. **Brand Personality** describes the personification of the brand by expressing its qualities as human qualities. Personifying a product is especially important if there is product or service parity in your industry as it may be the key element that differentiates your product from competitors. For example, when you think about buying something as mundane as batteries, would you buy Energizer, Duracell, or some other brand? Chances are, as you make that decision, you are subconsciously attracted to the brand personality, and this will influence your decision. Are you drawn more toward the cute, pink Energizer bunny that keeps going and going, or matter-of-fact Duracell, the strong copper-top battery?

When a brand is defined with human characteristics, you give your product or service a personality that people can relate to on an emotional level. **Brand Essence** can be defined as the values, emotions, and core elements used to describe a brand.

The most effective brands are charismatic. Emotions outweigh logic even when it comes to technical purchases. This is evidenced by people who desire an Apple computer instead of a PC despite the fact that the company he or she works for uses a PC platform.

People are drawn to brands that connect with their own personalities, or the person they aspire to be. Consider how brand personification applies to ski resorts in Colorado. Each resort conveys a distinct personality. Aspen would likely be a celebrity, Vail may be a refined and worldly traveler, and Arapahoe Basin is a Gen Y dude who enjoys adventurous skiing. In Colorado, where skiers have such close proximity to so many world-class resorts, brand identity helps skiers identify with their own personality and preferences. Skiers will choose a mountain resort that is relevant and meaningful to them or what they would like to be—glamorous, international, or adventurous.

Other aspects like symbols, logos, and tag lines anchor a brand and effectively tie brand identity to brand essence. The famous Nike swoosh communicates a sense of competition, speed, and performance and is easily recognized when disaggregated from the Nike name. It is so recognizable and effective that the brand identity functions in much the same way as ancient Egyptian hieroglyphs, conveying a meaning and personality through its logo design. McDonald's "Golden Arches" are recognizable around the world, as is Target's bulls-eye and Apple Computer's symbolic image of a fruit. Coca-Cola's strong image has become an international symbol of American culture, earning the number-one spot as the world's most valuable brand.

A strong brand name needs to be managed so the equity does not depreciate. Included in that task are continuous R&D, skillful advertising, and appropriate levels of trade and customer service throughout the distribution channel. And remember, *while brand management is usually a function of the marketing department, brand equity is the responsibility of everyone in an organization.*

## *Results of Strong Brand Equity*

- **Reduced marketing costs** as a result of a high level of consumer brand awareness and loyalty.
- **More trade leverage bargaining with distributors and retailers** because customers expect them to carry the brand. Typically only the top one or two national brands can command shelf space long-term. New brands are given a couple of months to prove their value.
- **Higher prices** because the brand has higher perceived quality.
- **Ability to launch brand extensions** to capitalize on credibility already established.
- **Protection against price competition** from other products.
- **Financial** contribution to company.

# 45

# Design Your Brand Personality and Essence

So far we have discussed how marketing successes are built on the foundation of positioning and branding. But what are some first steps in developing your own brand? You can use the following four-step creative process to describe your brand personality and essence:

1. Begin by thinking of preferred adjectives that describe your ideal brand image.
2. Consider your current brand image versus your desired brand image. Describe each and consider how far apart they are.
3. Describe your competitors and their brand identity using the same criteria. Describe their brand personality and brand essence. Think about how much they have invested in their total brand equity.
4. Consider your target audience. How will your brand identity and personality appeal to their emotional wants and needs? How significant and worthwhile is your product or service to their life?

Another way to evaluate your brand is to draw associations with already identified icons. Is your brand a Cadillac or a Jeep? Is your service more like a conservative Charlton Heston or a rebellious James Dean? Would a willow or an oak tree symbolize your brand's essence? What's your style? Are you Abercrombie, Armani, or Talbots? Are you more like sushi or steak? Comparisons to people, objects, or even other products and services help to further define your brand.

Branding and positioning are such vast topics that I recommend you read more on the subject. An "oldie but goodie" resource is *Positioning: The Battle for Your Mind* by Jack Trout and Al Reese. If you would like sage wisdom from one of the world's leading brand authorities, read *A New Brand World* by Scott Bedbury. Bedbury led branding and marketing for both Nike and Starbucks, so he knows what he's talking about. His perspectives are included in Section I, "Purpose," where he articulates that effective branding is aligned with a company's mission and values.

Another expert on the subject of branding is Mike Moser, a San Francisco-based branding expert and author of *United We Brand*. He worked with two of the fastest-growing companies in the world, Cisco and Dell, and in the following article, he shares his insights on how to build a brand.[1]

## Moser: Brand Roadmap Can Drive Company's Marketing

**Reece:** How would you describe the brand roadmap process you present in United *We Brand,* and why is it important to create a brand roadmap?

**Moser:** The process involves four steps: defining a company's core brand values, core brand message, brand personality, and brand icons. A brand roadmap helps everyone in an organization have a really clear idea of what the company stands for. Every decision that is made in a company can actually come from their brand values, which is why I start with values in the process. Most people equate branding with the external image of a company, not the internal values, and to me, that is where the greatest weakness is in companies.

**Reece:** How have you used the roadmap in the accounts you worked on?

**Moser:** I was the creative director on Dell Computers for 11 years. They were growing at an unbelievable pace and at one point they were hiring 150 people a week, and went from $280 million in sales to $20 billion. Added to that, we had a 53 percent turnover rate at the agency. There was no document that guided all the new people coming into the company, so this is what caused me to develop the brand roadmap. I worked with two of the four fastest-growing companies in the world—Cisco and Dell—so as new people were coming into the company, it was critical that they got up to speed in a day.

**Reece:** Did the brand change a lot in your time working on the Dell account?

**Moser:** No, and that's because Michael Dell was just so clear from the day he started the company. When you see a strong leader like Bill Gates or Steve Jobs at the top who has a strong vision and strong sense of what they stand for, and they stay at the helm, their company will have a strong brand. For example, Michael's model of eliminating the middleman and being accountable to every single customer, whether a customer was buying from him out of the back of his car, or when he had a $20 million company, remained the same. The value of accountability was huge for him.

**Reece:** How should the brand roadmap be communicated in a company?

**Moser:** It starts in the marketing department because those are the individuals who are responsible for the external image of the company, and it works back through the organization. The HR department might say the document is great because it defines the parameters of the values of the people they want to hire. The board of directors may like it because it attracts the kind of people they want on the board.

Then it goes to research and development. For example, if they work at Dell, they might say, "Hey, this gives us a good heads-up that if we are responsible for the one-to-one relationship with the customer, and if accountability is the key value, then we better make machines that are bulletproof." And this may start a conversation with engineering, and so on. That's how it moves through a company.

**Reece:** Your second step, core messaging, is probably the hardest part of the process because it's so hard to bring messaging down to three or four words. How do you advise companies to do this?

**Moser:** I ask the question, "If the company went away today, what would employees, suppliers, or customers say is missing in their lives? What is the emotional hit from that?" When you go through this exercise, there are generally one or two things that really stand out. For example, what would people miss about Nordstrom? It's not their products; it's the service. So this process leads to the core message and then you ask, "How are we going to express this core message to our various audiences?" That one message, that one sentence, should keep coming back.

**Reece:** How can a company that sells a commoditized product, such as computer storage or phone service, differentiate its services?

**Moser:** Not everything can be differentiated. That's when you get into personality and icons. Think of the company like a person. What differentiates them is their personality. For example, Motel 6 is virtually the same as Ramada Inn or another hotel along the highway. But because Tom Bodet is delivering that message with a charming, friendly, Southern twang, they are differentiating themselves in the marketplace.

**Reece:** Why don't more companies use a distinct voice or mnemonics to differentiate their brand since it's such a distinctive anchor?

**Moser:** I suppose it's because so many decisions like this are done by committee versus by an individual, and the personification of the brand often gets lost.

**Reece:** What are the most important characteristics to consider when developing the brand personality for a product or service?

**Moser:** Likeability. If you are trying to sell something, likeability is a key motivator. For example, Nike's personality is total commitment—"just do it." The icons they used were people who had done one thing well, and done it their entire life. They said, "In a whole culture that doesn't commit to anything, that moves from marriage to marriage, job to job, relationship to relationship, and location to location, we are going to stand for total commitment to one thing."

So that was their core message and they picked personalities who epitomized that. People like Tiger Woods, who has committed to one thing since he was 3 years old. Or Michael Jordan and John McEnroe. When I say likable, it doesn't mean not controversial. McEnroe is loud and abrasive, and leads with his emotions. Tiger Woods is quiet and introverted and just gets the job done. But the brand essence of Nike didn't change because they have these two opposite personalities.

**Reece:** Your fourth step on developing brand icons does not necessarily equate "icon" with "logo" or "packaging." It means much more than that in your definition.

**Moser:** To me it means the image of the brand that comes up in a person's mind, and through whatever senses the image comes up, are the icons for that brand. I'm stretching the literal meaning of icon, but if I walk by Mrs. Fields cookies, the smell of cookies can fire on that image in my mind.

**Reece:** So it can be a smell, a taste, a touch?

**Moser:** Yes, like Velcro. When you touch Velcro, it says Velcro. Anything that has to do with your senses takes your brand and externalizes it so it becomes a sensual experience for people.

# 46

# Customer Strategies

*"People have become relatively immune to messages targeted at them. The way to reach your customers is to create an experience with them."*

Successful companies have strong, focused customer strategies for retaining and growing the customer base they worked so hard to build. As we discussed previously, the best way to know if you are satisfying customers' needs, wants, and expectations is to ask them. Ongoing periodic surveys, advisory group discussions, and other means of engaging customers in a dialogue will help you stay on top of customer preferences.

Data analysis will help you understand the frequency and total value of customer purchases, customer retention rate, percentage of customer "wallet share," customer delight (are they satisfied enough to refer others to you?), and customer mind share (is your company the first to come to mind in a category when making a purchasing decision?). It will also help you spot buyer trends over time, as well as identify customers who are at risk of defecting to a competitor. As you become more accustomed to acquiring and analyzing this type of information, it will enable you to continuously innovate and improve your customer strategies.

## Customer Loyalty Objectives and Strategies

The key to creating successful customer relationship management strategies is to understand what you want to achieve. Customer retention is critical to the profitability and long term success of your business. The objectives and strategies you develop in this area will generate both short-term revenue and long-term success for your business. Here are a few to consider:

- **Increase Customer Retention.** As discussed previously, it is five times more cost effective and profitable to retain customers than it is to find new customers. The profitability of a customer increases over time, so one of your strategies should be customer retention.

- **Reward Loyal "A" Customers.** It would be wise to create strategies and programs that reward your best customers. Consider offering increasingly higher levels of rewards to customers who achieve a certain level of spending. For example, Nordstrom gives customers cash-back rewards based on what they spend. Hotels reward customers for their loyalty by awarding them free nights, double points during off-peak days, and upgrades.

- **Encourage Frequency.** A membership program can provide special benefits to its members. For B2B companies, the benefits can include access to research, informative newsletters, mentoring, and networking. For Business-to-Customer (B2C) companies, incentives and upgrades can keep customers engaged. Airlines do this by increasing benefits and rewards for frequent flyers.

- **Improve Customer Insight.** If you want to learn about the wants and needs of individual customers, or segments of customers, establish the mechanisms to gather this information fluidly and directly from customers. Develop communication programs and mechanisms that can be executed dynamically using your website, email marketing program, customer forums, and regular meetings that salespeople have with customers. Reward salespeople who create a closed loop feedback system to the marketing department, and reward customers by sharing the information you have learned with them—and of course, by taking action on the feedback they give to you.

- **Organize to Focus on Customers, Not Products.** This is a big goal if your company is currently organized around products. It could mean a restructuring of product teams and entire divisions. The first priority is to focus on sales and service to major customer accounts and valuable market segments. This may require a restructuring of the sales force to allow salespeople to spend more time with customers. Or it could mean switching from VAR or distributor relationships to a company sales force.

- **Deliver Knowledge and Expertise.** If a company differentiates itself from competitors based upon knowledge and service, then training programs and processes should be developed for the different audiences that interact with customers, including salespeople, marketing professionals, customer service, and operations teams. Don't forget to plan and budget training for suppliers, distributors, and partners that sell and work with customers. This needs to be done for each new partner, and on an ongoing basis to all partners, to increase knowledge of your solutions and stimulate sales.

- **Improve Service Delivery and Fulfillment.** When Wal-Mart initially introduced their inventory and supply chain requirements to vendors several years ago, suppliers scrambled to meet their needs. While most customers are not the size of Wal-Mart, you will have service delivery issues to fulfill. If delivery preferences, process integration, or logistics is a priority for customers, business processes may need to be redesigned to fulfill customer requirements. A customer that demands reliability and responsiveness may require an around-the-clock help line or reassurance that security and back-up systems are in place.

- **Implement Customer Segment Marketing Programs.** Refer back to Chapter 14, "Micro Perspective: Focus on High-Value Customers," where you completed the A, B, C, and Deadbeat Customer exercise. In the third and fourth parts of the exercise, you noted how service should be unique and delivered at increasingly higher levels for your best customers. You also noted that marketing programs should be unique for different customer segments. How will you service and market to different customer segments so you focus investments on your best customers? What is your strategy to migrate customers to a higher level?

- **Measure Customer Delight.** Create a system to gather ongoing customer feedback to continuously learn and make improvements across several areas of your business. You can implement the Net Promoter Score (explained in Chapter 15, "Love Your Loyal Customers"), implement polls and surveys on your website and social media, implement real-time focus groups to improve products or quickly adjust marketing messages and marketing programs, or use a combination of several methods.

- **Improve Customer Experience.** Customer experience has become an important way that company's differentiate and compete in commodity markets. What experiences can you create that will inspire customers to return again and again…and even pay more for? The Wynn and Encore hotels in Las Vegas stand out from the other hotels on the strip. The hotel's beautiful and unexpected visual elements captivate you the moment you enter. Intimate chill music enhances the experience and draws you into an environment you never want to leave. If you can create experiences like this, your customers will pay more for them.

- **Create a Customer-Focused Culture.** A great customer experience starts with great employee experience. Implementing strategies to nurture a healthy vibrant culture is the catalyst for creating great customer experiences. The Excellence Playa Mujeres creates a different and unexpected experience with their five-star all-inclusive resort. The lavish spa and fitness center and eight gourmet restaurants are luxuries usually not found in an all-inclusive resort. The best part of the experience however is the exceptional service from friendly, attentive staff. The world-class service and luxury surroundings are a first-class experience at an all-inclusive price.

You have learned about the importance of customer strategies throughout the book. As you develop your own strategies, give particular attention to those that will improve your culture and customer service.

# 47

# Listen and Respond

Dell Computers was once a company praised for the innovative approach they brought to the PC industry. The company was well-known for built-to-order PCs, competitive prices, and dependable customer service. But when Dell's sales began to fall and customer complaints were on the rise, it took a long time before Michael Dell stepped in to help stop the bleeding.

The Internet created a very public forum for customers to air their complaints, damaging Dell's once pristine image. The biggest complaints came from customers who were put off by customer service agents in off-shore call centers. In response to this, and for a price, customers now have 24/7 phone access from trained North-American-based technicians who will respond in two minutes or less.

To Dell's credit, they eventually responded to complaints, but with mixed reaction from customers. Dell says, "We listened, reacted, and changed. Dell Services offers access to qualified experts, fast response time, and great value." However, even though Dell professes "We're Back to #1," customers continue to log complaints on blogs and forums.

A Google search for "Dell Customer Service" reveals blog posts and stories that are less than flattering. In fact several are hostile remarks made by customers who are not just angry, but want to retaliate. This isn't the search result any company would want to surface on the first page of a Google search. What drives customers to the point that they want to seek revenge? Is it lack of response from a company or is it because they feel complete indifference or disregard for the bad experience they have caused someone?

What can you learn from this lesson? Customer retention is a whole lot easier than customer win-back. As your marketing and growth strategies succeed, make sure your customer service strategy keeps pace. Keep your finger on the pulse by monitoring both employee performance and customer feedback. How many reports or quarters of lagging sales will it take to get the attention of management? If the culture doesn't truly honor customers and continuous improvement, it is more likely that more time will be spent finger pointing than resolving problems.

## Emotion Is Viral

Dell is not alone when it comes to a damaging public outcry. It can happen to any company whether they are deemed good corporate citizens or not. The key question to ask is, "What drives the popularity of consumer-generated media?" At the most basic level is the emotional need to be heard. People who feel "wronged" want to be heard as much as they want to evangelize what they love. The Internet and social media are accessible and easy to use, and they provide a platform for those who want to voice an opinion—right or wrong, good or bad.

When people have a good experience, they will tell others. When people had a bad experience in the pre-Internet days, they told an average of 9–13 people. Now when people have a bad customer experience, they tell *thousands* of people. The Internet provides the platform and people provide the emotion and the stories. Why do bad stories resonate so well with the media and other people? Let me answer that question with an example.

Several years ago, June 16, 2006 to be exact, a man named Vincent Ferrari called AOL to cancel his father's AOL account. The call center agent protested against the request and asked Ferrari to explain his reasons for cancelling the account. Ferrari said his father didn't use the account and didn't even have the software loaded on his computer anymore. The agent continued to protest against Ferrari's request and proceeded to explain how many hours his father had used in the past and asked to speak with him. An infuriated Ferrari demanded the agent to "cancel the account," saying he didn't "know how to make it any clearer." What the agent didn't know was that Ferrari was recording the call and that he was an avid blogger.

Here's where the viral nature of the story takes over. Ferrari was so angry he shared his story on the Internet, which was picked up by CNBC. But that's not all. When CNBC reporters attempted to cancel an AOL account, a representative hung up on them. It took 45 minutes before the account could be cancelled. When Matt Lauer and other journalists conducted interviews and continued to report the story, Vincent Ferrari was launched into stardom.

That was 2006. In 2008, I checked to see if Vincent had become even more famous and a Google search returned nearly 300,000 results. By early 2010, Vincent had become even more famous. Search results doubled to 600,000. How did one guy command so much attention? Can a few call center agents inflict this much damage? Emotion is viral. It picks up steam when other people can empathize with the issue because they have had a similar experience.

It's also notable that some industries are "easy pickins." Do you recall our discussion in Section IV? Airlines, car rental companies, cable companies, phone companies, and so on, have a large customer base and have been slow to the draw when it comes to providing customer service. Even though a company may have implemented significant change in a response to prior incidents, the Internet can be rather unforgiving. Consumer-generated media spreads and events become magnified. Search engines have a *long* memory, leaving a lasting impression on your brand.

In Section V we will discuss ways that you can proactively respond to angry customers, and how to turn even the most hostile customer into a happy supporter.

# 48

# Customers Are Your Best Advisors

Creating a Customer Advisory Board can help you achieve several customer objectives. These types of forums are most often used by companies to gather customer insight, but depending upon how, where, and who is asked to participate, they are also a rewarding experience for your most valuable customers.

Many companies, large and small, hold customer advisory meetings quarterly or twice a year to gain a deeper understanding of customer needs and how to improve products, services, and relationships with customers. An advisory group consisting of top customers and thought leaders across several industry groups fosters an interactive discussion for everyone to learn from each other. When thought leaders are chosen from different industry segments, there is less concern about sharing sensitive competitive information; therefore, ideas and suggestions can flow freely.

A key benefit for companies that implement an advisory board is the ability for business leaders to hear, first-hand valuable information about key trends shaping an industry. This can be an important competitive advantage. Additionally, a unique setting and interactive discussion gives customers the opportunity to co-create innovative new solutions, creating a win/win situation for both companies. It benefits the customer's business and potentially adds to the revenue stream for the sponsor company if the solution is commercialized. As customers play a key role in driving innovation and product development, it will help businesses make important decisions about priorities, investments, technology, marketing, and sales strategies.

Hewlett-Packard (HP) is a great example of a company that began implementing a customer advisory program that has surpassed their expectations about the strategic value it has created over time. DreamWorks, the innovative film company founded by Stephen Spielberg, Jeffrey Katzenberg, and David Geffen, is a good customer of HP. During a customer advisory meeting, HP asked how they could improve the workstation that DreamWorks used to create animated films. The animators commented that they didn't like the USB ports on the back of the computer because it was not convenient to plug in other devices to the workstation. They didn't want to hassle with plugging equipment into the ports on the back of the computer; they wanted the ports to be on the front of the computer. The customers viewed this as a disruption to their work flow and asked HP if they could fix it.

HP wanted to please one of their most valuable customers, and in the scheme of things, the design issue was a fairly easy fix for HP. The fact that HP not only listened to the advice from DreamWorks, but acted on it, demonstrated to DreamWorks that they were more than just a customer to HP: They were a partner. In fact, they were so pleased that they suggested inviting some of their competitors to join the advisory group, some of whom used HP products and some who didn't. The advisory group grew to include all of the major Hollywood studios, including Pixar, whose Chairman and CEO was Apple's Steve Jobs. The CTO of Pixar participated in the advisory councils, putting aside the competitive nature of HP and Apple, and saw the value his company received as a member of the customer advisory group comprised of top industry thought leaders.

Perhaps the biggest outcome of the advisory group was that it created a customer-focused culture within the organization. HP has a typical organizational structure for companies its size. There is a "front-end/back-end" structure, where the product development is handled by one organization and the marketing and selling of the product is handled by a different organization. Getting customer input into R&D is difficult in this type of structure, and it is easy for product development to become internally focused on what they design, not necessarily what the customer wants and needs.

The advisory councils put the customers and their needs right in the face of the product designers. As a result, HP is very focused on designing customer needs-based products, and they are taking market share from competitors who design only cost-focused workstations.

# 49

# Customers Are Cocreaters

If your objective is to improve customer experience, there are several ways you can integrate customer experience into different parts of the value chain process, from product conceptualization to marketing. For example, you can create an interactive Web site that enables customers to customize products and make design suggestions. Ducati Motor Holdings, makers of the sexy Italian motorcycle, invite customers to visit their virtual Tech Café where they can present designs and ideas. Hallmark cards encourages customer to submit ideas and suggestions on both products and channels. Nike engages customers in coproducing products via their Web site. Volvo has been able to increase time to market by involving customers in virtual product concept tests during the product development process.[1]

For many years, the software industry has engaged customers to improve products as well as participate in the role of product support specialist by providing advice and support to their peers. This is often done through "user groups," which have become a critically important customer group in most software companies like Cisco and Microsoft. Software companies also have development groups where members develop new products that are an extension of the company's platform technology. Groups take on the role of product conceptualizer, designer, tester, and/or product marketer.

In all of these examples, customers play an important functional role that actually helps companies improve several parts of their business. Another outcome is improved customer experience and deeper customer relationships.

## The $1 Million Prize

Netflix launched the ultimate contest when it challenged customers and innovators to improve the company's ability to accurately predict movie preferences in the recommendation system by 10 percent. The prize: $1 million. This was a challenge that Netflix scientists had been working on for over a decade and were unable to solve. It took three years for a group of seven team members from Austria, Israel, Canada, and the U.S. to develop the winning algorithms. The group of statisticians, software and electrical engineers, and researchers and was originally comprised of three teams that competed against each other but decided to join forces in the eleventh hour to collaborate and win. In fact, the submission was entered just 24 minutes prior to the conclusion of the contest in July 2009, nearly three years after the launch of the Netflix Prize.

The contest was truly innovative on several levels. Netflix released private data consisting of 100 million anonymous movie ratings rated on a scale of one to five stars. Teams and contestants formed their own groups, many collaborating virtually around the world. The winning team had never met each other until they traveled to New York to collect their prize. The $1 million is a large sum to the winners, but was a relatively small investment for Netflix considering their own team had worked on cracking the code for over ten years. It's also a huge win for customers as the recommendation engine is one of the most important benefits of the Netflix service. Another surprising uniqueness of the competition is who owns the intellectual property. The winning team was required to publish its methodology so that other people and businesses could benefit. The team licensed its work to Netflix and is free to license it to other companies.[2]

The competition was so successful that Netflix immediately announced a second contest to win $1 million prize. This time the challenge is much harder: To predict movie enjoyment by members who do not rate movies. Demographic and psychographic data will be provided to contestants who will compete in the 18-month-long contest.

When companies collaborate with customers to solve problems, it opens the door to accelerate innovation and customer experience on several levels. The ideas presented in this chapter can be applied to any business in any industry to improve customer relationships and add value to all stakeholders. Develop customer strategies with an open mind and creative spirit. When you allow customers to challenge you to improve service and experience, your company will be better as a result.

## Customer Engagement: A New Business Model

Threadless is a company that has created an entirely new business model that is built entirely around the customer. In fact, the customer does all of the sales, marketing, and design for the company. Founder Jake Nickell has taken a commodity business, making T-shirts, and completely reinvented the company so the customer makes most of the decisions, and does so virtually. Nickell started the company like a lot of entrepreneurs do—by accident.

Nickell was a CompUSA salesperson who spent his evenings as a part-time art student. He enjoyed dabbling in Web design and conversing online with other like-minded illustrators who were part of Dreamless.org., an online forum for illustrators. Members passed designs back and forth to see who could create the best design. When Nickell won a design contest, it gave him the idea to make a real business of it. He teamed up with friend, Jacob DeHart, and they held their first T-shirt design contest in November 2000. Illustrators from the forum submitted designs for the contest and voted for their favorites. The $12.00 T-shirts sold out quickly because the customers designed them, liked them, and wanted to own what they had actually created. They also wanted to tell friends, family, and of course other designers to buy their designs. Since T-shirts designs sold out quickly, it eliminated unwanted inventory, a problem most T-shirt manufacturers and retailers are forced to deal with.

Artists loved having their designs selected and purchased by other designers because there were few places for designers to show their work. Word about Threadless spread in the design community, and by 2002, Threadless had sold $100,000 worth of T-shirts and built a community of 10,000 members. By 2006, sales had reached $18 million and members grew to an astonishing 700,000. In 2007, sales grew another 200 percent, to an estimated $30 million.[3] 2007 was the peak year for memberships with more than 200,000 members joining the community.

Threadless is a new business model that is entirely built around what the customer wants. Its shareholders are the community. If an innovative business model can be created based on something as ordinary as a T-shirt, what can you create with your customers?

# 50

# Product and Service Strategy

All products go through four distinct stages, called product life cycle (PLC) stages. Each step presents its own opportunities and challenges that should be addressed in your marketing strategy. It is important to correlate strategies according to the PLC stage because each stage presents different revenue and profitability implications, and places very different demands on the sales, marketing, operations, product, and supply chain departments of an organization. This section will outline issues and their corresponding implications to take into account as you develop product and service strategies.

## Product Life Cycle Stages

**Introduction:** As new products are introduced, sales tend to be slow (but not always). Profitability will be negative or minimal as significant costs are incurred to introduce the product in the marketplace.

**Growth:** As market adoption increases, revenues and profitability increase. This period of time can last many years.

**Maturity:** As market share increases and market penetration reaches saturation levels among buyers in your target market, sales revenue will peak and profits will level off or begin a slow decline. Competition usually increases and new strategies are needed to maintain sales.

**Decline:** At this stage, sales and profits decline after leveling off for the reasons stated above.

## Introduction

You want to be mindful of both the challenges and rewards of launching new products. If you are introducing a new product in a new market, the first mover advantages include the ability to capture new customers in desirable market segments, a higher likelihood of creating repeat customers, and the ability to position your product as the category leader in the customer's mind before competitors arrive on the scene. If you are marketing a technology product, technology leadership is especially important, and hopefully you have patents and trademarks as barriers to entry for other competitors.

One of the biggest disadvantages of launching new products is the high marketing costs to introduce the product. You need advertising and promotion to build awareness. And to further stress financial matters, R&D and manufacturing costs can be significant. Since sales start at virtually zero, little to no profit is realized during the initial introductory stage. To ease the impact on the bottom line, many businesses will implement a price skimming strategy (more on this later in the chapter) during the introductory stage to recoup the new product development costs. If you use the same distribution channels that you currently use for other products and services, this will help reduce costs as well as time to market.

Your initial goal should be to strategically move into one or two market segments. As these become successful, another product can be added to move into a new segment. When this is successful, the first product can be introduced into another market segment. This stair-step approach creates incremental growth to cross sell products into various market segments and build market share while reducing risk.

## Growth

The growth stage begins when there is a sharp increase in sale revenue. As sales increase and marketing costs decline or hold steady, profitability rises. Manufacturing costs decrease as production increases, which also contributes to profitability. Prices should remain the same or be lowered slightly as new competitors enter the market.

During the growth stage, you should move into target market segments and develop new products and services to sell to existing customers. Also look for ways to increase product quality by adding new features and/or product extensions. New strategic alliances and channel partnerships will expand your reach to new markets and new customers; therefore, distribution options should be evaluated.

As new competitors enter the market, advertising, promotion, and positioning messages will shift focus from creating market awareness to influencing buyer preference. Depending how aggressive the growth plan is, marketing costs can continue to rise as your company expands into new market segments to get a larger share of the market.

## Maturity

The maturity stage in the PLC lasts the longest and usually consists of two periods. The first period is stabilization and is marked by a leveling off of sales. This can be caused by several factors such as market saturation, increased competition, or the lack of any new distribution channels to sell products or services into. During the second half of the maturity stage, sales begin to decline. This is the result of factors that occur during the stabilization period, which is now compounded by customers who begin to switch to other competitive or alternative products.

As competition heats up, price cuts begin to take place in the market. Marketing and promotion costs increase as competitors battle it out for market share. Companies fight back by increasing R&D expenditures to design new and improved products and line extensions.

It is no surprise that this PLC period presents the biggest challenge for most companies. Some battle it out until there are only a few market leaders left while others retreat from the market to pursue more profitable products and markets. If you have a product in this stage, you should give careful consideration to the exit strategy and not be too quick to eliminate it. After all, significant time and expense has been expended to nurture the product to this point and many well known products can remain in the maturity stage for decades. Before pulling a product, exhaust all the options you have available to profitably market the product in either new market segments (vertical and/or geographic) or through new channels. For example, a product that has been sold exclusively in specialty stores could be sold in high-volume distribution channels.

Mature products can be extended by converting non-customers who are using a substitute product. An example is beer drinkers who switch to wine. Or morning cola drinkers who switch to energy drinks. A desirable strategy is to attract a younger customer base that has not yet experienced the product. They will become customers for a long period of time, and consequentially increase the time a product stays in the maturity PLC stage.

Another strategy to revive a product in the late maturity stage is to aggressively pursue your competitor's customers. This is done through differentiated positioning and sales promotions that provide incentive to try a new brand. Another strategy is to increase the rate at which a new product is consumed by repositioning it. Orange juice became known as a product that was "not just for breakfast anymore." Arm and Hammer, a product that has been around for decades, was repositioned as a refrigerator deodorizer. Popcorn is a healthy snack to eat anytime, not just movie food. "Got Milk?" was an effective strategy and marketing campaign that repositioned milk as a hip beverage endorsed by celebrities.

## Decline

This stage is marked by—you guessed it—steadily declining sales. A company with products in this PLC stage needs to decide if they want to discontinue the product or slowly reduce the resources that are allocated to support the product. If the latter is the course of action, a company would reduce the sales force that supports the product, stop or dramatically reduce the amount of advertising and promotion, and eliminate R&D investments. These changes will improve cash flow.

Products in decline require very little marketing and sales promotion. Consider directing your sales and marketing efforts toward distributors to persuade them to continue carrying your product. You can also direct more time and attention to the sales people who sell the product. As sales of a product decline, you may notice that sales people will begin to gravitate toward selling other more successful products. You may need to increase communication and sales incentive programs as a way to keep them interested and in the game.

If you decide to discontinue the product, be sure to evaluate all exit strategy costs to understand the true impact on the P&L. The decision to eliminate a product should not be taken lightly and usually sparks a lot of debate. Companies that do not have a clear product exit strategy tend to err on one extreme or the other. Some err on the side of keeping the product long after customer interest diminishes, using up precious internal resources. On the flip side are companies that drop the product too quickly, causing confusion with customers and employees. Ideally, key product stakeholders from multiple teams should meet to flush out every possible alternative prior to discontinuing a product. The lesson to learn in either case is to have a process established for exiting products *before* there is a need.

## Are You a Pioneer or a Follower?

Pioneers, the companies that are first to market, take on both the opportunity for huge success as well as significant risk. The biggest reasons companies pursue a pioneer or first mover advantage is because they have an opportunity to establish a market, creating not only market share, but establishing a premier brand in the customer's mind. If early adopters love the product, the company will continue to build market share and establish itself as a market leader before competitors begin to make a lot of noise.

Some companies prefer a follower strategy, which has many advantages. Pioneers incur significant costs to create and develop a new product, educate the market about the benefits, promote it through advertising campaigns, and establish distribution channels. Followers can enter a market behind pioneers who have just established a growing market. They can learn from the pioneers' mistakes and capitalize on customer demand and awareness that pioneers have already established. It's also a great strategy for companies that do not have the resources of large companies.

# 51

# Product Differentiation

The most effective brands are those that have a high degree of differentiation. Some product categories can be highly differentiated and others, especially commodity consumer products, are more difficult to differentiate. The next time you are in a grocery store, just take a look down the laundry detergent aisle or browse the dozens of toothpaste brands and observe how the vast array of choices can be so confusing.

That said, remember that a brand is created through differentiation and there are lots of ways you can do this creatively. Products can be differentiated based on size, form, performance, features, durability, reliability, ease of repair, design, and style.[1] Arizona Iced Tea was one of the first beverage companies to distribute a beverage product in a large can. Cell phone manufacturers promote "indestructible" mobile phones for reckless teenagers. Maytag stresses reliability of their appliances. Herman Miller promotes style.

Products are differentiated by several other factors in addition to just form and functionality. Brand is important, as are associations with distributors and third parties. Customer service, customer experience, and technical support are also important factors that attract buyers and drive them to endorse it and tell others about it.

Design has become increasingly important to consumers. Retailer Target observed this trend long before other retailers, using design as a point of differentiation. The company believes that design isn't limited to museums, and style doesn't have to be expensive to be attractive. This strategy has worked extremely well, and Target has extended this design strategy across several types of product lines, from Mossimo's design of women's clothing to Michael Graves' designs found in the kitchen aisle. A significant section of their Web site is devoted to showcasing designers and their philosophy. Restoration Hardware is another retail chain that has a similar emphasis on design and successfully executed the strategy in a direct marketing campaign.

The importance of product innovation and design can be seen by studying the creative new companies that are revitalizing even the most mundane of household categories, like soap and cleaning products. Two former schoolmates teamed up to create Method, a company that has exploded in growth through the successful application of product design.[2, 3]

## Method Products Make a Clean Sweep in Product Category

Eric Ryan and Adam Lowry are former high school roommates who have reinvented the household cleaning products category. Together they founded Method Products, a company that combines design and environmentalism, breathing new life into the mundane hand soap category when they introduced a product with style. The bottle was designed by Karim Rashid, an award-winning designer who names Prada as one of his clients. The clean, simple raindrop design was immediately embraced by consumers who were tired of hiding ugly soap bottles under their sink.

Not only does the product have style, it has substance. It is designed to pump soap from the bottom (so you don't have to turn it over to squeeze out the last little bit of soap), and it features a nice leak-proof spout so soap doesn't drip all over the counter. The team's goal now is to create products that are nontoxic and made from real—not chemical—plants. Lowry says, "One of the things that I think we're really proud of…is [how] the success that we've had in bringing green—and health-focused—products to the mass market [has] actually changed the market much bigger than our own footprint. One of the big goals with Method, and why design and sustainability are inextricably linked in our brand, is that if you don't have the design element, you're only going to appeal to people who are already green, so you're not actually going to create any real environmental change."

With sales of over $75 million, Method is sure to make a clean sweep in other household product categories.

## Design with a Purpose

When David Butler joined Coca-Cola in 2004, he walked into a product design conundrum. The world's most powerful brand had become diluted from decentralized marketing and a steady turnover in marketing leadership. Category sales were declining due to a constant barrage of new products in the non-carbonated market.

Big problems call for a big new approach. Butler has a new, refreshing approach to global branding and product design. First he made fundamental changes to the role of design in a global brand. At corporate headquarters, he stopped using the word *design* (because no one knew what it meant anyway) and created a three-page manifesto called

"Designing on Purpose" that spoke not about design, but about the language of the Cola-Cola culture: How to sell more product.

Butler said, "I wanted to show how you could create more value for the business through design….How do we sell more of something? How do we improve the experience to make more money and create a sustainable planet?"[4] Next, he focused his challenge around the following goals:

- Increase customer satisfaction for a product in a declining market that was moving away from carbonated beverages.
- Reduce the carbon footprint caused by a global supply and distribution chain.
- Offer more choices to consumers within the confines of limited space in fast food restaurants and cafeterias.
- Acquire accurate, real-time feedback on customer choices.
- Elegant Design "Make it look like a Ferrari" (the wish of CEO, Muhtar Kent).[5]

By applying systems thinking to achieve all these goals (and of course, the goal of selling more product), Butler created the Freestyle fountain, a beautiful and functional new piece of equipment that dispenses over 100 different types of Cola-Cola varieties. Not only is it unique in offering a vast number of products, it's also smart, enhances environmental sustainability, and is beautiful to look at. A built-in computer enables the company to monitor what, when, where, and the quantity of beverages consumed. It reduces the carbon footprint by replacing five-gallon bags of concentrate with 46-ounce cartridges. And looks? Beautiful, sleek, elegant, and useful—all words that describe the elements of great design.

Then Butler took on the even bigger challenge of unifying the Coca-Cola brand identity. Coke is a colossal brand with 450 brands sold in 200 countries through 20,000 retailers. More than 300 agencies work on the Coca-Cola brand. Over the years, marketing became decentralized and brand identity became diluted as each country put its own spin on localization. Butler worked with Todd Brooks, group design director for global brands, to develop a system that would provide unified brand identity while also providing the ability to localize concepts. The team came up with a set of brilliant and simple product design standards that could be used worldwide to localize marketing and sales campaigns instantly. They consisted of four brand assets and four design principles:

**Brand Assets:** Color red, the script font, ribbon, and bottle contour.
**Brand Principles:** Bold simplicity, real authenticity, the power of red, familiar yet surprising.

The result was the Design Machine, a unique tool that allows marketers to develop and customize their own marketing materials utilizing the four aspects of brand principles and brand assets in product design. It's part web-based design tool and part asset management system that enables customized point of sale design and delivery from anywhere in the world. Marketers simply pick a language, a product, and an occasion and the Design Machine sends the file for local approval and then to the printer for production. It's an elegant solution that drives brand standards, product innovation, and business value.

Mid-size and small businesses have their own marketing and brand challenges, especially when expanding into new markets and using new partners and distributors. If the world's leading brand can simplify their brand strategy, so can you. See if you can apply some of Coke's design principles to streamline your brand standards. As more companies expand their marketing programs through social media and affiliate marketing programs, a concise description of your brand essence will be more important than ever.

# 52

# Competitive Strategies

Understanding the drivers, objectives and strategies of competitors will help you position and formulate new strategies so you can either (1) take advantage of opportunities competitors don't pursue or don't yet realize, or (2) learn how to out flank them.

Your competitive analysis in Section II, evaluated and compared competitors based upon their size, customer base, market share, distribution channels, and other areas outlined on the Competitive Tracking Information worksheet in Chapter 26, "Competition: Keep Your Friends Close and Your Enemies Closer." You will now expand this information to create effective strategies to win market share. If you are in a highly competitive market, effectual competitive strategies are critical to win or maintain market share. You can create offensive competitive strategies in a highly competitive market, or defensive strategies in response to hostile competitors.

## Pick Your Battle Position

### Attack

A company that intends to compete with a market leader can choose this strategy to attack the market leader in one or more of the following ways:

- **Value Pricing:** A low price or short-term promotional discount gives your competitor's customers an incentive to either try your product or switch brands entirely.

- **Improved products and/or services:** Customers who seek the latest technology may respond to a "new and improved" version of an old product.

- **Geographical:** A customer may choose to do business with one company over another because it does a better job of serving local market needs. The flipside of this is to appeal to a customer's desire for convenience by offering several locations within a geographic market, or by winning their business by promoting powerful global capabilities.

- **Need Fulfillment:** If competitors have outdated solutions, poor service, inferior products, or otherwise fail to adequately serve customer needs, customers will flock to a business that offers a better solution.

**New Distribution Channels:** Distribution through new channels provides access to new customers and increases product availability. Large, well-known distributors can also strengthen a company's brand simply by selling the product. When Target began to sell Method products, the brand gained instant credibility and visibility. Method attracted a new consumer audience that was not previously interested in "buying green," so customers were won at the expense of well-entrenched consumer products companies.

Most strategies are a combination of several factors. For example, Frontier Airlines is one of the few profitable airlines remaining. After emerging from Chapter 11 in 2008, the company announced they were profitable again in January 2009. Frontier is a regional airline that serves the Western United States, typically in secondary markets. The company has been successful in taking on United Airlines for several reasons. Frontier's regional focus and operational efficiency by using only Airbus planes reduces maintenance and training expenses. Frontier operates primarily on a regional basis, so routes are more profitable than United, and they typically match United's fares. Not surprising, however, Southwest has decided to enter Frontier Airlines' market and is primarily competing based on lower prices.

## Flank

A flanking strategy identifies a gap in a competitor's ability to serve a market, or a weakness in a competitor's ability to reach a particular target market or geographic segment. For example, Apple's ongoing television campaign attacked Microsoft's operating platform—first Vista, then Windows 7—playing on the operational issues that plagued the company.

Enterprise Rent-A-Car focused on car rentals to individuals that needed quick, short-term access to a car. In highly fragmented markets, even market leaders can be challenged by a smaller competitor's strategy to offer a better product that meets the needs of a target segment.

## Defend

When a company is attacked, the competitor usually responds with a direct defensive strategy. A typical defensive strategy is to lower prices, increase advertising and promotion, or add product features that directly compete with a competitor's solutions. Microsoft's defense against Apple's flanking maneuver was to defend Windows Vista and Windows 7 as the hip choice of a diverse majority with the "I'm a PC" campaign.

The two companies continue to duel it out (with the bespectacled nerd and laid back guy in a T-shirt) in Apple's very public advertising campaign.

## Preemptive

A preemptive strategy seeks to either establish a market position or attack a competitor before it can make a big impact with their product. Companies deploy this strategy to dissuade competitors from introducing a new product or diffuse the impact that competitors may make. For example, when Apple introduced the iPod, the company announcement was made long before its arrival. Car companies are also famous for deploying this strategy in the fall to attract new car buyers.

## Substitute Product

Companies that offer an alternative solution for a specific need at a lower price provide a substitute to other category solutions. The product is usually positioned as a better value, or is perceived as a better alternative because it offers greater convenience and saves consumers valuable time. For example, the airline JetBlue offers short-distance commuters on the east coast as an alternative to driving or taking a train. During tax season, software companies will battle it out with H&R Block and other professional services firms to vie for your business.

## Retreat

Sometimes the best strategy to aggressive competitive action is to retreat from a market leadership position in a geographic market, target market segment, or industry vertical market. This strategy should not be perceived as defeat, but as a smart move against larger, well-entrenched competitors that simply have more resources and staying power. If the decision to retreat is made early enough, then valuable time, money, and resources can be saved, and energy can be redirected toward better opportunities. Fast-growing companies know that it is much smarter to play offense than defense.

Intel, a dominant player in the memory chip market, began to get hammered by Japanese chip manufacturers who could make the product much cheaper. In a bold move, Intel decided it would be wiser to lose this battle and focus on winning the war, so they closed this business to focus on new opportunities. Intel's microprocessor business was small at the time, but Andy Grove saw this was going to be the market of the future. Intel's microprocessor business is now a $270 billion business, and Intel has the largest market share at 12.2 percent.

# The Downside of Winning

It may not be obvious from the outset of devising a competitive strategy, but there are potential risks to winning a competitive battle. The most obvious are the increased expenses and bottom-line impact from fighting a long battle. This is caused by increased advertising and promotional spending, increases in operational costs resulting from serving more customers in expanded markets, and/or reduced brand equity following an ugly competitive war.

A competitive battle may result in price cuts, which likely impact margins and profitability, and perhaps consumer buying once prices inch their way back up. The best way to fight off competitors and avoid a bloody battle is through differentiation and positioning. As Kotler says: "Companies that forge a unique way of doing business gain lower costs, higher prices, or both. While their competitors increasingly resemble each other and are forced to compete on price, strategically positioned companies avoid the bloodbath by following the beat of a different drummer."[1]

Amen. As you read the remaining chapters in this section, you will learn several other strategies that can be parlayed into competitive differentiation.

Review the information that you gathered about competitors in Chapter 26. What areas present problems or challenges because competitors are pursuing the same target market or the same strategies? In what areas can you differentiate and innovate to create competitive advantage?

# 53

# Growth Strategies

With very few exceptions, every company wants year-over-year growth that is realized through increases in sales and market share. If the goal is rapid growth, it is best achieved through a strategy such as the acquisition of another company. Organic growth is upward business growth achieved incrementally with the successful execution of selling more products, establishing new target markets, or expanding geographical reach. Businesses that pursue organic growth are usually established companies in a mature market, or businesses that desire slower growth for a number of good reasons such as access to capital.

Exponential growth is a harder strategy to execute and takes focus. If your goal is to achieve rapid growth, consider the following strategies:

- Acquisition
- Strategic Alliances and Partnerships
- New Distribution Channels
- New Markets
- New Customers
- New Products

## Acquisition

Acquisition is the fastest way for companies to grow and quickly capture market share. It is also a good strategy for businesses that would like to enter new industries or expand into new target market segments because they can buy knowledge, expertise, brand, and customers instantly.

Crocs bought Finproject NA—the Canadian company that manufactured Crocs and owned the formula for Croslite—the unique, odor-resisting, spongy resin of which Crocs are made. This acquisition gave Crocs control over manufacturing and timing, lending a hand to their unique distribution system, which compared to most shoe companies is quick and customized. Retailers receive only the style they want at the quantity and color wanted, delivered in a few weeks. This method ensures that retailers aren't left with unsold Crocs, meaning they're never sold at a discount.[1]

If a merger or acquisition sounds easy, don't be fooled. The result is not always win/win and it takes considerable time, effort, and money to make them successful. The vast majority of acquisitions fail because company cultures are mismatched.

## Strategic Alliances and Partnerships

New alliances pave the way for entry into new target markets, geographies, and vertical markets. Like acquisitions, alliances provide access to an existing customer base, although this access will take cooperation and effort from both companies. Each company in the alliance benefits from the ability to offer a more robust product or service that will attract new customers, provide complementary services that offer greater customer benefits, and extend brand equity and good will to business partners.

## New Distribution Channels

The addition of different types of distribution channels can add significantly to a company's growth. VARs (value added resellers) and resellers can sell products through channels they have already established. In consumer markets, distribution into mass retailers like Wal-Mart, Costco, or Target can turn a product into a superstar in a very short period of time.

In Section III, "Analyze," you analyzed different types of distributors to reach new target markets and expand geographic coverage. Evaluate your distribution strategy to consider every possible path to market. Analyze the entire network in the value chain and how you can create strategies to expand awareness and sales. In some companies, a value network can literally comprise of hundreds of network partners who contribute to the delivery of a product. For example, Cisco Systems' value network is comprised of manufacturers, VARs, resellers, user groups, government entities, school systems and universities, and dozens of other partners.

## New Markets

Rapid growth can be achieved by entering new geographical locations (local, regional, national, or international), new target markets that reach new buyers, or new industry vertical markets. Growth into new markets always looks attractive, but it also means additional costs to customize a product, increased resources to provide operational support, and extra marketing and promotion expenses to make a new market aware of a product.

The following case study "Adobe Makes Lemonade Out of Lemons" describes how Adobe Systems created new markets for a beleaguered software product.[2]

## Adobe Makes Lemonade Out of Lemons

In 2003, Adobe Systems, Inc. had recently entered the Enterprise Software market. For some time, the company's electronic paper (such as Adobe Acrobat and PDF) product lines had been popular in government sectors that were heavily dependent on paper forms as a means of communicating with constituents. One Adobe product, Adobe Document Server for Reader Extensions, showed a lot of promise in the broader Enterprise Software market. The product effectively worked like a "postage meter". The product would take an existing PDF file and embed a hidden key into the file, which would then activate latent functionality in the freely distributed Adobe Reader software. As a result, the product effectively was a reverse licensing mechanism for Adobe Reader.

Adobe had positioned the Reader Extensions Server (RES) product exclusively to the Federal Government vertical market and the licensing options for the product were limited to a $75,000 per document option or a $1.5 million unlimited use license. In 2003, product-line revenues for the RES were less than $500 million and the product had fewer than five customers worldwide.

By 2003, Adobe believed that the addressable market for its flagship products— Adobe Photoshop and Adobe Acrobat—had been largely penetrated. The company believed that exploring new markets, such as Enterprise Software, were critical to achieve long-term revenue growth and expansion. The RES product was easily installed and easy to use. As such, Adobe recognized that it was a potential entry point product to cross-sell other, more sophisticated, Enterprise Software products. However, the exclusive vertical market focus and the narrow pricing models restricted Adobe's go-to-market options for RES.

Adobe determined that in order to use the RES product as a leverage point to cross sell its other Enterprise Software product lines, it must first overhaul the go-to-market strategy.

First, the vertical market focus on large government agencies was eliminated. The product messaging and positioning was recreated to showcase value propositions that were more horizontally oriented. Additionally, new vertical market messaging was created to support value propositions specific to other paper form-intensive industries such as Insurance, Banking, and Healthcare.

Second, the pricing model for the product line was re-worked to provide a lower entry point, as well as a tiered pricing structure that would enable customers to adopt the product with a limited initial investment, but grow their use over time. Regional pricing models were also created to gain entry into Asian and European markets. Packaging bundles were established to facilitate Adobe's core objective: to use the RES product as an entry point that would facilitate cross-selling and up-selling opportunities for the breadth of the Enterprise Software product suite.

Third, a worldwide roll-out of the go-to-market strategy was executed. New sales and marketing materials were provided to Sales and Field marketing organizations on a global basis. Sales teams in all of Adobe's geographic regions were trained on the new strategy, positioning, and pricing options.

What were the results? By the end of 2004, the first year after the implementation of the new go-to-market strategy, product-line revenues for the RES product were nearly $20 million. The product was successfully implemented at over 200 customer sites worldwide, including multiple enterprise site licenses that individually were worth in excess of $2 million in license revenues. At the end of 2005, product-line revenues had exceeded $35 million and were forecasted to grow 100 percent year-to-year for the subsequent two years.

## New Customers

In addition to targeting new markets and buyers, you can quickly expand your business by targeting and closing one or two key customer accounts. Securing a prestigious top-tier customer has the added benefit of attracting other customers similar in size and profile, which add to the reputation of a business. This can catapult a company into new levels of brand awareness and business growth.

The one precaution to keep in mind is the risk associated with putting too many eggs in one customer basket. It can deplete precious resources, and for smaller companies, the risk of losing one customer that contributes the majority of sales can be devastating. If you pursue this strategy, make sure you have the resources to fulfill demand and service needs. Then you can leverage this success and focus business development efforts on acquiring additional tier-one customers.

## New Products

The introduction of a new product that captures the hearts and minds of customers can result in an explosion of growth and sales. It can also lead to additional sales from other products and services your company offers.

Under Armour, the successful athletic-wear manufacturer, created a breakaway new product category that has evolved from founder and CEO Kevin Plank's grandmother's house to the shelf of 6,500 athletic retailers. Plank, tired of his cotton football shirts' moisture retention, commissioned a tailor to make tight-fitting undershirts from the same moisture-wicking material of which many cycling and football undershorts were made. Plank began marketing to college athletic teams, but his eyes were on the retail market. To attract big retailers, such as Dick's Sporting Goods, Plank tirelessly pitched to college and NFL football teams with the idea that their acceptance would provide Under Armour an "authenticity that advertising alone [couldn't] create."[3, 4] This strategy worked and sales grew from $17,000 in 1996 to an astonishing $55 million by 2005. By 2008, Under Armour's revenues grew to over $200 million and captured 75 percent of the $416 million market for tight-fitting athletic garments.[5]

Under Armour's initial strategy was niche-market penetration. Marketing was targeted to football teams, and then spread to other male athletes, women, youth, and in 2006, the $9 billion footwear market. The footwear market represents a very different and competitive market, so again Under Armour entered the market with a a highly specialized product: football cleats. It chose this comparatively small market ($250 million in the U.S.) because competing with Adidas and Nike in soccer shoes, for example, would be suicidal. Plank says Under Armour's primary goal in its release of football cleats was to authenticate itself as a footwear brand. By May 2008, Under Armour captured a 20 percent share in football cleats. They next gleaned an 11 percent share in the baseball and softball cleat market. The company recently expanded into the cross-training market, in direct competition with Nike. Under Armour released its first line of running shoes in early 2009, stimulating a new wave of competition.

In summary, the challenge—especially for disruptive companies that create new industries—is to grow beyond its niche and develop new products and innovations that capture new customers. At the same time, it requires tremendous focus to not be all things to all people.

# 54

# Innovation Strategies

This category of strategy development will not focus on one particular type of innovation, but several examples that are intended to challenge you to think about how your business can become more innovative in satisfying customer needs and growing into new markets. Every company—whether it is small or large, new or established, in a new growth market or a mature market—must consider how innovation will help them compete and thrive in the new economy. Innovation may create market differentiation, take costs out of the business, streamline processes, increase customer stickiness, and create new revenue streams. The following are a few models to evaluate as you consider strategies for innovation.

## Innovation Models

**Product/Service Innovation:** New features and functionality can be innovative, but disruptive innovation is the most compelling. It creates demand for products and services that people didn't even know they "needed." Apple's iPod and iTunes are examples of disruptive innovations that represent not just product innovation, but business model innovation as well.

**Solution Innovation:** Bundled or integrated products and solutions are customized to solve a customer problem. Apple's iPhone was bundled with AT&T's service to create the largest 3G network. Another example is Google's customized home page, which allows customers to integrate a wide variety of useful gadgets, custom information, and news feeds into their personal home page.

**Platform Innovation:** This strategy involves the use of established brands and solutions to create a new spin-off that is simplified, making it easier for others to use it. An example is the Linux open source operating platform and the subsequent Android software platform for mobile devices based on the Linux system, developed by Google and Open Handset Alliance.

**Process Innovation:** Redesigning core processes can create efficiency and customer value. Wal-Mart is a stellar example of process innovation with their inventory management and supply chain processes.

**Value Innovation:** Stripping away the cost of manufacturing or materials allows companies to sell an established product at a lower price. Consumer electronics is a category that has applied this concept by substituting lower-priced parts and materials to manufacture products.

**Customer Innovation:** This strategy involves creating new products and services to fulfill an unmet customer need. Examples include Motorola's introduction of the first cell phone and AOL's free email campaign to speed rapid adoption and use of email.

**Customer Experience Innovation:** Creating unique and valuable customer interactions with a brand are crucial to maintaining or expanding a customer base. Innovative product companies like Oakley and Converse enable customers to design products to reflect their individual style and preferences. This concept leverages mass customization, which uses technology and manufacturing processes to mass produce individual customized products and services. Customer Experience innovation is especially important in commodity products, as it results in differentiating the product from others in its category.

**User Innovation:** In this model, the customers are the key driver of innovation. Customers design, market, and sometimes sell products and services for a company. Threadless (highlighted in Chapter 49, "Customers Are Cocreators") is an example of a company based on user innovation.

**Crowdsourcing:** Similar to the User Innovation model, customers and/or users collaborate with companies to create solutions to problems. The difference between the two models is crowdsourcing facilitates collaboration with a group of people or among a community to solve a particular problem. Netflix is known for tapping into the power of a community to help it solve challenges.

**Marketing Innovation:** Digital media and new marketing channels are constantly evolving, which helps you reach more buyers and sell more products through social media, viral marketing, and affiliate marketing programs. As different people interact with the product, they can endorse it, influence others to use it, and add their own value to the solution, further customizing it for their audience.

**Organizational Innovation:** This is the structural redesign of how people in an organization work together to provide value to customers. An example is JetBlue's virtual call center that delivers high-quality customer service, while increasing employee satisfaction, by allowing agents to work from home.

**Brand Innovation:** This involves extending a brand into new areas. An example is UK-based Virgin, a company that has ventured in many different businesses in the airline, retail, and banking industries. Innovation is driven by founder Richard Branson, who is known for parlaying his individual style of risk taking and adventure into an attitude for business diversification.

**Syndication Innovation:** Syndicators bring together several sources of information and distribute it in useful ways to consumers who are interested in particular topics. Examples of syndicators are E*Trade, Alltop, and Mashable. The growing number of bloggers who distribute information via RSS are also syndicators of information.

**Distribution Innovation:** This is distributing products and services in a unique way, or creating disintermediation, which means bypassing traditional channels and marketing directly to consumers. Examples of this business model are eBay and Dell.

# 55

# The Long Tail

The distribution and sales channel of the Internet enables businesses to reach new niche markets by selling a large number of unique items in small quantities. The Long Tail describes a business model developed by Chris Anderson, editor of *Wired* magazine and author of *The Long Tail: Why the Future of Business is Selling Less of More*. A perfect example of this business concept is Amazon.com.

The average Barnes and Noble bookstore carries approximately 130,000 books. Store size limits the inventory of books that can be physically inventoried and sold, which essentially forces Barnes and Noble to carry a large inventory of the most popular books. On the other hand, Amazon is the largest bookseller, with two-thirds comprising "unpopular" or out-of-print titles. What makes this possible is a business model stripped of distribution, inventory, real estate, and other significant costs that are a burden to traditional retailers.

Netflix provides another example of how the Long Tail is an effective business model. Unlike competitors, Netflix can inventory and distribute a large number of obscure titles as well as popular movies. Netflix distributes approximately 2 million movies a day  An inventory of popular movies makes up the front of the demand curve, but the long tail of unpopular titles is far greater than the most popular titles. If you consider how the addition of a search and recommendation engine adds value to the business model, the Long Tail distribution to niche markets grows even longer (see Figure 55.1).

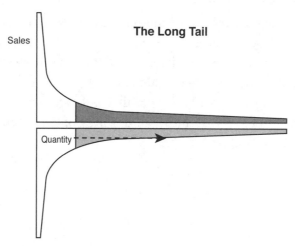

**Figure 55.1** *Long-Tail business model*

Other companies like eBay and iTunes have tapped into this successful business model, which is dominated by companies on the Internet. As more businesses begin to leverage the potential of the Long Tail, even large Internet businesses will begin to be affected by smaller online businesses that focus on niche products or niche target audiences.

The concept of the Long Tail business model is an ideal example of an integrated strategy that has no boundaries. Is it a niche target market strategy? A distribution strategy? A competitive strategy? A product strategy? Or perhaps it's a promotion strategy because it leverages social media. The answer to all of these questions is yes; depending on your strategy and approach, it can be all of the above. It's certainly innovation.

## New Revenue Streams and Business Models

A result of innovation is new business models. Many of these, especially Internet-based businesses, create and capture revenue in unique ways. Revenue streams can be generated through product and service transactions or through commissions from affiliate relationships. New revenue can also be produced by fees for memberships, subscriptions, licenses, installation, maintenance and service, click-through fees, and hosting or on-demand fees. In an online world where so much is offered for free, there is also unlimited potential for generating new revenue.

The Internet enables mass customization to be possible for both customers and suppliers. Online newspapers and online television channels such as Hulu are shaking up entire industries. Open-source software like Linux commands respectable market share, and new companies like Threadless are creating an open and collaborative business model built entirely around the customer.

Businesses are not the only drivers of innovative business models. Nokia estimates that by 2012, approximately 25 percent of web content will be user generated. Wikipedia and YouTube content is entirely user generated. As social networking and blogging software enable more collaboration and personalization, it will be interesting to see the evolution of Internet 3.0. Companies will discover that Internet marketing will no longer be about driving customers to their Web sites, but driving content to customers, enabling them to interact with it and add new value.

# 56

# Nurture a Culture of Innovation

Check out the values statement of any technology company, and you are likely to see that innovation is listed as one of the core values. But the desire for an innovative culture extends far beyond technology companies. A culture of innovation has become a requirement in today's rapidly changing environment. After all, isn't this the key to creating new revenue streams? Indeed it is, but few companies put meaningful effort into fostering a culture of innovation. If they did, they would undoubtedly create more innovative products and services, and also create new business value across all sectors of the business. Innovation is needed well beyond the confines of engineering, R&D, and product development teams. Increased innovation drives new business processes, new customer value, cost efficiencies, and strategies to compete and win in competitive markets.

In Chapter 40, "What Is Strategy?," I mentioned the value of Jim Collin's article on "Catalytic Mechanisms." Mechanisms are simply the means to build goals and good intention into processes increasing the likelihood of success. 3M has what may be the best-known example of a catalytic mechanism for innovation. The company prides itself on creating innovative new products, and wanted to build a mechanism for fostering creativity and innovation into their culture. By encouraging employees to spend up to 15 percent of their time on new projects, innovation stays top-of-mind for every employee.

Several other companies realize the value of investing time, money, effort, and mechanisms into their culture so employees drive innovation. BrightHouse, an innovative consulting firm, offers five "Your Days" so employees can get out of the office and spend time reflecting and recharging. This is in addition to the five weeks of vacation that every employee receives. The company also brings in a constant stream of people who are experts in their field to speak to the organization. The idea is to stimulate new thinking and get fresh perspectives so employees can apply this to new projects under development. Past speakers have included Edgar Mitchell, oceanographer Robert Ballard, as well as actors, professors, and even poets.[1]

Here are some other ideas to encourage innovation in your company:

- Rotate employees to work in other parts of the organization for a few weeks or months. This will give them an entirely new, holistic perspective of the business and probably several new ideas they can apply to their regular job.

- Present a bi-weekly or monthly seminar program with outside experts and leaders from different areas of the company. It doesn't have to be anything fancy; a brown bag luncheon works very well for this purpose. It shows employees that you care about their development, and the cross-functional interaction stimulates learning and new ideas for everyone.

- Establish communities of practice so employees can work together on topics they are passionate about, or a special problem or issue that is important for the company to solve. Too often problems stay in a boardroom of locked indecision when they could be quickly resolved by the people who are closer to the issue at hand.

- Encourage risk and celebrate failure. Many businesses want their employees to take well-calculated risks, but when situations don't go as planned, no one wants to talk about it. The same mistake is then made again by other people. To encourage risk, reward the person who stuck his neck out; make sure there is plenty of dialogue about what happened and why so others learn from the experience.

Creating a culture of innovation is an effective strategy every company can learn to implement. There are many small programs that can be developed to produce big results. But it must start with the desire and commitment to improve. Creating a culture of innovation is a strategy. It requires time, effort, and resources to effectively implement programs to drive change and innovation.

## Three Versus Drive Innovation and Growth

To summarize all the strategies covered so far in this chapter, I want to leave you with a final thought that may help you create and integrate your strategies. Nirmalya Kumar is a professor of marketing at London Business School. In his book, *Marketing as Strategy: Understanding the CEO's Agenda for Driving Growth and Innovation*. In the following interview, Kumar explains how companies use the three Vs: **valued customer**, **value proposition**, and **value network** as the mechanisms to fuel innovation and drive growth.[2]

## Kumar: Differentiate Company Marketing with Three Vs

**Reece:** The subtitle of your latest book (*Marketing as Strategy: Understanding the CEO's Agenda for Driving Growth and Innovation*) is something everyone wants to know about. What is the CEO's agenda for driving growth and innovation?

**Kumar:** There are two ways to get growth: Raise prices, which not many companies can do, [or] increase volume. The way to increase volume is to go into new countries, such as China and India, but there is a limit to this as well. The only way for true growth is to develop new products and services through innovation.

The biggest issue for a CEO is how to avoid competing on price, and how to keep prices from falling. The second issue is customer loyalty. The number of product and service choices for customers has increased dramatically, and customers have more access to information than ever before, so they can easily switch brands.

**Reece:** You make a strong case for changing the standard marketing focus around four Ps, to the three Vs: valued customer, value proposition, and value network. Tell us more about this concept.

**Kumar:** The four Ps are an essential part of marketing, but it's not enough to differentiate products based on the four Ps. Product, price, place, and promotion can easily be copied by competition. By focusing on the three Vs, a company can sustain differentiation.

"Valued customer" is a way to segment and target customers based on perceived value. "Value proposition" is how to competitively differentiate products and services to customers. "Value network" is how you deliver the value proposition to the target customer. It's a cross-functional orientation often referred to as the "value chain."

For example, at Starbucks, it's everything they do from the beginning of the value network, such as who they buy their beans from to providing a cup of coffee in the store. Wal-Mart is another example of creating a unique value network. Competitors can easily have the same products and prices as Wal-Mart, but not the business and distribution system.

**Reece:** How do companies develop a culture that fosters the type of radical innovation you describe, that in turn will create growth and innovation?

**Kumar:** This is a very difficult concept. To drive innovation, an entirely new value network is needed, and the only way I have found to do this successfully is to set up a completely different subsidiary. So you set up a different division whose only job is to maximize the value proposition. This is difficult because doing this requires using company resources, while also dealing with the constraints that keep them from making significant changes.

**Reece:** Hence your quote, "Let us keep all the cannibals in the family."

**Kumar:** Exactly. That is why so many airlines that launch a low-cost airline are not successful. Businesses face the same challenge. It's almost like killing the baby subsidiary even before the launch because they don't want the baby to flourish and become successful. If you have a new subsidiary, you want it to have the "kill attitude." Everyone needs to think, "I will do what is best for the subsidiary, even if it means killing the mother ship." The company needs to do whatever necessary to win in the marketplace.

**Reece:** What is the biggest industry ripe for change based upon a unique customer differentiator?

**Kumar:** Any company that has not used technology and can use it to reduce costs. The pharmaceutical industry trends are moving to low-cost countries where R&D and labor are cheap. The FDA has put so many restraints on R&D that I think companies are moving R&D to countries with a large knowledge base, such as China and India, where it can be done at a much faster rate. The accounting and financial industries will also see dramatic changes. A financial analyst does not need to sit in New York City. They can be anywhere the world.

**Reece:** If a company is after radical innovation, what is the best way to ensure success or test a new idea?

**Kumar:** They should get feedback, but it's a different kind of feedback. In a market-driving company, instead of asking customers what they want, they launch the new product. You know it's not perfect, but you launch it and see what kinds of customers stick. Then you watch them and observe them using it and come up with improvements that way. So instead of learning through research, you learn in the marketplace. You learn by doing.

# 57

# Sales Strategy and Plan

Several types of strategies have been discussed in this section and throughout this book. Now it's time to roll up your sleeves and create your own strategies to drive business growth. Let's start by developing a sales forecast. If you are creating a marketing plan for a new business and have not forecasted sales yet, you can create the forecast based on market demand and the marketing programs you will implement to drive demand. Established companies have a projected forecast that is based on prior year sales, new product and service introductions, market growth, and other factors.

Break down the sales forecast on a monthly or quarterly basis. This will provide everyone who is responsible for revenue and demand generation with greater focus and accuracy. Depending on the structure of your company, it is also advisable to further divide it to estimate revenue by customers, distributors, products, services, and/or industry segments. The final step is to define sales objectives for each sales person to develop commission plans.

One of the biggest disparities between sales and marketing departments is alignment and communication regarding sales objectives. In large companies, the sales department is crystal clear about sales goals, but the marketing department may only have visibility to lump sum quarterly and yearly sales goals. The marketing and sales teams must be aligned on a plan for revenue targets for existing customers, new customers, customer service programs, and other means of revenue generation. Then marketing can design programs to generate the right number of leads and conversions to achieve the sales targets.

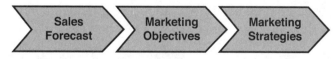

**Figure 57.1** *Creating sales and marketing objectives*

# Sales Strategy and Plan

A sales plan is an important component of a marketing plan. This describes objectives and the various types of strategy that will be implemented, such as customer acquisition, retention, and so on. It also describes what the sales team will need to be successful, such as training, executive level support, sales and marketing tools, and processes for communication. Use the following summary of topics to guide your development of an effective sales strategy and plan.

**Sales Objectives** (These should include sales by direct and indirect channels.)

**Sales Strategy** (What you are going to do in each market to achieve your sales goals?)

- Types of customers: Prioritize by value such as tier one, two, and three. Define sales by month, quarter, and year.
- Profiles of key customers and customer segments (include all the pertinent customer information you will need to achieve your sales goals).
- Major account sales strategy.
- New customer acquisition strategy (direct, sales, referral program, direct mail, tradeshow, partners, social media, and so on).
- Customer retention and loyalty strategy (what you are going to do to keep your best customers).
- Customer relationship management strategy.
- CRM software:
  - Data collection—what information should be gathered and entered into the system (industry, company size, geography, revenue potential, step in sales cycle, and so on)
  - Process and expectations
  - Reporting

## Sales Channels
- Define the goals, training needs, operational requirements, reporting, marketing support, joint sales process, and other key issues.

## Training and Support Needs
- Sales staff (define what sales skills your sales teams need to be successful, such as advanced sales training for high-end consultative selling, product training, industry briefings, technology, and so on).
- Training for other stakeholders (employees, partners, distributors, others).

- Executive-level support needs.
- Escalation process (criteria for escalating service issues and process for resolution).
- Other support needs (finance, admin, marketing).

## Sales and Marketing Tools

- Sales and marketing needs for each target market segment and major accounts.
- Define type of tools, such as PowerPoint slides, presentations by industry sector, sales channels, sales sheets, product data, and other materials.

## Sales and Marketing Alignment

- Monthly and/or quarterly operational meetings to review results.
- Closed loop process (sales, marketing, customer service, operations).
- Joint customer meetings (key customers and sales and marketing team members).
- Major account plans for key customers.
- Win/loss process and reviews: Establish disciplined process for sales and marketing teams along with other key stakeholder teams.

# 58

# Marketing Objectives Drive Strategy

Marketing objectives describe the specific goals that must be accomplished to reach sales goals. Do you recall how SMART goals were developed in Chapter 10, "Measurable Goals Drive Success"? Marketing objectives can be defined the same way.

A SMART objective is:

**Specific and Measureable:** Focused on a single, quantifiable goal.

**Motivating:** For employees, customers, and/or distributors.

**Achievable:** Is it realistic and attainable?

**Relevant:** Does the objective align with, and cascade from the company objectives?

**Trackable and Timebound:** How will the goal be measured and over what period of time?

Here are several examples of how to apply the SMART framework to create marketing objectives for different types of businesses:

1. B2B objectives focus on affecting the behavior of other businesses in your target market. An example might be:

   *Increase reorder rates in the financial services sector by five percent to $7 million to during the next six months.*

2. Retail objectives focus on affecting consumer behavior within a retail environment. They can be defined by geography, demographics, and other factors. An example of a retailer objective might be:

   *Increase sales per transaction among current purchasers, women 25–54, by 15 percent from $28 to $33 per year.*

   Or: *Increase sales traffic in the Boston market by 20 percent in the next six months.*

3. Consumer goods can focus on trade and consumer objectives. An example might be:

   Trade: *Increase distribution within the XYZ market chain from 20 stores to 40 stores by the second quarter of 2011.*

Consumer: *Increase purchases made by existing customers from 20 percent to 30 percent in the next 12 months.*

4. Manufacturing objectives can focus on consumer, retailer, distributor, or supplier objectives:

   *Increase sales for XYZ product in the western region by 12 percent within the next six months.*

   Or: *Distribute 18 percent more product through XXX in the European market in the first half of 2011.*

These are all quantifiable examples, but you may have qualitative examples as well. Be sure to write down all the objectives you would like to accomplish because your marketing strategies will be developed to achieve each of the stated objectives.

# 59

# The Art and Science of Developing Strategy

Now you are ready to create your marketing strategies. For each marketing objective, you will create at least one marketing strategy to achieve the objective, but most likely you will develop several strategies to achieve the objective.

The following steps will guide you to create strategies that leverage everything you have learned about your market, competition, customers, and opportunities. The steps are not intended to be done sequentially—although they can be—but rather to serve as a guideline so you consider the most critical factors in strategy development. Keep in mind that strategy is an art, but it you apply science and process it will be far less risky and much easier:

1. Determine if you will have different geographic strategies. You may need different local, regional, national, and/or international strategies.

2. Evaluate the need for short-term and long-term strategies. Determine if there is a need for seasonal strategies.

3. Analyze the Competitive Strategy Worksheet to fully understand the challenges associated with the competitive environment. This will lead you to take advantage of opportunities to differentiate your strategy.

4. Review the SWOT analysis you created in Chapter 11, "Situation Analysis and SWOT Analysis." What weaknesses and threats do you need to overcome? What strengths can you leverage? What opportunities do you wish to take advantage of?

5. Review financial objectives, company goals, and marketing objectives. Strategies will be developed to achieve them.

6. Develop customer, positioning, and target market strategies first. These strategies will drive your strategic direction in other areas.

7. Write strategies for each strategic area that applies to your company. Refer to the categories outlined throughout this section. Evaluate strategies to ensure they are aligned and integrated to achieve the overall company goals. Be specific and focused as you prioritize strategies. Determine what is *not* strategically important.

8. Summarize the sales forecast, sales plan, marketing objectives, and marketing strategies in the "Marketing Strategies" section of the Marketing Plan Template.

## Strategy Integration

As you read through this section, you may think that the lines and definitions between the various types of strategies described previously are blurred. This is a correct assumption. Growth strategies into new geographical markets could be considered target market strategies. A customer strategy might be considered a sales strategy or an innovation strategy. Or vertically targeted markets might be considered as part of a product strategy, and so on. What is important is not *what* you call a strategy, but *how well strategies are integrated to achieve your objectives*. Also be mindful that as the market environment changes, strategies need to change. If you operate a business in a volatile industry or market, it would be wise to create alternative or contingency strategies based on certain conditions occurring. This will enable you to quickly respond.

Strategies are also heavily influenced by the competency and leadership abilities of senior executives, the skills and commitment of employees, the company vision and culture, and of course, the financial strength and resources a company has available to execute a strategy. There are several moving parts and dependencies related to strategy formulation and execution. And remember, effective strategy is about making trade-offs and choices as you decide what you will do, and what you choose not to do.

## A Final Word

Entire books are devoted just to strategy, and there is more to learn beyond the content in this section. Develop an appetite for lifelong learning so you can adapt, change, and create new strategies to a continuously changing environment. Become a ferocious learner and read about successful strategies that other companies are deploying. Discuss new ideas and strategies with other business leaders. Look outside your industry for new ideas. Refine your strategies based upon results and customer feedback.

# P • R • A • I • S • E™ Marketing Process

## Strategize

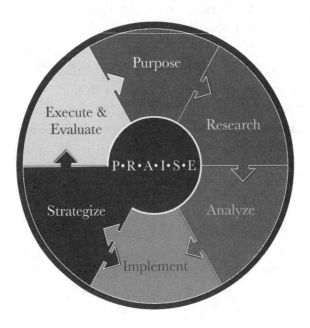

# Summary: Section IV

✓ Create a positioning statement for your products and/or services.

✓ Define your value proposition and the brand promise.

✓ Complete the four-step creative process to describe your brand personality and brand essence.

✓ Define competitors' strategies and analyze the challenges and opportunities this presents to your business. In the marketing plan template, define how you will approach these issues.

✓ Develop a sales forecast and a sales plan, making it as detailed as possible.

✓ Define specific marketing objectives that must be achieved during the planning period.

✓ Develop marketing strategies beginning with your customer, positioning, and target market strategies. Use the strategy process outlined in this section.

✓ Summarize all the preceding information in Section V of the Marketing Plan Template.

# Section V

# Implement:
# Traditional and New Media

*"If things seem under control, you're just not going fast enough."*
—Mario Andretti

During the course of working with CEOs, marketers, and entrepreneurs over the past 20 years, I have observed a consistent trait: They want to jump into execution without having a well thought out marketing plan. They want to implement some type of tactic to generate leads or sales. And therein lies the single biggest reason that most businesses fail. A tremendous amount of time, effort, and money is wasted because they don't do the foundational work to understand their customers, target market, positioning, or competitive market.

When businesses implement one tactic after the other and wonder why they are not effective, the root cause almost always points to the fact that they have not done the research to understand these issues.

A good analogy is visiting a doctor to find out why you aren't feeling well. If he or she makes a prognosis without first making a diagnosis, it would be called malpractice. The same is true with marketing. Implementing programs without first doing the foundational work is marketing malpractice. It's throwing money at something you are hoping will work.

The good news is you have done all the foundational work in previous sections of the process and you are armed with actionable knowledge you can apply to a tactical plan. If you have skipped ahead to this part of the process, you should bear this in mind. In this section you will:

- Improve the effectiveness and ROI of your marketing programs.
- Learn how digital marketing tactics and social media can generate brand awareness, leads, and improve relationships with customers.
- Understand the biggest trends in sales and marketing.
- Develop a tactical plan that defines and aligns sales and marketing programs to increase execution efficiency.
- Create an implementation calendar and marketing budget to forecast, track, and measure programs as they are executed.

As you develop a tactical plan to achieve the marketing objectives and strategies for your business, there are dozens of different types of tactics to consider. Some may be traditional types of marketing you have implemented before (see "Traditional Marketing Tactics" in the book resource section at www.MarketSmarter.com.), and others will be new types of digital media.

In Part I of this section, "Social Media, Digital Media, and Personal Communications," defines several types of digital media to communicate and engage customers.

In Part II, "Create a Tactical Plan with Execution Built-In," you will learn how to create a tactical plan to summarize all the details for each individual program you plan to implement. This includes specifics such as the program description, resource needs, budget, timeline, and projected ROI. A detailed tactical plan helps you align resources and is proven to improve tactical execution of the plan.

Before you dive into these sections, let's review key business trends and how they are impacting sales and marketing. We'll also look at the chief concerns of marketers and where they are choosing to invest precious marketing budgets.

# 60

# The State of Marketing Today

## Changes in Latitudes, Changes in Attitudes

Integrated marketing communications (IMC) is the application of multiple integrated communications media to reach customers. Marketing tactics like direct marketing, Internet marketing, social media, telemarketing, and sales promotions are optimized when they are aligned to create a seamless progression of marketing communication and touch points to customers. Consumers don't think about a brand as a marketing program or campaign. Ongoing, integrated marketing creates consistent branding, positioning, and messaging across all marketing communication and media to produce more impact and recall. But the burning question is, *"Where* will you reach potential buyers?"

In the past, it was much easier to market and predict consumer behavior than it is today. Here are just a few of the issues that make marketing much more difficult than is was in recent years:

- Consumer trust and confidence in organizations and institutions has declined significantly. Consumers turn to each other—sometimes even complete strangers—for advice and recommendations when making a purchase.
- Digital experiences and customer engagement are the biggest factors influencing consumer purchases and recommendations to others.
- The numbers of digital media choices grow and change every day, making it very difficult for marketers to learn while executing. Marketers must respond by retooling skills and ROI measures.
- Consumers of news and entertainment like the personalization and immediacy of digital media. A whopping 84 percent of consumers now say they rely on the Internet for news or information, 73 percent visit social networking sites on a regular basis, and 76 percent regularly watch video sites like Hulu and YouTube.

One of the biggest changes in recent years is where marketers are choosing to invest marketing funds. The growing use of digital media is driving marketers to invest in communication tactics that are more targeted and measureable. Advertising must reach consumers where they spend the most time, and it is increasingly away from television, newspapers, and other traditional media channels that were depended on for many years to reach the masses.

Media expert Jack Myers predicts that total advertising revenues will decline by 5.9 percent in 2010. This follows a 14 percent decline in 2009 and 5.8 percent decline in 2008, marking the first time in 40 years that advertising budgets will be down for more than three consecutive years. He notes this is historic because even in past recessionary periods, advertising budgets have shifted from advertising to sales, stimulating budget line items like sales promotions and retail allowances. The picture does not get brighter in Myers' 2011–2012 predictions of traditional advertising media. He estimates there will be further declines in newspapers, magazines, television, and radio advertising. Newspaper advertising is suffering the most, experiencing a 25 percent decline from 2002 to 2008 and a continued decline is forecasted through 2012. Although the age of one-way communication has given way to a new digital era of personal communication, media spending in traditional channels still far outweighs spending in new media alternatives.

## Facts, Stats, and Key Trends

The Chief Marketing Officer (CMO) Council conducts a yearly survey among its members who lead marketing across a broad variety of industries around the world. The CMO Outlook Report describes the biggest challenges and concerns of senior marketers and other executives in the organization. This report and several others published by the CMO Council (www.cmocouncil.org) are an excellent barometer of the changing business climate and how marketing professionals are shifting budgets and resources to respond.

The report states that top executives continue to demand that marketers grow market share while improving operational efficiency. In response to this request, marketers say they are focused on strategic cost cutting (not budget slashing) by improving operational efficiency, increasing customer experience and insight, and working with sales to drive revenue growth. This response is positive, however it appears there is still a disconnect between what executives want and where marketing chooses to invest time and resources. Marketers are not investing enough in marketing process improvements and operational systems that provide increased collaboration and marketing automation tools.

With so many evolving media choices, where should businesses invest their marketing budgets? What are the key trends that you need to know about that influence consumers and buyer behavior?

Let's take a look at several trends and issues that influence decisions of marketing and sales executives, as well as a few highlights that reveal where they are choosing to invest. These figures have been combined with additional industry facts to help you make decisions on a broad number of sales and marketing issues. You will find many other statics and trend information about specific marketing tactics as you read each chapter.

# Key Trends Driving Marketing

- 60 percent of marketers say they will fund increases in the company's interactive marketing budget by shifting money away from traditional marketing.[1]
- Search marketing, online display advertising, email marketing, social media, and mobile marketing collectively will grow to nearly $55 billion by 2014.[2]
- CMOs will focus on training and development for their existing staff to sharpen skills in digital media. Sixty-three percent say they will retrain staff versus hiring new talent or outsourcing.[3]
- Salespeople spend approximately 40 percent of their time preparing customer-facing deliverables while leveraging less than 50 percent of the materials created by marketing.[4]
- Marketers say they want to improve operations and analytics; however, only 9 percent of marketers say that they plan to create a deeper relationship with their IT department.[5]
- Customer experience and customer loyalty are critical to business success, yet only 17 percent of marketers oversee customer service and support responsibility.[6]
- Around the world, marketers estimate that 55 percent of their entire marketing expenditures failed to deliver results.[7]

John Wanamaker was famous for saying, "I know 50 percent of my advertising is wasted. I just don't know which 50 percent." This statement was made over 20 years ago and sadly, the problem continues to be one of the biggest issues plaguing businesses today. The estimated marketing wastage rate (MWR) averages 45 percent for B2B marketers, and where budgets are smaller, strategies are more niche, and campaigns are running via fewer media channels. The estimated MWR rises to 65 percent for B2C marketers, and where budgets are often larger and teams have to take more innovative, riskier, and creative media approaches to find new ways to differentiate their brands.

Let's see what one of the leading experts in integrated marketing communications and marketing analytics has to say about this subject. Don Shultz was named by *Sales and Marketing Magazine* as one of the most influential people in sales and marketing in the 21st century. (The list also includes Dale Carnegie, Henry Ford, and Edward Deming.) Shultz is a professor of Integrated Marketing Communication at Northwestern University and the author of nine books that focus on integrated marketing communication and measuring brand communication ROI.

This interview with Shultz that was conducted in 2001, yet as you can see by the figures stated previously, the issue remains as relevant today as it was then.[8] He offers insight and advice that every business can apply to improve their marketing effectiveness.

## Expert Discusses How to Measure Marketing

**Reece:** Most of your research and work has been focused around two words that most people don't normally link when they talk about marketing: measurable marketing. Why have you chosen to become a pioneer in the area of ROI measurement?

**Shultz:** In the mid '70s, we were just beginning to see the complexity of the data from the grocery industry. I was fascinated by the correlation of what was spent, the price, how deals and discounts affected an outcome, and how that drove consumer behavior.

I wrote my dissertation on advertising response functions and for 25 years, I studied marketing analytics, then database marketing and how all these fit together. Integrated marketing communication evolved out of this.

My interest is focused on this: How much should be invested in a brand, how it should be invested, and the ways a company gets its investment back.

**Reece:** So what is the magic formula? How much should a company spend?

**Shultz:** It's how much you invest, not how much to you spend. The key is to figure out how to value a customer and how much to invest in acquiring and maintaining that customer. Advertising is just the surrogate.

**Reece:** What are the critical elements to evaluate and consider when determining this?

**Shultz:** First, how much is a customer worth now and what is the income flow from that customer today? Secondly, what are the opportunities in the future? What share do you presently serve? What must be done for maintenance to keep that customer?

**Reece:** Marketing control is shifting from marketers and manufacturers into the hands of the consumer. What implications does this have for businesses?

**Shultz:** It changes the whole focus of the organization. Companies need to figure out what to say to customers and the easiest and fastest way to get this message to them. The challenge is to listen to customers. Most companies are good at talking, but not at listening. What they need to do is refocus the organization to have response devices to measure customer response over time.

Most companies have a campaign mentality. They think about communication with a customer in terms of a campaign that runs for 7 or 13 weeks. The problem is the customer is continuously in the market. Companies need to totally flip their way of thinking about marketing to their customers. What do customers want to hear and need to hear? When do they need to hear it and where do they need to get the information?

**Reece:** In your book, you state that in today's multi-faceted marketplace, that marketing elements often cannot be measured separately as there is synergy among them. What's a marketer to do then to accurately measure ROI?

**Shultz:** It's very difficult to break out each media and evaluate it on an individual basis. Don't look just at the specifics of direct mail vs. a newspaper ad. It's the entire brand communication program. People tend to want to get finite before they have an understanding of whether or not it's working.

Advertising managers, promotion managers, and public relations directors are all concerned with defending their turf instead of working together to create a greater synergistic outcome.

**Reece:** What's new in the area of measuring the ROI for marketing?

**Shultz:** The recognition that we need marketing metrics. We can no longer spend money and trust it will work. Marketing lately has been driven by dot-coms using old communication methods. The old model was to give the creative department free reign and to spend money on itchy creative. Or it was unrealistic media spending like buying Super Bowl ads. Or it was basing decisions entirely on what worked historically. It's different now. Companies need to figure out what works now.

**Reece:** Measuring attitudes and behaviors were once the primary methods for predicting an outcome. What methods do you recommend today?

**Shultz:** The question is how to integrate behavioral data with attitudinal data. These are typically separate marketing groups today, and they need to work together.

For example, we may know how a customer thinks, but not why. We may know how a customer behaved, but not what caused the behavior. We will move from using attitudes to predict behavior to using attitudinal data to explain behavior. It's the linkage of attitude and behavioral data that is powerful.

**Reece:** More than any other area in an organization, marketing is considered to be a mysterious "black hole" where money goes in, yet only a portion of it accounts for a measurable return. Do you believe this will change and, if so, what will be the catalyst?

**Shultz:** Yes, for two reasons. Marketing companies are creating new methodologies and systems, like demand mapping, to create more accountability. They are unlocking this mysterious black box to enable a greater understanding of brand valuation, customer value, and growth potential.

Accounting guys are insisting on this. When this happens, marketers will become big players. Accountability is something marketing has avoided for many years, and that will need to change.

# Part I

## Social Media, Digital Media, and Personal Communication Tactics

Web 1.0 offered consumers the ability to access information and opened the door to ecommerce as users embraced the convenience and depth of products and services offered on the Internet. Consumers learned to trust making transactions online and for many people, this became their preferred way to browse, compare, and purchase products and services.

Web 2.0 evolved into a much more robust and interactive experience. The Internet facilitates a very effective and efficient way to communicate with customers, prospects, employees, channel partners, investors, and a variety of other stakeholders. For marketers, the Internet became an inbound and outbound sales channel, as well as a distribution channel for marketing, replacing more expensive methods of marketing communication like direct mail.

The evolution to Web 3.0 is driven by mobility, live streaming video, virtual apps, cloud computing, social media, and other technologies that can be accessed from anywhere in the world through a growing variety of devices. A globally connected work force and society drives an intense need for virtual connectivity and collaboration.

Digital experiences create customer affinity and top line revenue growth. 64 percent of consumers say they made their first purchase from a brand because of the digital experience they have with it.[1] Digital experiences have a dramatic influence on purchases. According to the 2009 Razorfish Digital Brand Experience Study, 97 percent said a digital brand experience influenced whether or not they bought a product or service.[2]

Marketers who use a combination of digital media can move customers much faster through the sales cycle (awareness, trial, purchase, recommend) as a result of brand interaction and experience. The chapters in this section will show you how.

# 61

# Digital Base Camp: Create a Great Web Site

A Web site is ground zero for digital marketing. Although marketers have moved away from promoting their Web site home page like a billboard or brochure, it's a digital base camp for linking to content, directing inquiries, posting comments, distributing marketing and sales material, and hosting microsite landing pages in an email campaign.

Customer engagement has changed the way people interact with a Web site. The homepage is often the place visitors engage on a blog, or they may visit the "workroom" of a site to custom design a product or submit product ideas. Web site home pages feature blogs prominently and many Web sites are now created on platforms designed for blogs (like WordPress and Typepad), so site owners can make a blog the main focus and easily change the content on their own.

Your company Web site is a fast and efficient means for people to research and learn about products, services, people, and companies before making a buying decision. In business markets, it can be a central point for presenting thought leadership. In consumer markets, even if buyers don't purchase online, they will do research to compare features and prices before making a purchase.

It's more important than ever to create a captivating Web site that is designed for multiple uses and different types of users. Web sites are a focal point for collaboration and document sharing, networking, gathering information and research, broadcasting, developing products and services, and delivering knowledge, training, and development.

As you update your business Web site, evaluate all the potential ways you can use your site to make your business more efficient and productive. Consider four broad areas for content design and Web site development: informational, transactional, participative, and collaborative.

Because people have become accustomed to a self-serve world, make it easy for them to access and download standard information such as product and service brochures, staff directories, job postings, directions, calendars, and event information. Transactions should be streamlined as well. Make it simple for people to register for events and Webcasts, sign up for newsletters, download reports, register for training, take a course, make payments, order products and services, or fill out and submit an application.

Encourage participation and collaboration through your Web site by developing a blog to communicate with customers and respond to their needs and requests. Create a workroom for clients to streamline work on projects. Host Webinars and live events for prospects, customers, and employees. Post presentations, podcasts, and videos that inform, educate, and/or sell.

Your Web site will be the primary conduit from which many of your other marketing programs will flow. All of the other new media tactics that are described in this section can be integrated with your Web site. But before moving on to other types of digital media, let's review a few points that will help you design a more effective site.

## Design for User Experience

Designing an effective Web site begins by focusing on the customer experience. Usability is critical and the site should be designed around how customers will read, search, and find information. Start by mapping out how customers interact with your site. Evaluate recent Web metrics to discover how the most popular pages are prioritized and try to infer what series of decisions users make. If you design the site this way instead of following the typical hierarchy of Web site navigation frames, you should arrive at a simple but elegant framework that is geared to how customers make decisions.

Users like simplicity and they want information delivered fast. They want to view sites that are free from clutter, easy to read, intuitive to navigate, quick to download, and protective of their privacy. A user also wants to be able to contact a company through multiple means such as email or by phone, and often they want multiple choices of interaction (click to chat, call now, and so on) if help is needed.

If a customer is a repeat visitor to your site, make use of cookies to welcome customers back by using information the customer has already provided. When shopping online, the user expects to see product details and pictures, pricing information, shipping costs, and delivery information. She also wants an easy-to-use shopping cart with the ability to add and delete items, pay through a secure site, and receive an order confirmation via email. The ability to track delivery is also becoming more important to consumers.

If your goal as a B2B company is to build a database of people who are interested in your products and services, you will probably need to offer something of value, such as a free report or article, to encourage registration. Ask users if they are interested in receiving information from your company so you have their permission to send it to them. It will also help you understand their needs so you can customize information based on individual preferences and cultivate a relationship with your customers.

One of the most important factors to keep in mind as you develop a Web site and other types of digital marketing is that everything is connected. If your goal is to target customers that make ample use of mobile devices, consider this in your initial design and strategy. Design a Web site version for mobile devices.

## Make Your Web Site Interactive and Targeted

Web sites are evolving beyond simple, static pages. Interactive capabilities enable consumers to experience and interact with your brand, which facilitates the opportunity for them to emotionally connect to your products and services. Interactivity captivates a user's attention quickly, and you can lead the user to a purchase decision by giving them exactly the information that you want them to see.

Even flat collateral materials can become interactive. Use multimedia to create interactive brochures which allow readers to turn pages in a company brochure, product catalog, or other sales collateral materials. Tutorials, videos, and interactive slide shows keep users engaged in the content as it educates, informs, or entertains.

As marketers use a growing number of digital marketing channels to reach consumers, the use of microsites is becoming more important. Microsites are Web site landing pages that take the visitor to a specific part of a company Web site, or even to a completely different Web site and URL. Microsites are a much more effective way to target market, advertise, and direct promotions than simply listing a company Web site in marketing materials. For example, if you wanted to advertise a training seminar to customers and prospects, it is much more effective to promote a Web site with messaging and content for the program than it would be to list a company URL and hope the visitor will find the training program buried deep within the site. The fewer the clicks, the better.

Companies also use microsites to extend their brand. Smirnoff Vodka created a site where visitors can interact with a "virtual bartender" to mix any combination of ingredients to see if various combinations would taste good together. The user selects the combination of ingredients and the virtual bartender drinks the concoction and makes a face to convey his approval, disapproval, or disgust.

Burger King's "subservient chicken" Web site featured an actor dressed in a chicken costume who would respond to commands made by the user. If the user asked the chicken to "do jumping jacks" or "jump up and down on the couch," the chicken responded. The promotion was designed to promote a new chicken sandwich, as well as Burger King's brand message of "Have it Your Way." More than 54 million people visited the site during the initial launch week and the average person spent eight minutes on the Web site.

Developing online communities, blogs, and resources in a company's Web site encourages personal communication with customers. For example, a consumer product company may want to create special communities of interest, such as new mothers wanting to exchange ideas through a discussion forum or by joining a new mother's online community. Such sites usually feature a vast array of resources for similar topics as a way to provide value to customers.

## Integrated Technologies Deliver Better Customer Service

If your company Web site facilitates decisions for complex sales like a site that helps students decide which college to attend, you should consider integrating customer service technologies to improve the customer experience. Live chat offered via the Web or phone provides instantaneous gratification to customers who wish to speak with someone who will help them find what they need. Studies show that companies that use this technology see an increase in sales of 25 percent or more and an 80 percent improvement in customer satisfaction. Companies can chose from a variety of live chat technologies:

1. Online chat enables users to click a button to "chat online with a customer service representative." It's a simple way for a customer service agent to answer questions and exchange information with the customer in real-time.

2. An option to "talk with a live person" is a great alternative for customers who prefer to speak to a real person and ask questions. If a customer prefers this option, she simply clicks on the phone icon and in less than a minute their phone rings and a service representative is there to help.

3. Sensory technology detects if a customer is shopping on the Web site. A chat window appears and a service representative asks, "May I help you find what you are looking for?" It's as if the customer walks into a store and is greeted by a salesperson. This type of technology is used by customers who prefer personal assistance. It's an ideal option for companies that offer hundreds of products because customers won't have to click though dozens of pages to find what they need.

Implementing a technology like the integrated sensory technology shouldn't create the image of a salesperson stalking a customer. If the customer replies that he or she is "just looking," then the salesperson can say, "Just let me know if you need help." Companies that use this technology report that engaging in live chat with a customer greatly increases the probability of a sale. It is reported that upwards of 70 percent of online orders are terminated before finalizing the sale at checkout. If you review Web reports and see that your company has a similar situation and you are losing potential customers, you should add this technology to your CRM capabilities and test if it makes a difference in customer conversion rates (in other words, if it transitions lookers to buyers). You can also use a survey tool, such as Biz Rate, to evaluate a customer's experience and measure satisfaction levels right after he purchases from your Web site.

## Provide Value For Free

From day one, the democratization of the Internet provided free and easy access to information. When someone visits a Web site, they want to find what they are looking for, and almost always expect to find something of value to them—for free. This doesn't mean give away services for free, it means providing value through ideas and access to information.

For example, if you have a resource section on your Web site, you can provide links to other Web sites that are relevant to your customers. This could include information resources, reports, white papers, articles, associations and organizations, tools and gadgets, podcasts, and so on. If your company produces Webinars or newsletters, you may want to list an archive so people can find information on certain topics pertaining to your business.

You can also communicate information about social causes that are important to your company. For example, Patagonia, a Seattle-based company that sells outdoor clothing and sports gear, is known for their passionate support of environmental causes. They post videos about these issues and concerns on their Web site; in turn, these videos help them build their brand by creating an emotional connection with their customers.

# 62

# Search Engine Marketing (SEM) and Optimization

Most of the marketing executives I talk with have incurred significant scar tissue as a result of learning how to optimize pay-per-click advertising. Changing rules and experimenting with different keywords made for difficult buying decisions. The marketers that have figured this out are buying specific keywords and investing former paid search dollars in Search Engine Optimization (SEO).

Search marketing accounts for the largest share of interactive spending, accounting for 59 percent of the overall interactive advertising budget. Annual growth rate is predicted to be 15 percent, rising to $32 billion by 2014.[1]

Another issue marketer's face is determining which search engines will best appeal to their target audience. This is important since 47 percent of Internet users say search engines are the way they find products and services and more than 90 percent don't go beyond the first page of search results. Internet users have become accustomed to using search and 85 percent of online consumers use it at least weekly. For this reason, SEM and SEO are critically important to marketing and sales efforts. Here are some steps you can take to increase your likelihood of success:

- Plan for SEM and SEO from the first day the Web site is being designed.
- Choose words and phrases you believe people would use to search for your product or service. Different words will appeal to different buyers, so choose both technical terms as well as words describing business benefits.
- Prioritize words and consider grouping words by categories for the purpose of campaign management. Check web analytic resources to learn how often specific search words and phrases were used. The more a search term is used, the more you will pay.
- Develop microsite landing pages for specific messages, offers, and campaigns. This page can have links back to your Web site for additional information. Another advantage of a microsite is that you can easily track results by using different Web site addresses linked to a specific advertising medium and message.
- Although Google commands an impressive share, you will probably want to test other search engines to determine what your target audience will respond to, and which search engine brings you the best ROI. Yahoo!, Bing, and other search engines have lower market share than Google, but ad rates tend to be more

affordable, and some advertisers say they get a better ROI with search engines like Yahoo!.

- Track and measure key metrics such as click-through rate, conversion rates (by word, phrase, or ad size), cost-per-click, and cost-per-conversion.

Expect a learning curve as you experiment with different types of online marketing. Even seasoned marketing professionals need to remain flexible as they learn what works and what doesn't, and experiment with different types of ads and media buys. Effectiveness must be constantly monitored because customer preferences change quickly. Most "novel" types of ads tend to lose their effectiveness over time as users are inundated with them across the Web.

## Optimize Your Web Site

The term search engine optimization (SEO) and search marketing are becoming interchangeable. SEO is an Internet marketing strategy companies apply to their Web pages so search engines can find them easily, hopefully ranking their website high on a search results. Search engines index Internet sites by sending out "spiders" that log words, pages, and sites so when a keyword or keywords are entered into a search engine such as Google, the most relevant sites are served to the user. The spiders scan sites to look for where the keywords appear, such as in a headline or in text copy, and how frequently they appear. Words in headlines and those that appear multiple times earn higher rankings. Rankings are also determined by the number of click-throughs as well as links to and from the site. Each link is essentially a vote, and each vote is weighed based on the site's popularity. Thus, getting blogs, articles, and links that point to your site is very valuable for SEO purposes.

As search engines become increasingly more sophisticated, it becomes more difficult to figure out the optimal way to rank sites higher in search engines. The strategies that savvy Web marketers used a month ago may not necessarily work next month because the search engine rules changed.

# 63

# Online Advertising

Advertisers love interactive marketing because it is more effective and more targeted, while also being less expensive than traditional media. Even big brand advertisers are aggressively pursuing interactive media. Kimberly-Clark launched Huggies Pure and Natural diapers without TV advertising to reach a more targeted audience of digital moms.[1]

An important question to ask as you evaluate where to spend your marketing dollars is: "What are the most effective ways to advertise online and what kind of results should I expect?" The following topics describe the most popular forms of online advertising and new media advertising.

## Display Advertising

Online advertising skyrocketed in 2000, reaching $8.2 billion, then dropped with the dot-com bust, and leveled out at $7.3 billion in 2003. Since then, the pace of display advertising has been growing and is expected to reach approximately $12 billion in 2010. Display advertising, including online video, is expected to grow 17 percent CAGR to reach nearly $17 billion in the U.S. by 2014.

Display advertising is comprised of contextual ads, static images, rich media, and online video. It can be purchased in a variety of sizes, including banners, rectangles of various sizes, skyscrapers, buttons and more. When a user clicks on the display ad, they are linked to the advertiser's Web site or a microsite landing page designed specifically for the advertised offer. To view results on some of the most popular sizes, visit the AdRelevance section in Nielsen Media's Web site (www.adrelevance.com). The use of rich media in display advertising is used in about one-third of all display spending because it increases user engagement and leads buyers through the purchase process.

Reports on consumer preference for online advertising results vary widely. Seventy-nine percent of users say they click on ads, and 26 percent made an online purchase as a result of clicking on an online ad. Incentives like coupons and contests drive interest.

Forty-seven percent say they participated in online contests or sweepstakes during the past 12 months, and 31 percent said they use online coupons.[2] Incentives also play a big role in social media. Of the people who said they follow a brand on Twitter, 44 percent say access to deals is the primary incentive. Results are similar on Facebook and MySpace, where 37 percent say they "friended" a brand to get access to special deals.[3]

Marketers are eager to invest in performance-based media buys that are measurable compared to other types of ad spending. Forrester reposts that marketers currently invest 60 percent of display advertising budgets in pay-per-click buys versus impression-based buys, and will continue to do so because it is easier to measure ROI.

## Sponsorships and Affiliate Advertising

Web sites that promote products and services online for another company participate in affiliate marketing. Affiliate marketing is a very cost effective way for companies to reach potential buyers who match their target audience because it is similar to adding a sales force, but without the expense. Affiliate marketers earn a commission when a buyer makes a purchase or takes action. Typical payment structures are Cost Per Lead (CPL), Cost Per Action (CPA), and revenue sharing, which is what the affiliate earns as a percentage of the purchase. Affiliate fees generally range between 5 percent and 20 percent and may vary based on the volume of purchases made.

Amazon.com is probably the most well-known affiliate program, because it was one of the first to ever be established. When a business promotes select books on their Web site that are relevant to their business, they might feature a link to Amazon.com. If the user buys a book as a result of a link from the site, the company earns 6 to 15 percent of the selling price.

Affiliate programs are booming as more businesses pursue affiliate marketing as a key component of their strategy. The referral fee is akin to paying a sales commission but without the hassle and expense of hiring and managing a sales force. Another advantage is the extended brand presence created by affiliates.

Affiliate programs require good tracking software to track leads and sales made by each affiliate. For this reason and others, companies may choose to work with an affiliate network. Large affiliate networks usually provide tracking, reporting, ad hosting, and the ability to engage a large number of affiliates. Affiliate networks act as a third party between the merchant and the affiliates, and they usually charge businesses a percentage of the commission earned by affiliates.

Sponsorships can be an effective way to position your company's products and services on Web sites that feature a synergistic product or target the audience that you would like to reach. Sponsorships can be purchased on news, finance, entertainment, and a variety of special interest Web sites. The sponsor pays a fee and receives acknowledgment in the form of advertising or promotion for paying a fee to sponsor an event, a service, content such as a report, or other service. For example, a financial services business might be interested in sponsoring part of a financial news Web site. If you market a consumer product targeted to women, you may wish to sponsor content that will reach a large number of people in your target market, such as the Oprah Web site. Or a manufacturer of golf clubs such as Calloway might purchase a replay segment of the PGA tournament on a news or sports Web site. There are many different types of sponsorship and each is unique in terms of the benefits rewarded to sponsors.

## Ad Exchanges

One of the best opportunities in digital advertising has been the proliferation of advertising exchanges. An advertising exchange is an auction-based platform that allows buyers and sellers of online advertising to transact directly with one another. This highly flexible business model allows advertisers to more effectively purchase and target their advertising by buying inventory based on their impressions in real-time.

Another benefit is the flexible pricing model. Instead of negotiating lengthy contract terms and making purchases on a cost-per-thousand basis—a process that has been in place for decades—advertisers can set variable prices for certain types of inventory and different types of target markets, which provides for more specific targeting.

This completely changes the game with respect to buying a certain program or time slot and paying a set rate. Advertisers can align pricing to the target market impressions and anticipated return.

This is good news for both advertisers and for ad exchange portals like Google DoubleClick, Yahoo! Right Media, AOL's BidPlace, Microsoft AdECN, and others that are eager to tap into this emerging market. As marketers demand more and more performance-driven marketing investments, budgets will no doubt shift to those with measurable returns.

# 64

# Email Marketing

Email continues to be a very strong and effective means of communicating with customers by offering promotional offers and discounts, encouraging participation and registration to attend company events, introducing new products and services, facilitating improved customer service, and sending informative and educational newsletters. Email marketing is growing because it has many benefits:

- Minimal cost compared to direct mail, which requires additional economic and environmental costs associated with designing, printing, and mailing.
- Messages and offers can be highly personalized to individuals.
- Programs can be implemented quickly to provide immediate results and sales.
- Links embedded in the message can direct readers to a Web site or microsite landing page to learn more about the offer.
- Email is an effective way for people to pass information along to others.
- Email marketing can integrate other types of media such as video, audio, and social media.
- Web analytics allow for easy tracking of metrics and results.

Email marketing is an effective marketing tool that is widely used and accepted by both businesses and consumers. The ability to target individual messages combined with decreasing costs of delivery make email marketing very cost effective. Forrester Research reports that 97 percent of marketers use email marketing, and spending will grow about 11 percent CAGR to reach $2 billion in the U.S. by 2014.[1]

Fortunately, most of the bad raps associated with email marketing have disappeared as new email marketing protocols have emerged. Opt-in/opt-out marketing, also called permission marketing, is a practice conscious companies use to encourage open communication with customers and potential customers. When purchasing a list, make sure it contains only opt-in subscribers who have asked to receive information. Being perceived as a "spammer" hurts your reputation with customers and potential customers. It can also wreak havoc with Internet service providers who are enforcing stricter standards and have the power to cut off the privilege of businesses that abuse protocols or are simply unaware.

An important component of email marketing is giving people the right to opt-out of receiving information from your company at any time. This is easy to execute by simply placing a message at the bottom of a communication to unsubscribe to future communication.

Successful marketing is the result of creating a learning relationship with your customers. Continuously ask them what they are interested in receiving information about, and tailor marketing campaigns to their individual preferences. Also create an easy mechanism so email recipients can update email addresses as they change jobs and/or email addresses.

Even though subscribers choose to opt-in, sometimes email advertising and promotions can eventually be perceived as too frequent or annoying by subscribers. For example, I once received emails from Williams Sonoma on a bi-weekly basis. When I decided I was getting too many emails from them, I chose to opt-out, or unsubscribe. I was surprised when I hit "submit" and a message popped up asking me why I wanted to unsubscribe. When I clicked on one of the three options, "receiving too many emails," another message asked if I would like the option to receive emails once a month or once a quarter. Once a quarter was perfect for me, and Williams Sonoma kept me as a customer.

Email marketing is highly measurable so it is easy to test response to campaigns with different messages and price points. Advertisers can also test what days of the week and time of day recipients are most likely to respond (usually the highest is Monday and the lowest is Friday). Email campaigns generate approximately a three to ten percent click-through to the Web site or landing page, and an average five percent conversion rate.

Other techniques can be applied to increase email marketing effectiveness. The most important factors that drive successful execution of email marketing are similar to direct mail: the target audience, the message (in the subject line and email text), and the offer.

---

One of the biggest challenges of email marketing is managing a CRM system and database that will assist in creating customized and relevant messages to individuals, as well as tracking results. Marketers need access to real-time information that enables them to create more customized and relevant information to customers, while also streamlining the reporting, analytics, and integration of information to learn more about customers.

---

# 65

# Mobility Marketing

Consumers want to access brands through alternative channels and mobile phones are quickly becoming the preferred choice for communication. Most people don't leave home without their mobile phone, which often functions as a television, radio, CD player, camera, and computer. It's easy to see why mobility marketing is on the minds of marketers everywhere.

Several factors are converging to create the perfect storm driving mobile adoption. Mobile devices are smaller, faster, and have robust functionality. Pricing for service, both phone and data, has dropped significantly. Creative and interesting applications are one of the biggest factors driving mobile adoption. And of course, social networking is the fuel that speeds interest in applications as people are eager to share "the next big thing" with friends and family.

## Widgets, Gadgets, and Mobile Applications

As applications and gadgets are designed for the Web, there is now equal consideration given to applications on mobile devices. Since our mobile phone goes wherever we are, it's natural we crave the same functionality and personalization on our mobile devices as we get from our desktop. Use of applications on mobile phones has exploded as developers designed creative, fun, and helpful applications that streamline and add value to our lives.

Apple launched the Apple iPhone 3G and Application Store in July 2008. By January 2009, 15,000 applications were available, and by January 2010, the number had exploded to well over 100,000, and more than 2 billion applications had been downloaded. It's clear people are hungry for applications that add functionality, productivity, and entertainment to their lives. The growing use of applications also fuels the need for robust mobile devices. When a new Apple iPhone was released, more than 3 million were sold in the first day alone. Other providers have launched application stores for their own devices, eager for a share of this lucrative market. Google's release of the much-awaited Android-powered phone will no doubt drive the application market even faster.

Social media networks that were once relegated to the Web are now mobile. Mobile video from sites like YouTube grew by more than 50 percent in 2009 and continues to rise. Facebook created $45 million mobile users in only an eight-month period, and Twitter has created several mobile apps like Tweetdeck that let users update Tweets from anywhere. Approximately 20 percent of updates are made from mobile devices.

Developers are rushing to design applications that will help marketers serve the growing demand for mobile advertising and the consumers that want special promotions delivered to them. Advertising networks like AdMob will localize content for advertisers so they can make location-specific offers. Do you need an application that will let you register your presence in a certain geographical location? There's an app for that. Do you own a business that needs to target people in certain locations (say, a fast food restaurant chain)? There's an app for that, too.

As mobile phones go wherever we are, localization weighs in as an important factor for both consumers and businesses. Because mobile phones took first place over households with television and Internet access, marketers are looking for a way to capitalize the sheer reach of this medium.

## A Growing Tidal Wave of Opportunity

While mobile advertising is still a small category representing only $561 million in 2010, a minuscule percentage of total advertising expenditures, it is one of the fastest-growing categories with a projected growth rate of 27 percent a year for the next five years.[1] As text messaging use continues to rise, especially in Europe and Asia where text messaging is used by over 80 percent of subscribers, mobility marketing is taking off.

It's still unclear exactly how mobile users will embrace advertising. Sixty-six percent of users say that advertising on this media is annoying.[2] Other marketers say they have success with mobile text messaging if the message is short, targeted, relevant to the user, and interactive with a call to action. For example, a shopper at a local mall that receives a message for a discount at her favorite store is likely to appreciate a personal text to receive 20 percent off on purchases that day. Restaurants and nightclubs might offer customers a free drink. A consumer product company might offer a coupon for a free trial when the consumer is asked to enter a special promotion code. Or a music artist or store could offer a free ringtone or music download.

As marketers experiment with different types of advertising, a combination of text messaging and promotion might just be the key. If 47 percent of online users participate in online contest or sweepstakes, and 31 percent use online coupons, then mobile users may embrace it too.

## How Companies Use Mobile Phones to Drive Business

Mobile devices are also a great way for companies to provide education and training relevant to the user. I worked with a company that delivered bite-sized training over mobile phones as a way to stay connected to their sales force and deliver product training. A question with three multiple choice answers was served to the salesperson's mobile phone. The user selects an answer and is told if it's right or wrong. It then displays the answer and serves up the next question. For salespeople who find it difficult to schedule time for online learning, this was a great mechanism to deliver training on the morning commute or while waiting in a client's lobby.

John Edwards used mobile marketing heavily during his presidential campaign run. At events and rallies, he would invite people to pull out their cell phone and asked them to enter a short code. His campaign organizers could then add the mobile numbers to their campaign list and text messaging network. Edwards was able to raise thousands of dollars using mobile marketing as a tactic to connect with his endorsers.

As you evaluate new methods of marketing to tap into the power of this media, it would be wise to examine new applications and their use among your target audience. For example:

With **Shop Savvy**, a phone is now a bar code scanner that can be pointed at any item to receive a price comparison from nearby retailers as well as online retailers. This application combines brick and clicks comparison shopping and urges businesses to find another value proposition besides "low price."

**Mint Financial Services** lets you manage your entire financial portfolio by tapping into 7,500 U.S. financial institutions. User accounts synchronize investments, account balances, expenses, and other financial data to deliver service offers from financial institutions that are customized to the user's assets and investments. When Mint became the top finance application within 24 hours of launch on iTunes, it threatened disintermediation in the financial institution market.

**Zillow.com** is an application with tons of potential in the real estate market. Home buyers and industry professionals can quickly download information on the value of homes by neighborhood, see current listings, and search comparables to see what homes have recently sold for. Click on a listing to see details on the home size, square footage, taxes, past pricing information, and other data.

# 66

# Social Media: Build Your Brand and Connect with Customers

The rapid rise of social media may be the most important evolution to impact marketing in decades. It changes everything. It enables businesses to influence new buyers (rather than sell to them), interact and engage with customers (instead of having a one-way dialogue), and it puts the consumer in control of shaping and influencing a brand (not marketers).

The next several chapters will highlight the key trends driving social media, summarize the benefits of the most popular social networks, and describe the metrics and results of businesses that are using it to market and sell. As I send this book to my editor for publishing, I am keenly aware that by the time it is in your hands, the social media environment will have already changed. The only thing that is certain is it's here to stay. Time will tell us how effective it will be as a customer loyalty strategy and lead generation tactic. Read on to learn what we know so far. As social media moves more mainstream, I encourage you to experiment and take an active role in its evolution.

## A Shift of Power

Digital media channels have given new meaning to The First Amendment, a privilege that is not only practiced in America, but around the world. Social networks, blogs, media aggregators, and dozens of different types of digital media provide channels for consumers to have their voices heard. This has changed the entire landscape of marketing, and the bottom line is that power has shifted to consumers who now have the ability to interact and influence brands. Consumers can influence how fast a new product is adopted and liked, and they can bring a company to its knees when they set out to damage a brand. When videos like the "Comcast sleeping technician" are posted and shared, it's easy to see how the power of one consumer-generated video can affect a brand.

Consumer-generated media is everywhere. YouTube gives users power and control to upload, download, post, and share videos to inform, persuade, educate, and entertain others. Media sites like Digg and StumbleUpon give consumers the power to review and vote on content they believe is the most important or interesting. On sites like Wikipedia, content is completely created by a community of users.

What drives the popularity of consumer-generated media? At the most basic level is the emotional need to be heard. People that feel "wronged" want to be heard as much as they want to evangelize what they love. The Internet and social media is so accessible and easy to use, it provides a platform for those that want to connect, communicate, and drive change.

Social media and social networking is also referred to as social influence marketing (SIM), which describes the *business benefits* of social media. It is not only a channel through which people can experience and interact with your products, services, and company, it expands the reach and multiplies the influence consumers have. This creates momentum around how brands are interpreted and have meaning.

Communication on social media platforms is transparent and perceived as much more authentic than traditional advertising and marketing. When consumers embrace a brand, they turn into its greatest promoters, bringing a level of legitimacy and authenticity to your brand that you couldn't possibly buy.

Businesses must get comfortable with releasing control and step into the role of *leading* and *guiding* the brand. Smart marketers are tapping into the real power of digital media by engaging in conversations with customers, guiding their experiences with the brand, and giving them the tools to help raise awareness and market their brand.

Encourage interactive dialogue with customers and prospects by posting a blog on your Web site. You will actually have more control than you would if customers had to go elsewhere to blog when they have something to say about your company. It also gives you the opportunity to respond to ideas, inquiries, and complaints much faster than traditional methods.

For example, when Dell was presenting at a national conference and the PC literally burst into flames, word quickly spread on Twitter. Dell could have chosen to issue a press release and suffer through days of agonizing backlash. Instead, the company quickly communicated on Twitter to explain the situation and the buzz was quickly dispelled. Not only was a PR nightmare averted, but you could argue that it helped their image because they were so responsive and transparent about the incident.

The speed and sheer reach of digital media spreads news and events like wildfire. It has catapulted people like Susan Boyle into instant stardom, and it has garnered some commercials with the same status as Super Bowl ads. When the People for the Ethical Treatment of Animals (PETA) advertisement for the Super Bowl was declined by the networks because it was too provocative, the ad was distributed online and may have been seen by even more people because it was shared across social media networks. Dozens of online media and news channels featured the story on their home pages.

Millions of people saw the commercials and forwarded the message to friends, family, communities, and organizations using social media—and all this was free. Sure beats a million-dollar Super Bowl commercial.

## The Real Value of Social Media

As marketers move deeper into becoming owners of customer experience, they will begin to see the important role social media marketing plays in customer engagement with brands: It facilitates real-time conversations that build closer customer relationships.

Marketers embrace social media because it can help them accomplish many goals. It can increase their understanding of how customers use and value their brand, monitor customer satisfaction, improve customer experience, and launch marketing programs and campaigns. It also helps in the area of product development. Customers are the best source for innovative new ideas, and social media gives them a channel to share suggestions to improve products and business processes.

All of these benefits explain the real value of social media. It's not trying to figure out how to "sell more" by leveraging advertising campaigns into social media, or trying to assess ROI using traditional marketing measures. The evolution of social media will no doubt create opportunities for monetization. *My point is that the opportunity and benefits social media provide are much more than that.*

If your goal is to position your brand expertise, it won't happen overnight in the social media space. Just as face-to-face networking is relational and takes time and effort to foster, so does social networking. But imagine the difference over time. If you attend an event with 100 people in the room, you'll be lucky to connect with five people in a meaningful way. If you spend the same amount of time in an evening on social networking platforms, you may connect with ten times as many people.

Keep in mind that social media requires practice, patience, and persistence to build a network and awareness. What works for one company does not work for another. There are differences in business markets and in consumer markets, as well as in industry and company size. As you experiment, keep in mind that there are a few principles that cut across every sector. The list in the following section, "Social Media Principles," summarizes what I believe are the most important right now.

These principles are simple, yes, but they are not always easy to execute. Some require effort and others a great deal of discipline. The early adopters of social media set up a pretty good ecosystem. As we all take a role in its evolution, let's all do our part to keep it that way.

## Social Media Principles

- **Listen.** Social media is all about listening to what people are saying, hearing what is important to them, and engaging them. Listening tells you what people want to know. If you monitor what is being said, it will tell you if a need is being fulfilled or not. If not, then you have something to write about.

- **Learn.** Social media requires an insatiable appetite for learning. If you read reports from analysts and other sources, you will learn what's working and where people spend their time. It will also spark new ideas and give you insight and perspective. There are dozens of tools and analytics that will help you measure results and decide where to invest your efforts in the future.

- **Engage.** "Social" means engagement. If your goal is to build a huge following of friends or followers, you have to ask: What's the objective? What will you get in return? An auto-follow tool that gets you thousands of followers may do little to add value to your business if they never engage with you. On the other hand, another school of thought practiced by many avid Twitter-ers is to live by the law of numbers and get as many followers as possible. Who is to say who's right? Only time will tell—in the meantime, you decide. Interact, engage, and share your expertise with others.

- **Transparency.** Social media is incredibly transparent. What you do and say is visible to the world. Your actions have a direct reflection on your reputation, your company culture, and the quality of your relationships. Personalization and the quality of transparency is one of the most attractive features of social media. Keep in mind that digital media has a long memory—but if you are authentic and honest, you will be just fine.

- **Live by the Golden Rule.** "Do unto others as you would have them do unto you" is a principle to live by every day. And in the world of social media, its expected. Take a moment to comment on a blog that someone obviously invested time to research and write if it benefited you in some way. Share valuable information and content with others who would benefit from it. Thank people who open their network to you or make introductions that help you.

- **Give More Than You Take.** Early social media pioneers could have had an attitude of scarcity, but thankfully, they didn't. Give freely and believe that what goes around comes around. What you give, you get back in spades.

- **Brand Authenticity.** Consistency of brand promise is important across all media platforms. In social media marketing, it is reflected in what you say in forums, the content you develop, the programs you execute, and the relationships you establish with people and businesses. Social media is a rich space to share videos, podcasts, blogs, groups, ebooks, wikis, or other tools to express and share your knowledge, creativity, and humor—whatever your gifts are.

# 67

# What We Know So Far: Surprising Statistics

Although social media adoption has grown exponentially, it's still in its formative years. A few of the biggest questions on the mind of marketers and business owners are: How do I measure the value of social media? What are the best platforms I should use to reach my customers? Can I generate leads? How much time and money and how many resources should I invest in it?

We'll be able to answer these questions much easier in a couple years, but what we can do right now is examine the trends shaping social media and social networking through 2014. We can also analyze results so far to see what areas are gaining the most momentum.

The Center for Marketing Research at the University of Massachusetts Dartmouth has studied the adoption of social media for three years (2007–2009). The study tracks familiarity and adoption of social media with the Inc. 500, a list of the fastest-growing companies in the United States.[1] Six types of social media were studied: blogging, podcasting, online video, social networking, message boards, and wikis. The results show skyrocketing growth of social media. Here are a few of the highlights:

1. The Inc. 500 reports that social media is "very important" to their business and marketing strategy. This almost doubled in one year, with 44 percent saying social media is a primary part of their business and marketing strategy. Ninety-one percent use at least one social media tool.

2. Social networking is the most popular, with 75 percent of the Inc. 500 very familiar with it. A surprising 52 percent of Inc. 500 companies use Twitter.

3. Forty-five percent of the Inc. 500 now blog, compared to 39 percent in 2008. The use of blogs increased to 45 percent in 2009, and 44 percent of companies that do not currently implement a blog intend to have one.

4. Social media is regarded to be highly effective for companies across the board. Success measures are defined as hits, comments, leads, or sales. Twitter is reported as successful 82 percent of the time and all other tools achieved at minimum an 87 percent success rate.

5. Social media is used for brand and company monitoring by 68 percent.

I like this report because it trends three years of data. It's also a great barometer of what the fastest-growing companies in the U.S. consider to be the most important and how fast they are adopting various types of social media.

## Business Results from Social Media

Marketers are not hesitating to invest in social media. Over 73 percent of chief marketing officers say they will increase budgets for social media solutions.[2] Forrester predicts social media will have the steepest growth over any other media channel. Investments will grow at 34 percent CAGR over the next five years and are estimated to reach $3 billion by 2014.

What do businesses hope to gain from social media investments? According to the "Social Media Marketing Industry Report," the number-one benefit of social media is generating exposure for a business.[3] The top three benefits for social media ranked in priority are 1) increasing exposure for my business (81 percent); 2) increasing traffic/subscribers (61 percent); and 3) building new business partnerships (56 percent).

This was followed closely by an increase in search engine rankings (52 percent) and generating qualified leads (48 percent). The all important question of "Did it help you close business?" was cited as a benefit by 35 percent of respondents.

It's interesting to note there appears to be a direct relationship between the amount of time spent weekly on social media and the amount of experience a person has with it. Ten percent of experienced marketers average a whopping 20 hours or more per week, and this same group also claims to close more business than light users. If you can't devote that kind of time to social media, you will be relieved to know that marketers spending six or more hours per week claim "exceptionally positive results."

It's also useful to look at what hinders adoption of social media. Company culture influences a company's social media usage. Most large companies govern communications with a very tight leash, and this extends to social media. Some marketers participate in social media under the radar and others follow protocol which tends to get caught up in corporate governance and legal teams. Risk tolerance and fear are a few of the key issues slowing adoption of social media.

# 68

# Measuring the Effectiveness of Social Media

We have already had considerable discussion about the lack of discipline and knowledge that is needed to measure traditional media. It appears that social media might provide even more of a challenge for some marketers. According to one IDC study, only 25 percent of direct marketers have a strategy for measuring social media ROI. On the other hand, some marketers report that they find it easier to track leads from social media. As marketers become more accustomed to using different types of social media, I predict they will find it much easier to track social media than traditional media.

One of the challenges of measurement is making sure you are measuring the things that matter, as well as linking measurements to the right objective. If the goal is awareness, the number of forwards can be evaluated, but they don't necessarily shed insight on how it drives purchasing behavior.

Another measure is customer engagement, which is defined as time spent on content generated from social media, pass-along value, and how this correlates to revenue. RazorFish, a global interactive agency, studied the effects of engagement with applications and gadgets by people who discovered the application from a media source and those who accessed it from a friend. People who discovered the application via a friend are two to four times more likely to download the application, are two to eight times more likely to spend money on the client site and have an average order that is 10 to 30 percent higher than those who are exposed only through media.[1]

RazorFish is doing further research and development on tools that will assist businesses in understanding the key elements of social media ROI. Using a tool called the Generational Tag, RazorFish tracks how users pass viral media on to their friends, how their friends respond and forward messages, and the value of each successive group (generation) that receives and passes along the message element. The Generational Tag is a set of code that tracks the viral spread of widgets and gadgets in social network platforms (such as Facebook) and non-social network environments (such as desktop applications). To use this new measure, the SIM must have shareable elements (applications, gadgets, and so on) that are associated with people (see Table 68.1).

**Table 68.1**  Measuring Social Media

| Value Driver/Generation | Measurement and Optimization |
|---|---|
| Impressions and engagement generated through media | Downloads and conversion behavior/intent to purchase |
| Incremental reach/pass-along value | Model and measure total number of pass-along viewers |
| Value of endorsement effect | Views, users, downloads, and conversion behavior/intent to purchase |

As more companies develop innovative solutions for tracking and measuring the effects of social media, there is little doubt that businesses will be eager to adopt them.

In the meantime, we know that one of the most important components of social media is the viral nature of the media when a message is passed among friends, family members, colleagues, associates, and other communities. Each of these people or groups of people are influencers who can raise brand awareness, add value through endorsements, and recommend or influence purchasing decisions.

Whether you are dipping your toe in social media marketing or have already jumped in with both feet, the best strategy is to experiment. The rules of the road for social media are still being written, but that doesn't mean you should sit back and wait. Experiment and adopt strategies that are being used successfully by other companies. Keep in mind that what works for one business is different from another based on integration of other marketing programs, budget, target market, and other circumstances.

## Operationalize Social Media

Social media has scaled to the point that businesses should establish both a budget and resources to oversee this important function. It should not be thought of as a poor step-child that receives whatever is left over after other marketing dollars are allocated. Remember, if social media is used to drive product development, research, and customer service, as well as add value to other areas of the business, then it would be wise for several departments to contribute budget and resources to social media strategy and execution.

The marketing department will usually drive social media strategy, and marketers should take an active role in guiding others in the organization to learn and contribute. Ongoing learning helps everyone become better marketers and in turn, the company builds a stronger brand. The marketing department can provide education and training, share best practices, provide guidelines for use, and establish systems for closed-loop communication internally and externally, as well as create the systems for reporting and measurement.

Even the CEO should have a role in social media. CEOs of companies that were early adopters to this media have been very successful in shaping and growing their brands. Comments on a blog or Twitter are much more authentic than comments made through a press release.

Content generation is another area that needs to be built into the marketing operations plan. It requires planning and development to create a library of content so it is not an afterthought after a program is launched. Who will be responsible for writing content? Will you post original content or will you pull from other sources? What types of media such as video, podcasts, webinars, and photos can be used? Use pre-established branding guidelines to guide development of the content and format.

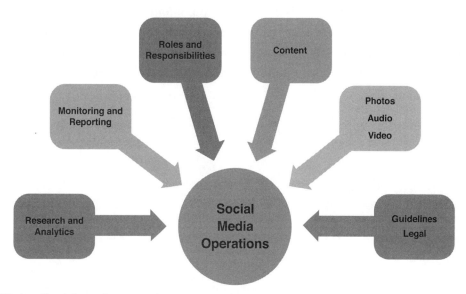

**Figure 68.1** *Social media operations*

Sales and marketing departments should use social networking to listen to the voice of the customer, as well as monitor what is being said about competitor's products and services. It's a valuable research tool that should be used collaboratively by sales and marketing teams to keep their pulse on the market. Several online tools for monitoring customer feedback such as YackTrack, Yelp, and Get Satisfaction are excellent services to monitor what is being said about your company, as well as competitors.

If your goal is to collect customer feedback dynamically tools like WuFoo, PollDaddy, and TwtPoll are good real-time research tools. SuggestionBox.com is another tool that facilitates the collection of ideas from customers. It encourages customers to rate their favorite ideas (externally on the site) and employees to rate ideas and suggestions internally. Employees can respond to customer ideas privately, and there is a mechanism to notify customers when their idea has been implemented. Download a widget and the service is featured on your company website.

If you have an online store, consider using RatePoint, a service with several customer service and feedback tools. Like some of the other services, customers can post a review, and if the review is negative, you can reach out to the customer to resolve the issue before a comment is made public. RatePoint verifies reviews to make sure they are legit, and in the process verifies contact information that you can use for ongoing customer communication. Communicating with and learning from your customers has never been easier—so no more excuses!

Make it easy for your customers to find you and your company in lots of different places. Place buttons for tools so it's easy to share content on your Web site, blog, articles, and other areas where you post online content (Digg, Twitter, Delicious, RSS feeds). This will help others share and amplify your content. Include your social network profile link in your email signature and on business cards so people can easily find you.

# 69

# Social Media Networks

As more people begin to use social media, it will ultimately be the users who define which social networking sites will make it and which ones won't. As new sites come and go, you will need to experiment to find the best social networks that work for you and your business. Some people swear by LinkedIn and others prefer Twitter, Facebook, MySpace, or a more targeted network like NING. It just depends on your business and industry. It's also a matter of personal preference and the networks that clients, prospects, colleagues, and business associates use.

Remember, the value of social media is connecting and communicating. It will be more effective to be selective rather than spread your efforts across too many networks. If you try to take on too much, chances are you'll find it overwhelming or not as effective as you would if you were to prioritize your efforts.

The following information summarizes the key benefits and attributes of the three of most popular social media preferences: LinkedIn, Facebook, and Twitter.

## LinkedIn

While MySpace and Facebook are extremely popular and have larger networks, LinkedIn has found a niche with business professionals who use the platform to network and market their business. It has also become an effective network for communities, associations, and organizations.

LinkedIn has grown to over 52 million members and professes to have the "world's largest audience of affluent, influential professionals." In addition to networking, finding and staying connected with people in your personal network is a key benefit of LinkedIn. Despite how many times people change jobs or email addresses, they stay connected through LinkedIn, and for this reason alone it is a valuable business networking service. It synchronizes with Microsoft Outlook contacts, so as you add new contacts, you can also add them to your LinkedIn database and build your network.

Your personal profile page generally includes information about your company and brand, and it should succinctly communicate your personal brand and work experience. Many people use LinkedIn for finding new jobs and careers, to seek referrals and endorsements, and to give referrals to others. When people want to hire an individual with specific skills, they might ask for recommendations from people they trust in their network. Like other social networking tools, the more you use it, the more valuable it becomes. You need to invest time to add connections, give or ask for referrals, and keep your profile current. You can also start or join a group to connect with people in organizations, associations, and universities to build your network. Participate in the groups you join. You can comment or start a blog post, make announcements to the group, ask questions to help with research, and participate in several other ways. All of these things will also improve your Google page rank since your profile can be searched.

## Facebook

Facebook was launched in 2004 as a social network exclusively for Harvard Students. Within just four months, 30 colleges had joined the network. Today there are more than 300 million active users from 170 countries.

Nielsen reports that Facebook is the number-one social networking site. Over 4 million users become fans of Facebook's public profile page *every day*. As the average user has 100 friends linked to their site and adding more each day, Facebook continues to grow exponentially. It's also popular among the one million developers who have developed more than 52,000 applications.

For businesses that want to tap into the power of Facebook, it's important to apply a few marketing basics. First of all, understand that the audience is still young demographically and skews more heavily toward females. If you sell power tools, Facebook probably won't be your first choice in brand building. But if you are thinking like Victoria's Secret, you will have success. The fan page created to promote their PINK line has been extremely successful because it aligns perfectly with the demographics of Facebook.

Victoria's Secret was also successful because they effectively promote their Facebook page, as well as links to their MySpace page, on the PINK website landing page. By promoting multiple ways that consumers can connect with the brand, it builds fans across all platforms.

When a fan page was created by two passionate Coke enthusiasts, the company could have leveled a velvet hammer in an attempt to control the site content. Instead, they rewarded the two fans with a trip to Coke headquarters in Atlanta. This created even more passion and enthusiasm for the brand and other successful groups rallied around Coke. By giving up some control and letting fans influence the brand, Coke now has the number-one product fan page on Facebook.

Like other social networking sites, the practice of providing valuable resources to users, as well as offering coupons, incentives, or contests, creates pass-along value. Give your fans something to talk about and watch your idea take fire.

## Twitter

If you believe in the premise that short, quick bits of information are valuable, maybe even more valuable than long bursts of information, then you will love Twitter, a micro-blogging service founded in 2007. Twitter is growing in popularity faster than any other social networking service. Within a year, more than 2.2 million accounts were generated.[1] By June 2009, Web-tracking firm Compete reported that Twitter had grown an astounding 1,928 percent in just a year.

People use Twitter to answer the question, "What are you doing?" with far-ranging topics from eating a donut to announcing a new product launch. They also share information about people, companies, news stories, products—really anything.

Twitter may be thought of as frivolous by some people, but it has been used for important causes. Twitter helped free an American from an Egyptian jail, provided the latest news on events like the San Diego fire, and broke industry news such as the financial crisis. It's also used for raising money for charities and promoting a brand. Celebrities love Twitter. Ashton Kutcher has nearly 4 million followers, and Oprah, Obama, and Britney all have a huge number of followers.

Twitter is a marketing channel to build your brand, create customer loyalty, and leverage the power of social influence. It is easier than ever before for people to endorse a product or a company in their personal network. Of course, the flip side of that is it's also very easy for consumers to vilify a company.

Many businesses that were quick to embrace Twitter now have a small army of avid followers. Jet Blue (@jetblue) and Home Depot (@TheHomeDepot) are just a couple that Twitter. Topics range from employee interests and community involvement to resolving customer service issues. But beware: Pimping products is considered bad behavior. The way to build your brand is through personal customer communication, community interests, social causes, and being a helpful resource to people.

A common way to use Twitter and build your own army of followers is to make ample use of the retweet function, which is a lot like forwarding an email to people in a database. According to Dan Zarella, a social, search, and viral marketing scientist, nearly 70 percent of all retweets contain a link to a news source, article, blog, website, or content of value. It's difficult to say something meaningful in 140 characters or less, so it's much more effective to link to valuable content such as breaking news, "How To's," and instructional content. Other avid Tweeters swear that tweeting unusual or strange content garners the most comments and retweets. What's unusual and strange you might ask? A tweet about a boy born with two heads, a cat that can sing, an ant colony that is taking over the world, or a Jerry Springer moment (did anyone say "National Enquirer?").

If you want more helpful hints, check out the Twitter Guidebook on Mashable or other helpful online resources. Start using some of the latest and greatest Twitter applications like Tweetdeck to sort, search, respond, organize, and manage your Twitter activities. And don't forget to download a mobile Twitter application like Twitterific so you can Tweet to your heart's content from anywhere your mobile device takes you.

Guy Kawasaki is the author of several bestselling books and the CEO of Garage.com, a Silicon Valley-based company that funds and works with early stage start-ups. He offers more helpful hints on how to use and optimize Twitter. As an early Twitter evangelist with a huge following, he is qualified to be "Trusted Twitter Tutor." Here is his advice to help you get started.

## How to Use Twitter as a Twool

**1. Forget the "influentials."** The Internet's democratization of information means that the "nobodies" are the new "somebodies." It is better to have a legion of "nobody" devotees than an occasional somebody, and enough attention from the "nobodies" will demand the "somebodies'" attention.

**2. Defocus your efforts.** The goal is to reach the masses because you never know who can help you and how. Twitter's an easy and inexpensive way to reaching the masses, making a defocusing market strategy both plausible and profitable.

**3. Get as many followers as you can.** Those who argue that it's the quality, rather than the quantity, of your Twitter followers that matters aren't using Twitter as a tool. It's the law of big numbers—your chances of reaching the tipping point increases with the number of followers you have. Also, you might want to try to prevent domain name squatting, and secure both your name and your company's name. People are more inclined to follow a person than a company, but you may want both.

**4. Monitor what people are saying about you, your company, and your product.** You can do this with Twitter's searches, which you can bookmark for convenience. You can also use Tweetdeck to create and follow a search, or Twilert.com for email notification of search results. As a marketing tool, it is a quick and efficient way to communicate and sincerely help those who are pissed off, confused, or have unanswered questions in regards to you or your company. By simply monitoring what people are saying about you, you're using Twitter better than 95 percent of companies.

**5. Ask for help.** Don't be shy about asking people on Twitter to spread the word for you. The worst someone can say is "no," but more often you'll be surprised by the number of people who are willing to not only help you, but go out of their way to do so—whether it's spreading the word or offering helpful suggestions.

**6. Make it easy to tweet on your behalf.** Twitterfeed allows you to post any RSS feed as your own tweet. A Twitterfeed was created for Alltop where people could sign up to allow Alltop to automatically post Alltop news as their own tweets. Initially, 177 people signed up, and another 280 signed up for the free copy of Kawasaki's new book, *Reality Check*, totaling 450 people. These people had 140,000 followers—can anyone say *free marketing?* This is nothing short of IT evangelism, though it can unintentionally get out of hand, as you'll see later.

**7. Create an email list.** When people follow more than one person who has a Twitterfeed (as described previously), they'll receive duplicate posts. In this case, to ameliorate this issue, Alltop created the Alltop news and announcements email list, which allows recipients to decide whether they want to edit it, tweet it, or email it to others. This tool attracted more people than the Twitterfeed by not taking over their feeds and by giving them the power to sift through their outgoing material.

**8. Make it easy to "post to Twitter."** You can increase the traffic to your website by placing a "Post to Twitter" link on each page, or article, or whatever. If a viewer likes the content, she or he can click on the "Post to Twitter" button, which then opens a preconfigured tweet you could send to followers. Digg, Delicious, and Yahoo! Buzz buttons are other instant-click ways you can spread the word.

**9. Offer advice deals to Twitter users.** You can offer special deals to your Twitter followers, who I'm sure will love that you're rewarding them for their loyalty, and allow them to share their great experiences with you with their followers. Special offers via Twitter are an efficient and fun way to extend your special offers to a large base.

**10. Tell the complainers where to go.** Some followers may harangue you for using Twitter as a tool, but remember: Following you is completely optional, and if they don't like your use of Twitter, they can follow someone else more Twitterly "upright." Period.

Source: GuyKawasaki.com

## Social Bookmarking Sites

Bookmarking sites lets users search, tag, organize, and share Web pages on the Internet. A tag is simply a word to describe a bookmark, and on sites such as Delicious, your bookmarked tags are organized by topic. Similar to social networking, social bookmarking sites like Delicious have become a popular way for people to share information with each other. Bookmarks are saved by the user and made public by sharing them with specific people in their network. Most sites let viewers see other bookmarked content that is similar to a tag and some include the number of people who have bookmarked the site, as well as the ability to add comments. Some social bookmarking sites also provide web feeds with topics organized by tags.

Digg is an example of a different type of social bookmarking service that can be used to promote news stories about your company. By sending an article to customers and potential customers, or posting it on another web site, people can choose to Digg (or promote) a story if they like it. If a post receives enough "Diggs" from influential members, it is launched on the first page, creating instant fame for you and your company. Like Twitter, Digg can be used to build your company brand. Digg has 30 million users a month, so you can communicate with customers, prospects, or anyone who may have suggestions or ideas for your company.[2]

Another type of social bookmarketing site is StumbleUpon, which helps users find and share Web sites. When clicking the Stumble! button, the network delivers pages matched to your personal preferences. These pages have been recommended by the others with similar interests in the database of over 8 million users. When users rate sites they like, it automatically shares them with like-minded people in the network. StumbleUpon's value proposition is that they deliver higher quality Web pages than other search engines because they are rated by members and sorted by personal interests and preferences. The database stays current as old or low-quality sites are removed if their ratings become too low.

Another nice benefit of social bookmarking is that tags help search engine rankings. To learn about other social bookmarking sites, consult the Social Media Tools section in the Social Media Strategy and Planning Guide (www.MarketSmarter.com).

# 70

# The Blogosphere

Blogs are booming in popularity as a public relations and marketing tool. Technorati, a blog index, sites that more than 133 million blogs have been written and posted by people and companies to reflect perspectives on a particular topic, event, or news story. Over 900,000 people write and post articles every day. Blogs can be served up on an existing Web site, a separate Web site, delivered via email, or subscribed to using an RSS feed. This makes it easy to add frequently read blogs to a personal home page.

Businesses don't create blogs to necessarily sell products or solutions, although this is often the outcome. The main purpose of a blog is to connect users and readers with the personal brand of a person or company. People subscribe to blogs because they get value from the content, not because they are being sold something. A blog gives like-minded people an opportunity to talk directly with people who share similar interests, and post ideas about specific topics.

Seth Godin is a bestselling author of several marketing books, including *Permission Marketing*, *The Purple Cow*, and several others. Both marketers and business owners can gain valuable insight from his blog posts, which he updates almost every day. What does Godin get out of writing a daily blog? At a minimum, he has the opportunity to connect with people, learn from them, and test ideas. He also communicates his expertise. If people are interested in learning more, they can click on links to buy books or hire him for speaking engagements.

Godin is also the founder of Squidoo, a community of "lenses." Lenses are pages created by users (lensmasters) that aggregate and share everything on a topic of interest. Pages are called lenses as each person's lenses are focused on a topic. Users can create multiple lenses focused on different topics. As of January 2010, Squidoo has more than 1 million lenses and 800,000 visitors a day. Squidoo is free to use. Revenue comes from advertising and affiliate links. The company donates 5 percent of earnings to charity, 45 percent is allocated to company overhead, and the remaining 50 percent goes back to charity or the people who build lenses (their choice).

Squidoo is an interesting community of eclectic ideas and topics. It's another way to build your community and create interest around a passion. The point of Squidoo is not to sell something, but to engage, entertain, and find people who share your passion and interests.

Alltop is an online magazine that aggregates and sorts information from all over the Internet. It's one of the best places on the Web to find content spanning a huge number of categories, as well as to see the issues are the most important to people. List your blog in the Alltop Directory to help raise visibility and awareness. It's a unique site where you are sure to find new readers.

When blogs are well written and executed, they become a very effective marketing strategy. They provide a fabulous forum for talking with customers (think real-time research). Visitors of a blog share a common interest (you, your company, or your products) and they enjoy giving tips and advice that improve the experience for others. For this reason, blog posts can be updated with new information from your company, as well as by customers who enjoy sharing their opinion and helping others. If you allow members to comment and share their own content, it not only helps the content development effort, but more importantly it creates goodwill, builds your brand, and creates relationships with your current and future customers.

New software, such as WordPress and TypePad, has made it easy for anyone to quickly create and update their own blog with no HTML experience needed. Through the use of templates and the framework for the content management system, anyone can author their own blog. In fact, many businesses and professionals choose to create a blog site instead of a traditional Web site because it is so easy to use and to update content.

Evaluate how other companies are facilitating and implementing blogs to get ideas for your business. Check out the previously mentioned examples as well as blog lists, such as Blogcast, Technorati, Bloggapedia, and the extensive listings compiled by Peter Kim.

Here are a few things you can do to improve your results from implementing a blog:

- Even before you create a blog, define your blog strategies and process.
- If you create a blog, you will need to commit to posting updates (one to five times a week is ideal). Create a plan for the topics you will blog about, and if you can, create a library of content that you can access.
- Submit your URL and RSS feed to blog directories, RSS directories, and search engines.
- Share your knowledge and expertise with others in your industry. As your network increases, you will see other blogs link to and reference your blog.
- Respond to comments and questions and thank other bloggers who reference your material or link to your site.
- Promote and market your blog as you would a product or service. Include the blog address on your business card and other marketing materials. Market your site using social media networks and through channels that can post your blog within a larger portal that is relevant to your target audience.
- Actively research high-ranking blogs and Web sites and exchange links.

## Getting Started

In the next chapter, you will use a tool, the "Social Media Strategy and Planning Guide," that will help you bring all the components of social media together to develop your strategy and plan. The tool follows the same planning process you have been using throughout this book. You will start with defining the objectives you want to accomplish and finish with tactical tools and ROI evaluation metrics. If you follow this process, it will ensure you are developing your strategy before you get into the fun tactical tools of social media.

# 71

# Social Media Strategy and Planning Guide

Decision-making framework of the PRAISE Marketing Process.

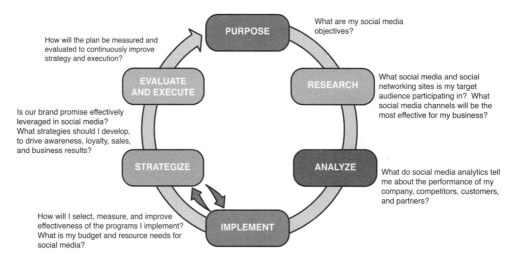

**Figure 71.1** *Decision-making framework*

## Social Media Strategy

The same process that helps businesses develop an operational marketing plan can be applied to create a social media plan. The P•R•A•I•S•E Marketing Process is a decision-making framework that will guide you through social media planning, execution, and measuring results.

Just like any other marketing strategy you implement, your plan for social media must start with your objectives and strategy. What do you want to accomplish and why? If you are going to invest in social media or allocate resources from another tactic, then you should have a sound business strategy for doing so. The investment in social media is small compared to other types of marketing, but it requires an investment of time. It also requires a commitment to experiment, measure results, and adjust as you learn. It takes time to build a social media presence and a community. It's not simply a commitment to "blog twice a week and tweet five times a week." The true investment is time spent listening, engaging in conversations, monitoring feedback, researching competitors and trends, developing content, building customer relationships, and measuring results.

The following guidelines will assist you in defining what you want to accomplish with your social media presence, what research and analysis is needed to develop effective strategies, the types of social media programs that will be the most effective for your business, and how to measure results so they continuously improve.

## PURPOSE

### Purpose: What Do You Want to Accomplish?

What is your purpose for engaging in social media? What are your objectives?

How will you define success? Is your goal to generate leads, brand awareness, drive sales, or establish expertise? Is your objective to increase customer engagement with your brand or to build a large community of subscribers and followers (see Figure 71.2)?

**Figure 71.2** *Social media objectives*

## RESEARCH

### Research: Who Is Your Target Audience and Where Will You Find Them?

Social media is all about connecting with prospects, customers, and like-minded people. How would you define them? Are they using social media? Where will you find them and what social media networks do they use? Do they engage in blogs? After you answer these questions, consider what the audience currently knows about you and how you can leverage this to expand your presence. Once you have identified who you want to reach, then you can discover how to communicate with them on different types of social media.

### Research to Listen, Understand, and Respond Effectively

Social media requires research to discover what is being said about you, your company, your brand, customers, competitors, and trends. Equally important is learning. The social media ecosystem changes and evolves daily, so listening and learning are an ongoing part of the social media process. Research will help you understand what types of social media are the most effective for your business. It will also shorten your learning curve as you discover what works and respond more quickly to adjust strategy and tactics.

## ANALYZE

### Analyze: Statistics, Media Tools, Metrics, and Trends

Although social media is relatively new, there are a vast number of analytics tools that will assist you in research and analysis. An extensive list of social media tools can be found in the "Social Media Tools and Tactics" section of this guide to determine what search engine and management tools will streamline your understanding of the market. (Note: Download the "Social Media Tools and Tactics" section of this guide. It is revised often, and you can find it in the resource section at www.MarketSmarter.com.)

Analysis will help you determine what strategies will yield the best results, as well as select the metrics for monitoring performance. Will it be number of subscribers, comments, views, actions, retweets, followers, links, leads, media mentions, or something else? Will you compare your presence to competitors, industries, or best practices? How will you know if you are attracting the people who matter?

**STRATEGIZE**

### Strategize: Create Your Game Plan

Social media strategies cascade from your business goals and marketing objectives. Like any other marketing strategy, social media strategy is developed to affect the actions of the target audience you wish to reach. It also reflects a consistent brand position and messaging.

### Positioning: Articulate Your Brand Promise

In social media, it's more important than ever to have a succinct value proposition (think 140 characters on Twitter). Your brand promise must be simple and it should be parallel across media channels. Regardless of whether you have a blog, Facebook page, or Twitter profile, you should make it easy for customers and prospects to understand what you are passionate about and quickly surmise if you are important to their community.

### Presence: Select the Types of Social Media to Use

Now that you have answered some important questions, it will be much easier to develop social media strategies and select tools to reach your target audience and establish your brand presence.

For example, if your strategy is to position you or your company as thought leaders, demonstrating this on a blog would be a good strategy. To reach your key influencers, you will link, comment, post, report, and affiliate your brand in a reputable and respectful way with them. To reach a large number of people in your target audience, you can participate in social networking sites they use. To get maximum exposure for your blog and create a community of followers, you can actively participate to develop community, which means listening, engaging, and responding. You may want to create videos and podcasts that will share your knowledge of particular subjects and demonstrate your expertise. Then you can add social media tools that will help you amplify your content (see the "Social Media Tools and Tactics" section).

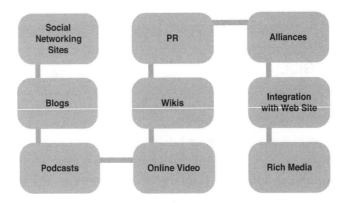

**Figure 71.3**  *Social media strategy and tactics*

Summarize your social media strategies and check to make sure they are integrated and aligned with your other marketing programs.

## IMPLEMENT

### Implement: Develop a Tactical Plan

Now that you have developed strategies based on the objectives you want to achieve, you will develop social media tactics to achieve your strategy. Later in this chapter, you will create a tactical plan that describes how you will operationalize and execute it.

The attributes and benefits of each type of social media can be described in a similar way as other types of advertising and marketing. For example, a magazine would have a specific profile describing its content, style, audience, circulation, readership, shelf life, geographic coverage, advertisers, and so on. Social media tactics can be described using similar criteria.

Your research and analysis should lead you to the best type of social media to use in order to reach your target audience and achieve you objectives. The list of social media tools in the "Social Media Tools and Tactics" section, as well as the information presented throughout Section V, will help you select and create the social media tactics to achieve your objectives.

The plan should describe what tactics you will use, the resource needs, how tactics will be measured, and projected ROI. Also include budget, time frame, and who is responsible for execution.

One of the key benefits of social media is that much is available for free or is low cost. Your budget may include videos, podcasts, and Webinars that you want to post in social media and distribute through links. The sales promotion budget may include discounts and offers made to friends and followers on Facebook and Twitter. Other items may include analytics and reporting tools, third-party software and services for rating customer satisfaction, consulting or agency fees, and internal staff resources to manage social media.

Although social media is relatively new, it has advanced to the point where it deserves a share of budget and resources to execute the strategy. Headcount is required. At a minimum, a budget for staff (internal or external) is needed to execute the strategy. If it's done in the margins, then who is responsible when the strategy is not executed?

## EXECUTE AND EVALUATE

### Execute: Link Strategy and Execution

Now it's time to operationalize your plan so it can be executed more efficiently. Your social media strategy should outline clear roles and responsibilities. Who creates blog content? How much time will it take to develop it? What ramp time is needed to create a library of content for posting? How often should posts be made? How many hours a day or week are required to participate and build a community? Who monitors customer engagement and satisfaction? Who responds to customer requests? These are just a few of the questions you need to answer.

### Company Culture: Social Media Roles and Policy

If you are just beginning to formalize your social media strategy, one of the first things you will need to decide is who in your company will participate and what type of guidelines should be developed for content and messaging. What topics can people comment on and what topics are taboos? How much time can people spend with social media?

Engage the legal department early to understand their opinion and risk tolerance. It's a good idea to clearly define this upfront as well as establish some guidelines to avoid a train wreck later.

### Evaluate: Metrics

Ongoing review is critically important. Your social media strategy should outline ROI metrics and the research and analytics that are needed to make decisions. Who is responsible for doing this important activity? How often will strategy and metrics be reported and adjustments made? Social media and other marketing program results should be evaluated in the quarterly operations review.

Define your criteria for success. Some of your goals may be overarching, others much more granular and tied to specific metrics. Review the following list of social media metrics and select those most relevant to your success criteria. Assign specific goals that you can track and measure through analytics and reporting.

Social media metrics generally fall into the three areas of Awareness, Loyalty, and Sales (see Figure 71.4). Social media is also used to achieve other company goals like employee recruiting. Metrics such as number of referrals and number recruited can be tied back to social media.

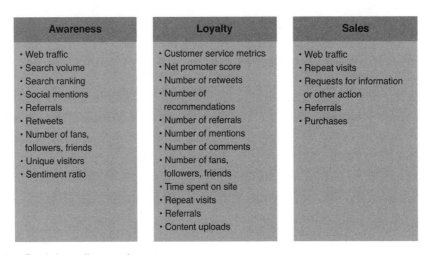

**Figure 71.4** *Social media metrics*

## Reporting and Adjustments: Experimentation Criteria

Evaluate programs often to ask questions such as: Where are we getting our greatest response? Do we know why? What messages resonate with our customers and prospective customers the most? Are messages on Twitter more effective when retweeting, using a hashtag (#), or creating pass-along value?

As social media evolves, it requires a healthy appetite for experimentation. Different strategies and tactics work for different types of businesses. If you don't experiment how do you know how much *more* effective your strategy can be?

# 72

# Word of Mouth: Viral Marketing and Buzz

Word of mouth, also referred to as buzz marketing and viral marketing, is the most desirable type of marketing you can hope to create. Word of mouth marketing has been a tactic savvy marketers have used for years, and the proliferation of digital media has made this tactic a primary component of many marketing programs. As we have discussed throughout this section, marketers are integrating viral marketing into social media, email marketing, and several other programs to generate excitement around a brand, promote a new product, or get publicity.

Viral marketing is facilitated by providing customers with the tools to share emails, videos, and other types of online communications with friends, family, and business colleagues because it is funny, creative, and/or relevant to their interests. The recipients then send the message to others in their network, who in turn send it to others in their network. This can be a highly effective way to create an install base of customers (especially for a software or an Internet company such as AOL or LinkedIn) while also building brand recognition.

## Stunts and Pranksters

Unique new forms of word of mouth are being created by consumers. One example is the recent formation of "pranksters" who gather for impromptu stunts and perform what looks like a choreographed spontaneous act. A typical stunt involves 50 or more people who learn online or through social networks about a stunt that will take place in their city. Some of the acts are funny, some are considered art, and some are just weird. In one stunt, a group of young adult twins gathered to create a "human mirror" in a New York subway. The twins sat across from each other on the subway car and mirrored the other twin's movements.

From a marketer's perspective, what is so interesting about the stunts is they are often focused around a brand. For example:

- In Manhattan, 80 people dressed in Best Buy uniforms of blue shirts and khakis slacks and descended upon a Best Buy store. The only purpose was to walk around and confuse customers (and of course, the real Best Buy employees).

- In New York, 111 shirtless men walked into an Abercrombie and Fitch store to say they were shopping for a shirt.
- At a Taco Bell restaurant, pranksters posing as both employees and customers went to the restaurant and froze in place.

A video of the Taco Bell stunt was made and used in a viral marketing campaign for the Fruitista Freeze drink and was viewed 500,000 times online. A spokesperson for Taco Bell said, "We thought it was brilliant."[1] To view a few of the latest videos check out: http://improveverywhere.com/video/.

But most groups form stunts simply want to entertain themselves and have no commercial intent. Stunts are formed loosely by different groups around the world and go by the names Improv Everywhere, San Diego-based Scene Diego, The Urban Prankster Network, Boston-based Banditos Misteriosos, GuerillaLA, and many others.

If marketers can figure out a way to channel the activity of urban pranksters, it is a new way to create exposure for their brand—especially if it's captured on video, as the Taco Bell video was, so it can be spread virally.

## Historical Milestone

For the first time in history, word of mouth and viral marketing was a crucially important element of a political campaign. In the last presidential election candidates from both parties urged Americans to vote and make a difference in the election resulting in the largest voter turnout in 90 years.

The organization MoveOn is an organization comprised of 5 million people who individually fund causes in the areas of education and advocacy on important national and congressional issues. The organization includes MoveOn.org Political Action and MoveOn.org Civic Action.

MoveOn.org Political Action created a message about "getting out to vote" was pure genius. Many of you reading this probably received the video in an email that was forwarded to you by a friend with the subject line "Don't let your friends lose the election." It is a streaming video of a news report (from CNNBC) announcing the election has just been won by one vote. The story then unveils the global impact and rage of other voters who discover who the culprit is (drum roll): *you.*

The person who forwards the video could easily customize the video with names of their personal friends. The sender just entered as many email recipients as they wanted, and in one click, sent a customized video to everyone they selected. The video used the email recipient's name in newspaper headlines and in captions under various news videos of people around the world expressing outrage about this one nonvoter. The video was a hit because it was creative, hilarious, and the message focused on one point: the importance of everyone voting in this election. It was successful as a viral marketing program because the creators gave people the tools they needed to easily customize a message and send it to their personal network. In the month before the election, the email had been forwarded to 6.3 million people and it was being forwarded to 30 new people per second.

---

## Viral Marketing: A Case Study from Obama

Perhaps no better example of integrated communications and new media comes from Barack Obama's campaign to win the 2008 Presidential race. Great marketing campaigns are expected from companies like Apple and Nike, but who would ever think such a great marketing case study would come from a politician? Regardless of which side of the political fence you are on, you have to agree that the results of this political campaign can teach everyone about the power of viral marketing, grassroots marketing, and branding. Here are just a few of the ways Obama has used viral marketing:

- When Clinton donated $5 million to her campaign, Obama asked his supporters to quickly match it. Within 24 hours, $8 million was donated to Obama's campaign.

- By the second quarter of 2008, Obama raised $31 million—$10 million more than Clinton raised. Obama's online fundraising alone contributed $10 million during this time.

- More than 258,000 people donated to Obama during this same period of time in small increments of $100 or less, creating a base for donors to contribute again and again.

- More than 9,500 volunteers signed up to host individual fundraising Web sites. As friends and family responded and forwarded the message and Web site on to their friends, actual donation amounts often surpassed the pledge.

- Obama uses messages created by other people in blogs, Web sites, and events to demonstrate that the people created his brand.

- Obama's messaging makes extensive use of the words "you" and "we," creating transparency and authenticity.

- An online raffle offered tickets for $5 to win a dinner for five with Obama.

- Obama hosted several low-cost fundraising events throughout the country, some as low as $25 per person, attracting thousands of people.

- A music video about Obama created by the Black Eyed Peas generated nearly a million views per day online. Obama put it on his Web site and generated even more hits.

- Obama's nearly $1 million spent on a 30-minute infomercial in October 2008 created new supporters in his critical hours. He invited people to connect with him by texting him or visiting his Web site.

- During the final weeks of the election, Obama's campaign purchased space in the popular Madden NFL 09 Xbox 360 game, and nine other video games to target this notoriously difficult segment (male 16-30). The ad appeared on billboards and stadium signs in games that were using the Xbox Internet service in the major swing states. In the racing game "Burnout Paradise" racers drive by a billboard that features Obama's photo and the words "Early Voting Has Begun. VoteForChange.com."

- Obama makes extensive use of social networking platforms to communicate his message and solicit donations.

- Obama's brand and logo has already reached the status similar to Nike and Apple. The circular mark with the flowing red and white stripes with a rising "O" sun can be recognized without his name attached to it.

Sources: Devin Leonard, "Obama's Web marketing triumph," CNNMoney.Com; Karen Tumulty "Obama's Virtual Marketing Campaign," Time.com; David Folkenflick, "Obama Ad Blitz Unprecedented," NPR.org; MoveOn.Org Political Action, http://pol.moveon.org/.

Obama's successful use of digital marketing earned him the title "Marketer of the Year" from *Inc. Magazine*. Regardless of your political affiliation you must agree that Obama's digital marketing team made brilliant use of the new media tools and channels that are available.

Obama's marketing continues to be impressive post-election. His Web site is a hub of activity to and from which other mediums are directed. It's continuously updated to keep loyal activists inspired and engaged.

He also communicates regularly through a blog (www.whitehouse.gov) and Twitter. He discusses his perspective on important issues and encourages citizens to take action.

The most impressive take-away from this case study: Who would have thought that marketers would be learning a lesson in marketing from a politician?

# 73

# Public Relations

Bill Gates once said, "If I had only a dollar, I would spend it on public relations." Public Relations (PR) is an effective and inexpensive means of communicating and building credibility for your business, and it should be a part of every marketing plan. As both a distribution channel and a rich source of information, the Internet has changed the way we communicate and market products, people, and companies. It has been the driving force behind the significant transformation of the PR industry. Once an industry based on "who you know," the process for PR was fairly formulistic. Now it is more complex in some ways (the number of online distribution sources and need for SEO-enabled releases), and in other ways, it has become easier because anyone can learn how to create effective PR for their business. PR can be implemented at a fraction of the cost of advertising and many tactics incur little to no cost at all.

Public relations is intended to build awareness, goodwill, and influence public opinion across several stakeholder groups, including employees, media, shareholders, community, customers, and other audiences. PR, also known as marketing public relations, is directed toward a company's target markets in order to build awareness, inform and educate, and build the brand.

As the lines between marketing, PR, and social media are blurred, the PR strategy you develop will be integrated with other strategies and tactics to define how you will market your brand. Blogs and social media like Twitter may be part of a business' PR strategy. Webinars and events are also an effective way to provide value to stakeholder audiences while also building the brand and customer relationships. A news release sent to the media through news wires can influence your target market, be posted on the company website, or sent directly to journalists and the media.

## What's New, Who Cares?

Reporters, news directors, media sites, magazines, online news sites and a myriad of other online and offline sources are always looking for newsworthy stories to cover. Think about it—the news media *must* find and write stories to fill space in print and online publications every single day. Writers and editors are grateful when successful business owners reach out to give them ideas for stories that interest their audience.

It's up to you to actively promote your business and to provide the means for them to find you.

The most important principle of PR is to make sure the story you are pitching is something meaningful and interesting to the audience. A news release about how great your product is only serves the purpose of saying "look how great my product or company is." It's boring and self-serving. If your news release talks about how your product or service changed or improved the life of your customer, that's interesting. If your release demonstrates how your product or service ties into an important trend, that's appealing. Develop a story from the audience point of view to make it compelling.

Another significant change in the field of PR is the ability to target a large number of people with your message. The new rules of PR include search, reach, and frequency. Here's how to apply these concepts to maximize success.

## Search

Successful PR is driven by the mechanics of the Internet, namely search. To maximize search engine optimization and reach interested customers and reporters, you need to understand the mechanics. A news release must use keywords and phrases, as well as links, so it reaches people who are interested in a specific topic. For example, if you are in the financial services industry, keywords must be used so your release finds the people who have flagged this topic. Keyword search terms should also align to those on your Web site. We'll cover more on this in the "Mechanics" section later in this chapter. The important thing to keep in mind is that you cannot reap the benefits of reach and frequency unless you maximize the effectiveness of search.

## Reach

News releases that were once directed only to writers and editors are now also directed to customers, consumers, potential customers, and business leaders. Now you can reach hundreds of targeted buyers and influencers through mass distribution via search engines, Web sites, RSS feeds, portals, and wire services like PR Newswire, a news distributor for over 50 years. PR Newswire (www.prnewswire.com) can distribute your message to over 5,400 Web sites, news portals, and other information sources. The service can also distribute to 500,000 media outlets through their international network. Other distribution services include PRWeb (www.prweb.com); Business Wire (www.businesswire.com); and Marketwire (www.marketwire.com). Distribution services will send your release to broad news sites and portals (like Google and Yahoo!) or target specific vertical industries such as finance or healthcare.

## Frequency

The new rule of frequency is driven by RSS feeds, an endless supply of news sources on the Internet, and the growing number of people searching the Internet. The more frequently you send news releases, the greater the odds your audience will find you. The most important thing to keep in mind is that news release content should be directed to a specific target audience. While distribution of a news release is broad, the message should clearly convey a specific need to a target audience that would be interested in your idea. Here are a few ideas for topics to promote:

- Introduce a new business or new locations based on business growth.
- Launch new products or services (include an example of a business or person benefiting from it).
- Describe how your company's solution aligns with a new business trend.
- Awards and honors bestowed on your company or someone in your firm.
- Special events such as conferences, Webinars, and seminars.
- New articles, white papers, blog, report, etc. and its benefit to the target audience.
- How your company's solution created specific outcomes and results with a customer or strategic alliance.
- Charitable sponsorships and company involvement.
- Executive personnel changes such as new executives joining the company or senior executives assuming new roles.

## Pitching Your Story

If you are targeting a story in a specific publication, the most important question you need to ask yourself is, "Why will this publication be interested in my story?" If you can't answer that question, you probably don't have a story. Just as you customize messaging for target audiences, you need to customize your content and pitch for publications.

Create a database of local, national, and international industry contacts. Do your research to find out whom to contact and keep the database current. Different reporters cover different "beats" or topics. Make notes about the types of stories reporters like to cover. When talking to reporters it might be helpful to refer to a similar story the reporter wrote and why you believe your story would interest them. Cultivate relationships with reporters, journalists, editors, and other media authorities. Over time, you can become a trusted resource and advisor to a reporter looking for an authority in your area of expertise. Have you ever noticed how a newspaper or news show will interview the same expert over and over when there is a newsworthy event on that topic? That's because they have developed a relationship as a trusted advisor.

# The Mechanics

The following information will take you through several of the mechanics of PR including how to create a news release or news advisory, what to include in a media kit, and the basics of distribution and search criteria.

## Search Criteria

Just as your Web site is optimized for search engine optimization, the same rules are true for optimizing who reads your news release. It is critically important to tag your release with specific keywords that would interest your target audience. This will make sure news sites and search engines send it to all the people that have signed up for RSS feeds based on those keywords and phrases.

Selecting the right key words and phrases must be approached from your customers' point of view. What words would they use to search for your product or service? What needs are they trying to fulfill? Optimize the news release so it contains key words that correlate to the key words in your Web site. Also remember to include the most important information and search terms paying particular attention to the headline and first paragraph.

## Links

Similar to keywords and phrases, search engines like links. If you have links in your news release that connect to your Web site, this will help increase your marketing and sales results. First of all, every time someone clicks on a link from a news release to go to the company Web site, it increases search engine rankings. Secondly, it can help close sales. If a link goes to a landing page that has been designed to appeal to the needs of the buyers interested in those key words and phrases, then you have an opportunity to provide targeted messaging and an offer to a potential customer.

## News Release

A news release is a good PR marketing tool to inform the media about a newsworthy event. It must be factual, informative, and direct. Use the following guidelines to help you develop the content:

- The headline should be short and compelling. Use keywords for SEO.
- The first paragraph is critical. It must give the reader a broad overview of your intent and compel the reader to read on. Use keywords to flag search engines.

- Customize the content for the audience of the news media. Reporters like stories that are localized.
- Focus on only one or two messages. Ideally there is only one.
- Use quotes to help tell your story and to add credibility.
- Humanize your story to make it more interesting.
- Use an example of how a customer benefited from your products or services.
- Avoid industry jargon and acronyms unless they are clearly defined.

## News Advisory

A news advisory is an announcement about an upcoming event such a press conference, seminar, conference, or event. It is sometimes used to provide the media with informational updates such as the availability of new photos, interviews, and other content beneficial to the media. A news advisory is different from a news release because it does not tell the whole story. It is simple and provides enough information to encourage the media to take action. It should contain a headline, what the event is, why media should attend, when and where the event takes place, a URL web address where more information can be found, contact information (email and phone numbers), and the source of the news advisory.

## Media Kit/Media Room

If you have ongoing public relations and analyst relations needs, you should create a basic media kit that can be customized for events, meetings, conferences, and reporters' needs. A Media/PR Kit, or "Press Kit," was once distributed in hard copy form, such as a folder with data sheets on the company, key executive profiles, photographs, and so on. While these are still used for events like industry conferences and analyst events, many companies have moved to an online media room that contains most of these same items. Your company Web site is the perfect place for this.

Marketing effectiveness comes from making it easy for customers to find you. The same is true if you are targeting reporters and editors. Make it easy for them to download information about your company so they can write a story. They'll appreciate this and it will also streamline your marketing operations processes.

Here is a list of items you may want to include in a media room/PR kit. Develop the most appropriate items for your business:

- A Company Fact Sheet (in PDF format) that includes basic information most reporters want to know about (industry sector, products and services, company officers, number of employees, revenues, locations, year founded, historical milestones, and so on).
- Biographical information about the business owner(s), senior executives, and board of directors.
- Articles previously published in newspapers, magazines, or trade journals.
- Product and service data sheets.
- Detailed product and/or service descriptions (written from the customers' perspective).
- Case studies describing the benefits customers have realized as a result of working with your company or using your products/services.
- Customer quotes and testimonials.
- Photographs of people, products, events, or company locations/stores. Label photos clearly.

## You Got the Story…Now What?

Once you are successful in getting a news story or article written about your company, you need to market the coverage you received. Use the story in your sales and marketing programs. You must keep in mind that some people will hear the broadcast or read the article, but the vast majority of the people that you really want to see it—customers and potential customers—will not. Post it on your Web site. Send an email with a link to the article or broadcast. Order reprints of the article and mail it to clients. Make it part of your collateral materials. Give it to your sales force to give to customers. You worked hard to get the coverage, so shamelessly promote your business!

# Part II

## Create a Tactical Plan with Execution Built-In

Every marketer, indeed every business, is concerned with measuring the effectiveness of their marketing programs. In this section, you learn how to create a comprehensive tactical plan that not only makes marketing and sales more accountable, it helps you improve tactical execution.

In the book resources section of www.MarketSmarter.com, you can download and learn how to use several new tools to help you more effectively measure individual marketing programs, as well as align marketing programs with stages in the sales funnel. You will find the Marketing Program ROI and Sales Funnel Analysis worksheets are instrumental in helping you to create a more effective implementation plan and budget. After you begin to apply this methodology and process to your marketing programs, you begin to see immediate improvements:

> **Sales Funnel Analysis:** This tool will help you analyze how the steps in the sales cycle correlate to marketing strategy and execution. Do programs target qualified buyers? Do they generate enough leads? Do they create too many leads resulting in lost opportunity because the sales force is not staffed to follow up? How many proposals were converted to closed sales? Each stage in the sales funnel should be analyzed for its effectiveness.

> **The Marketing Program ROI:** This worksheet is a "what if" tool that can be used to plan and test new marketing programs. It helps you prioritize programs based upon projected ROI and it provides justification for budgets and expenses. Best of all, this tool will help you improve the skill with which you predict and measure results over time. Use the worksheet on the next page to plan and evaluate individual marketing programs. This information can also be used in the Implementation Calendar that follows it.

# Marketing and Sales Program ROI Analysis

For both planning and measurement purposes, conducting an ROI analysis of all marketing and sales programs is the best way to learn and optimize future programs. It helps to prioritize what programs should be continued or eliminated, and it provides justification for budgets and expenses. A solid ROI analysis process that is matched to diligent results tracking will lead to better program planning, ROI predictability, and marketing ROI optimization over time.

Fill in the worksheet with the results of your past sales and marketing programs to analyze results. The worksheet can also be used to plan and estimate future programs.

| Program Name | Program Cost (PC) | Impressions (I) | Response Rate (RR) | Leads (L) | Lead Conversion (LC) | Qualified Leads (QL) | Win Conversion (WC) | Wins (W) | Total Revenues (TR) | Program ROI |
|---|---|---|---|---|---|---|---|---|---|---|
| | Include all expenses | Number of people you reach/ contact | % of people who take initial action | I x RR | % who meet qualification criteria | L x LC | % of people who buy | QL x WC | Revenues from all wins | (TR/PC): 1 |
| Email | $5,000 | 55,000 | 1% | 550 | 10% | 55 | 9% | 5 | $32,500 | 6.5:1 |
| | | | | | | | | | | |
| | | | | | | | | | | |
| | | | | | | | | | | |
| | | | | | | | | | | |
| | | | | | | | | | | |
| | | | | | | | | | | |

# 74

# Make Marketing Measurable

The tactical plan is developed after your sales plan, marketing objectives, and marketing strategies have been defined. It describes the details of each marketing program which will make your plan actionable and operational (meaning you use it to guide daily decision making). For each program you will define who is responsible for executing the plan, when it will be executed, how much the program will cost, and the projected ROI.

If you have not projected ROI for sales and marketing programs in the past, or have not been disciplined about doing so, now is the time to start. I'm always amazed at how few companies track marketing programs using a disciplined process. The good news is if you start using this process now, a year from now you will have a good baseline to work from. You will be surprised how quickly you learn and improve with every program you execute.

This section of your marketing plan will change the most because as strategies are executed and marketing programs are implemented, marketing tactics may need to be updated. Large companies that have many marketing programs may wish to pull this section out of the larger marketing plan and use it as a separate document that is updated as marketing programs are executed. You can call it a Tactical Implementation Plan, a Go-to-Market Plan, or anything else that fits with the language and culture of your business.

## Individual Tactics Description

The following template is a way for you to organize and plan each of your tactical programs. Adjust this template as necessary to list all the activity steps and costs associated with each tactic. Also estimate revenue and ROI for each tactic using historical information if you have it. If you don't, then make your best prediction. As you begin to use this process to predict, measure and track programs, you will quickly learn and improve the results of your sales and marketing programs. Duplicate this template for each of your tactical programs. The actual numbers can be recorded in the Implementation Calendar.

**Table 74.1** Marketing Program Template

| Tactic Name: |
| Purpose: |
| Program Objectives: |
| Description: |
| Target Audience: |
| Messaging / Positioning |
| Total Estimated Budget: |
| Total Targeted Revenue: |
| Projected ROI: |

| Activity | Timeline | Estimated Budget | Resource |
|---|---|---|---|
| | | | |
| | | | |
| | | | |
| | | | |

You should repeat this template for each program you plan to implement. If you would like to see an example of how this template is filled out, visit the "Real-Time Marketing" book resources section of www.MarketSmarter.com.

 **Marketing Tip**

Large companies with many tactical programs may wish to pull this section out of the plan and distribute it as a Tactical Plan Brief. This helps the marketing and sales teams stay on top of programs and easily update the document. If you do this, be sure to keep the master tactical plan as a part of your overall marketing plan.

# 75

# Implementation Calendar and Budget

The Implementation Calendar and Budget is used to summarize tactical programs for a specific period of time (monthly, quarterly, or yearly). This is a good way to report sales and marketing programs by summarizing the projected costs, leads, qualified leads, and projected revenue for each tactical program, and a campaign as a whole. At the end of each quarter you will find this is an excellent tool to compare your projections against actual results.

The worksheet example presents an annual calendar and budget, presented monthly. You can customize this form to present quarters on each page or even just a single month, depending on the number of programs your business executes. Using this worksheet also allows you to enter a minimal number of assumptions to quickly provide a view of the projected results. You can see which programs are providing the most impact, and make adjustments accordingly.

**Worksheet Instructions:**

1. Enter the average lag time for your sales cycle and time to revenue in months for:
   - Lead to qualified lead
   - Qualified lead to close
   - Close to revenue
2. Enter the average revenue per sale, split out by:
   - One-time, up-front revenue
   - Monthly recurring revenue
3. Enter conversion ratios for:
   - Each tactical category for lead to qualified lead
   - The average qualified lead to close ratio
4. Enter costs and associated leads, by month, for each tactic:
   - If working this process manually, complete the rest of the timeline by tactic by entering the associated qualified leads (using the appropriate ratio assumption), close (using the average qualified lead to close ratio), and revenue (multiply the number of closes by the average revenues).

The automated version of this worksheet (at www.MarketSmarter.com) will use the entered assumptions to automatically calculate the qualified leads, closes, and associated revenue in the correct time period.

## Implementation Calendar and Budget

**Assumptions / Date Entry Fields**

| Lag Time | Months |
|---|---|
| Lead to Qualified Lead | 1 |
| Qualified Lead to Close | 3 |
| Close to Revenue | 1 |

| Revenue | $ |
|---|---|
| One-time revenue | $ 50,000 |
| Monthly recurring rev per Sale | $ 7,500 |

| Conversion Rates | % |
|---|---|
| Leads to Qualified Leads | |
| Events | 25% |
| Executive Events | 80% |
| Web/SEO | 6% |
| Email | 10% |
| DM | 10% |
| PR/Other | 5% |
| Avg QL to Close | 15% |

| | Jan | Feb | March | April | May | June | Total |
|---|---|---|---|---|---|---|---|
| **Trade Shows** | | | | | | | |
| Cost | $    - | $ 80,000 | $    - | $    - | $ 30,000 | $    - | $ 110,000 |
| Leads | - | 150 | - | - | 100 | - | 250 |
| Qualified Leads | | - | 38 | - | - | 25 | 63 |
| Closed | | | | - | - | 6 | 6 |
| Revenue | $    - | $    - | $    - | $    - | $    - | $    - | $    - |
| **Email Marketing** | | | | | | | |
| Cost | $ 7,500 | $ 7,500 | $ 7,500 | $ 7,500 | $ 7,500 | $ 7,500 | $ 45,000 |
| Leads | 75 | 75 | 75 | 75 | 75 | 75 | 450 |
| Qualified Leads | | 8 | 8 | 8 | 8 | 8 | 38 |
| Closed | | | | - | 1 | 1 | 2 |
| Revenue | $    - | $    - | $    - | $    - | $ 57,500 | $ 57,500 | |
| **Direct Mail** | | | | | | | |
| Cost | $ 125,000 | | | $ 125,000 | | | $ 250,000 |
| Leads | 1,000 | | | 1,000 | | | 2,000 |
| Qualified Leads | | 100 | - | - | 100 | - | 200 |
| Closed | | | | - | 15 | - | 15 |
| Revenue | $    - | $    - | $    - | $    - | $ 862,500 | $ 862,500 | |
| **Web/SEO** | | | | | | | |
| Cost | $ 7,000 | $ 7,000 | $ 7,000 | $ 7,000 | $ 7,000 | $ 7,000 | $ 42,000 |
| Leads | 60 | 60 | 60 | 60 | 60 | 60 | 360 |
| Qualified Leads | | 4 | 4 | 4 | 4 | 4 | 20 |
| Closed | | | | - | 1 | 1 | 2 |
| Revenue | $    - | $    - | $    - | $    - | $ 57,500 | $ 57,500 | |
| **TOTALS** | | | | | | | |
| Cost | $ 139,500 | $ 94,500 | $ 14,500 | $ 139,500 | $ 44,500 | $ 14,500 | $ 447,000 |
| Leads | 1,135 | 285 | 135 | 1,135 | 235 | 135 | 3,060 |
| Qualified Leads | - | 111 | 49 | 11 | 111 | 36 | 318 |
| Closed | - | - | - | - | 17 | 7 | 24 |
| Revenue | $    - | $    - | $    - | $    - | $    - | $ 977,500 | $ 977,500 |

# Implement

## P • R • A • I • S • E™ Marketing Process

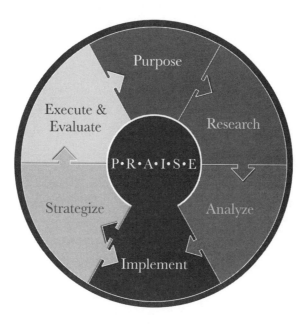

## Summary: Section V

✓ Complete the Marketing Program ROI worksheet for each tactic you plan to implement. This will help you project ROI, and you will use this information in Section VI, "Execute and Evaluate," to create a ROI Optimizer.

✓ If you do not currently track ROI for marketing programs *start now!* What gets measured will improve, so begin a process for systematically projecting ROI and measuring the actual results. A year from now, you will have some history to reflect upon and make wiser decisions.

✓ Complete the Social Media Strategy and Plan.

✓ Create a tactical plan using the template provided. Outline the marketing programs you plan to implement and include a description of the program, resource needs, time frame, budget, and projected ROI.

✓ Transfer your programs and budget to the Implementation Calendar and Budget to provide a consolidated view of programs. Update this at least quarterly.

✓ As sales and marketing programs are implemented, use the Sales Funnel Analysis worksheet to track and measure success.

# Section VI

# Execute and Evaluate:
# Create a Culture of Execution

*"The fact is culture eats strategy for lunch.... You can have a good strategy in place, but if you don't have the culture and the enabling systems to implement that strategy...the culture of the organization will defeat the strategy."*
—Dick Clark, former CEO of Merck

As you know now, creating a marketing plan takes significant effort, especially if this is the first time you have developed one. But it's execution of the plan that will make your business successful. This concept may sound simple enough, but lack of execution is one of the biggest reasons companies fail to achieve their objectives. There are several reasons why this happens, and we will discuss these pitfalls and how to avoid them in this section.

In addition to increasing your execution skills, you will also learn how to evaluate your marketing plan using several tools and processes. Ongoing evaluation of your plan is a critical component of keeping it updated in real-time, and you will learn a simple process to do this. As the market changes and marketing programs are executed, you will be able to quickly adjust your strategies and tactics. In this section, you will:

- Understand why so many companies fail to execute strategy and what to do about it.
- Learn an effective process to integrate sales, marketing, and service teams.
- Use new tools and processes to evaluate specific elements in each section of the P•R•A•I•S•E Marketing Process.
- Learn how to predict and measure the outcome of marketing and sales programs to targeted customers.
- Measure success to both quantifiably and qualitatively assess the effectiveness of your plan.
- Identify the most critical areas of your plan to track and update frequently in real-time.

- Learn a process to integrate marketing planning with operational reviews.
- Create top-down and bottom-up alignment of your entire demand chain using the ROI Optimizer.
- Learn why culture drives financial performance.
- Learn how to create a company culture focused on accountability and execution.
- Create a process to communicate, review, and update your plan, which will help you execute better than 90 percent of companies.

# 76

# The Problem with Marketing

Borrowing from Rodney Dangerfield, I would say the biggest problem in businesses today is "Marketing Gets No Respect." If marketing is viewed simply as a department that implements campaigns and "creative stuff," how can the organization possibly hope to align around customer needs? If the purpose of marketing is to understand and meet the needs of customers, what gets in the way of this happening?

It's the organization's perception of marketing that needs to change.

In Section I, "Purpose," I referred to Peter Drucker's quote that the most important functions in a business are marketing and innovation. Marketing and innovation are the drivers to understand and fulfill customer needs, and without satisfied customers to buy a company's products and services, a business would cease to exist. So with all the technological innovations and creative new thinking around the world, why is it that perceptions and advancements in how we think about marketing have not kept pace? If we all buy in to the commonsense wisdom of Peter Drucker's statement, *why don't organizations give more respect to marketing?*

*Marketing is uniquely positioned to align the entire organization around the customer.* To do so, marketing must take a leadership role to redefine the definition of marketing, and the CEO must ensure that marketing has a seat at the executive table. In large companies, the person leading marketing, the Chief Marketing Officer (CMO) must have the same stature as a COO or CFO (not just a title). A similar principal applies in small and mid-sized companies, regardless of what title is used. Organizations need to think beyond marketing as simply a department because the role and meaning of marketing has evolved way beyond this. It's much more complex and comprehensive as we have discussed throughout this book. It's time for CEOs, marketing and sales professionals, and other business executives to work together to create a new definition of marketing. This role should include priorities such as leading change, deepening the organization's understand of customers and how to build loyalty, and implementing new communication and alignment processes to improve strategy execution.

*"Marketers who don't learn the language of quality improvement, manufacturing, and operations will become as obsolete as buggy whips. The days of functional marketing are gone. We can no longer afford to think of ourselves as market researchers, advertising people, direct marketers, strategists—we have to think of ourselves as customer satisfiers—customer advocates focused on whole processes."*
—Daniel Beckham

On the next few pages we will discuss some of the biggest issues related to marketing today. My intention is not to point fingers at marketing, sales, CEOs, or any other functional role. I have personally held positions in all of these roles and each gave me a different perspective about marketing. The sum of all these experiences is what led me to think about marketing in a different, more holistic way.

It's time to start a conversation about what marketing really means, not just as a role, but as a way of managing the business. It may require you to think very differently about budgeting, organizational structure, how teams work together, and how results are measured. In this redefined role, everyone aligns around customer needs.

## How to Fix the Biggest Problems in Sales and Marketing

Marketing and sales effectiveness is an issue on the mind of every business leader. Most of the issues that hamper effectiveness have been around for a long, long time. If you have several years of business experience under your belt, you will look at these problems and, like me, wonder why the heck they persist. None of them are especially complex, but they do take effort to fix. These issues are just as persistent in many small companies as large ones, but the scale is different. If you work in a large company, you might think it's easier to solve world hunger than fix some of these issues, but you will see that even the smallest changes will make a big difference. I speak from experience—you can tackle and fix these issues!

The biggest problems in sales and marketing boil down to issues in five main catagories—and if you can solve them, you will greatly improve your company's success in several areas:

1. Break down sales and marketing silos to increase collaboration, effectiveness, and customer value.
2. Improve the selling process to sell higher in the organization and increase revenue.

3. Increase access to information and facilitate cross-functional conversations to improve customer knowledge and experience.

4. Train all stakeholders, internal and external, to think like marketers.

5. Change the process for measuring marketing and sales programs to create more effective and predicable outcomes.

## Break Down Sales and Marketing Silos

According to a recent CMO Council report, only 16 percent of sales and marketing departments believe they are "extremely" collaborative. Marketing and sales often operate as completely separate silos with little collaboration. If a company wants to be customer-focused, these two teams must work together to improve their understanding of customer needs. This involves joint planning on market strategy and major account plans. This seems obvious, yet most companies don't take the necessary steps to resolve this problem. Let's see what each party can bring to the table to improve the effectiveness of both sales and marketing teams.

Marketers can improve CRM system data and customer analytics to make sure that the right kind of information is being collected about customers. Improving processes for data collection, analysis, and reporting will ensure strategy and decisions are made by an informed group of customer stakeholders. Marketing must also lead *internal* branding and communications programs and *teach* everyone in the company about what it means to be marketing and customer-focused. This requires a focused and comprehensive internal branding campaign that is not event driven, but part of the company culture. When marketers facilitate discussions with people and teams across the company, everyone has a shared understanding of what drives business success, and that everyone has a role in marketing.

What about the sales department? What can salespeople do to break down the silos between marketing and sales? As the principal liaison between a company and its customers, salespeople are the primary stewards of the customer relationship. The first and most important step is to actively engage marketers in customer meetings. The marketing team cannot develop effective sales and marketing programs if they don't have a shared experience working with customers. It is unrealistic for salespeople to expect them to create effective marketing programs with information that has been handed down or gathered only from marketing surveys. Marketers need real face-to-face time with customers in order to understand their biggest challenges and pain points. Since salespeople usually "own" the customer relationship, they should initiate this first step. The head of sales should mandate and promote a strong relationship between his/her sales team and the marketing team.

A huge benefit of joint sales meetings is sales and marketing professionals each have a different perspective, and both are equally valuable. Salespeople have an established relationship with customers and deep customer knowledge. Marketers will look not only at the immediate customer's challenges, but how these issues impact entire industries. Marketers can then apply research to understand if a customer's challenges are similar across an industry, and contrast how well your company is able to solve these issues. This will help them identify gaps in your product/service offerings, as well as create more effective marketing programs and communication to customers and industry segments. The obvious benefit for salespeople is that this will enable them to sell more effectively to more customers in an industry segment.

Sales and marketing teams should collaborate on the revenue goals and the marketing and sales plan. If the marketing department has only a target revenue number and little visibility into how the number will be achieved, how can they create effective marketing programs that will help salespeople achieve their goals? There is an old saying "Good marketing makes selling irrelevant" but this statement is seldom a reality for most businesses. Effective communication is needed by both teams. If marketing and sales teams work together on planning, strategy, execution, and reporting, it will solve most of the problems caused by operational silos. Productivity will improve, and so will sales results.

In good economic times, it's important for marketing and sales to work together to increase organizational knowledge of industries and customers. During difficult economic times, it becomes even more critical. Budgets are tighter and decision making tends to be much slower. This makes it imperative to approach the sales and marketing process in a new way that is much more collaborative and customer-centric.

## Change the Sales Pitch, Win New Business

In addition to revenue generation, companies are looking for ways to cut costs and improve efficiencies. For salespeople that understand how to do both, it presents a big opportunity to expand customer relationships. Customers want to do business with people who understand their specific needs. To win complex sales, salespeople must go beyond "consultative selling." They need to dig deep to understand the issues their customers face, and offer knowledge and creative new ways to solve a customer's biggest strategic business issues and challenges. This type of strategic selling is very different from solution selling. The salesperson takes a genuine interest in providing strategic advice to help customers improve sales, or recommending operating efficiencies, or improving bottom-line performance measures.

A salesperson who is focused on delivering this kind of value to customers may recommend not only products and services, but new distribution channels, strategic alliances, or even strategic changes to the customer's business model.

This requires salespeople to have knowledge of industry issues that affect their customer's individual situations, and this is where a marketer can really help a salesperson. A good marketer can research and analyze important industry facts and trends that will help customize solutions for individual customers. If the sales and marketing team has tackled the organizational silo issue and is working collaboratively, each party brings different skills to the table and both are needed to create compelling, customized business solutions and sell at higher levels in the organization.

This reveals another benefit of a collaborative sales approach. When a salesperson sells at higher levels in an organization, it will give them exposure to several new areas of a client's business to which they previously did not have access. This can lead to increased revenue on a per customer basis without discounting prices because customers receive more value. The result is increased profitability and market share as a result of improved customer relationships and increased account penetration. This is good news for companies that are hungry and aggressive about winning new business from entrenched competitors.

## Organize Around Customers, Not Products

Sales effectiveness is one of the most important measures of business growth. Despite the recession, many companies have not lowered sales expectations. Even during the most difficult period of the recession, the average sales growth target was 18 percent and targets continue to be aggressive as the economy struggles to recover. What fuels this optimism?

Nearly 75 percent of sales leaders believe that double-digit sales increases will be realized from adopting a consultative, business-centric approach to solving customers' problems. The problem is they have a difficult time executing this strategy. Why is it that only 31 percent have been successful in adopting this approach, despite the strategy and the rationale to do so? The issue is not the salesperson's style or sales methodology, but the larger systemic issue of how businesses are organized.

Here's the problem: Although sales leaders want to sell solutions (not just products or services) and sell at higher levels in their customers organizations, *their own companies are still organized around products instead of around customers.* The problem grows even worse in large companies. According to the Sales Talent Management Benchmark study, only 9 percent of companies with over 1,000 salespeople are business-centric instead of product-centric.[1] When companies are focused on selling products instead of what customers need, it leads to all kinds of problems—and one of the biggest is unrealized sales opportunities. Another more visible issue is dissatisfied, confused customers.

When I worked for a very large company several years ago, I had lunch with one of our biggest customers and a few of our company executives. After a tense 20 minutes of conversation, the customer leaned over and whispered to me, "If I didn't have nine sales people from your company calling on me, we wouldn't even be talking about this problem. Don't any of these guys talk to each other?"

Later when I told the primary salesperson about the customer's comment, he just shook his head and responded that he was well aware of the problem. Salespeople from several different business units and from different geographies were all fighting to get a piece of the customer's business. In essence, they were all competing against each other. He then said something equally horrifying: "I know exactly how our customers feel. I have 12 different division leaders calling on me to see how much I will be selling for their division."

If you work in a large company, start a conversation and build a business case for how changes in the organizational structure will drive knowledge and collaboration that will lead to increased customer satisfaction and account penetration. Teams are working toward the same desired outcomes—improved customer relationships, sales, marketing and operational effectiveness, and of course, increased revenue. What gets in their way of achieving these goals is the organizational silo structure that breaks down communication. It's also the way compensation is structured. If changes are made to the budgeting process and how revenue is recognized across company divisions, this may be the fastest way to drive change.

If you own a small to mid-sized company, you should seriously consider these facts and assess your own organizational structure. If your company is not organized around customers so that every department can work collaboratively to solve customers' problems, your business is lacking efficiency and effectiveness—and most likely sales opportunities. It will also affect the pace of growth in your business. Organize around customers instead of products as early as possible, and you will see improvements in agility, responsiveness, and results—both internally and externally.

## Collaborate, Automate, and Get Smart

As customers continuously interact with a brand, there is an increased need to share customer information across multiple teams to improve customer knowledge. This will drive improvements in customer experience, customer service, and ultimately loyalty—the key driver of business growth and profitability. Making improvements in this area makes absolute sense, right? The reality is only 12 percent of sales and marketing teams say that they have access to integrated, real-time information about customers that would enable them to make informed decisions to improve sales and marketing programs and communication to customers.[2]

As we discussed, one of the issues that inhibits sharing information is organizational silos, but an equally important issue is the lack of processes and systems to share customer information.

Some businesses use CRM systems (like salesforce.com) to gather basic customer information about interactions, but what is missing is information about customer *experience* across different parts of the organization. A marketer may know which customers responded to a campaign, and sales people may know what the customer purchased, but they do not understand customer reaction and interaction with the brand as a whole. For example, how do customers find and respond to information on the company Web site? What kind of experience did they have with customer service representatives? What kinds of questions did the customer ask and what were the concerns? Were they resolved? What follow-up is required and how is this communicated to salespeople?

Customer service and support are critically important to customer experience, a responsibility that should fall under the responsibility of marketing, yet only 17 percent of marketers oversee this important function.[3] The same questions asked above can be asked about communication between a customer and the billing department, fulfillment, operations, technical support, and other parts of the organization.

It is the *culmination of a customer's experiences with a brand* that drives satisfaction and loyalty. Information should be collected and shared about customer experience through a CRM system, and internal communications processes should create a closed-loop system to analyze and discuss results on an ongoing basis. But the problem with many large companies is they may collect the data but lack processes to share information and discuss the results. This leads to the next obvious problem, which is lack of results and poor ROI from marketing, sales, and customer service programs. As programs are implemented, they're not optimized, so ROI is far less than what was projected.

You can guess what happens next: finger pointing. The marketing department gets blamed for a poorly designed program, the sales team is accused of not having the right sales skills or poor follow-up, and the customer service team is charged with not having deep relationship skills. Sound familiar? Then, make a change to collaborate, automate, and get smart.

Most small businesses have basic CRM software, but if you don't, you can see by the example above that the issues of data collection, analysis, and sharing are very important. This can be done by putting the processes in place to improve collaboration, even if the processes are manual. Determine what information needs to be tracked and reported, and schedule regular meetings to discuss key customers.

As processes are reviewed, make sure that handoffs are defined between all the departments that interact with customers, including marketing, sales, customer service, and other parts of the organization. There should also be a process regarding expectations related to documentation, last customer conversation, and next actions required. Not only will this streamline and improve efforts across teams, it will increase knowledge and cultivate organizational learning.

One of the most important conversations that teams can have is asking the question, "What drives customer satisfaction and what drives customer loyalty?" As each team answers the question, it creates a shared understanding of what each team must do, individually and collectively, to improve the value that your customers receive.

A collaborative process should also include an analysis of the solutions each customer buys, and how to cross-sell and up-sell additional solutions. An easy and effective way to increase existing customer sales is to improve your customers' understanding of the full range of products and services your company offers. CEOs are often shocked to learn how many customers are simply not aware of the company's full range of solutions. This realization usually occurs after learning that a piece of their customer's business is going to a competitor. The good news is that when this issue is identified and resolved, it can create surprising increases in sales and customer profitability.

Take a moment and answer this question: *If your company implemented just one of these ideas, what difference would it make?*

## Marketing Is Not a Department

If knowledge is a competitive advantage for your business, then you need a commitment to develop knowledge as a core competency. Sharp business leaders know it is wise to cultivate sales skills and knowledge in the people who work with customers. After all, personal selling and customer service are the attributes that give companies their competitive advantage. People need more than basic skills training. They need to understand company goals and the *business reasons* behind decisions. For example, if marketing, sales, and customer service levels are aligned to customer segments (remember A, B, C, and D customers?), then front-line employees need to understand why some customers are "A" customers and others are "C" or "D" so they can make better decisions about how to service them.

Several departments need training to understand how your company segments markets and targets customers. For example, what is the profile of an ideal customer? How does your company's solution solve the needs of your customers? Why does customer loyalty and retention matter? How should customer issues be flagged and/or escalated? What is the value and importance of key customers?

Businesses must not forget to invest in the systems and training to help other stakeholders become successful. Distributors, strategic alliances, and other channel partners need training that extends beyond "features and benefits" training on products and services. Sales partners are an extension of your company, so they should have knowledge of the company's core values, customers, growth strategies, mutual goals and expectations, and a closed-loop system to communicate new ideas back to the company.

Customer stakeholders need to know what information is important to track and measure, as well as how to report and share what they learn. When everyone has the knowledge and tools to do all of these things, they become much more effective in servicing customers.

## Measure Marketing, Continuously Improve

*"Marketing is like a millstone around my neck."*
—Anonymous CEO, McKinsey Quarterly

*"Marketing is increasingly living a lie in my organization."*
—Anonymous CEO, PWC Survey

*"Marketing is divorced from the operational world."*
—Anonymous CEO, Synesis

Executives have long suspected that much of the money they spend on marketing in their companies is wasted. Marketers are under a lot of pressure. The vast majority report that demands to improve marketing efficiencies have significantly increased. Is this news surprising? Of course not. Companies have been asking for more measureable marketing for decades. Despite the growing concern, the problem persists. The reason behind the problem: One-third of companies have little or no understanding of their true marketing costs, and very few have a disciplined process to measure marketing.

When companies fail to create a system to predict, measure, report, and improve marketing, decisions are based on assumptions, which can be misguided. As a result, sales suffer, and money that could be directed toward investments in profitable growth is squandered away.

How bad is it? In one report, only 23 percent of B2B technology companies "fully agree" that their direct marketing activities are systematically measured. Wow—direct marketing is pretty easy to measure. What does this mean for other marketing program measurement? Only 9.3 percent of marketers rate their e-metrics and measurement capabilities as excellent.[4] It's no wonder marketing continues to be such a problem for companies today.

Another disconnect is the budgeting process. The criteria and method that is used to budget marketing and project ROI is often incorrect. All of these factors define why we need a new approach to marketing. Executives, marketers, and finance teams must work together to change the old out-dated methods of budgeting and ROI measurement. In the remaining chapters in this section, you will learn more effective processes that will help you develop a new approach to budget and measure marketing and fix this long-standing problem at last. Is this easy? I wish I could say yes, but the processes you are about to learn require effort and disciple to execute.

Let's start by looking at the budgeting process first. The next chapter describes a holistic, collaborative, and more accurate way to budget and plan for marketing expenses. It will help you understand the true cost of marketing, which has a direct effect on how results are measured.

In Chapter 79, "ROI Optimizer: Increase the Effectiveness of How Marketing Is Measured," you will learn a new process to measure the effectiveness of your marketing using the ROI Optimizer. But this process does even more than measure marketing results. By linking and measuring all the elements in the demand chain, it actually helps you continuously improve and even predict the results of marketing and sales.

# 77

# Asset-Based Marketing Measurement

Let's step back to get a broader picture to understand the context of how sales and marketing budgets are established and therefore measured. Is the budget based on individual department goals and marketing programs/campaigns, or is the budget based on the integrated activities to improve customer and market share? These are key questions.

Marketing budgets are often based on departmental budgets that are divided among project expenses to implement a marketing program or campaign. The results, or ROI, are based on the sales generated during the time the program is implemented (revenue generated less marketing expense). This method is overly simplified and is not a good measure of marketing effectiveness. Several others factors must be considered.

In a typical sales process, many people have a direct impact on the ultimate sales results. Marketers create demand. Salespeople close the deal. Call center agents fulfill orders and service customers. Fulfillment and operations teams handle distribution. Accounting invoices customers correctly and in a timely manner, and customer service agents respond to customers' problems, issues, and concerns. Departments across an organization have a role in the execution of programs.

If several parts of the organization are responsible for executing programs that drive customer satisfaction and customer experience, then it only makes sense that several departments should jointly contribute to the planning and budgeting process. Multiple teams should also weigh into how programs are measured. A company objective (increasing customer loyalty) is an integrated activity that needs the support and commitment from several departments, managers, and executives (see Figure 77.1). When mutual objectives are established, budgeting, execution, and measurement become an integrated process, which results in increased success for the entire company.

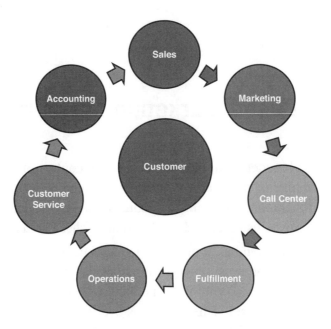

**Figure 77.1** *The true cost of marketing: measuring what matters*

## Holistic Marketing Measurement

Peter Doyle, author of *Value-Based Marketing*, makes a compelling case for different marketing measures other than simply increased sales and market share. He argues that businesses should focus on shareholder value rather than profit maximization, which is the typical business metric that is used. A focus on profit maximization leads to short-term sales, market share, and profit increases (all attractive goals), but it also leads to cost cutting to see a quick hit to the bottom line. *Actions like these do nothing for the long-term value for the firm.*

What if marketing was viewed as an *investment* to build the brand and customer relationships that enabled growth into new markets? Marketing assets like brand equity, customer relationships, and partner relationships are investments in long-term growth and profitability. All of these factors also impact employee satisfaction and loyalty, which result in reduced turnover and better customer satisfaction—two areas that drop directly to the bottom line. If we adopt this approach, marketing is not simply perceived as a cost or evaluated by the success of a single program. It becomes an investment in the long-term growth and profitability of the organization, and an integral component of the entire management process.

Holistic or value-based marketing requires a great deal of collaboration and consensus within a leadership team. It requires a clear and compelling vision of mutually shared goals, and it requires patience for profits. If the vision of a leadership team extends only to the next quarter, the business will never attain what it is capable of achieving.

This type of approach to budgeting and measurement has benefits that far exceed long-term growth. A holistic approach such as this helps to resolve several of the other long-standing issues with marketing discussed so far in this section. When multiple business leaders agree on strategy and mutually fund projects as investments, it changes how teams work together. It improves how people communicate and collaborate. It expands the value customers receive. Bigger problems can be tackled and solved, and this leads to deeper customer relationships.

Isn't it time to change the way we think about marketing?

## Key Performance Measures

Every company uses a different set of individual or collective measurements to evaluate the health of their business. Metrics may include revenue; profitability; earnings before interest, taxes, depreciation, and amortization; cash flow; gross margin; return on sales; operating margin; and other metrics. In addition to these business metrics, there are several you can use to measure marketing:

- Percent increase in net new customers
- Percent improvement in customer satisfaction
- Customer lifetime value
- Customer retention/defect rate
- Marketing program ROI
- Conversion rate
- Return on objectives

Marketing metrics can be analyzed in several different ways to get an increasingly deeper level of granularity to help you refine your understanding of the business (see Figure 77.2). You can analyze a portfolio of products, individual products and services, industry segments, customer segments, individual customers, channel partners, marketing campaigns, and marketing programs. This data can be analyzed again by business units, divisions, and/or geographic regions. The level of analysis will depend upon the complexity of your business, the resources you have to collect this data, and the level of detail you wish to use to evaluate your business.

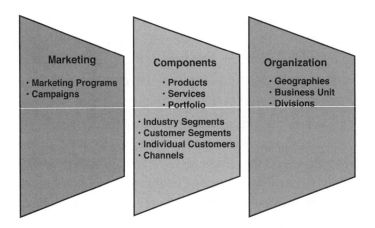

**Figure 77.2**  *Marketing metrics*

In addition to the holistic marketing measures previously discussed, you now have several other components and metrics that you can choose from to measure business results. Now we will look at several other methods you can use to evaluate and measure your marketing plan. The evaluation elements in the next chapter, "Evaluate: What Is Measured Improves," are real-time marketing measures that will help you analyze and adjust your plan as it is executed.

# 78

# Evaluate: What Is Measured Improves

You will be pleasantly surprised to learn that you have been automatically building a measurement and evaluation process into your marketing plan. Each step of the P•R•A•I•S•E Marketing Process has components that will help you evaluate the effectiveness of your plan as it is executed.

## Purpose

*Goals and objectives* were defined in the first section of your marketing plan. Now that you have completed the marketing planning process, you need to revisit the goals to see if they are still relevant or if they need to be adjusted:

- Are the goals still relevant and realistic given what you have learned through your research and analysis?
- Have you established both short-term and long-term goals?
- Do you have buy-in and commitment from leaders across the business?
- Are the goals linked to the larger goals of the organization?

Goals should be specific and measurable so that you can evaluate your progress toward achieving the stated goals and update them as your business situation changes.

*Mission, vision, and values* are timeless but there are times when they need to be updated to reflect leadership, market, or customer changes:

- Are the vision, mission, and values of the company defined?
- How will the vision be communicated so everyone in the company is clear about where the company is headed?
- How will values become such an integral part of the business that it drives, supports, and nurtures the behavior in all employees?
- Is there congruency between the internal brand and external brand?
- Do employee performance reviews include measures of accountability and demonstration of core values?

The *SWOT analysis* that you created as part of your situation analysis is a tool that can be used in the yearly planning cycle. Use this at the start of strategic planning meetings to get a quick consensus of the company's strengths and weaknesses relative to external threats and new opportunities.

## Research

*Customer research* is an ongoing activity. Customer surveys and interviews may only be done once or twice a year, but there are several mechanisms you can build into your plan to continually measure customer satisfaction and loyalty with respect to your product and service offerings. Interactive voice response (IVR) will help you evaluate the effectiveness of customer service agents, as well as listen and understand the issues that concern your customers. Consider how you can integrate Web-based feedback (quick surveys, blogs, forums, etc.) to stay current and connected to customers. Continuously refine your understanding of why your customers buy and what motivates them. Consider hosting a customer advisory board to get in-depth information about how to improve your business on an ongoing basis. Most important, get out of the office and in front of customers to observe them interacting with your products and services. You may learn more this way than with a dozen surveys!

As you learn through ongoing customer interactions, apply this information to improve customer experience and to increase the success of marketing communications and programs.

*Customer segments* should be analyzed in operations reviews so everyone can contribute their knowledge and experience from working with customers. It will also create a collective understanding of who the most important customers are to your business. Evaluate how well the CRM plan is being executed. Is the sales team doing an effective job of targeting and selling to "A" customers? Is the number of customers in this category increasing? If you had a goal to migrate "B" customers to "A" customers, was the strategy effective? What new strategies should be developed to impact customers in the "C" and "D" categories? Based upon a refined understanding of customers, will this change the target market profile?

*Competitive updates* are easy if you divide the responsibility for collecting this information across several people. In operations reviews, people can report changes and strategic adjustments can be made. As new competitors are identified, your team can respond quickly.

*Macro-environmental* trends are easier to monitor when several people are tracking various topics and issues. If this information is collected on an ongoing basis as described in Section II, "Research," your strategies and plan can be updated real-time in quarterly operations meetings.

## Analyze

*Break-even and target profit* are dynamic and change as the factors that impact these measures change. Evaluate pricing for your solutions compared to industry benchmarks and competitors' pricing. These metrics can be evaluated as financials are updated, or during the quarterly marketing and operations review.

Continuously look for new ways to add *customer experience*, thereby adding *value* and the potential to raise prices. You may wish to do the "Finding New Value" worksheets once a year to evaluate strategic changes in response to changing conditions.

*Distribution channels* require analysis in several areas. Were the goals for each channel met for revenue, profit, and margin? If not, what will you do to improve results? Do channels need additional training? Are there any issues related to channel conflict or compensation? Do marketing programs create too many or too few leads? For some businesses, channel partners represent the most important aspect of their marketing mix. Build relationships and create ongoing value with your trusted partners. Include them in company meetings and events and share information with them to build a mutual understanding of customers and your business.

## Implement

The *Implementation Calendar and Marketing Budget* are updated as programs are executed. In quarterly reviews the program results should be reported and analyzed. The results may require changes in messaging, targeting, price, media, creative, and other areas. Marketing is a process of continuous learning by tracking results, understanding the underlying factors that created the results (whether they are positive or negative), and making adjustments.

Remember, most businesses are looking for a marketing program that will be a "magic bullet" to produce new customers. The real secret is rigorously measuring and analyzing results and making improvements based upon a closed-loop continuous learning process.

The *Marketing Program ROI* worksheet is a "what if" tool that can be used to test new marketing programs. This worksheet should be used in conjunction with the sales funnel analysis worksheet and the ROI Optimizer.

*Sales funnel analysis* will help you analyze how the steps in the sales cycle correlate to marketing strategy and execution. Do programs target qualified buyers? Do they generate enough leads? Do they create too many leads resulting in lost opportunity because the sales force is not staffed to follow up? Analyze the number of proposals that were created and how many were converted to closed sales. Each stage in the sales funnel should be analyzed for its effectiveness.

## Strategize

*Strategies* should be assessed and updated in every quarterly review meeting. The performance measures and market reports on the topics previously mentioned will dictate if strategies need to be adjusted. New competitive information may require attention to competitive and pricing strategies. Trends and customer analysis may signal that strategic changes must be made. Customer feedback may reveal the need for a new service. A new product innovation may create growth opportunities in new markets. As products evolve through the lifecycle, they require new distribution channels, pricing, and marketing.

## Evaluate and Execute

The *ROI Optimizer* is a process you will learn in the next chapter that will link and measure all the elements in the demand chain. It is an invaluable tool that will help you not only assess the effectiveness of marketing programs, but will also identify specific areas and dependencies in the demand chain where improvements can be made. By improving the success of marketing and sales strategies and tactics, you will be able to make better decisions and grow your business at a faster pace.

The *Balanced Scorecard* is another tool you will use to measure the effectiveness of targeted objectives. It will help you align people and processes to meet customer needs, thereby achieving financial goals. An overview of this process is described later in this section.

*Culture assessments* will create specific measures you can use to improve year-over-year results in several areas of your business. Several companies can help you create and administer assessments. Look for those that will link employee and customer satisfaction with business performance metrics. You can also follow the ten "Culture Rules" at the end of this section to design and monitor your own programs.

# 79

# ROI Optimizer™: Increase the Effectiveness of How Marketing Is Measured

The MarketSmarter ROI Optimizer is a methodology for connecting, visually and mathematically, all the components of the demand chain to give managers and executives the ability to dramatically improve the efficiency, effectiveness, and predictability of their entire demand chain. An organization's demand chain is comprised of the sales, marketing, and service organizations, and the activities and programs that are implemented to consumers, to a sales force, and through various channels such as distributors, wholesalers, and strategic alliance partners.

The ROI Optimizer provides a framework for planning, managing, and measuring every entity and activity within the demand chain. It is made up of five primary elements that, when linked, provide a holistic picture to gain insight about what is working and what is not working. These elements are: (1) the revenue and quantity goals for the number of products sold, sales goals for sales and distribution channels, target customer segments, and sales and marketing programs that will be implemented; (2) the products or services that you sell; (3) the sales channels that sell them (sales force and the distributors, resellers, and other channels you sell your products through); (4) the goals for target customer segments; and (5) the marketing and sales programs you will implement to reach all audiences.

An important benefit of the ROI Optimizer is that it provides a clear picture of how sales, marketing, and service organizations must work together to achieve the best results. Departments have clear objectives about what is needed to stimulate demand and support for every other section of the demand chain.

Additionally, the ROI Optimizer creates a continuous improvement cycle so people can learn from every program that is implemented and improve over time. Optimization occurs when the existing situation is analyzed for its contribution to the overall goals of an organization. If you set this up in a spreadsheet, multiple scenarios can be quickly created to evaluate different versions of what is most effective regarding the mix of products, channels, customers, and marketing and sales programs.

The first time you use the ROI Optimizer, it will take some getting used to because it's a different way of thinking about linking marketing and sales activities to the company's overall goals. But do you want to base your decisions upon linking the demand chain, or on the accuracy of your intuition? Measuring marketing and sales ROI also takes discipline, but you will see improved ROI and continuous improvement. As you learn more each time you use the ROI Optimizer, it will become easier over time to predict results.

The ROI Optimizer is a solution to the problem that plagues most organizations—particularly marketers. As you read in earlier chapters, the ability to measure marketing is the nemesis of every marketer. It's a real-time marketing tool that can significantly reduce the time to develop, justify, manage, and measure plans, and it can increase the ROI for any sales and marketing program. In short, it will help you market smarter and improve results.

## ROI Optimizer™ Process

The following process will help you visually connect all the components of your demand chain to improve the efficiency, effectiveness, and predictability of marketing and sales programs. The ROI Optimizer will be created with information defined in five areas:

- Goals
- Products and services
- Sales channels
- End users
- Marketing and sales programs

Figure 79.1 depicts the basic flow of the ROI Optimizer, and the dependencies between each section. Complete each step following the directions outlined in each section.

**NOTE:**

- Numbers have been rounded.
- Definitions for terms used in the ROI Optimizer are defined at the end of Step #5 "Define Marketing and Sales Programs."
- The Marketing ROI Optimizer™ is flexible and can be customized to your business needs.

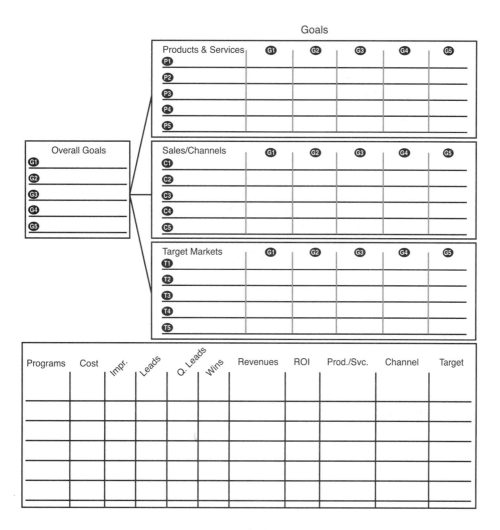

**Figure 79.1**   *The ROI Optimizer*

## Step 1: Set Your Goals

Define overall sales goals, which should include at least the basics: quantity and revenue. Keep in mind that the more specific your goals are, the more they can be measured and improved over time.

Goals can include the number of products you want to sell, the size or revenue goals for target customer segments (which defines the opportunity for possible sales), and specific sales goals for each of the sales and distribution channels (see Figure 79.2).

- Define revenue and quantity goals for products/services, sales channels (direct and indirect), and end user market segments.
- Make your goals quantifiable. For example:
  - Reach $5.2 million in revenue by the end of your fiscal year.
  - Obtain 230 new customers, including service plans for 175.
  - Sell 45% of yearly revenue goals through indirect channels ($2.3M).
  - Recruit 50 resellers by March 1st.

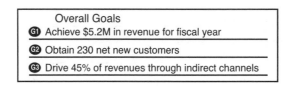

**Figure 79.2**  *Define goals*

## Step 2: Products and Services

- List all of your products and services.
- Map your products to the previously identified goals.
- Make sure your cumulative product goals equal your overall goals.
- For example:
  - Achieve $1.0M in revenue from the Basic Package and 31% of Enhanced Package revenues ($1.9M) through the direct company sales channel.
  - Attain 36% of indirect channel revenues from the Enhanced Package totaling $840K (represents 45% of overall revenue goal).
  - Shift 100% of service fulfillment to channel partners, resulting in 64% of indirect channel revenues ($1.5M).
  - Obtain 175 new Enhanced Package customers, all with a service plan.

| Products & Services | G1 Revenues | G2 New Customers | G3 Channel % |
| --- | --- | --- | --- |
| P1 Basic Package | $1.0M | 55 | 0% |
| P2 Enhanced Package | $2.7M | 175 | 36% |
| P3 Maintenance Services | $1.5M | 175 | 64% |

**Figure 79.3**  *Define products and services*

## Step 3: Define Sales Channels

- Identify and list all the sales organizations and channels, both direct and indirect, that the products are sold through, including an inside sales team, major account sales, distributors, resellers, strategic partners, and other channels.
  - Depending on the complexity of your sales channels and how specifically you would like to measure your results, you should define each specific sales channel. (Note: Reports can group sales channels like online catalogs, marketing affiliates, and manufacturers' representatives so they roll up to one number for a category like "online sales channels," but each channel needs to be measured individually first.)
- Map your sales channels to the previously identified goals.
- Make sure your cumulative sales channel goals equal your overall goals.
- For example:
  - Attain $2.9M (55%) of revenues through direct sales.
  - Attain $2.3M (45%) of revenues through indirect channels.
  - Gain 39 new customers through Partner A, 32 new customers through Partner B.

| Sales/Channels | G1 Revenues | G2 New Customers | G3 Channel % |
|---|---|---|---|
| C1 Direct Sales | $2.9M | 159 | 55% |
| C2 Partner A | $1.3M | 39 | 25% |
| C3 Partner B | $1.0M | 32 | 20% |

**Figure 79.4**  *Define sales channels*

## Step 4: Define Target Customer Segments

- Identify and list each discrete customer segment you will be targeting. Target segments may be defined by demographic, vertical industry, company size, number of employees, geography, type of asset, job title, and other criteria.
- Map your target customers to the previously identified goals.
- Make sure your cumulative target market goals equal your overall goals.
- For example:
  - Attain 46 percent of revenue from existing customers in the primary market segment (Segment A).
  - Utilize channel partners to get 46 percent of revenues from Segment A, 31 percent from Segment B, and 23 percent from Segment C.
  - Achieve 23 percent of revenue from small and medium businesses in the technology sector (Segment C) (see Figure 79.5).

| Target Markets | G1 Revenues | G2 New Customers | G3 Channel % |
|---|---|---|---|
| T1 Segment A | $2.4M | 110 | 46% |
| T2 Segment B | $1.6M | 65 | 31% |
| T3 Segment C | $1.2M | 55 | 23% |

**Figure 79.5** *Define target customer segments*

## Step 5: Define Marketing and Sales Programs

- Define what percentage of your goals (for example, revenue or wins) will be derived from marketing and sales programs versus other sources (that is, upgrades from existing customers, existing channel sales contacts, and so on).
- For example:
  - Drive 20 percent of revenues, or $1.0 million, from marketing and sales programs.
  - Achieve 160 wins from these programs.
- List the tactical marketing and sales programs you plan to implement to achieve your *program-driven* (as opposed to overall) goals.
- For each program, include the estimated cost, projected number of impressions, leads, qualified leads, wins, revenue goals, and resulting ROI (see "Definitions" for how to calculate ROI).
- Map each program to a specific product/service, sales channel, and target market segment.
  - Note: Each program should map to a single product/service, channel, and target customer segment. If programs overlap multiple areas, repeat the program listing as needed.
- Define the goals you would like to achieve for each marketing and sales program. Note that each program needs to have its own goal, and that these will roll up to provide you with a campaign-level view.

Defining each program in this manner provides insight into the total costs associated with each marketing activity, how each program is designed to achieve the best result, and how each program is quantitatively based upon impressions, response rate, and conversion rates (see Figure 79.6). For example:

- Conduct a $15,000 telemarketing campaign to convert 150 leads into 35 qualified leads, resulting in 15 wins to drive an estimated $97,500 in revenues.
- Conduct a joint seminar with Channel A to target Segment A with B Package offer, resulting in $39,000 in estimated revenues for an ROI of 3.9:1.

| Programs | Cost | Impr. | Leads | Q. Leads | Wins | Revenues | ROI (n:1) | Prod./Svc. | Channel | End Users |
|---|---|---|---|---|---|---|---|---|---|---|
| Telemarketing | $15k | N/A | 150 | 35 | 15 | $97.5k | 6.5 | Enh. Package | Direct | Segment A |
| Email Campaign | $5k | 55k | 550 | 55 | 5 | $32.5k | 6.5 | B. Package | Partner A | Segment B |
| Joint Seminar | $10k | 1.5k | 150 | 30 | 6 | $39.0k | 3.9 | B. Package | Partner A | Segment A |
| Online Advertising | $6k | 1M | 400 | 40 | 4 | $26.0k | 4.3 | Enh. Package | Partner B | Segment B |
| Tradeshow | $20k | 300 | 75 | 30 | 6 | $39.0k | 1.9 | Enh. Package | Direct | Segment A |
| Maint. Email | $3k | 2k | 75 | 50 | 15 | $30.5k | 10.2 | Maintenance | Partner B | Segment C |

**Figure 79.6**  *Define marketing and sales programs*

## Definitions

**Impressions:** The total number of people who are exposed to your marketing program. (Impressions could be Web page views, for example—not necessary who is "targeted.")

**Leads:** The number of people who respond to the program.

**Q Leads:** Qualified leads fit the specific description a company uses to define a qualified lead (for example, interest and ability to purchase).

**Wins:** The number of closed sales/contracts.

**ROI (n:1):** Return on Investment calculated by dividing the estimated revenue by cost. (For example, 10:1 ROI means the return was 10 times the investment.)

## Top-Down and Bottom-Up Analysis

By taking a cumulative view of all programs, you can ensure that your programs are sufficient enough to meet your previously stated program-driven goals for revenues for each product/service, channel, and target market. Perform an analysis on your anticipated results by reviewing the cumulative results broken down by product/service, channel, and end-user markets.

For example: The overall revenue goal of $5.2 million and $1.0 million is from the Basic Package. If you anticipate 20 percent of that revenue to come from marketing and sales programs, your tactics for the Basic Package need to account for $200,000 in revenues. However, the programs only provide estimated revenues of $71,500, which prompts the questions:

- Is your Basic Package revenue goal realistic?
- Can you achieve more than 80 percent of your revenue goal for the Basic Package from non-marketing related activities?
- What other marketing and sales activities can be added to make up the shortfall?
- Do you have enough of a budget to support the additional programs that would be required to meet the revenue goal?

This analysis should be repeated for every product/service, sales channel, and target market. The ROI Optimizer tool provides an immediate insight into whether your programs are sufficient to meet your goals.

In addition, while performing the analysis of the bottom-up estimates versus the top-down goals, you need to continuously check your assumptions to make sure they make sense (see Figure 79.7). For instance:

- Does Partner A have the expertise and contacts to drive 150 leads at a joint seminar?
- Is online advertising the best method for driving revenues from the Enhanced Package?

**Products & Services**

| Products & Services | G1 Revenues | G2 New Customers | G3 Channel % |
|---|---|---|---|
| P1 Basic Package | $1.0M | 55 | 20% |
| P2 Enhanced Package | $2.7M | 175 | 36% |
| P3 Maintenance Services | $1.5M | 175 | 64% |

**Overall Goals**

| Overall Goals | |
|---|---|
| G1 Achieve $5.2M in revenue for fiscal year | |
| G2 Obtain 230 net new customers | |
| G3 Drive 45% of revenues through indirect channels | |

**Sales/Channels**

| Sales/Channels | G1 Revenues | G2 New Customers | G3 Channel % |
|---|---|---|---|
| C1 Direct Sales | $2.9M | 159 | 55% |
| C2 Partner A | $1.3M | 39 | 25% |
| C3 Partner B | $1.0M | 32 | 20% |

**Target Markets**

| Target Markets | G1 Revenues | G2 New Customers | G3 Channel % |
|---|---|---|---|
| T1 Segment A | $2.4M | 110 | 46% |
| T2 Segment B | $1.6M | 65 | 31% |
| T3 Segment C | $1.2M | 55 | 23% |

| Programs | Cost | Impr. | Leads | Q. Leads | Wins | Revenues | ROI | Prod./Svc. | Channel | End Users |
|---|---|---|---|---|---|---|---|---|---|---|
| Telemarketing | $15k | N/A | 150 | 35 | 15 | $97.5k | 6.5 | Enh. Package | Direct | Segment A |
| Email Campaign | $5k | 55k | 550 | 55 | 5 | $32.5k | 6.5 | B. Package | Partner A | Segment B |
| Joint Seminar | $10k | 1.5k | 150 | 30 | 6 | $39.0k | 3.9 | B. Package | Partner A | Segment A |
| Online Advertising | $6k | 1M | 400 | 40 | 4 | $26.0k | 4.3 | Enh. Package | Partner B | Segment B |
| Tradeshow | $20k | 300 | 75 | 30 | 6 | $39.0k | 1.9 | Enh. Package | Direct | Segment A |
| Maint. Email | $3k | 2k | 75 | 50 | 15 | $30.5k | 10.2 | Maintenance | Partner B | Segment C |

**Figure 79.7** *Top-down and bottom-up analysis*

## Demand Chain Optimization

Once you have created your ROI Optimizer, it can be evaluated and optimized. Because elements in the map are linked and quantified, everything can be measured. This means that every time you execute a program, it can be improved the next time. Most businesses don't measure marketing, and if you don't, the goal is to start now. You can only get better if you begin to track and measure now. The ROI Optimizer can simplify and automate the process, and help track real results to analyze programs and adjust assumptions for future planning.

Schedule quarterly reviews to share results and assess the next steps in improving performance. Demand generation is dynamic, not static, so don't plan once and wait to change strategies and tactics until next year. Update the ROI Optimizer quarterly, and monthly if you execute many programs and have the ability to measure often. As you apply the ROI Optimizer process, you create a culture of accountability, high performance, and continuous improvement.

# 80

# The Balanced Scorecard

The missing links between strategy development and strategy execution are communication and alignment. The Balanced Scorecard and Strategy Map are fabulous tools that will help you improve these two critical links. It will create and communicate a shared understanding of strategy, resulting in alignment. Alignment across multiple teams enables greater flexibility in creating and communicating new strategies based on changing market, competitive, and technological conditions.

A few years ago, *Fortune Magazine* published a shocking statistic that stated only ten percent of employees understand their company's strategy.[1] This is consistent with other findings. Research from Harvard professors Robert Kaplan and David Norton, creators of the Balanced Scorecard, reveals that 95 percent of employees are not aware of, or do not understand, their company's strategy.[2] Furthermore, their research also discovered that 85 percent of executives typically spend less than one hour per month discussing strategy. With statistics like this, it's no surprise that most companies complain about their inability to execute strategy.

The Balanced Scorecard is a more meaningful and effective method for describing, measuring, and communicating strategy than traditional methods. In fact, it is so effective that nearly 70 percent of the Fortune 500 have adopted it. But you don't have to work in a large company to reap the rewards from using the Balanced Scorecard. One of the advantages to small and mid-sized companies is that the process will be easier to manage. There are many benefits of the Balanced Scorecard. It will help you:

- Translate strategy into operational terms.
- Describe and measure both leading and lagging indicators.
- Describe and measure intangible assets.
- Uncover a flawed strategy or one that is missing critical elements.
- Facilitate budget decisions by focusing on holistically funding initiatives.
- Define time-based measures of the strategy.
- Illustrate a holistic view of the organization.

Balanced Scorecards have four distinct perspectives: Financial, Customer, Process, and Learning and Growth. Strategy Maps translate the strategy, objectives, initiatives, and measures into the four quadrants. Succinctly summarized it would answer the question:

*What skills and knowledge do people need (learning and growth) to create and implement strategic processes (internal processes) that will create value for our customers (customer value), thereby achieving our financial goals (financial)?* Answering each part of this question will link and align strategic initiatives and goals in each of these four areas.

Strategy maps can be developed around strategic "themes," which are the three to four overarching goals for your business. For example, if a theme is to "increase customer loyalty," then you would need to consider the knowledge and training that employees need to achieve the goals of this theme. It may include training to understand customer lifetime value (CLV), customer segmentation, and other factors. Processes to measure CLV, segmentation, customer profitability, and CRM would need to be established. In the customer sector, you would need to determine what customers value the most so they can be retained and identify the programs to nurture customer relationships. In the financial sector, you would create financial targets and objectives that are tied to increased profitability as a result of increasing customer loyalty.

For each theme that is developed, establish objectives, strategies, and programs. Work top-down and bottom-up to make sure each of the areas are aligned to achieve the stated objective (see Figure 80.1)

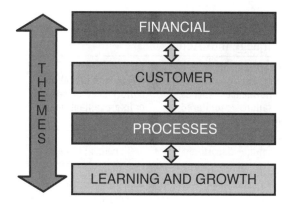

Source: Adapted from "The Balanced Scorecard: Translating Strategy into Action," Robert S. Kaplan and David P. Norton. Permission to reproduce granted by author.

**Figure 80.1**   *The Balanced Scorecard*

The overall business strategy map is created first. The strategy map cascades to other stakeholder groups, such as divisions, business units, and/or teams, so they can align their objectives to the overall organization objectives (see Figure 80.2). This creates alignment of objectives across the entire company, and it also creates accountability and ownership as objectives cascade to the individual level.

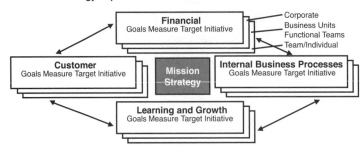

Strategy Maps Cascade to Business Units and Individuals

Source: "The Balanced Scorecard: Translating Strategy into Action," Robert S. Kaplan and David P. Norton. Permission to reproduce granted by author.

**Figure 80.2** *Strategy map cascade*

The Balanced Scorecard translates strategy map objectives into strategic initiatives, measures, and targets. The strategic initiatives form the action plan that enables the targets to be achieved, and execution of the strategy is managed through execution of initiatives. On completion of strategy development, it cascades to teams and individuals where strategy is translated into individual performance metrics.

Table 80.1 summarizes how a low-cost airline might describe their objectives in the customer and internal process categories.[3]

**Table 80.1**   Translating Strategy into Action

| Objective (What is the strategy intended to do?) | Measurement (How is performance—success or failure—monitored against objectives?) | Target (What is the level of performance or rate of improvement needed?) | Initiative (What key action programs are needed to achieve targets?) |
|---|---|---|---|
| Fast ground turnaround | —On ground time<br>—On-time departure | —30 minutes<br>—90 percent of the time | —Cycle time optimization |
| Attract and retain more customers | —# Repeat customers<br>—# of customers | —70 percent<br>—Increase 12 percent annually | —Implement CRM system |
| Flight is on time | —FAA on-time arrival rating | —#1 | —Quality management |
| Lowest prices | —Customer ranking | —#1 | —Customer loyalty program |

As initiatives are executed, they are measured against the targeted performance measures. Over time, this process enables an organization to become more precise in predicting and measuring strategy execution.

As you can see in Figure 80.3, the Strategy Map and Balanced Scorecard follow a process that is aligned to the P•R•A•I•S•E Marketing Process. Mission, vision, and values create the context and foundation. This is followed by strategy, implementation, and measurement. The two processes implemented together will help you link planning, strategy, execution, and evaluation metrics to continuously improve results.

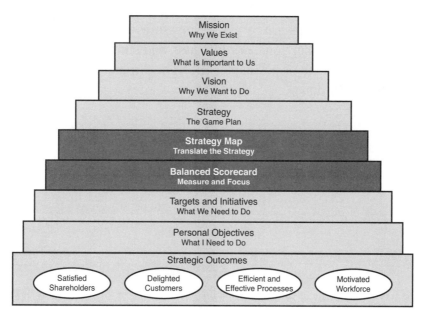

Source: "Strategy Maps: Converting Intangible Assets Into Tangible Outcomes," Robert S. Kaplan and David P. Norton. Permission to reproduce granted by author.

**Figure 80.3**  *Balanced Scorecard and Strategy Map Process*

## What Is Measured Improves

The ROI Optimizer, Balanced Scorecard, and Strategy Maps are tools you can implement to improve planning and execution. There are similar components in the processes:

- Visually translate strategy to operational terms by mapping it
- Align the organization and its activities to the strategy
- Link measures across the organization and demand chain
- Increased success of strategy execution

The Balanced Scorecard combined with the ROI Optimizer and other methodologies you have learned throughout the P•R•A•I•S•E Marketing Process will increase the effectiveness of strategy development, communication, and execution. The tools and processes are not difficult to use, but they do take discipline to develop and manage. Like your marketing plan, after they are complete, they are continuously updated as strategy is executed. If you like the concepts of the Balanced Scorecard and Strategy Maps, I suggest you read Kaplan and Norton's books on these subjects. A complete listing of their books can be found at www.MarketSmarter.com.

A business can no longer govern by simple measures of revenue, profitability, and margin. You can't manage what you can't measure, and strategy must be measured differently now than it was in the past. Chapter 81, "The Art and Science of Execution," focuses on *how* things get done.

# 81

# The Art and Science of Execution

The final part of this section will describe how you can create a culture of execution. The process will explain how to increase efficiency, effectiveness, and business results by aligning people, processes, and operations to your plan, which is the roadmap to successful business growth.

The word "execution" has generated a lot of buzz the past few years, but what does it really mean? The best description I have seen is from Larry Bossidy, chairman and former CEO of Honeywell, and international and vice chairman of GE. It can be found in the book he coauthored with Ram Charan, *Execution: The Discipline of Getting Things Done*:

> *Execution is a systematic process of rigorously discussing how's and what's, questioning, tenaciously following through, and ensuring accountability. It includes making assumptions about the business environment, assessing the organization's capabilities, linking strategy to operations and the people who are going to implement the strategy, synchronizing those people and their various disciplines, and linking rewards to outcomes. It also includes mechanisms for changing assumptions as the environment changes and upgrading the company's capabilities to meet the challenges of an ambitious strategy.*

I had an opportunity to talk with Larry Bossidy a few years ago, and he shared his thoughts on how process-based strategy and execution have given the companies he has lead a competitive advantage.[1] You can apply the same concepts to improve the effectiveness of your business. The following article shows what he had to say.

## Former GE Chief Shares His Thoughts on Management Trends

**Reece:** You have written one of the best and most concise books I have read regarding how to run a more effective company. Why do you believe leaders have such a difficult time executing on what many believe are basic leadership skills?

**Bossidy:** I think CEOs are being pulled in lots of different directions and as a consequence, they don't apply themselves to what will ultimately decide whether they keep their job or not. It isn't that these principles are new notions, but they are more complicated to execute than they were ten years ago just because of the marketplace in which we are in. So if they don't pay enough attention on one hand and it's more difficult to implement on the other, then there are performance issues, and as a consequence, CEO turnover is up higher than it's ever been before.

**Reece:** Do you see this trend continuing?

**Bossidy:** I think the answer is yes. CEOs are conducting themselves very differently than they did five years ago. They know this is a relatively slippery slope, and that they have to pay more attention to things than in the past, so I think that will improve performance. On the other hand, I think the world gets ever more competitive. It's challenging and turnover may not be as high as it was the last three years, but it will be high.

**Reece:** You describe execution as much more than tactically getting things done. Is the heart of execution really planning and executing against that plan?

**Bossidy:** The heart of execution is making sure things happen. In other words, it has to be a discipline we call creating and sustaining and energizing around making things happen. There are so many companies that philosophize and wonder and have unimplementable ideas. And the ones who are successful are those who get an idea, do an evaluation whether it will fit in the company, put a timetable on it, and get it done.

**Reece:** How do you keep your plan alive in the organization?

**Bossidy:** Most assumptions made during planning don't turn out as expected because we are not able to see things clearly. Keep it refreshed and put a contingency plan together. Quarterly, sit down and look at the plan and identify those things that have changed and what midcourse corrections are needed to keep it alive and relevant. For example, if you have a big target and the world falls apart, you change the target. Don't have people chasing a target that is never going to happen. So you keep the challenge refreshed as well so people have a chance to find fulfillment.

**Reece:** What specific methods do you use to evaluate both strategy and execution?

**Bossidy:** Did we make our goals? Did we keep our commitments that we said we were going to make? There are so many companies that commit to goals they never make. And they find lots of reasons they didn't make them including lots of excuses. The fact of the matter is you judge how well you are doing by whether you made your commitments or not.

**Reece:** Is there a specific scorecard or key indicators that you use?

**Bossidy:** Yes, and the metrics change every year. I want three measures all across the company. Those companies with ten goals, ten measurements, don't know what they are talking about. It's too many for people to concentrate on.

**Reece:** As a CEO, you have been very involved in marketing in your organizations. What do you believe are the biggest marketing challenges businesses face today?

**Bossidy:** Selling to product teams that demand more. They want economically priced products and they also want a better product built for them. The quality standard has gone up. Also, companies once kept customers for years. Loyalty is not near what it used to be.

**Reece:** You provide several examples throughout your book of companies that chose the wrong strategy at the wrong time. How would you suggest companies create an accurate strategy given these uncertain times?

**Bossidy:** With a lurch back to realism. Basically, strategies that failed were unrealistic to begin with. In other words, if you look at companies that are going into an entirely different area that they know nothing about and there are different customer dynamics, they don't succeed. That's why we use the AT&T story in the book. Yes, they had a big strategic problem in the sense of a declining telephone business, but they didn't know anything about cable.

**Reece:** I have read about your case for companies to eliminate the COO position in their companies. How is this being received?

**Bossidy:** Theory is this: The CEO can't be divorced from the things the COO is doing. Often times when that exists the CEO is involved in external matters and strategy, and the COO is involved in operations, and that's a dangerous separation to make. The CEO is supposed to be involved with both of those things. I think it's unnatural to divide them, and sometimes when they are divided, there is a friction that begins to develop. The CEO and COO each have their camp and it doesn't provide for a very efficient and effective organization.

**Reece:** As you consider your vast career as a CEO, what do you consider to be the single most important concept you use to govern your leadership and how do you want to be remembered?

**Bossidy:** Two things. You don't ever think of a legacy until you retire. But if I had a legacy, it was one, that I grew a lot of people who learned to run their own companies as CEO. I have a lot of pride in that. And two, I think I have a reputation for being fair and equitable. Not everybody liked me, but I was straightforward and candid with everybody.

**Reece:** What's next for you?

**Bossidy:** Writing another book. I run a venture capital company in California and oversee a couple of companies. I'm on a couple of boards. I'm as busy as I want to be. But I don't have the 7-to-9 schedule every day anymore. You have to keep growing. You hope the day you die you learn something. You make your own life dynamically.

Successful execution of your marketing plan is dependent on the processes you put in place to manage it. You have learned several processes to keep your marketing plan updated throughout this book. Now you will learn a system that brings everything together to help you evaluate your plan and integrate it with other areas of your business.

# 82

# Real-Time Marketing Planning

Real-time marketing planning is the process of making ongoing updates to sections of the plan so that it is always fresh and responsive to changing market conditions. In today's market, once-a-year planning is not effective. It needs to be linked to operational processes so the planning process becomes of the responsibility of everyone, not just marketing. Most companies have a quarterly operational review, and this is the best possible way to integrate marketing, planning, and operations.

Figure 80.1 integrates each step of the P•R•A•I•S•E Marketing Process into a yearly and quarterly operations review. The top headings define the sections of your marketing plan and how often they should be updated. The bottom section describes the types of meeting to accomplish each task, and recommends the roles of people who should participate.

The *research* and *analyze* components of the plan can be updated on an ongoing basis using the process outlined in Section II. Depending on your company's size and structure, individuals or teams can gather and report on these items.

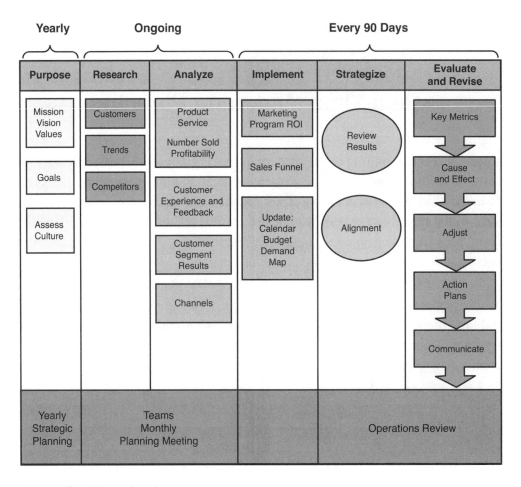

**Figure 82.1**   *Real-time planning process*

One of the most important outcomes of this planning process is collaboration and alignment of team members. It creates more accountability and ownership when cross-functional teams are involved in the process of strategy development, reporting, and adjusting the plan based on results. It creates an entirely different level of engagement than traditional methods of planning.

Overlay this process with your business operations process and make adjustments as needed for your business. If you have a very small business, use the resources you have so that responsibility of sales and marketing does not fall to just one person.

# 83

# Create a Culture of Execution

Consulting firm McKinsey & Company believes that there are seven key elements that drive successful business practice, all of which begin with the letter "S." Strategy, Systems, and Structure are viewed as the "hardware," while Style (common thinking and behavior), Skills, Staff, and Shared Values are considered the "software" of business success. It's interesting that four of the seven attributes are "soft" elements, yet comprise the majority of business success criteria. These attributes describe a company's culture and they are the "glue" to drive successful execution of your plan.

Extensive research proves that company culture drives business performance. It's a fact that companies that focus on creating a thriving culture are the most successful. A culture that values accountability and execution requires commitment. It also helps to have a framework. The ten principles are short, concise guidelines that you can use to create a culture that is focused on execution, integrity, and accountability.

If your goal is to create a high-performance company, you cannot choose to implement just a few of these principles and hope for the same results as you would if you followed all of them. Implement these top ten "rules" to create a healthy, innovative, and responsive company where *Culture Rules!*

## Culture *Rules!* 10 Principles to Drive Business Success... and Have More Fun

## 1. It's the Economics, Stupid.

Rule number one is to create passionate believers. This starts at the top. The CEO and senior executives must passionately believe that culture is the most important driver of a company's ability to execute and win in the market. Otherwise, culture initiatives will fail to get off the ground, let alone sustain any momentum. If senior leaders don't get it, forget it. They must be act on and support culture change—not just talk about it.

I learned this lesson the hard way. Several years ago, I worked in a company where we were beginning a large cultural change effort. Some of the top executives were on board and some weren't. The CEO clearly understood the importance of culture but his ideas were not shared by everyone on the executive team. One day, one of his direct reporters (who was third in command in the company) pulled me aside during a meeting and asked, "Why are you working on that fluffy people shit?" Clearly this individual was not on board. But this one person was responsible for leading thousands of people and responsible for half of the company's revenue. If he didn't believe in the value of culture, how could the program possibly be successful? Although the CEO was a strong believer, somehow his passion and enthusiasm were not embraced by even those closest to him.

One of the questions I am asked most often is, "How do I convince company leaders that we need to focus on developing our culture?" If you want to be the catalyst for change in your company, I recommend that you start by making a *business case* for change. The best place to start is by simply sharing the facts about how culture is the driver of business growth. There is a preponderance of evidence to support this fact which will help you get even the most conservative business leaders on board. All the data points to one simple fact: *Companies with strong corporate cultures outperform other companies.*

Some of the best research on the link between company performance and culture was done by management and leadership expert John Kotter of Harvard Business School. He and colleague John Heskett conducted a study to correlate the financial results of culture improvement programs. Here are the results:[1]

- Revenues grew more than four times faster.
- Job creation rates were seven times higher.
- Stock prices grew 12 times faster.
- Profits were 750 percent higher.
- Net income grew more than 700 percent.
- Return on equity increased.
- Sales rates improved.
- Customer satisfaction more than doubled.

In another study, Success Profiles, a performance measurement company, studied the business practices of more than 600 companies over eight years and found a critical link between business practices related to culture and performance outcomes including employee turnover, profit per employee, and revenue growth.[2]

Denison Consulting is another organization that has done extensive research to link culture to superior business performance. In a study of 950 businesses, Daniel Denison and colleague William Neale found a correlation between culture and bottom line financial performance measures including profitability, quality, innovation, sales growth, market share, employee satisfaction, and customer satisfaction.[3]

So aside from the commonsense reasons to create a healthy company culture, you now know key financial facts to create a business case for change. If you believe that the culture in your company drives business success, start by helping others understand what culture means and why it's important.

## 2. Walk the Talk

Leadership flows from the top down in organizations. Leaders inspire and teach others to lead through their own actions. Great leaders possess extraordinary communication skills and foster trust through an open and transparent leadership style. They let people know what is expected of them and why it matters. They energize people by describing the larger vision while focusing on short-term accomplishments and quick wins that create momentum. They set milestones and follow through to make sure people keep their promises, commitments, and deadlines. If a roadblock prevents a person from executing the plan, a leader helps him or her create an alternative solution that will work under the changed circumstances.

Leaders take every opportunity they can to lead by example and "walk their talk." If they say risk and innovation are important, they not only show this in their actions, but also encourage and support others who take initiative. A culture of risk and innovation can only be created by allowing people to make mistakes, and even celebrating them if they lead to positive change.

Leaders turn every situation into an opportunity to teach others. By addressing an issue in front of a team, people learn how to make decisions and take initiative quickly and effectively. The lessons learned will help everyone, both individually and collectively, improve their performance over time. This is the essence of a learning organization.

Senior leaders must be decisive; once a commitment is made, urgency and action plans must be made and followed through. One of the biggest frustrations in companies both large and small is indecision. It can paralyze a department, a division, or even an entire company.

Leaders know that competitive advantage is temporary, so their goal is always to create a flexible, adaptive organization. They teach others how it's done through systems, processes, and actions.

## 3. Integrity, Accountability, and Trust

If your goal is to create a culture of execution, then integrity, accountability, and trust must be woven into the fabric of the company culture. These values are the foundation for getting things done.

Accountability is doing what you say you will do. If leaders demand accountability, then they are accountable to others. They keep their promises and feel a sense of personal responsibility to do so. Personal accountability doesn't just create better results in the area of execution, it creates a culture of trust. Trust, in turn, creates confidence. When people trust and believe in each other and in the senior leaders they follow, they begin to see what's possible. They have increased faith in the company purpose and vision. They begin to expect what they believe in—and guess what? Science proves that people get what they expect.

Live by the Golden Rule, which is to do unto others as you would have them do unto you. Yes, this sounds like the basics your mother taught you, and she was right. Be nice, be fair, don't lie. It's easy enough to say the words, but action is everything. Integrity is about honesty and truthfulness.

These personal characteristics are in short supply these days. Consumer skepticism is at an all-time high, and who can blame folks for being skeptical? Executives from Enron, Qwest, Tyco, and other once-respected firms are now in jail. The life savings for loyal employees in some of these companies has been wiped out. Other industries have also been hit hard. Banks and mortgage companies created an unrealistic housing market, causing it to crash. Well-established companies like Lehman Brothers and Merrill Lynch experienced devastating losses or ceased to exist. U.S. automakers, once a pillar of strength in America, now depend on the government for bailouts as the industry reinvents itself. We are in our first global recession and the stock market has reacted with volatile swings. U.S. unemployment levels have reached a 14-year high with over 15 million Americans unemployed, nearly 10 percent of the U.S. workforce.

Trust was once a given, but now it seems more and more people are from Missouri, the "Show Me" state: They need to be shown they can trust others before they do. So what can you do? Create a company that values transparency, and then make it real by fostering open and honest communication. If you do this, it will cultivate a culture of accountability, trust, and integrity, and you will be doing your part to help rebuild faith in business.

## 4. Create a Compelling Vision

If you want to create a kick-butt culture but you're not certain where to focus your efforts first, here is the answer. Research proves that companies that clearly define their mission, vision, and guiding principles, and communicate them consistently across the organization, have significantly higher profit per employee than companies that do not. A survey by Success Profiles found that the average profit per employee increased from

$7,802 to $27,401 in companies that make mission, values, and communication a best practice in their organization.

One of the most interesting results in the Denison study was that one attribute—mission—stood out more than any others, impacting six out of the seven performance measures.[4] These are profitability, sales/revenue growth, market share, quality, employee satisfaction, and customer satisfaction.

This study is fabulous news for companies that are driven by purpose. The key to driving strategy and execution is a message that communicates the higher purpose of the organization. This is accomplished by creating a compelling vision that inspires everyone toward a common purpose and mission.

Bring the vision alive by making it visible in as many ways as possible. For example, post a strategy map or vision board on the walls of conference rooms. Frame visual reminders and pictures that celebrate achievement toward milestones. For example, Zappos has an entire wall framed with T-shirts that celebrate the company's million dollar milestones…from 1 million to the first $1 billion.

Strategy describes how a company will achieve its vision and purpose. It communicates what must be achieved and the initiatives and tactics describe how it will be implemented. Priorities and personal objectives are linked to strategy. Through regular dialogue, employees understand the link between purpose, strategy, and their own activities. When performance metrics are tied to the execution of activities, this creates personal accountability and a stake in the outcome.

In a high-performance culture, people make commitments focused on priority objectives. There is active discussion about what to do, as well as what to stop doing. This dialogue creates not only focus, but alignment, because there is strong communication about what must be collectively achieved.

## 5. Product Myopia Is the Death Spiral

One of the biggest reasons behind a company's inability to innovate and adapt to change is a structural flaw. It is caused by organizing the company around products, not customers. Often this creates product or service silos that only accentuate the problem because each department or division has a myopic view of its own products and markets. It drives people to defend their turf and focus on achieving revenue targets for their division instead of creating an integrated portfolio of solutions to fulfill customer needs. It wastes precious internal resources and is counterproductive to developing solutions that customers need. The result is lost opportunity—that is, revenue.

A result of aligning around customers instead of products is customer knowledge. A company will stay one step ahead of customers because it understands their needs so well. Because the company understands customer needs so well, it is more keenly aware of the broader market of substitutes available to customers, which makes it more competitive, flexible, innovative, and responsive. In contrast, a product-focused company will always be spinning to catch up to changing customer needs and market conditions.

If you look closely at the most innovative product/service companies (Google, Apple, and Zappos, for example), you will observe that the focus is not actually on the cool *products*, it's on fulfilling *customer needs*. Google delivers a simple user interface for search, making it as easy and intuitive as possible for people to find what they are looking for. Apple delivers customers an *experience* that drives the need for products consumers didn't even know they needed. Zappos is not just a shoe store; it is a service company that happens to sell shoes and clothing.

## 6. Love Is the Killer App

When a company treats employees, customers, shareholders, vendors, and suppliers, and the community with equal respect, they build long-term sustainable competitive advantage. Do you remember the Firms of Endearment case study? The companies that embraced and honored all stakeholders returned 1,025 percent to investors, versus 122 percent for the S&P 500.

All five stakeholder groups are important to the success of a business; however, I do think employees deserve some special attention. After all, they are on the front line with customers every day, so if your goal is to provide great customer service, you have to realize that this is not possible without your employees. They also interact with vendors and suppliers, and they are the face to the community and shareholders. Employees are a critically important component of your brand. Everything they do and say is a direct reflection on the quality of your brand.

Invest in employees by providing them with education and training so they can learn new ways to create even more value for your company. Create a cross-functional training program so people will understand the business holistically. Some of your best ideas will come from people after you do these things.

Celebrate successes often. Reward and recognize employees for the things they do to make your company better. When times are tough, engage them in the problem-solving process. This fosters loyalty in the toughest of times when folks are overworked, and it will help you retain your best employees in the best of times when other businesses try to win them over. You will be surprised at the lengths people go to support a mission they believe in and associates they call their friends.

Give your employees respect, live by the Golden Rule, and give them lots of love. Yes, I said love. Think about it: Most people spend far more time with coworkers than they do with their own family, so you should love them like family. You'll be amazed at what you get in return. Remember, you get what you give.

## 7. Feedback Is the Breakfast of Champions

What do you suppose is the number-one reason for poor performance? It's probably not what you think. The answer is poor or insufficient performance feedback.

A study by The Conference Board reveals that poor or insufficient performance feedback is a surprising 60 percent of the reason for low performance. This fact is substantiated by other studies as well. Companies that give employees ongoing feedback experience higher revenue growth. In fact, businesses scoring high in this area experience above 50 percent revenue growth per year. Companies that performed well in feedback and engagement saw revenue growth jump from 18.6 percent to 113.1 percent.[5]

When Jack Welch was CEO of GE, he consistently drilled the value of performance feedback into executives and managers. Performance reviews are not a once- or twice-a-year event. He rightly contends that if someone is not performing well and needs to be fired, it should never come as a surprise. Employees value ongoing feedback, and when leaders get into the habit of giving regular feedback, they find that employees will actively seek feedback and be more engaged. Not only does it make more sense to develop employees, it's every leader's responsibility. If you want a great culture, make this principle a central part of your plan.

## 8. Relentless Communication

If 95 percent of a company's strategy is not executed, what is one of the primary reasons for this abysmal statistic? The best way to answer this question is to ask another question: How well do people understand what the strategy is? Think about it: If people don't understand the strategy, how can they possibly be expected to execute it?

The most common mistake companies make is insufficient communication. Businesses must learn to share the plan and encourage people across the organization to ask questions so they really understand it. Sharing is not a presentation of the company's highlights in an all-hands meeting once a quarter. People need to hear about the strategy *all the time*. They need to understand where the company is going and why. They need feedback about the specific results of programs they have already executed. If results fail to achieve the expected goals, communicate *why*. Engage them in resolving issues and developing new ideas. Don't be afraid to confront the facts and realities. It's what people don't know that makes them fearful.

Most importantly, remember that communication is a two-way street. It doesn't happen through a monologue, but through the opportunity to interact and ask questions. Improved execution is the result of people understanding what the strategy is and what their role is in making it happen. This sounds like commonsense wisdom but statistics prove otherwise. Perhaps if more companies knew that increased communication drives increased financial performance, they would build a strong communication plan into their business plan.

Success Profiles found another benefit of communication. Companies that have strong communication programs that educate, inform, and engage employees see a drastic reduction in employee turnover. Businesses that do not score well in this category see a direct correlation in employee turnover and company performance. They had 25.8 percent employee turnover versus only 10.2 percent in companies that score high in this area. As you can see, companies with poor communication had nearly twice the employee turnover, so even slight improvements in the frequency and clarity of communication have a profound impact on employee turnover.

Here's a simple rule of thumb: It's simply impossible to "over communicate" your company direction and strategy.

## 9. Link Planning to Operations

You now know that the best way for a company to grow its business is to have a plan. How often should the plan be updated? The answer is all the time. When a plan is completed, it must be evaluated, measured, and adjusted based on what was learned. Throughout this process, you have learned several processes for real-time planning. The mechanism to update strategy and the plan is two meetings that link planning and operations. This is the most simple and effective way to accomplish this important task:

1. **Monthly Strategy Meeting:** Do you know that 85 percent of executives typically spend less than one hour per month discussing strategy? It's not enough. Set aside two to four hours for a strategic discussion once per month. Discuss and analyze critical issues affecting the business. Select only one or two topics so that the discussion is focused and progress is made. You will learn that another important outcome of this meeting is greater alignment across teams.

2. **Quarterly Operations Meeting:** Set aside one or two days once a quarter, preferably offsite. The agenda should include a review of results against the objectives, an analysis of the cause, and adjustments to the plan. Look ahead to the short- and long-term strategy and objectives and what must be accomplished. Review elements of the plan such as trends, customers, and competitors making adjustments as necessary.

It's imperative that research and reports are distributed in advance of both meetings. People need to come prepared to actively participate and discuss issues. Encourage a creative dialogue that focuses on problem solving and innovation.

## 10. Marketing Is Not a Department: It's a State of Mind

Yes, of course, marketing is a department, but it's much more than that. It's a perspective. Do you recall Peter Drucker's wisdom? He said the most important components of a business are marketing and innovation. If you create a culture where everyone thinks like a marketer, this stimulates innovation to solve more customer needs.

Marketing is a state of mind, a perspective that needs to be learned and shared by *everyone* in the company so it is integrated into the culture. This is how companies win. When you get everyone thinking about customers, your company has to become more innovative and competitive. In fact, you won't be able to stop it.

How do you get everyone to be more customer-focused? Give them education, training, and a process for closed-loop feedback. Encourage people to spend time observing customers using your products and services. Make sure there are mechanisms and processes in place so people can share what they learn.

One of the most powerful things you can do to stimulate a marketing mindset companywide is get customers engaged in the business. Ask customers to join all-hands meetings to share their opinion about what they like and listen to their suggestions for areas that can be improved. You won't believe what this does for your employees—and for your customers, who will feel like they are a real partner, a valuable part of your team and your company's success.

# Evaluate and Execute

## P • R • A • I • S • E™ Marketing Process

## Summary: Section VI

✓ Define the key performance measures for your business, including specific marketing measures.

✓ Evaluate the major components and decisions made throughout the planning process. Use the evaluation components in the P•R•A•I•S•E Marketing Process model outlined in this section to guide you.

✓ Use the ROI Optimizer to link all the elements of your demand chain—products and services, sales teams, channels, target markets, and marketing programs.

✓ Check for top-down and bottom-up alignment.

✓ Consider using the Balanced Scorecard as a tool to drive alignment across the organization. Evaluate how it will help you communicate strategic direction and track priorities and key measures.

✓ Use the Real-Time Planning Process to identify the most critical areas of the plan to update and define the process to do so.

✓ Use the 10 principles in "Culture Rules!" as a guide to develop a culture plan and internal branding campaign with senior leadership and develop the cultural mechanisms that will drive accountability, execution, and financial performance.

✓ Define a process to review, communicate, and update your plan.

# 84

# Now It's Up to You

You now have everything you need to create profitable and sustainable growth in your business. You know how to evaluate your marketing plan, in whole and in part, using several processes and performance measures. You have also learned how the ROI Optimizer, Balanced Scorecard, and Strategy Maps will help you describe, measure, and communicate strategy so that people can understand and execute it. Execution is not hard when you know the ingredients that make it successful.

You now have in your hands the principles and processes to create a real-time marketing plan, a roadmap for increasingly higher levels of growth in your company. You have also learned to create a company with purpose, character, and a culture people really love and want to be a part of.

Now it's time to put it to work. As you develop and implement your plan I would love to hear about your discoveries, challenges, successes, and results. *My inspiration comes from knowing how YOU benefited from the experience of learning and applying something new.* Good luck!

# Endnotes

## Chapter 1

1. Tom Olivo, "Increasing Profits Through Mission, Vision, and Guiding Principles," Success Profiles. www.successprofiles.com.

2. Ken Blanchard and Sheldon Bowles, *Raving Fans* (New York: William Morrow and Company, 1993).

3. Brian McCormick, "National Leader of the Month," Leader Network.org, www.leadernetwork.org/ken_blanchard_april_07.htm.

4. Ibid.

5. Ibid.

## Chapter 5

1. Donovan Robertson, "My Story 2.0," *Zappos 2008 Culture Book*, page 469. ©2010 Zappos.com, Inc.

## Chapter 6

1. Sandra Sucher and Stacy McMans, "The Ritz-Carlton Hotel Company," *Harvard Business Review*, Volume 9-601-163 (2005), page 12.

2. Ibid.

## Chapter 8

1. http://www.firmsofendearment.com.

2. Mike Taylor, "2008 CEO of the Year New Belgium's Kim Jordan: Tapping a Collective Energy." www.cobizmag.com/articles/2008-ceo-of-the-year/.

3. Source: *Denver Business Journal*, May 31, 2004.

4. Monique Reece, "Just Do It" Campaign Among Bedbury's Accomplishments," Denver Business Journal, May 31, 2004.

## Chapter 15

1. Philip Kotler and Kevin Keller, *Marketing Management* (Pearson Education, Upper Saddle River, New Jersey: 2006), page 156.

2. Reichheld, Fredrick, *The Ultimate Question (*Boston, Massachusetts: Harvard Business School Press, 2006), page 15.

3. Philip Kotler and Kevin Keller, *Marketing Management* (Pearson Education, Upper Saddle River, New Jersey: 2006), page 148.

4. Reichheld, Fredrick, *The Ultimate Question* (Boston, Massachusetts: Harvard Business School Press, 2006), pages 32–33.

5. Reichheld, Fredrick, *The Ultimate Question* (Boston, Massachusetts: Harvard Business School Press, 2006), page 37.

## Chapter 23

1. Clayton Christensen, Scott Cook, and Taddy Hall, "Marketing Malpractice, the Cause and the Cure," *Harvard Business Review*, Volume 83, Number 12 (2005), page 76.

## Chapter 28

1. Source: Sharon Brant. Adapted from the presentation "Research Methodologies."

## Chapter 29

1. Max Chafkin, "Kevin Rose of Digg: The Most Famous Man on the Internet." Inc.com. http://www.inc.com/magazine/20081101/keeevviin.html.

2. Brian Brown, "Guide to Using Technorati to Find Blogs About Your Industry," Business.com. http://www.business.com/guides/using-technorati-to-find-blogs-about-your-industry76.

## Chapter 32

1. Renee Mauborgne and Kim Chan have studied this concept extensively. For further information about how to create uncontested market space, I suggest you read *Blue Ocean Strategy*.

## Chapter 33

1. Clayton Christensen, Scott Cook, and Taddy Hall, "Marketing Malpractice, the Cause and the Cure," *Harvard Business Review*, Volume 83, Number 12 (2005), page 78.

## Chapter 35

1. The Risk Management Association develops new techniques and products for consumers to understand and limit credit risk, market risk, and operational risk. www.rmahq.org/RMA/.

## Chapter 40

1. Diane Anderson, "When Crocs Attack: With a Battle Plan Based on 'Thinking Bigger Than You Are,' the Maker of the World's Ugliest Shoe Takes the Footwear Business by Storm," *Business 2.0 Magazine*. http://money.cnn.com/magazines/business2/business2_archive/2006/11/01/8392028/index.htm.

2. Michael Porter, *Competitive Strategy: Techniques for Analyzing Industries and Competitors* (New York: Free Press, 1980), Chapter 2.

3. Philip Kotler, *Marketing Management* (Upper Saddle River, NJ, Pearson Education, 2006), page 54.

# Chapter 42

1. Diane Anderson, "When Crocs Attack: With a Battle Plan Based on 'Thinking Bigger Than You Are,' the Maker of the World's Ugliest Shoe Takes the Footwear Business by Storm," *Business 2.0 Magazine*. http://money.cnn.com/magazines/business2/business2_archive/2006/11/01/8392028/index.htm.

# Chapter 45

1. Monique Reece, "Moser: Brand Roadmap Can Drive Company's Marketing," *Denver Business Journal* (December 26, 2003). http://denver.bizjournals.com/denver/stories/2003/12/29/smallb5.html.

# Chapter 49

1. Satish Nambisan and Priva Nambisan, "How to Profit from a Better 'Virtual Customer Environment,'" *MIT Sloan Management Review*, 49:3 (2008), page 54.

2. "Netflix Awards $1 Million Netflix Prize and Announces Second $1 Million Challenge," Netflix News Release, New York, 2009.

3. Max Chafkin, "The Customer Is the Company," *Inc. Magazine*, June 2008. http://www.inc.com/magazine/20080601/the-customer-is-the-company.

# Chapter 51

1. Philip Kotler and Kevin Keller, *Marketing Management* (Upper Saddle River, NJ, Pearson Education, 2006), page 319.

2. Sarah Van Schagen, "Fighting Dirty," www.grist.org/cgi-bin.

3. Linda Tischler, "Pop Artist David Butler," *Fast Company Magazine*, pages 91-97.

4. Ibid.

# Chapter 52

1. Philip Kotler, *Marketing Insights From A to Z* (Hoboken, NJ: John Wiley and Sons, Inc., 2003), page 173.

# Chapter 53

1. Anderson, Diane (February 16, 2007). "When Crocs Attack: With a Battle Plan Based on 'Thinking Bigger Than You Are,' the Maker of the World's Ugliest Shoe Takes the Footwear Business by Storm," *Business 2.0 Magazine*. Retrieved January 6, 2009, from http://money.cnn.com/magazines/business2/business2_archive/2006/11/01/8392028/index.htm.

2. Adobe case study submitted by Ryan Hunter.

3. John Carey, "Under Armour a Brawny Tee House? No Sweat." *Business Week*, May 25, 2006. http://www.businessweek.com/print/smallbiz/content/may2006/sb20060525_601534.htm.

4. Gregory, Sean (2008). "Under Armour's Big Step Up [Electronic Version]." *Time*, *171*, pages 44–45.

5. Chuck Salter, "Protect This House," *Inc. Magazine*. http://www.fastcompany.com/magazine/97/under-armour.html.

## Chapter 56

1. Leigh Buchman, "Innovation: How the Creative Stay Creative," *Inc. Magazine*, June 2008. http://www.inc.com/magazine/20080601/innovation-how-the-creative-stay-creative.html.

2. Monique Reece, "Kumar: Differentiate Company Marketing with Three Vs," August 27, 2004. http://denver.bizjournals.com/denver/stories/2004/08/30/smallb4.html.

## Chapter 60

1. Shar VanBoskirk, "U.S. Interactive Marketing Forecast, 2009–2014," Forrester Research, Inc.

2. Ibid.

3. Ibid.

4. Glen Peterson, *The Profit Maximization Paradox: Cracking the Marketing/Sales Alignment Code* (BookSurge Publishing, 2008). http://www.discoverelementthree.com/ images/news/E3_WhitePaper_5MarketingStrategies.pdf.

5. CMO Marketing Outlook.

6. Ibid.

7. CMO Council, Facts and Stats, http://www.cmocouncil.org/statistics/spend.asp?View=all.

8. Monique Reece, "Expert Discusses How to Measure Marketing," *Denver Business Journal*, August 24, 2001. http://denver.bizjournals.com/denver/stories/2001/08/27/smallb7.htm.

9. Garrick Schmitt, "RazorFish Digital Brand Experience Study 2009," RazorFish. http://feed.razorfish.com/.

## Section V, Part I

1. Garrick Schmitt, "RazorFish Digital Brand Experience Study 2009," Razorfish. http://feed.razorfish.com/downloads/Razorfish_FEED09.pdf.

2. Ibid.

## Chapter 63

1. Jack Neff, "New Huggies, Old Spice Launches to Go TV-Free," *Advertising Age*. http://adage.com/article?article_id=136419.

2. "IDC U.S. Consumer Online Behavior Survey Results," http://www.idc.com.

3. RazorFish Digital Brand Experience Study, 2009.

## Chapter 64

1. Shar VanBoskirk, "U.S. Interactive Marketing Forecast, 2009–2014," Forrester Research, Inc., pages 11–12.

## Chapter 65

1. Shar VanBoskirk, "U.S. Interactive Marketing Forecast, 2009–2014," Forrester Research, Inc., pages 14–15.

2. Caroline Dangson, IDC, "Consumer Attitudes About Advertising and the Implications for Advertising on Social Networks," 2008, pages 13–19.

# Chapter 67

1. Nora Ganim Barnes, Ph.D. and Eric Mattson, "Social Media in the 2009 Inc. 500: New Tools and New Trends," The Center for Marketing Research, University of Massachusetts, Dartmouth, pages 1–7.
2. Shar VanBoskirk, "U.S. Interactive Marketing Forecast, 2009–2014," Forrester Research, Inc., July 30, 2009, page 13.
3. Tim McAtee, *The State of Social Media Marketing*, MarketingProfs Report, December, 15, 2009. http://www.marketingprofs.com/articles/2009/3246/the-state-of-social-media-marketing-by-the-numbers-a-sneak-peek.

# Chapter 68

1. Marc Stanford, PhD, "Social Influence Measurement: What's It Worth? Modeling and Creating Measurable Outcomes of Social Media Engagement," RazorFish Digital Outlook 2009, pages 138–144.

# Chapter 69

1. "How Micro-Interactions Are Changing the Way We Communicate Online," RazorFish, Digital Consumer Behavior Study, 2008.
2. Max Chafkin, "Kevin Rose of Digg: The Most Famous Man on the Internet," *Inc. Magazine*, November 2008. http://www.inc.com/magazine/20081101/keeevviin.html.

# Chapter 72

1. Ellen Gamerman, "The New Pranksters," *Wall Street Journal*, September 12, 2008, Weekend Journal, W1 and W12.

# Chapter 80

1. Charles Bloomfield, "Bringing the Balanced Scorecard to Life: The Microsoft Balanced Scorecard Framework," White Paper, Insightformation, Inc.
2. Robert S. Kaplan and David P. Norton, "The Office of Strategy Management," *Harvard Business Review*, October 2005, page 1.
3. Robert Kaplan and David Norton, *Strategy Maps, Converting Intangible Assets into Tangible Outcomes* (Boston, Massachusetts, Harvard Business School Publishing Corporation, 2004), page 53.

# Chapter 81

1. Monique Reece, "Former GE chief shares his thoughts on management trends," *Denver Business Journal* December 20, 2002. http://denver.bizjournals.com/denver/stories/2002/12/23/smallb6.html.

# Chapter 83

1. John Kotter, and Heskett, "Corporate Culture and Performance," Riverside, NJ:  Free Press Publishing, 1992.

2. Tom Olivo, Business Best Practices Study, Success Profiles. www.successprofiles.com.

3. Carolyn J. Fisher, "Like It or Not: Culture Matters," ARC International, LTD.

4. Ibid.

5. Tom Olivo, Business Best Practices Study, Success Profiles, www.successprofiles.com.

# Workshops and Training Programs

MarketSmarter LLC is a marketing and management firm that provides advisory services and training to help companies realize predictable, profitable business growth. We specialize in helping companies create a culture of execution and implement real-time business planning processes to continuously innovate and grow while avoiding risk. Businesses learn how to create a dynamic culture that inspires innovation, employee commitment, and customer loyalty.

MarketSmarter's ROI Optimizer™ helps businesses measure and improve results of marketing and sales programs by linking all the elements in a demand chain. It provides a framework for planning, managing, and measuring programs resulting in continuous improvement.

## Personal Training and Coaching

MarketSmarter is best known for the MarketSmarter Growth Plan Workshop, a program that has helped hundreds of businesses learn and grow to the next level.

If you are interested in working with other business professionals to apply the concepts in this book to develop a marketing plan, you can enroll in a class at www.marketsmarter.com. You can choose to attend a workshop in person or virtually using Web and audio conferencing, or have us facilitate a corporate workshop for your team. You can also receive one-on-one personal coaching to develop your marketing plan.

As alumni of the program, you have access to a network of marketing and business professionals who share ideas, support each other, and develop lasting partnerships and friendships. Alumni also receive new tools and resources, and are eligible to participate in the MarketSmarter Growth Roundtable.

## Corporate Training and Workshops

Are you interested in developing a thriving, company culture that is described as innovative, customer focused, and results oriented? Does your company consistently achieve objectives, attract highly knowledgeable employees, and have loyal customers who are *Raving Fans*?

MarketSmarter works with companies who desire to have a healthy, thriving, vibrant culture. We can help you develop leaders, improve collaboration and alignment, increase customer satisfaction, and achieve new levels of growth.

MarketSmarter also facilitates programs for sales, marketing, and service teams. Our philosophy is to teach as we advise so people can learn and apply new skills to current projects underway. All programs are highly customized to achieve the specific needs of your organization.

Programs include marketing and business planning, customer loyalty, making marketing measurable, creating a culture of execution, branding, organizational change, and many other topics. Send us an email that describes your challenges and what you would like to achieve: Monique@marketsmarter.com.

## Speaking

Monique Reece is a frequent speaker at industry conferences, organization and trade associations, and company events. She delivers highly engaging keynotes and workshop topics that are customized for every audience. If you are interested in having her speak at your next conference, please email Monique@marketsmarter.com.

# Real-Time Marketing for Business Growth
# Free Resources and Tools

Marketing is dynamic and constantly changing. We are too. Visit our Web site where you can download worksheets, templates, tools, and case studies by visiting the *Real-Time Marketing for Business Growth* book resource at www.MarketSmarter.com.

## *Real-Time Marketing for Business Growth* Book Resources

Download worksheets, examples, case studies, sample marketing plans, and other tools that are designed to help you implement the strategies and tactics in this book. A few of the tools you will find include:

- Marketing and Sales Program ROI Analysis
- Sales Funnel Analysis
- Implementation Calendar and Budget
- Selected Book Chapters
- Break-Even and Target Profit Analysis Worksheets
- Sales Planning Guide
- Tactical Plan Template
- Real-Time Planning Tools
- Research Guides
- *Culture Rules!* ebook
- …and much more!

## Social Media Strategy and Planning Guide

Download and share the *Social Media Strategy and Planning Guide.* This comprehensive resource explains a process for developing your social media strategy and tactical programs. Learn about new social media tools to help you implement, measure, and analyze results. This guide is updated often to provide you with new tactical tools, analytics programs, and management tools to help you create and execute your social media plan.

## Research Resources Guide

Download the *Research Resources Guide,* a comprehensive list of research resources on a wide variety of topics. Shorten your learning curve and save time by knowing where to look for valuable information that will help you turn data into actionable knowledge.

*Competitive Research Guide* is a guide that will direct you to the most relevant sources for competitive intelligence.

## Articles, Tools, Templates, and Products

Download tools, templates, worksheets, and products to access a growing number of resources to help you with marketing, sales, strategy, leadership, and culture.

## MarketSmarter Blog and Newsletter

Subscribe to our blog and newsletter via RSS or email to access new articles, get fresh new insight, and share ideas with other business leaders.

## Business Coaching

MarketSmarter helps business owners tackle their biggest business challenges and achieve their goals. Receive personal coaching or attend a training session.

Would you like to develop a growth plan using the process outlined in this book? Attend the MarketSmarter Growth Plan Workshop to develop your plan as you collaborate and network with other CEOs, marketers, and business professionals.

Collaborate and network with CEOs, marketers, and sales professionals who have attended the MarketSmarter Growth Plan Workshop. To learn more, visit our Web site.

# Appendix

# Marketing Plan Template

**Cover Page:** Insert your company logo and the time frame for the plan. Optional: Insert the date the plan was created and by whom.

**Page Two:** Executive Summary

This should be a one- to three-page summary written after everything else is complete. Include a definition of the plan, purpose, and audience.

## I. Purpose

### Company Purpose

- Mission
- Vision
- Values

### Company Goals

- Summarize one- to three-year goals.

### Situation Analysis

- Brief overview of company's current situation (may include market and competitive factors, or reference to past performance)
- Key issues and business drivers
- Brief product and service description (if not stated already)
- SWOT Analysis

# II. Research

## Market Opportunity Analysis

Market Analysis

- Market and industry analysis (market situation, needs, trends, growth)

Company Analysis

- Market share, size, and growth potential
- Resources/Alliances
- Product analysis (sales, profits, etc.)

Customer Analysis

- Revenue/Profits by segment

Summarize A, B, C, D Customer Analysis

- Summarize buyer behavior/customer wants and needs.
- Summarize findings from primary research and "Why People Buy" worksheet.
- Summarize actions to refine understanding of customers.

## Macro-Environmental Analysis

- Summarize findings from research into macro-environmental issues that are relevant (legal/political, economic, social/cultural, demographic, ecological/professional, technological).
- Define contingency plans as needed.

## Market Segmentation and Target Markets

Market Segments

- Market sizing

Primary and Secondary Target Markets

- Define specific details of primary and secondary target markets.

## Competitive Analysis

- Define major competitors.
- Define competitive situation summarizing key observations; use the Competitive Information Worksheet as a guide.

# III. Analyze

## Products and Services

- Summarize products and services (include features, benefits, and value proposition).
- Product strategies.

## Pricing Strategy

- Summarize observations from expansion and vulnerability analysis.
- Summarize decisions and observations from Pricing Map.
- Pricing analysis (break-even, target profit, and so on).
- Pricing strategies:
  - Finalize upon completion of Strategize section.

## Distribution Strategy

- Current channels (size and importance).
- Identify future channels for growth.
- Strategic alliances.
- Distribution strategies:
  - Finalize upon completion of Strategize section.

# IV. Strategize

## Sales Analysis and Projections

- Summarize revenue, profit, and key performance indicators, including historical figures and projected revenue for one- to three-years.

## Sales Objectives

- Summarize sales projections.
- Summarize sales objectives and plans.

## Sale Strategy

- Define strategies to achieve sales objectives (includes details for specific customers, industries, geographies, etc.).
- Summarize the sales plan. (Use the Sales Strategy and Planning Guide.)

## Marketing Objectives

- Summarize marketing objectives.

## Marketing Strategies

- Define positioning strategy.
- Summarize target market, customer, product, price, distribution, promotion, competitive, growth, and innovation strategies.

# V. Implement

## Tactical Implementation Plan

## Marketing Programs

- Summarize new media, social media, and traditional media promotion strategies.
- Define tactical programs and plan:
  - Include description, resource needs, timeline, estimated cost, and projected ROI.

## Marketing Budget

- Summarize and/or insert Marketing Budget.

## Implementation Calendar

- Summarize and/or insert Implementation Calendar here.

## Measuring Marketing and Sales Effectiveness

- Marketing program ROI.
- Sales funnel analysis.
- Define key marketing and business metrics.

## VI. Execute and Evaluate

### Execute

- Align marketing plan to operating plan.
- Integrate with Balanced Scorecard (if applicable).
- Define real-time components of marketing plan.
- Create a timeframe for periodic reviews and updates; link it with operational planning.
- Summarize how plan will be executed, including key processes and roles and responsibilities.
- Define the communication plan to key stakeholder groups.
- Define Culture Plan.

### Evaluate

Financial Metrics

- Operating cash flow
- Net profit/net income
- Return on sales
- Other metrics

Evaluation Components: Summary measurement criteria in each step of P • R • A • I • S • E Model and plan for ongoing evaluation:

- Purpose
- Research
- Analyze
- Implement
- Strategize
- Execute and Evaluate

Marketing ROI Optimizer

# Index

## Numbers

**3M, culture of innovation example, 199**
**80/20 rule, 32**

## A

**Abercrombie and Fitch, viral marketing example, 262**
**accountability in culture of execution, 321-322**
**acquisition as growth strategy, 189**
**activity-based cost, 51**
**Adobe, new markets example, 191-192**
**advertising exchanges, 229**
**advertising spending statistics, 214**
**advisory boards, customers on, 172-173**
**affiliate advertising, 228**
**airline industry, poor customer experience, 64**
**alliances/partnerships, 139-140**
  as growth strategy, 190
**Alltop, 102**
**Amazon**
  affiliate advertising, 228
  distinctive delivery example, 118
  long-tail business model example, 197
**analysis**
  business expansion, 106-107
  disruptive innovation, 110-113
  distribution channels
    *channel conflict, 137*
    *checklist for, 137-138*
    *evaluating, 130-132*
    *real-time channel development, 133-135*
    *selecting, 129-130, 136*
    *types of, 131-132*
  elements of, 105
  evaluating, 297
  pricing strategy, 121-124
    *factors affecting, 122*
    *mapping customer value to, 122-124*
    *objectives, 121-122*
    *training industry example, 124*
  revenue/cost analysis, 127-128
  social media strategy, 256
  strategic alliances/partnerships, 139-140
  substitute products/services, 108-109
  value creation process, 114-120
**analyst firms for real-time research, 102-103**
**Analyze stage (P•R•A•I•S•E Marketing Process).** *See* **analysis**
**Anderson, Chris, 197**
**Andreessen, Marc, 63**
**Andretti, Mario, 211**
**AOL, customer service example, 170-171**

Appel, Joel, 58, 69, 135

Apple

customer advisory board example, 173

customer-centric example, 324

flank strategy example, 186

preemptive strategy example, 187

applications for mobile devices, 232-233

Arizona Iced Tea, 181

Arm and Hammer

broadening potential market example, 115

primary research example, 94

art and science of strategy development, 208-209

Artful Frame Gallery, customer buying reasons example, 66

attack strategy, 185-186

# B

B2B (busienss-to-business) target markets, 74

Balanced Scorecard (BSC), 33, 298, 308, 311-312

Barnes and Noble, long-tail business model example, 197

Beckham, Daniel, 282

Bedbury, Scott, 27-29, 162

Best Buy, viral marketing example, 261

Blanchard, Ken, 4-5, 23, 95

blogs, 251-252

real-time research with, 102

*Blue Ocean Strategy* (Monbourge and Chan), 111

Bodet, Tom, 164

bookmarking, 250

Bossidy, Larry, 313-316

bottom-up analysis in ROI Optimizer, 305-306

brand equity, 159-161

brand essence, 159-160

designing, 162-165

brand innovation, 195

brand personality, 159-160

designing, 162-165

brand positioning in social media strategy, 257

brand roadmaps, Mike Moser interview, 163-165

brand strength of purpose-driven companies, 27-29

brands

designing, 162-165

ingredient branding, 153

Mike Moser interview, 163-165

positioning strategy, 154-155, 157

*brand influence factors, 157*

*characteristics of success, 158*

*creating positioning statements, 156*

*elements of positioning statements, 155-156*

*examples of positioning statements, 157*

*types of, 154-155*

worth of, 159-161

Branson, Richard, 196

break-even point, evaluating, 297

brewery example, purpose-driven companies, 25-26

BrightHouse, culture of innovation example, 199

Brooks, Todd, 183

BSC (Balanced Scorecard), 33, 298, 308, 311-312

budget statistics, 215

budget worksheet for tactical plans, 275-276

budgets
  basis for, 291-292
  evaluating, 297
  value-based marketing, 292-293

Burger King, Web site interactivity, 222

Bush, George W., 63

business case for changing corporate culture, 319-321

business expansion, analysis of, 106-107

business models
  customer engagement business model, 175-176
  long-tail business model, 197-198

business value, 110

business-to-business (B2B) target markets, 74

Butler, David, 182-184

buyers, broadening potential market, 114-115

buying, determining reasons for, 66-68

buzz marketing, 261
  pranksters, 261-262
  in presidential elections, 262-264

## C

calendar worksheet for tactical plans, 275-276

Campbell's, market penetration strategy example, 152

car rental industry, poor customer experience, 64

Chan, Kim, 110-111

channel conflict, 137

channels
  channel conflict, 137
  checklist for, 137-138
  evaluating, 130-132, 297
  as growth strategy, 190
  real-time channel development, 133-135
  selecting, 129-130, 136
  types of, 131-132

Charan, Ram, 313

Chief Marketing Officer (CMO) Council, 214

Christensen, Clayton, 75-76

Citizen's Bank, customer experiences, 61

Clark, Dick, 279

Clinic Service Corporation
  mission statement, 6-7
  positioning statement example, 157

CLV (customer lifetime value), 51

CMO (Chief Marketing Officer) Council, 214

**Coca-Cola**

brand equity of, 159

"designing with a purpose," 182-184

Facebook example, 246

**cocreaters, customers as, 174-176**

**Cohort, market segmentation example, 79**

**collaboration**

between sales and marketing, 283-284

on CRM, 286-288

**Collins, Jim, 146**

**Colorado ski resorts, brand personality example, 160**

**commitment to core values, Zappos example, 14-16**

**communication**

in culture of execution, 325-326

of values, 23

**communications industry, poor customer experience, 64**

**company culture, 12**

customer-centric culture, creating, 57-60

employee turnover statistics, 20

Ritz-Carlton example, 17-18

*employee training program, 18-20*

in social media strategy, 259

Zappos example, 12

*commitment to core values, 14-16*

*customer service, 13*

**company culture assessments, 298**

**company culture of execution, creating, 319**

business case for, 319, 321

communication, 325-326

customer-centric service, 323-324

employee recognition, 324-325

integrity, accountability, trust, 321-322

Larry Bossidy interview, 313-316

leadership by example, 321

linking planning and operations, 326

marketing as state of mind, 327

performance feedback, 325

vision, 322-323

**company culture of innovation, encouraging, 199-202**

**company purpose**

culture, 12

*customer-centric culture, creating, 57-60*

*employee turnover statistics, 20*

*Ritz-Carlton example, 17-20*

*in social media strategy, 259*

*Zappos example, 12-16*

customers as raving fans, 3-4

elements of, 2

employees as heart of business, 4-5

evaluating, 295-296

intentional versus dysfunctional, 5

mission statements

*elements of, 6*

*examples of, 6-7*

*as inspiration, 7*

profits and, 2-3

values

*behavior, effect on, 11*

*commitment to, Zappos example, 14-16*

*communicating and executing, 23*

*defining and prioritizing, 21-23*

*evaluating, 295*

*measuring, 23*

*personal and professional values, relationship between, 11*

vision statements, 8-10

**company values**

behavior, effect on, 11

commitment to, Zappos example, 14-16

communicating and executing, 23

defining and prioritizing, 21-23

evaluating, 295

measuring, 23

personal and professional values, relationship between, 11

**competitive advantage.** *See also* **differentiation**

with disruptive innovation, 110-113

training to maintain, 288-289

value creation process, 114-120

**competitive research**

tracking competitors, 87-89

types of competitors, 86-87

**competitive strategies, 185-188**

attack strategy, 185-186

defensive strategy, 186

flank strategy, 186

preemptive strategy, 187

retreat strategy, 187

risks of success, 188

substitute product strategy, 187

**contests, Netflix example, 174-175**

**Converse, customer experiences, 61**

**Cook, Scott, 53-54**

**core messaging, 164**

**core values**

behavior, effect on, 11

commitment to, Zappos example, 14-16

communicating and executing, 23

defining and prioritizing, 21-23

evaluating, 295

measuring, 23

personal and professional values, relationship between, 11

**corporate culture.** *See* **culture**

**costs**

fixed costs, 127

variable costs, 127

**CRM (customer relationship management), 55**

collaboration on, 286-288

strategy implementation, 55-56

**Crocs**

acquisition example, 189

mass market example, 151

**crowdsourcing, 195**

**Cru Vin Dogs, passion example, 30-31**

**cultural information, researching, 92**

**culture, 12**

customer-centric culture, creating, 57-60

employee turnover statistics, 20

Ritz-Carlton example, 17-18

*employee training program, 18-20*

in social media strategy, 259

Zappos example, 12

  *commitment to core values, 14-16*

  *customer service, 13*

**culture assessments, 298**

**culture of execution, creating, 319**

  business case for, 319-321

  communication, 325-326

  customer-centric service, 323-324

  employee recognition, 324-325

  integrity, accountability, trust, 321-322

  Larry Bossidy interview, 313-316

  leadership by example, 321

  linking planning and operations, 326

  marketing as state of mind, 327

  performance feedback, 325

  vision, 322-323

**culture of innovation, encouraging, 199-202**

**customer advisory boards, 172-173**

**customer delight, customer satisfaction versus, 52**

**customer engagement business model, 175-176**

**customer experience**

  creating, 61-62, 115-116

  evaluating, 297

  Golden Rule in, 64-65

  poor customer service, 63-65

  sharing information about, 286, 288

**customer experience innovation, 195**

**customer innovation, 195**

**customer lifetime value (CLV), 51**

**customer relationship management (CRM), 55**

  collaboration on, 286, 288

  strategy implementation, 55-56

**customer satisfaction, customer delight versus, 52**

**customer segments, defining in ROI Optimizer, 303-304**

**customer service**

  based on customer segmentation levels, 47

  designing Web sites for, 223-224

  Orange Glo example, 58

  poor service, 63-65

  response by, 169-171

  Ritz-Carlton example, 59

  Zappos example, 13

**customer strategies, 166-168**

  customer advisory boards, 172-173

  customer service response, 169-171

  customers as cocreaters, 174, 176

**customer surveys**

  creating, 96-97

  online surveys, 97-98

**customer value, 110**

  mapping to pricing strategy, 122-124

**customer-centric culture**

  creating, 57-60

  product-centric versus, 285-286

**customer-centric service, in culture of execution, 323-324**

**customers**

loyalty, 50

*CLV (customer lifetime value), 51*

*Intuit example, 53-54*

*NPS (Net Promoter Score), 52-53*

*penalization for, 65*

market segmentation

*based on product role, 75-78*

*Globus example, 79-81*

new customers as growth strategy, 192

power shift with social media, 235-237

primary research

*creating customer surveys, 96-97*

*developing plan for, 96*

*online surveys, 97-98*

*quantitative versus qualitative research methods, 94-95*

as raving fans, 3-4

real-time customer research, 69-70

reasons for buying, 66-68

segmentation, 44-49

skepticism of, 63-64

target market identification, 71-73

*B2B target markets, 74*

**customization, designing Web sites for, 222**

## D

**decline stage (product life cycle), 179-180**

**defensive strategy, 186**

**defining**

core values, 21-23

secondary research plan, 93

**DeHart, Jacob, 176**

**delivery process, distinguishing from others, 117-118**

**Dell**

customer service example, 169

social media example, 236

**Dell, Michael, 163**

**demand, forecasting, 83-85**

**demand chain, 299**

optimization, 307

**demographics, 72**

researching, 91

**Denison Consulting, 320**

**Design Machine (Coca-Cola), 184**

**"designing with a purpose," Coca-Cola example, 182, 184**

**detractors, 53**

**development framework for strategy, 147-148**

**differentiation, 164.** *See also* **competitive advantage**

in positioning statement, 156

in product strategy, 181-184

**Digg**

social bookmarking, 250

trendsetting example, 117

**digital media**

advantages of, 219

email marketing, 230-231

mobility marketing, 232

*applications for, 232-233*

*examples of, 234*

*growth rate, 233*

online advertising, 227
  *advertising exchanges, 229*
  *affiliate advertising, 228*
  *display advertising, 227-228*
  *sponsorships, 229*
public relations, 265-270
social media, 235
  *blogs, 251-252*
  *Facebook, 246-247*
  *LinkedIn, 245-246*
  *measuring ROI, 241-244*
  *operational budget for, 242-244*
  *power shift with, 235, 237*
  *principles of, 238*
  *social bookmarking, 250*
  *statistics, 239-240*
  *strategy formulation, 254-260*
  *Twitter, 247-249*
  *value of, 237*
viral marketing, 261
  *pranksters, 261-262*
  *in presidential elections, 262-264*
Web sites, 220-221
  *integrated customer service
    technology, 223-224*
  *interactivity, 222-223*
  *mass customization, 222*
  *search engine optimization, 225*
  *targeted markets, 222-223*
  *usability design, 221*
  *value-added services, 224*
**direct competitors, 86**

**display advertising, 227-228**
**disruptive innovation, 110-113, 194**
**distribution channels**
  channel conflict, 137
  checklist for, 137-138
  evaluating, 130-132, 297
  as growth strategy, 190
  real-time channel development, 133-135
  selecting, 129-130, 136
  types of, 131-132
**distribution innovation, 196**
**distribution services for public
  relations, 266**
**Doyle, Peter, 292**
**DreamWorks, customer advisory board
  example, 172**
**Drucker, Peter, 61, 110, 281, 327**
**Ducati Motor Holdings, 174**
**dysfunctional purpose, intentional
  purpose versus, 5**

# E

**early adopters, attracting, 151-152**
**ecological information, researching, 91**
**economic information, researching, 91**
**Edwards, John, 234**
**elections, viral marketing in, 262-264**
**email marketing, 230-231**
**emotions, effect on customer service
  reputation, 170-171**
**employee recognition in culture of
  execution, 324-325**
**employee turnover statistics, 20**

**employees**

in customer-centric culture, 57-60

as heart of business, 4-5

Ritz-Carlton training program, culture example, 18-20

understanding of company strategy, 308

**Enterprise Rent-A-Car, flank strategy example, 186**

**entrepreneurship**

brand strength, 27-29

Cru Vin Dogs example, 30-31

New Belgium Brewery example, 25-26

profitability, 24

*Firms of Endearment (FoE)*, 24-25

**environmental factors, researching, 90-93**

**environmental impact, New Belgium Brewery example, 25**

**Evaluate and Execute stage (P•R•A•I•S•E Marketing Process).** *See* **evaluation; execution**

**evaluation**

of Analyze stage (P•R•A•I•S•E Marketing Process), 297

with Balanced Scorecard, 308-312

of distribution channels, 130-132

of Evaluate and Execute stage (P•R•A•I•S•E Marketing Process), 298

of Implement stage (P•R•A•I•S•E Marketing Process), 297-298

of Purpose stage (P•R•A•I•S•E Marketing Process), 295-296

of Research stage (P•R•A•I•S•E Marketing Process), 296-297

with ROI Optimizer, 299-307

of Strategize stage (P•R•A•I•S•E Marketing Process), 298

**evaluation stage (social media strategy), 259-260**

**exclusive distribution strategy, 131**

**execution**

creating culture of, 319

*business case for, 319-321*

*communication, 325-326*

*customer-centric service, 323-324*

*employee recognition, 324-325*

*integrity, accountability, trust, 321-322*

*Larry Bossidy interview, 313-316*

*leadership by example, 321*

*linking planning and operations, 326*

*marketing as state of mind, 327*

*performance feedback, 325*

*vision, 322-323*

evaluating, 298

real-time marketing planning, 317-318

of values, 23

**execution stage (social media strategy), 259**

***Execution: The Discipline of Getting Things Done* (Bossidy and Charan), 313**

**expansion, analysis of, 106-107**

**experiences**

creating, 61-62, 115-116

evaluating, 297

Golden Rule in, 64-65

poor customer service, 63-65

sharing information about, 286-288

**experiential marketing, 28**

**experimentation in social media strategy, 260**

**exponential growth strategies, 189**

**external brand strength, 27-29**

## F

**Facebook, 246-247**

**Federal Express, positioning statement example, 157**

**feedback**

in culture of execution, 325

importance of, 95

**Ferrari, Vincent, 170-171**

**Firms of Endearment (FoE), 24-25**

**fixed costs, 127**

**flank strategy, 186**

**focus groups, 69-70**

**FoE (Firms of Endearment), 24-25**

**follower strategy, 180**

**forecasting demand, 83-85**

**Foss, Bill, 30**

**frame of reference in positioning statement, 156**

**frequency in public relations, 267**

**Frontier Airlines, attack strategy example, 186**

**Fruit Growers Association, market penetration strategy example, 152**

## G

**gadgets**

for mobile devices, 232-233

for Web sites, 222

**Gates, Bill, 265**

**Generational Tag, social media ROI example, 241**

**Globus, market segmentation example, 79-81**

**goals**

BSC (Balanced Scorecard) categories, 33

categories, 33-34

evaluating, 295

setting in ROI Optimizer, 301-302

SMART goals, 32, 206

**Godin, Seth, 110, 251**

**Godiva Chocolatier, market penetration strategy example, 152**

**Golden Rule in customer exerience, 64-65**

**Google**

customer-centric example, 324

social networking example, 101

**"green" initiatives, New Belgium Brewery example, 25**

**Grove, Andy, 187**

**growth opportunities, analysis of**

business expansion, 106-107

disruptive innovation, 110-113

distribution channels
  *channel conflict, 137*
  *checklist for, 137-138*
  *evaluating, 130-132*
  *real-time channel development, 133-135*
  *selecting, 129-130, 136*
  *types of, 131-132*
  elements of, 105
  evaluating, 297
  pricing strategy, 121-124
    *factors affecting, 122*
    *mapping customer value to, 122-124*
    *objectives, 121-122*
    *training industry example, 124*
  revenue/cost analysis, 127-128
  social media strategy, 256
  strategic alliances/partnerships, 139-140
  substitute products/services, 108-109
  value creation process, 114-120
**growth stage (product life cycle), 178**
**growth strategies, 189-192**
  acquisition, 189
  new customers, 192
  new distribution channels, 190
  new markets, 190-192
  new products, 192
  strategic alliances/partnerships, 190

# H

**Hallmark, 174**
**Herman Miller, 181**

**Heskett, John, 320**
**holistic marketing metrics, 292-293**
**HP (Hewlett-Packard), customer advisory board example, 172-173**
**Hsieh, Tony, 12-15**

# I

**imaginative innovation, 119**
**IMC (integrated marketing communications), 213**
**implementation**
  advertising spending statistics, 214
  email marketing, 230-231
  evaluating, 297-298
  mobility marketing, 232
    *applications for, 232-233*
    *examples of, 234*
    *growth rate, 233*
  online advertising, 227
    *advertising exchanges, 229*
    *affiliate advertising, 228*
    *display advertising, 227-228*
    *sponsorships, 229*
  public relations, 265-270
  relationship with strategy, 143
  social media, 235
    *blogs, 251-252*
    *Facebook, 246-247*
    *LinkedIn, 245-246*
    *measuring ROI, 241-244*
    *operational budget for, 242-244*
    *power shift with, 235-237*

*principles of, 238*

*social bookmarking, 250*

*statistics, 239-240*

*strategy formulation, 254-260*

*Twitter, 247-249*

*value of, 237*

tactical plans

*creating, 274*

*implementation calendar and budget worksheet, 275-276*

viral marketing, 261

*pranksters, 261-262*

*in presidential elections, 262-264*

Web sites, 220-221

*integrated customer service technology, 223-224*

*interactivity, 222-223*

*mass customization, 222*

*search engine optimization, 225*

*targeted markets, 222-223*

*usability design, 221*

*value-added services, 224*

**Implementation Calendar, evaluating, 297**

**implementation calendar and budget worksheet, 275-276**

**Implement stage (P•R•A•I•S•E Marketing Process).** *See* **implementation**

**impressions, 305**

**indirect competitors, 86**

**ingredient branding, 153**

**innovation**

disruptive innovation, 110-113

imaginative innovation, 119

**innovation strategies, 194, 196**

culture of innovation, 199-202

long-tail business model, 197-198

models for, 194-196

**inspiration in mission statements, 7**

**integrated customer service technology, designing Web sites for, 223-224**

**integrated distribution strategy, 131**

**integrated marketing communications (IMC), 213**

**integration of strategies, 209**

**integrity in culture of execution, 321-322**

**Intel, retreat strategy example, 187**

**intensive distribution strategy, 131**

**intentional purpose, dysfunctional purpose versus, 5**

**interactivity, designing Web sites for, 222-223**

**internal brand strength, 27-29**

**internal competitors, 87**

**Internet distribution strategy, 132**

**introduction stage (product life cycle), 177-178**

**Intuit, customer loyalty example, 53-54**

**iPhone, trendsetting example, 117**

## J

**JetBlue, substitute product strategy example, 187**

**Johnson's, market penetration strategy example, 153**

**Jordan, Michael, 165**

**Jordon, Kim, 25**

**justification in positioning statement, 156**

# K

Kaplan, Robert, 308

Kawasaki, Guy, 107, 248

The Ken Blanchard Company, response after 9/11 attacks, 4-5

Kent, Muhtar, 183

keywords in public relations, 266-268

Knight, Phillip, 27

Kodak, market penetration strategy example, 152

Kotler, Philip, 110, 145

Kotter, John, 320

Kraft, market penetration strategy example, 152

Kumar, Nirmalya, 145, 200-202

Kvietok, Frank, 69

# L

Landmark Theaters, customer experience example, 115

Launch Pad

    real-time channel development example, 133-135

    real-time customer research example, 69-70

leadership by example, 321

leads, 305

Lebesch, Jeff, 25

legal factors, researching, 90

lenses, 251

Levitt, Theodore, 75

LinkedIn, 101, 245-246

LinkExchange, 14

links in public relations, 268

The Long Tail: Why the Future of Business is Selling Less of More (Anderson), 197

long-tail business model, 197-198

Louis Vuitton, customer experience example, 116

Lowry, Adam, 182

loyalty of customers, 50

    CLV (customer lifetime value), 51

    creating customer experiences, 61-62

    Intuit example, 53-54

    NPS (Net Promoter Score), 52-53

    penalization for, 65

# M

macro research, 42, 71

    competitive research

        *tracking competitors, 87-89*

        *types of competitors, 86-87*

    environmental factors, 90-91, 93

    forecasting demand, 83-85

    market segmentation

        *based on product role, 75-78*

        *Globus example, 79-81*

    target market identification, 71-73

        *B2B target markets, 74*

Madoff, Bernie, 63

Malcolm Baldridge National Quality Award, 17

market leadership (pricing objective), 121

market penetration strategy, 152-153

market segmentation

    B2B target markets, 74

    based on product role, 75-78

Globus example, 79-81

target market identification, 71-73

**market share penetration (pricing strategy), 121**

**market size, identifying, 83-85**

**marketing**

budget statistics, 215

current trends in, 213-215

improvements needed in, 282

*collaboration on CRM, 286-288*

*customer-centric organization, 285-286*

*metrics, 289-290*

*sales and marketing collaboration, 283-284*

*strategic versus solution sales, 284-285*

*training to maintain competitive advantage, 288-289*

metrics

*in Analyze stage (P•R•A•I•S•E Marketing Process), 297*

*Balanced Scorecard, 308-312*

*in Evaluate and Execute stage (P•R•A•I•S•E Marketing Process), 298*

*in Implement stage (P•R•A•I•S•E Marketing Process), 297-298*

*performance measures, list of, 293-294*

*in Purpose stage (P•R•A•I•S•E Marketing Process), 295-296*

*in Research stage (P•R•A•I•S•E Marketing Process), 296-297*

*ROI Optimizer, 299-307*

*in Strategize stage (P•R•A•I•S•E Marketing Process), 298*

perception of, 281-282

ROI measurement, 216-218

as state of mind, 327

**marketing and sales programs, defining in ROI Optimizer, 304-305**

***Marketing as Strategy: Understanding the CEO's Agenda for Driving Growth and Innovation* (Kumar), 200**

**marketing budgets**

basis for, 291-292

evaluating, 297

value-based marketing, 292-293

**marketing innovation, 195**

**marketing objectives, strategy and, 206**

**Marketing Program ROI worksheet, 271, 297**

**markets, new markets as growth strategy, 190-192**

**Marquis Banking Partners, competitive research example, 88**

**Mashable, 102**

**mass market penetration strategy, 150-151**

**maturity stage (product life cycle), 178-179**

**Maytag, 181**

**McCarty, Tyler, 93**

**McConnell, Mac, 66**

**McEnroe, John, 165**

**McKenna, Regis, 98**

**measurable goals**

BSC (Balanced Scorecard) categories, 33

categories, 33-34

evaluating, 295

setting in ROI Optimizer, 301-302

SMART goals, 32, 206

**measuring.** *See also* **metrics**

marketing effectiveness, 271

values, 23

**media room, creating, 269-270**

**Method Products**

attack strategy example, 186

differentiation example, 182

**metrics**

improvements needed in, 289-290

marketing budgets, basis for, 291-292

marketing metrics

*in Analyze stage (P•R•A•I•S•E Marketing Process), 297*

*Balanced Scorecard, 308-312*

*in Evaluate and Execute stage (P•R•A•I•S•E Marketing Process), 298*

*in Implement stage (P•R•A•I•S•E Marketing Process), 297-298*

*performance measures, list of, 293-294*

*in Purpose stage (P•R•A•I•S•E Marketing Process), 295-296*

*in Research stage (P•R•A•I•S•E Marketing Process), 296-297*

*ROI Optimizer, 299-307*

*in Strategize stage (P•R•A•I•S•E Marketing Process), 298*

in social media strategy, 259-260

value-based marketing, 292-293

**micro research, 42**

customer loyalty, 50

*CLV (customer lifetime value), 51*

*Intuit example, 53-54*

*NPS (Net Promoter Score), 52-53*

customer segmentation, 44-49

**microsites, 222**

**Microsoft, defensive strategy example, 186**

**million-dollar prize (Netflix) example, 174-175**

**Mint Financial Services, mobility marketing example, 234**

**mission, evaluating, 295**

**mission statements**

elements of, 6

examples of, 6-7

as inspiration, 7

**mobility marketing, 232**

applications for, 232-233

examples of, 234

growth rate, 233

**Monbourge, Renee, 110-111**

**Moser, Mike, 162**

interview with, 163-165

**MoveOn.org, 262**

**Mrs. Fields, brand imaging example, 165**

**Myers, Jack, 214**

# N

NAICS (North American Industriy Classification System), 85

Naisbitt, John, 39

Net Promoter Score (NPS), 52-53

Intuit example, 53-54

Netflix

distinctive delivery example, 118

long-tail business model example, 197

million-dollar prize example, 174-175

value creation process example, 110

NetJets, distinctive delivery example, 118

New Belgium Brewery, purpose-driven companies example, 25-26

*A New Brand World* (Bedbury), 162

news advisories, writing, 269

news aggregators, 99-100

news releases, writing, 268-269

niche markets, 149-150

Nickell, Jake, 175

Nielsen Media Research, 85

Nike, 174

brand strength example, 27-29

branding example, 165

customer experiences, 61

Nisbet, Scott, 79

North American Industry Classification System (NAICS), 85

Norton, David, 308

NPS (Net Promoter Score), 52-53

Intuit example, 53-54

# O

Oakley, customer experiences, 61

Obama, Barack, 263-264

objectives

evaluating, 295

for social media, defining, 255

observational research, 75

one-to-one marketing, 55

collaboration on, 286-288

strategy implementation, 55-56

online advertising, 227

advertising exchanges, 229

affiliate advertising, 228

display advertising, 227-228

sponsorships, 229

online survey tools, 97-98

operational budget for social media, 242-244

operations, linking with strategy, 326

opt-in/opt-out marketing, 230

Orange Glo, customer service example, 58

Oreck, Diana, 17

organic growth strategies, 189

organizational innovation, 195

# P

Pareto principle, 32

partnerships, 139-140

as growth strategy, 190

passion, Cru Vin Dogs example, 30-31

passives, 53

Patagonia, 224

performance feedback in culture of execution, 325

performance measures, list of, 293-294

permission marketing, 230

personal values, relationship with professional values, 11

personification of brands, 159-160

  designing, 162-165

pet food example, niche markets, 149

PETA (People for the Ethical Treatment of Animals) Super Bowl ad, social media example, 236

Phelps, Ron, 6

pioneer strategy, 180

pitching stories in public relations, 267

Pixar, customer advisory board example, 173

Plank, Kevin, 192

platform innovation, 194

PLC (product life cycle) stages, 177-180

policies for social media strategy, defining, 259

political factors, researching, 90

Pollard, William, 42

PollDaddy, 101

Porter, Michael, 143-145

positioning in social media strategy, 257

positioning statements

  creating, 156

  elements of, 155-156

  examples of, 157

positioning strategy, 154-157

  brand influence factors, 157

  characteristics of success, 158

  creating positioning statements, 156

  elements of positioning statements, 155-156

  examples of positioning statements, 157

  types of, 154-155

*Positioning: The Battle for Your Mind* (Trout and Reese), 162

Post-its, mass market example, 150

potential market, broadening, 114-115

power shift with social media, 235, 237

PR (public relations), 265-270

PR kits, creating, 269-270

PR Newswire, 266

pranksters in viral marketing, 261-262

preemptive strategy, 187

presence, social media type selection, 257-258

presidential elections, viral marketing in, 262-264

pricing map, 122-124

pricing strategy, 121-124

  factors affecting, 122

  mapping customer value to, 122-124

  objectives, 121-122

  training industry example, 124

primary research, 42

  creating customer surveys, 96-97

  developing plan for, 96

online surveys, 97-98

quantitative versus qualitative research methods, 94-95

**prioritizing core values, 21-23**

**PRIZM (Potential Rating Index by Zip Codes), 79**

**process development for strategy, 147-148**

**process innovation, 194**

**product development process, 107**

**product innovation, 194**

**product life cycle (PLC) stages, 177-180**

**product role, market segmentation based on, 75-78**

**product strategy**

differentiation, 181-182, 184

PLC (product life cycle) stages, 177-180

**product-centric organization, customer-centric versus, 285-286**

**products**

listing in ROI Optimizer, 302

new products as growth strategy, 192

**professional information, researching, 91**

**professional values, relationship with personal values, 11**

**profit maximization (pricing objective), 121**

**profitability**

of loyal customers, 50

of purpose-driven companies, 24

*Firms of Endearment (FoE), 24-25*

**profits, purpose and, 2-3**

**promoters, 53**

**psychographics, 72**

**public relations, 265-270**

**pull strategy (distribution channels), 130**

**purpose**

culture, 12

*customer-centric culture, creating, 57-60*

*employee turnover statistics, 20*

*Ritz-Carlton example, 17-20*

*in social media strategy, 259*

*Zappos example, 12-16*

customers as raving fans, 3-4

elements of, 2

employees as heart of business, 4-5

evaluating, 295-296

intentional versus dysfunctional, 5

mission statements

*elements of, 6*

*examples of, 6-7*

*as inspiration, 7*

profits and, 2-3

values

*behavior, effect on, 11*

*commitment to, Zappos example, 14-16*

*communicating and executing, 23*

*defining and prioritizing, 21-23*

*evaluating, 295*

*measuring, 23*

*personal and professional values, relationship between, 11*

vision statements, 8-10

Purpose stage (P•R•A•I•S•E Marketing Process). *See* purpose
purpose-driven companies
  brand strength, 27-29
  Cru Vin Dogs example, 30-31
  New Belgium Brewery example, 25-26
  profitability, 24
    *Firms of Endearment (FoE), 24-25*
push strategy (distribution channels), 130
Putten, James, 51

## Q

Q leads, 305
Qik, 63
qualitative research methods, 94-95
quantitative research methods, 94-95

## R

rapid growth strategies, 189
Rashid, Karim, 182
raving fans, customers as, 3-4
*Raving Fans* (Blanchard), 4
reach, in public relations, 266
real-time channel development, 133-135
real-time customer research, 69-70
real-time marketing planning, 317-318
  linking operations and strategy, 326
real-time product development, 107
real-time research
  analyst firms for, 102-103
  integrating with other research, 103
  news aggregators, 99-100

with social media, 100
  *blogs, 102*
  *social networking, 100-101*
  *tools/gadgets, 101*
RedShift Framing, mission statement, 6
Reese, Al, 162
Reichheld, Fredrick, 52
research
  CRM (customer relationship management), 55
    *strategy implementation, 55-56*
  customers' reasons for buying, 66-68
  evaluating, 296-297
  goals of, 42-43
  importance of, 40-41, 43
  macro research, 42, 71
    *competitive research, 86-89*
    *environmental factors, 90-93*
    *forecasting demand, 83-85*
    *market segmentation, 75-81*
    *target market identification, 71-74*
  micro research, 42
    *customer loyalty, 50-54*
    *customer segmentation, 44-49*
  primary research
    *creating customer surveys, 96-97*
    *developing plan for, 96*
    *online surveys, 97-98*
    *quantitative versus qualitative research methods, 94-95*
  real-time research, 69-70
    *analyst firms for, 102-103*
    *integrating with other research, 103*

*news aggregators, 99-100*

*with social media, 100-102*

secondary research plan, defining, 93

**Research stage (P•R•A•I•S•E Marketing Process).** *See* **research**

**research stage (social media strategy), 256-257**

**Restoration Hardware, 181**

**return on investment.** *See* **ROI**

**retreat strategy, 187**

**revenue forecast, creating, 203**

**revenue/cost analysis, 127-128**

**rituals, 23**

**Ritz-Carlton**

culture example, 17-18

*employee training program, 18-20*

customer service example, 59

daily rituals, 23

**The Ritz-Carlton Gold Standards, 18**

**The Ritz-Carlton Leadership Center, 17**

**Roberson, Donavon, 15**

**ROI (return on investment)**

defined, 305

measuring, 216-218, 271

of social media, 241-244

**ROI Optimizer, 298-307**

demand chain optimization, 307

goals, setting, 301-302

marketing and sales programs, defining, 304-305

products and services, listing, 302

sales channels, defining, 303

target customer segments, defining, 303-304

top-down and bottom-up analysis, 305-306

**Rose, Kevin, 117**

**Ryan, Eric, 182**

## S

**sales**

collaboration with marketing, 283-284

strategic versus solution sales, 284-285

**sales channels, defining in ROI Optimizer, 303.** *See also* **distribution channels**

**sales funnel analysis, 298**

**Sales Funnel Effectiveness worksheet, 271**

**sales programs, defining in ROI Optimizer, 304-305**

**sales strategy, 204-205**

**Samuels, Denzil, 8-9**

**Schultz, Horst, 19**

**Schultz, Howard, 1, 27, 157**

**search, in public relations, 266-268**

**search engine marketing (SEM), 225**

**search engine optimization (SEO), 225**

**secondary research, 42**

**secondary research plan, defining, 93**

**segmentation**

of customers, 44-49

*defining in ROI Optimizer, 303-304*

market segmentation

*B2B target markets, 74*

*based on product role, 75-78*

*Globus example, 79-81*

*target market identification, 71-73*

**selecting**

distribution channels, 129-130, 136

social media types, 257-258

strategy, 145

**selective distribution strategy, 131**

**SEM (search engine marketing), 225**

**SEO (search engine optimization), 225**

**service innovation, 194**

**service strategy.** *See* **product strategy**

differentiation, 181-184

PLC (product life cycle) stages, 177-180

**services, listing in ROI Optimizer, 302**

**Sheraton Hotels, market segmentation example, 75**

**Shop Savvy, mobility marketing example, 234**

**Shultz, Don, 215**

interview, 216-218

**silos, breaking down, 283-284**

**SIM (social influence marketing), 236**

**Situation Analysis, 35**

**skepticism of customers, 63-64**

**ski resorts example, brand personality, 160**

**skimming strategy, 151-152**

**SMART goals, 32, 206**

**Smirnoff Vodka, Web site interactivity, 222**

**Smith, Brad, 54**

**Snellgrove, Jay and Mary, 30**

**social bookmarking, 250**

**social influence marketing (SIM), 236**

**social information, researching, 92**

**social media, 235**

blogs, 251-252

Facebook, 246-247

LinkedIn, 245-246

measuring ROI, 241-244

operational budget for, 242-244

poor customer service and, 63

power shift with, 235-237

principles of, 238

real-time research with, 100

*blogs, 102*

*social networking, 100-101*

*tools/gadgets, 101*

social bookmarking, 250

statistics, 239-240

strategy formulation, 254-260

*brand positioning, 257*

*evaulation stage, 259-260*

*execution stage, 259*

*experimentation in, 260*

*objectives, 255*

*research stage, 256-257*

*roles and policy, 259*

*selecting social media types, 257-258*

*tactical plan, 258-259*

*target audience, 256*

Twitter, 247-249

value of, 237

**social networking, real-time research with, 100-101**

solution innovation, **194**

solution sales, strategic sales versus, **284-285**

**Southwest Airlines**

customer experience, 64

value creation process example, 111

**sponsorships, 229**

**Sprint, market penetration strategy example, 152**

**Squidoo, 251**

**Starbucks**

brand influence factors, 157

brand strength example, 27-29

channel conflict example, 137

**start-ups, importance of research, 41**

**statistics**

advertising spending, 214

display advertising, 227

employee turnover and company culture, 20

employee understanding of company strategy, 308

marketing budgets, 215

Obama presidential campaign, 263

social media, 239-240

**stories**

pitching in public relations, 267

vision statements as, 10

**strategic alliances/partnerships, 139-140**

as growth strategy, 190

**strategic sales, solution sales versus, 284-285**

**Strategize stage (P•R•A•I•S•E Marketing Process).** *See* **strategy**

**strategy**

art and science of development, 208-209

brand equity, 159-161

brands, designing, 162-165

competitive strategies, 185-188

*attack strategy, 185-186*

*defensive strategy, 186*

*flank strategy, 186*

*preemptive strategy, 187*

*retreat strategy, 187*

*risks of success, 188*

*substitute product strategy, 187*

customer strategies, 166-168

*customer advisory boards, 172-173*

*customer service response, 169-171*

*customers as cocreaters, 174-176*

development framework, 147-148

employee understanding of, 308

evaluating, 298

explained, 145-146

growth strategies, 189-192

*acquisition, 189*

*new customers, 192*

*new distribution channels, 190*

*new markets, 190-192*

*new products, 192*

*strategic alliances/partnerships, 190*

innovation strategies, 194-196

*culture of innovation, 199-202*

*long-tail business model, 197-198*

*models for, 194-196*

integration, 209

linking with operations, 326

marketing objectives, 206

positioning strategy, 154-157

*brand influence factors, 157*

*characteristics of success, 158*

*creating positioning statements, 156*

*elements of positioning statements, 155-156*

*examples of positioning statements, 157*

*types of, 154-155*

product strategy

*differentiation, 181-184*

*PLC (product life cycle) stages, 177-180*

relationship with implementation, 143

revenue forecast, creating, 203

sales strategy, 204-205

selecting, 145

for social media, 254-260

*brand positioning, 257*

*evaluation stage, 259-260*

*execution stage, 259*

*experimentation in, 260*

*objectives, 255*

*research stage, 256-257*

*roles and policy, 259*

*selecting social media types, 257-258*

*tactical plan, 258-259*

*target audience, 256*

target market strategies, 149-153

*market penetration strategy, 152-153*

*mass market penetration, 150-151*

*niche markets, 149-150*

*skimming strategy, 151-152*

**strategy maps, 309-311**

**StumbleUpon, 250**

**stunts in viral marketing, 261-262**

**substitute product competitors, 86**

**substitute product strategy, 187**

**substitute products/services, analysis of, 108-109**

**Success Profiles, 320**

**SurveyMonkey, 98**

**surveys**

creating, 96-97

online surveys, 97-98

**survival pricing (pricing strategy), 121**

**sustainability, New Belgium Brewery example, 25**

**SWOT Analysis, 35-36**

evaluating, 296

**syndication innovation, 196**

## T

**Taco Bell, viral marketing example, 262**

**tactical plans**

creating, 274

implementation calendar and budget worksheet, 275-276

social media strategy, 258-259

**Target, product differentiation example, 181**

**target audience for social media, defining, 256**

**target customer segments, defining in ROI Optimizer, 303-304**

**target market**

customer segmentation, 44-49

*defining in ROI Optimizer, 303-304*

designing Web sites for, 222-223

identifying, 71-73

*B2B target markets, 74*

market segmentation

*B2B target markets, 74*

*based on product role, 75-78*

*Globus example, 79-81*

*target market identification, 71-73*

**target market strategies, 149-153**

market penetration strategy, 152-153

mass market penetration, 150-151

niche markets, 149-150

skimming strategy, 151-152

**target profit, evaluating, 297**

**technological information, researching, 92**

**Technorati, 102**

**TED (United Airlines subsidiary), value creation process example, 111**

**threadless, customer engagement business model example, 175-176**

**tiered distribution strategy, 131**

**top-down analysis in ROI Optimizer, 305-306**

**traditional media spending statistics, 214**

**train example, imaginative innovation, 119**

**training industry example, pricing map, 124**

**training programs, Ritz-Carlton culture example, 18-20**

**training to maintain competitive advantage, 288-289**

**Treacy, Michael, 145**

**trendsetting, 116-117**

**Trout, Jack, 162**

**trust in culture of execution, 321-322**

**Turner, Ted, 117**

**Twitter, 100-101**

explained, 247-248

tips for using, 248-249

**TwtPoll, 101**

## U

**Under Armour, new products example, 192-193**

**United Airlines**

attack strategy example, 186

value creation process example, 111

*United We Brand* (Moser), 162

**Upshaw, Lynn, 154**

**usability, designing Web sites for, 221**

**user innovation, 195**

## V

**value, mapping customer value to pricing strategy, 122-124**

**value creation process, 110-120**

broadening potential market, 114-115

creating customer experiences, 115-116

distinctive delivery process, 117-118

imaginative innovation, 119

trendsetting, 116-117

**value innovation, 195**

**value network, 200**

**value propositions, 157, 200**

**value-added services, designing Web sites for, 224**

**value-based marketing, 292-293**

**valued customers, 200**

**values**

behavior, effect on, 11

commitment to, Zappos example, 14-16

communicating and executing, 23

defining and prioritizing, 21-23

evaluating, 295

measuring, 23

personal and professional values, relationship between, 11

**variable costs, 127**

**Velcro, brand imaging example, 165**

**Victoria's Secret, Facebook example, 246**

**viral marketing, 261**

pranksters, 261-262

in presidential elections, 262-264

**vision**

in culture of execution, 322-323

evaluating, 295

**vision statements**

Denzil Samuels example, 8-9

as stories, 10

**Volvo, 174**

# W

**Wanamaker, John, 215**

**Web 1.0, 219**

**Web 2.0, 219**

**Web 3.0, 219**

**Web sites, 220-221**

integrated customer service technology, 223-224

interactivity, 222-223

mass customization, 222

search engine optimization, 225

targeted markets, 222-223

usability design, 221

value-added services, 224

**Welch, Jack, 325**

**widgets**

for mobile devices, 232-233

for Web sites, 222

**Wiersema, Fred, 145**

**Williams Sonoma, email marketing, 231**

**Wilson, Edward O., 105**

**wins, 305**

**Wirth Business Credit, macro-environmental factors example, 93**

**Woods, Tiger, 165**

**word-of-mouth marketing, 261**

pranksters, 261-262

in presidential elections, 262-264

**The World Business Forum, 62**

**WuFoo, 101**

**Wyckoff, Luke, 11**

# X–Z

**Zappos**

culture example, 12

*commitment to core values, 14-16*

*customer service, 13*

customer-centric example, 324

vision example, 323

**Zarella, Dan, 247**

**Zillow.com, mobility marketing example, 234**

**Zoomerang, 98**